Brig Jacob's book captures the urgency and vision of building a smart, self-reliant ammunition ecosystem. A timely guide for India's defence manufacturing journey.

Shri Sanjay Hazari, Chairman and Managing Director, Munitions India Limited

*

A timely and insightful work that highlights the urgent need for synergy between industry, users, and policymakers. Brig Jacob brings clarity and conviction to the complex pursuit of ammunition self-reliance.

Lt Gen S K Upadhya, PVSM, AVSM, SM, VSM (Retd), former Master General Sustenance

*

Brig Jacob makes a smart and elegant argument: in future wars, anything that moves must be automated and everything that fires must be intelligent. Intelligent automation must be the credo of A SMART, AATMANIRBHAR BHARAT!

Lt Gen Raj Shukla, PVSM, YSM, SM (Retd), former GOC-in-C ARTRAC & Member, UPSC

*

Ammunition remains the Ordnance Corps' enduring core competency, demanding precision and deep expertise. Biju's book is an insightful contribution that reinforces the nation's drive towards a smart, self-reliant ammunition ecosystem.

Lt Gen Gautam Moorthy, PVSM, AVSM, VSM, (Retd), former Director General Ordnance Services

*

This book captures the evolving essence of ammunition as a warfighting enabler. Brig Jacob's insights bridge operational need with manufacturing depth- vital India's future readiness.

Lt Gen D P Pandey, PVSM, UYSM, AVSM, VSM (Retd), former GOC 15 Corps

*

Brig Jacob builds on his earlier work, Shaping India's Arsenal, with a sharper focus on smart munitions and resilient supply chains, offering a valuable contribution to India's evolving defence policy discourse.

Dr. Laxman Behera, Special Centre for National Security Studies, JNU

*

Passionate and purposeful, Brig Jacob offers a strategic blueprint to make India a global leader in ammunition manufacturing.

Shri Ashish Kansal, FICCI Co-Chair National Committee on Defence & Chair for task force on Defence exports

*

SMART ATMANIRBHAR ARSENAL
FOR
VIKSIT BHARAT 2047

Also by Brig (Dr) Biju Jacob, VSM ....

Shaping India's Arsenal: The Path to Self-Reliance in Ammunition Manufacturing

Publisher: Pentagon Press LLP, New Delhi

SMART ATMANIRBHAR ARSENAL
FOR
VIKSIT BHARAT 2047

A blueprint to transform India into a global ammunition manufacturing powerhouse with secure supply chains and smart munitions ecosystem

Brig (Dr) Biju Jacob, VSM

Foreword by

Lieutenant General Dhiraj Seth, PVSM, AVSM
General Officer Commanding-in-Chief, Southern Command

PENTAGON PRESS LLP

First published in 2026 by
PENTAGON PRESS LLP
206, Peacock Lane, Shahpur Jat
New Delhi-110049, India
Contact: 011-26490600

Typeset in AGaramond 11.5 Point
Printed at Aegean Offset Printers, Greater Noida

ISBN 978-81-993527-3-5

www.pentagonpress.in

This book is a tribute to the values of selfless service and creative innovation that strengthen the foundations of a secure, self-reliant and Viksit Bharat. It is my humble offering to a future where India not only safeguards its sovereignty but leads the world in shaping the ammunition technologies of tomorrow!

CONTENTS

Foreword *xiii*

Preface *xv*

Abbreviations *xix*

1. Scenario 2050! A Vision 1

2. Drawing Insights for Ammunition Management from Recent Conflicts 5
   Introduction 5
   Complexities of Ammunition Management 6
   Key Lessons from Recent Conflicts 7
   Case Study Insights 13
   Challenges and Innovations in Ammunition Management 16
   Key Takeaways 18

3. Unmanned Dominance: The Drone Revolution in Warfare 19
   Historical Evolution of Drone Warfare 21
   Global Trends in Drone Development 23
   Technology Trajectory: Drone Warfare 29
   India's Drone Ecosystem 31
   Challenges for India 34
   Relevance of Supply Chains 36
   Integrating Drone Ecosystem with Ammunition Industry 37

4. Building a Robust Ecosystem for Smart Munitions Manufacturing 39
   Evolution of Smart Munitions in Modern Warfare 39
   Characteristics of Smart Munitions 40
   Advantages of Smart Munitions in Warfare 41
   Evolution of Conventional Ammunition to Smart Munitions 42
   Global Dependence on Smart Munitions and India's Challenge 44
   Key Technological Advancements in Smart Munitions 46

Importance of Smart Munitions for Indian Army 48
Global Landscape of Smart Munitions Development 51
Current State of Ammunition Manufacturing and R&D in India 54
Strengthening R&D Ecosystem for Smart Munitions 58
Priority Technology Thrust for a Smart Munitions Ecosystem 61

5. Securing Ammunition Input and Raw-Material Foundations for Self-Reliance 63
Introduction 63
Overview of Ammunition Manufacturing in India 65
Key Input Materials for Ammunition Manufacturing 67
Sources and Supply Chains of Input Materials in India 70
Key Challenges in Material Availability 72
Global Best Practices and Comparative Insights 75
Recent Developments and Indian Initiatives 77
Recommendations and the Way Forward 79
Conclusion 81

6. Leveraging Geopolitical Synergies to Secure Ammunition Supply Chains 83
Introduction 83
Geopolitical Landscape and Ammunition Manufacturing 84
Overview of Key Global Players and Alliances 84
Geopolitical Tensions and Their Impact on Ammunition Supply Chains 84
Strategic Partnerships: Case Studies 86
Technological Innovations and Their Role in Strategic Partnerships 87
Economic and Industrial Impacts of Strategic Partnerships 89
Impact on Local Economies and Employment 90
Challenges and Barriers to Effective Partnerships 90
Future of Strategic Partnerships in Ammunition Manufacturing 92
Recommendations for Strengthening Strategic Partnerships 93

7. Harnessing AI for Optimising Ammunition Supply Chains 96
Introduction 96
Leveraging Ammunition Supply Chain with AI 97
Quantitative Assessment of Ammunition Logistics in India 100
AI in Ammunition Supply Chain Optimisation 101
Challenges and Prospects 104
Ammunition Supply Chains Insights from Country Case Studies 108
Applications of AI in Ammunition Supply Chains 110
Recommendations for Strengthening the Ammunition Supply Chains 112
Conclusion 115

8. Leveraging Industry 4.0 to Modernise Ammunition Factories 117
Introduction 117
Legacy Ammunition Production in India: OFB and the DPSU Transition 117
Industry 4.0 Technologies and Their Relevance for Defence Manufacturing 118
Roadmap for Transition: From Legacy Systems to Smart Ammunition Factories 121
Challenges and Risks in Modernisation 123
Conclusion 125

9. Transforming Defence Corridors into Engines of Self-Reliance 126
Introduction 126
Evolution of India's Defence Industrial Base and the Role of Corridors 127
Concept and Genesis of Defence Corridors in India 130
Key Defence Corridors 132
Strategic Contributions of Defence Corridors to Self-Reliance 134
Exports, Foreign Direct Investment (FDI), and Global Positioning 139
Challenges and Strategic Interventions for Optimisation 141
Future Prospects and Conclusion 147

10. Reimagining Ammunition Quality Assurance for Modern Manufacturing 149
Introduction 149
Quality Assurance and the Changing Character of Warfare 150
India's Ammunition QA Landscape 152
Towards a Transformed QA Paradigm 155
Advanced Testing and Inspection Technologies 156
Lessons from Experience 158
Conclusion 160

11. Munitions Without Missions: A Growing Dilemma in India's Ammunition Manufacturing 162
The Paradox of Ammunition Self-Reliance 162
Historical Evolution of Ammunition Manufacturing in India 163
Expansion and Role of the Ordnance Factory Board 165
Calls for Reform and Structural Critiques 167
The Emerging Dilemma 172
Why This Matters and How to Realign? 177
Conclusion: Strategic Payoff 179

12. Integrated Ammunition Nodes: A Strategic Framework for R&D and Manufacturing 181
Introduction 181
Historical and Contemporary Context 182
Concept of Integrated Ammunition Nodes 184

Integrated Ammunition Nodes: A National Grid for Smart Munitions 187
Implementation Roadmap 191
Governance and Quality Assurance 193
Risks and Mitigation 195
Conclusion 196

13. Building an Agile Ammunition Acquisition System for Rapid Technological Integration 198
Introduction 198
Technological Obsolescence 199
Historical Insights and Current Landscape of Defence Procurement 200
A Double-Edged Sword 202
Way Ahead for Agile Acquisition System 203
Policy Reforms Needed 204
Technology-Based Procurement for Ammunition 206
Conclusion 209

14. Way Forward: Ten Missions, Metrics, and Transformation Plan 211
Introduction: From Vision to Execution 211
Defining Missions 212
Metrics for Success 224
Missions-to-Metrics Matrix 229
Transformation Plan 230
Policy and Governance Enablers 236
Conclusion 238

NOTES 240

APPENDICES

Ammunition Raw Materials and its Applications 267

Components of 155 mm HE Ammunition 270

Index 273

FOREWORD

India stands today at a defining stage in its strategic evolution. As the nation advances through *Amrit Kaal* towards the vision of ***Viksit Bharat 2047***, it enters a phase of deliberate transformation—one that demands not only economic progress but also comprehensive national security preparedness. In this journey, building credible, sustainable and indigenous defence capability is not merely desirable, it is imperative for safeguarding national interests in an increasingly uncertain world.

The Hon'ble Prime Minister Shri Narendra Modi's recent articulation of **JAI—Jointness, Atmanirbharta, and Innovation**, provides a clear and compelling framework for national defence preparedness in the coming decades. Jointness ensures operational synergy across land, air, maritime, space and cyber domains; *Atmanirbharta* secures strategic autonomy by reducing external dependence; and Innovation guarantees technological relevance in an era of rapidly evolving warfare. These principles are no longer aspirational—they are operational necessities for our Armed Forces.

The success of **Operation SINDOOR** is a powerful validation of India's evolving military capability and doctrinal clarity. It showcased precise, integrated and decisive combat power anchored in indigenous technology and joint-force execution. Complementing this momentum, the Indian Army has rightly designated this period as the "**Year of Reforms—Transformation for the Future,**" underscoring the urgency of adopting cutting-edge technologies, restructuring processes and enhancing long-term readiness.

In this context, Brigadier Biju Jacob's work, "**Smart Atmanirbhar Arsenal for Viksit Bharat 2047**", is both timely and relevant. Ammunition remains the currency of deterrence and the backbone of sustained combat operations, yet it receives limited attention in strategic discourse. This book fills that critical gap. It traces the evolution of ammunition from a traditional production model to a **future-ready smart ecosystem** enabled by digital manufacturing, predictive logistics, precision engineering and secure supply chains.

The author's concept of **Integrated Ammunition Nodes** is one of the most compelling propositions of this work. It envisions a unified ecosystem that links research institutions, industry partners, start-ups, quality assurance agencies, logistics networks and the Armed Forces in a seamless feedback loop. This integrated model reinforces a simple but profound truth—strategic readiness is not built in factories alone; it is engineered through **institutional collaboration, user-driven design and mission-linked innovation.**

The chapters unfold a structured progression—from lessons of modern conflicts to the transformative potential of unmanned systems, artificial intelligence, additive manufacturing and Industry 4.0. The work explores how defence corridors can transition into true innovation clusters, how governance can ensure accountability without stifling agility and how India can secure ammunition self-reliance without losing focus on quality, safety and long-term sustainability.

What distinguishes this work is its **balance of imagination and realism.** It recognises that transformation in ammunition manufacturing cannot be achieved by policy directives alone—it demands a **culture of collaboration, long-term investment in R&D** and **strategic clarity**. The **missions-to-metrics framework** proposed in the book offers a pragmatic roadmap for measurable progress.

This volume mirrors the confidence of a rising India, an India determined not just to participate in the future of warfare but to shape it. It invites policymakers, industry leaders, military professionals, scholars and young innovators to engage with an essential question: *How does India build decisive military capability with indigenous strength?*

In conclusion, this book recognises that **Atmanirbharta is a journey, not a slogan.** It calls for strengthening indigenous inputs, securing critical materials, nurturing design capability, scaling manufacturing capacity and creating global standards of excellence. More than a technical study, it is a **strategic roadmap** for building a secure, resilient, and future-ready India by 2047.

This work is a valuable contribution not only to defence literature but to India's national security vision. It deserves attention, reflection, and action.

Jai Hind!

Lieutenant General Dhiraj Seth, PVSM, AVSM
General Officer Commanding-in-Chief, Southern Command

PREFACE

This book builds upon the foundation laid in my earlier work, *Shaping India's Arsenal*, which underscored the urgent need for self-reliance in conventional ammunition manufacturing. In recent years, through my writings in various defence journals, I have consistently advocated for comprehensive reforms in India's ammunition ecosystem, structurally, technologically, and institutionally. With the onset of *Amrit Kaal* and the rapid evolution of warfare, driven by smart munitions, autonomous drones and AI-enabled weapon systems, it became imperative to craft a broader, forward-looking strategic roadmap. This volume reflects that vision, integrating the hard-won lessons of recent global conflicts with India's aspirations for *Viksit Bharat* 2047, and proposing a future-ready ecosystem rooted in indigenous innovation, secure supply chains, and collaborative R&D.

India stands at a defining moment in its defence industrial journey. The nation's pursuit of self-reliance in ammunition manufacturing is not merely an economic or technological aspiration—it is a strategic imperative tied to national security, sovereignty, and global stature. Ammunition, though the lifeblood of combat power, has rarely received the intellectual and policy attention it deserves within India's strategic discourse. The prolonged battles of attrition in Ukraine, the rapid devastation enabled by drones in Nagorno-Karabakh, and the asymmetric strikes in the Middle East all demonstrate the same truth: the strength of a nation's ammunition supply chain defines the credibility of its military power. For India, with its volatile frontiers and dual-front contingencies, this truth has sharper implications. Dependence on imports, recurring quality issues, and reliance on outdated production models are not merely administrative inconveniences; they are vulnerabilities that cut to the heart of national security.

This book, therefore, seeks to reposition ammunition at the centre of India's strategic imagination. Its purpose is not only to diagnose dilemmas but also to map pathways for resilience, reform, and innovation. The central claim advanced throughout is that ammunition must be recognised as a strategic doctrine rather than a mere logistical commodity. To build this argument, the chapters unfold in a sequence that moves from imagination to reality, from disruption to reform, and from diagnosis to transformation.

The journey begins with *Scenario 2050: A Vision*, which looks ahead to the evolving grammar of warfare and compels us to ask what ammunition will mean in a world of intelligent, networked, and contested battlespaces. This forward-looking imagination is anchored by *Drawing Insights for Ammunition Management from Recent Conflicts*, where lessons from Ukraine, Nagorno-Karabakh, and the Middle East reveal how resilience, attrition, and adaptation now define the outcomes of wars.

From this foundation, the discussion moves to disruptive realities. *Unmanned Dominance: The Drone Revolution in Warfare* illustrates how drones are transforming doctrines and reshaping the demand profile for ordnance, while *Building a Robust Ecosystem for Smart Munitions Manufacturing* and *Securing Ammunition Input Material Foundations* together argue that India's response must combine technological sophistication with assured access to critical materials. Recognising that India cannot achieve resilience in isolation, *Leveraging Geopolitical Synergies to Secure Ammunition Supply Chains* situates the debate within the global canvas of partnerships, co-production, and diplomatic alignments. Complementing this outward gaze, two chapters turn inward to technology and manufacturing: *Harnessing AI for Optimising Ammunition Supply Chain* explores how predictive analytics and smart logistics can transform efficiency, while *Leveraging Industry 4.0 to Modernise Ammunition Factories* shows how digital twins, additive manufacturing, and automation can elevate production quality.

Industrial geography and institutional design form the next layer of analysis. *Transforming Defence Corridors into Engines of Self-Reliance* examines how industrial hubs can become ecosystems of innovation and synergy, while *Reimagining Ammunition Quality Assurance for Modern Manufacturing* emphasises that sovereignty is meaningless without reliability. The book then pivots to a critical diagnosis in *Munitions Without Missions: A Growing Dilemma in India's Ammunition Manufacturing*, which highlights the paradox of substantial capacity without mission orientation. From here, the narrative shifts to frameworks of reform. *Integrated Ammunition Nodes: A Strategic*

Framework for R&D and Manufacturing in India proposes new models of collaboration across industry, research, and users, while *Modernising Indian Defence Procurement* makes the case that procurement reform is indispensable to aligning missions with capacities.

The volume concludes with *Way Forward: Missions, Metrics, and Transformation Plan*, a synthesis that translates analysis into a roadmap. It outlines clear missions, measurable indicators, and institutional reforms that can guide India's ammunition sector towards the vision of *Viksit Bharat 2047*. The ambition here is not simply to suggest adjustments but to advocate for transformation building an ordnance ecosystem that is sovereign, adaptive, and globally competitive.

This book is intended for a wide audience: policymakers seeking to align defence priorities with strategic imperatives; industry leaders grappling with the risks and opportunities of ordnance innovation; scholars interested in linking ammunition debates with wider security discourses; and practitioners whose operational needs make this subject urgent rather than abstract.

Written at a moment when India stands at a threshold, the arguments advanced here insist that the credibility of national security in the twenty-first century will be decided not only by platforms or doctrines but by the strength of its ammunition ecosystem. To neglect this domain is to undermine the very foundations of strategy. To reform it is to ensure that India's vision of *Viksit Bharat 2047* is matched by the resilience, innovation, and readiness of its defence industrial base. If there is one argument that unites these chapters, it is this: ammunition is not merely a commodity of war, it is the anchor of sovereignty, preparedness, and national power.

ABBREVIATIONS

AI	Artificial Intelligence
AMPC	Anchor MIL + Private Consortium
ANNs	Artificial Neural Networks
ARDE	Armament Research and Development Establishment
ATT	Arms Trade Treaty
AVIC	Aviation Industry Corporation of China
AWEIL	Advanced Weapons and Equipment India Limited
BARC	Bhabha Atomic Research Centre
C4ISR	Command, Control, Communications, Computers, Intelligence, Surveillance & Reconnaissance
CAD	Central Ammunition Depot
CAD	Computer-Aided Design
CAG	Comptroller and Auditor General
CATS	Combat Air Teaming System
CBM+	Condition-Based Maintenance Plus
CWC	Chemical Weapons Convention
DAP	Defence Acquisition Procedure
DARPA	Defence Advanced Research Projects Agency
DCMA	Defence Contract Management Agency
DDP	Department of Defence Production
DGFT	Directorate General of Foreign Trade
DICs	Defence Industrial Corridors
DLA	Defence Logistics Agency
DoD	Department of Defence
DPA	Defence Production Act
DPEPP	Defence Production and Export Promotion Policy
DPP	Defence Procurement Procedure

DPSUs	Defence Public Sector Undertakings
DRDO	Defence Research and Development Organisation
DTIS	Defence Testing Infrastructure Scheme
EEL	Economic Explosives Limited
ERCA	Extended Range Cannon Artillery
FDI	Foreign Direct Investment
FPV	Cheap First-Person-View
GPSs	Global Positioning Systems
GSQRs	General Staff Qualitative Requirements
HAL	Hindustan Aeronautics Limited
IAI	Israel Aerospace Industries
IAN	Integrated Ammunition Nodes
ICDs	Interface Control Documents
IDDM	Indigenously Designed, Developed and Manufactured
iDEX	Innovations for Defence Excellence
IDF	Israel Defence Forces
IMUs	Inertial Measurement Units
INS	Inertial Navigation Systems
IoTs	Internet of Things
ISR	Intelligence, Surveillance, and Reconnaissance
ISTAR	Intelligence, Surveillance, Target Acquisition, and Reconnaissance
ITARs	International Traffic in Arms Regulations
ITIs	Industrial Training Institutes
JDAM	Joint Direct Attack Munitions
JMC	Joint Munitions Command
JSSs	Joint Services Specifications
LAC	Line of Actual Control
LGBs	Laser-Guided Bombs
LoC	Line of Control
MALE	Medium-Altitude Long-Endurance
MEMS	Micro Electromechanical Systems
MIL	Munitions India Limited
ML	Machine Learning

MoD	Ministry of Defence
MoEFCC	Ministry of Environment, Forest and Climate Change
MPCC	MIL–Private Coordination Cell
MRO	Maintenance, Repair, and Overhaul
MSMEs	Micro, Small and Medium Enterprises
MTCR	Missile Technology Control Regime
NAA	National Ammunition Authority
NAAI	National Authority for Ammunition and Industry
NCW	Network-Centric Warfare
NDMG	National Defence Material Grid
NDT	Non-Destructive Testing
OEM	Original Equipment Manufacturer
OFB	Ordnance Factory Board
PESB	Propellants and Energetics Safety Board
PESO	Petroleum and Explosives Safety Organisation
PGK	Precision Guided Kit
PGMs	Precision-Guided Munitions
PLI	Production-Linked Incentive
PLM	Product Lifecycle Management
PPPs	Public-Private Partnerships
PSM	Process Safety Management
PSU	Public Sector Undertaking
QA	Quality Assurance
QC	Quality Control
R&D	Research and Development
RFPs	Request for Proposals
SAAW	Smart Anti-Airfield Weapon
SCOMET	Special Chemicals, Organisms, Materials, Equipment and Technologies
SDB	Small Diameter Bomb
SPARC	Strategic Partnerships for Ammunition Resilience Consortium
SPM	Strategic Partnership Model
STANAGs	Standardisation Agreements
TBP	Technology-Based Procurement

TDF	Technology Development Fund
TNDIC	Tamil Nadu Defence Industrial Corridor
TNPO	Tri-Node Program Office
ToT	Transfer of Technology
TQM	Total Quality Management
UAV	Unmanned Aerial Vehicle
UPDIC	Uttar Pradesh Defence Industrial Corridor
VCOAS	Vice Chief of Army Staff
WWR	War Wastage Reserve

1

Scenario 2050! A Vision

As India moves through the *Amrit Kaal* towards the centenary of independence in 2047, the question of what its strategic environment will look like in 2050 is not speculative indulgence but a necessary exercise in preparedness. The grammar of warfare is evolving, shaped by the interplay of technology, geopolitics, and resource competition. For India, a nation positioned at the crossroads of the Indo-Pacific, this transformation is not only a military challenge but also an opportunity to redefine its place in the global security order. Scenario building for 2050 forces us to imagine the contours of future battlefields and in doing so, to rethink the role of ammunition, supply chains, and self-reliance as the decisive anchors of national power.

The Changing Grammar of Warfare

The battlefields of 2050 are unlikely to be defined by large formations clashing across deserts or plains. Instead, they will be dominated by intelligent, networked, and autonomous systems. Unmanned aerial swarms will saturate skies, loitering munitions will blur the line between platform and payload, and autonomous underwater vehicles will patrol critical chokepoints in the Indian Ocean. Precision, persistence, and adaptability will matter more than sheer numbers.

The domains of war will multiply. Traditional land, sea, and air battles will be intertwined with operations in space, cyberspace, and the cognitive sphere. Conflicts will be fought not only to control territory but also to dominate narratives, disrupt decision-making, and undermine morale. Artificial intelligence, quantum computing, and neuro-interfaces will create command-and-control architectures that operate at machine speed, far beyond human reflexes. In this environment, ammunition will no longer be an inert stockpile of shells and cartridges; it will be an ecosystem of smart, modular, and adaptive systems co-designed with their delivery platforms.

The Indian Strategic Imagination of 2050

On land, the Indian soldier of 2050 will no longer fight alone. Equipped with exoskeletons and supported by semi-autonomous drones, infantry units will be extended by swarms of loitering munitions that can scout, strike, and self-destruct in coordinated waves. Ammunition will be lightweight, networked, and precision-guided, designed to integrate seamlessly with ground drones and robotic vehicles. In the air, loyal wingman drones will accompany manned fighters, providing both defensive shields and offensive firepower. Solar-powered high-altitude platforms will remain aloft for months, acting as persistent ISR nodes and communication relays. Drone swarms will execute suppression of enemy air defence missions at scale, ensuring air denial without risking manned aircraft. Here, India's ammunition ecosystem will need to produce warheads that are not only precise but also scalable, miniaturised for micro-drones, yet lethal enough to neutralise hardened targets.

At sea, the Indian Ocean will be guarded less by fleets and more by networks of unmanned underwater vehicles, smart torpedoes, and intelligent mines capable of distinguishing friend from foe. Surface drones will escort carrier groups, while aerial drones will extend the range of surveillance across vital chokepoints. Ammunition production will thus include a wide array of maritime-specific payloads, from lightweight depth charges to AI-guided torpedoes. In the space and cyber domains, India will operate constellations of satellites linked by quantum-secure networks. These will direct not only drones and missiles but also electronic warfare payloads capable of disrupting enemy communications and navigation systems. Ammunition will extend into the electromagnetic spectrum, where jammers, decoys, and directed-energy systems are produced and deployed alongside kinetic rounds. The cognitive domain will emerge as an equally contested battlefield. Information-disrupting drones will manipulate communications, generate deepfake avatars, and create psychological dislocation in enemy ranks. In parallel, morale-sensing systems will provide India's commanders with real-time assessments of troop resilience, enabling tailored psychological operations. In this future, ammunition is as much informational as it is physical, designed to strike minds as well as machines.

Strategic Balance

The offensive dimension of India's 2050 scenario is underpinned by swarm tactics, modular ammunition, and AI-integrated strike systems. Yet offensive capability must be balanced by robust defence. India will require a *Sudarshan Chakra*, like defensive dome, multi-layered systems combining missile interceptors, electronic warfare suites, laser weapons, and AI-driven radars that create a shield around cities, military bases, and strategic corridors. The balance between projection and protection will be essential if India is to deter adversaries across multiple domains.

Equally vital will be the resilience of supply chains. Wars of 2050 will be long and attritional, and the ability to replenish stocks of smart munitions, sustain drone swarms, and ensure the availability of critical inputs like energetics and rare-earth materials will determine endurance. Here, India's integration of defence corridors, public-private partnerships, and indigenous innovation will play a decisive role. By positioning itself as a trusted supplier of smart munitions to friendly nations across the Global South, India can also extend strategic influence while reinforcing its own industrial base.

The credibility of such futuristic projections is already visible in India's operational practice. The successful conduct of *Operation SINDOOR* in May 2025 demonstrated how India has begun integrating indigenous drone warfare, layered air defence, and electronic warfare into real-time combat scenarios. Without crossing international boundaries, Indian forces neutralised hostile systems loitering munitions, AI-enabled surveillance, and counter-UAS grids, achieving precision strikes with no loss of assets. The operation also highlighted the role of satellite networks, integrated command-and-control, and the resilience of indigenous production lines. As noted in official accounts, this mission not only blunted adversarial attempts but also showcased India's capacity to fuze technology, doctrine, and industry in a seamless manner. In many ways, *Operation SINDOOR* foreshadows the battlespace of 2050, where swarm tactics, modular ammunition, and indigenous innovation converge to create both deterrence and dominance.

The Essence of 2050

The imagined battlefield of 2050 is one where human courage and machine cognition fuze into a single combat architecture. Soldiers are no longer burdened by shortages or exposed recklessly to attrition; they are augmented by technologies that extend reach, precision, and protection. Ammunition, once thought of as a consumable, becomes a force multiplier in its own right which is adaptive, intelligent, and seamlessly integrated into doctrine. For India, this scenario is not fantasy but a roadmap for imagination-driven planning. If the reforms and innovations outlined in this book are pursued with clarity and urgency, the India of 2050 can be a nation whose defence posture reflects both resilience and vision. Its ammunition ecosystem will no longer be a constraint but a source of confidence, enabling India to safeguard its sovereignty, project power responsibly, and contribute meaningfully to global stability. This is the essence of strategic imagination *vis-à-vis* to see beyond present dilemmas and prepare for a future where India's defence capabilities match its aspirations as a *Viksit Bharat.*

2

Drawing Insights for Ammunition Management from Recent Conflicts

Introduction

In the evolving landscape of modern warfare, the management of ammunition stands as a pivotal element that can significantly influence the outcome of military engagements. As conflicts become increasingly complex, with asymmetric warfare and hybrid tactics, the strategic importance of effective ammunition logistics cannot be overstressed. The capacity to supply, maintain, and manage ammunition effectively not only ensures operational success but also supports the broader strategic autonomy of nations engaged in protracted conflicts. This necessity has become even more pronounced with the introduction of advanced technological weaponry and the heightened pace of engagements, which demand rapid logistical responses. The management of ammunition, encompassing its procurement, storage, distribution, and utilisation, plays a pivotal role in shaping the outcomes of conflicts and determining the capabilities of armed forces.[1] As technology evolves and geopolitical dynamics shift, the significance of ammunition management in contemporary military operations has only grown more pronounced. Recent conflicts in Ukraine and Israel offer poignant examples of the critical role that ammunition management plays in modern warfare. In Ukraine, the ongoing conflict in the eastern regions has highlighted the importance of maintaining adequate ammunition stockpiles to sustain prolonged engagements and counter asymmetric threats.[2] Similarly, in Israel, where the country faces constant security challenges, the effective management of ammunition resources is essential for safeguarding national security interests and maintaining deterrence against adversaries.[3]

Ammunition management encompasses a broad range of activities, from the procurement and storage of munitions to their timely distribution and the maintenance of stockpile integrity. As recent conflicts demonstrate, the ability to manage these aspects efficiently often dictates the agility and effectiveness of a military force. For instance, disruptions in ammunition supply chains have historically led to critical setbacks on the battlefield, highlighting the vulnerability of relying heavily on external suppliers.[4] Moreover, the strategic placement and security of ammunition stockpiles have become central concerns as adversaries increasingly target these assets to cripple their opponents' operational capabilities.[5,6] Munitions management is further complicated by the need to tailor supplies to specific geographic and climatic conditions. In regions like India, where military operations span deserts, plains, forests, hills, high mountains, and glaciers, the diversity in environmental conditions demands a versatile approach to ammunition logistics. Moreover, the type of conflict, whether short and intense, static or mobile, or prolonged wars of attrition, further influences the types and quantities of munitions required. Effective management strategies must, therefore, be adaptable to these variables, ensuring that forces are adequately supplied under all conditions.

Complexities of Ammunition Management

An effective ammunition management is therefore crucial for maintaining not only the continuity and efficiency of military operations but also for ensuring national security and sovereignty. The balance between self-sufficiency in ammunition production and the complexities of global supply chains presents significant challenges and strategic considerations for defence policies. This chapter asserts that proficient ammunition management is essential for operational success and strategic autonomy in contemporary conflicts. The complexity of 'Munitions' in modern warfare is underscored by the diverse range of ammunition types required across different combat scenarios. This includes standard infantry weapons and a wide array of artillery shells, rockets, anti-tank and anti-personnel munitions, guided missiles, MANPADS, and specialised equipment, such as, range finders, drones, and precision-guided munitions. These diverse requirements highlight the intricate challenges in managing munitions effectively to maintain the fighting capacity of military formations across varied geographic and operational contexts. By analysing recent conflicts, this chapter aims to highlight the implications of ammunition logistics on modern warfare and offer insights into developing more resilient and effective defence strategies.

This section defines and explores the foundational concepts crucial to understanding ammunition management in the context of modern warfare. Ammunition management involves the comprehensive process of acquiring, storing, distributing, and maintaining ammunition supplies to ensure military forces can conduct operations efficiently.[7] It is a critical component of military logistics, which is concerned with the detailed coordination of complex operations involving many people, facilities, or supplies. In military contexts, specifically, logistics is the science of planning and carrying out the movement and maintenance of forces, which directly influences combat readiness and operational success.[8]

Key Lessons from Recent Conflicts

Modern warfare is characterised by the utilisation of contemporary technology and tactics, such as, cyberspace and artificial intelligence, making the management of resources like ammunition increasingly complex and strategic.[9] The concept of self-reliance in military contexts refers to a nation's capacity to produce essential resources for its defence without external assistance, which is pivotal for maintaining sovereignty and security in volatile geopolitical climates.[10] Additionally, Research and Development (R&D) in military technology focuses on improving existing munitions and developing new technologies to address emerging threats and operational requirements.[11] Effective R&D practices can lead to significant advancements in ammunition technology, enhancing a nation's military capabilities and strategic positioning. The integration of cyber capabilities and Artificial Intelligence (AI) into ammunition management offers significant advancements in efficiency and accuracy. AI-driven systems can optimise the logistics of ammunition supply chains by predicting demand, automating inventory management, and streamlining distribution processes. Moreover, cyber capabilities enable enhanced real-time data collection and analysis, providing military forces with actionable insights to make informed decisions on the battlefield. This ensures that the right type and quantity of ammunition are available precisely when and where they are needed, reducing waste and improving combat readiness. Key lessons for ammunition management from recent conflicts are as follows.

Importance of Ammunition Stockpiles

The strategic importance of ammunition stockpiles in military history is well-documented, illustrating how critical they are to the success and sustainability of military operations. Historically, the availability or scarcity of ammunition has frequently been a decisive factor in the outcomes of conflicts. For example, during World War II, the Battle of the Bulge showcased the critical role of ammunition stockpiles. As German forces pushed into the Ardennes, their initial success was stymied partly due to shortages in ammunition, which severely hampered their ability to sustain their offensive.[12] Similarly, during the Yom Kippur War in 1973, Israeli forces faced critical shortages of ammunition on the Golan Heights front, which almost led to a catastrophic defeat. Emergency resupply operations from the United States proved pivotal in turning the tide in Israel's favour.[13]

These historical instances underscore the strategic value of maintaining robust ammunition stockpiles. Effective stockpile management ensures that a military can sustain operations over prolonged periods, particularly under siege or cut-off conditions. Furthermore, ample stockpiles allow for greater flexibility and responsiveness to unexpected tactical situations or sudden escalations in conflict intensity.[14] In modern warfare, where conflicts can escalate quickly and logistical lines can be targeted, having significant reserves of ammunition is more crucial than ever.[15] For instance, the conflict in Ukraine since 2014 has highlighted how essential robust ammunition stockpiles are for sustaining long-term military operations. Ukrainian forces, initially facing shortages, significantly improved their combat effectiveness as international support helped to rebuild and enhance their ammunition reserves.[16,17]

Similarly, during the 2020 Nagorno-Karabakh conflict, the rapid depletion of ammunition reserves critically impacted the defensive capabilities of Armenian forces, contrasting sharply with Azerbaijani forces, who benefitted from well-stocked and well-managed ammunition supplies.[18] This disparity was a decisive factor in the conflict's outcome, illustrating how ammunition stockpiles can shift the balance of power in warfare. The strategic management of ammunition stockpiles also involves complex considerations of safety, security, and sustainability. For instance, NATO exercises regularly incorporate logistics simulations to address these challenges, ensuring that member states can coordinate and manage their ammunition stockpiles effectively in joint operations, especially with the return of high-intensity conflict in Europe.[19]

Significance of Research and Development in Ammunition Production

Research and Development in ammunition production is a critical driver of technological innovation, significantly impacting the efficacy and strategic capabilities of military forces.[20] Advancements in ammunition technology not only improve the performance characteristics of munitions but also enhance their safety, reliability, and adaptability to diverse combat situations.[21]

The recent advancements have included the development of guided munitions, which increase the precision of strikes and reduce collateral damage.[22] The introduction of programmable ammunition, which can be set to detonate at specific times or distances, revolutionises urban and asymmetric warfare scenarios, allowing forces to engage targets with unprecedented accuracy and minimal risk to civilian populations.[23] Additionally, the integration of advanced materials has led to the creation of lighter, more durable ammunition that can withstand harsh environments while maintaining performance integrity. To further improve the effectiveness of R&D in ammunition production, a more integrated approach between centralised and decentralised models should be considered. Centralised R&D can streamline the innovation process by consolidating resources and expertise, while decentralised R&D, located closer to production facilities, can foster rapid prototyping and iterative testing. Additionally, extensive field testing and direct feedback from frontline troops are crucial in refining ammunition technologies to ensure they meet the operational demands of modern warfare. This feedback loop is essential for adapting to the dynamic requirements of combat situations, ensuring that newly developed munitions are both effective and reliable.

The strategic advantages provided by these innovations are manifold. Enhanced precision and reliability directly contribute to the tactical effectiveness of military operations, allowing smaller units to carry out missions with a higher probability of success and lower risk of unintended consequences. Moreover, the development of environmentally friendly ammunition, which reduces the toxic residues left on battlefields, addresses growing environmental and health concerns, potentially reducing the long-term impact of military engagements on ecosystems.[24,25] Furthermore, R&D in ammunition production also leads to better resource efficiency. Innovations that extend the shelf-life and stability of munitions can lead to significant cost savings and logistical advantages as stockpiles become easier to manage and maintain over extended periods. This contributes to enhanced strategic autonomy, as forces can rely on a consistent and dependable ammunition supply in prolonged conflicts. R&D efforts should be geared towards creating adaptive systems that can respond to the varying demands of the battlefield. Military forces can maintain flexibility in their operations by focusing on modularity and interoperability in ammunition design. Furthermore, integrating user feedback from combat operations into the R&D process can significantly enhance the applicability and effectiveness of new technologies. This user-centred approach ensures that innovations meet theoretical specifications and perform optimally in real-world scenarios.

The continuous investment in R&D is crucial for maintaining a competitive edge in modern warfare, where technological superiority often determines the outcome of conflicts. As the nature of warfare evolves, the demand for more sophisticated and versatile ammunition will continue to drive innovation in this field.

Imperative of Self-Reliance in Ammunition Production

Self-reliance in ammunition production is a critical aspect of national security and defence strategy, particularly in an era where geopolitical tensions frequently influence the availability of military supplies. The economic and strategic rationale for self-reliance is based on the need to reduce dependency on foreign entities, which may become unreliable partners in times of political or economic turmoil. Nations that maintain robust domestic ammunition production capabilities are better positioned to handle sudden escalations in conflict without facing the risks associated with supply chain disruptions.[26,27]

For instance, the United States maintains one of the world's most comprehensive domestic ammunition production capabilities, which not only supports its military operations but also provides a significant buffer against international supply chain vulnerabilities. This self-sufficiency enables the US to execute military operations without reliance on external sources, enhancing its strategic autonomy and operational readiness.[28] In contrast, smaller nations often struggle with the high costs associated with establishing and maintaining extensive ammunition production facilities. For countries like Estonia, which rely heavily on imports for military supplies, the lack of self-reliance in ammunition production can pose significant risks during geopolitical crises.[29] Such dependencies may force these nations to make strategic compromises to secure the necessary resources. Comparatively, nations like India have recognised the strategic disadvantage of dependency and are aggressively pursuing policies to enhance their domestic defence production capabilities. The Indian government's "Make in India" initiative, for example, includes significant investments in local defence manufacturing, aiming to achieve greater self-reliance and reduce imports by fostering domestic innovation and production.[30]

This comparative analysis illustrates that self-reliance in ammunition production not only strengthens national security but also enhances a nation's ability to conduct independent military operations without the constraints imposed by international supply dynamics. The strategic advantage provided by domestic production capabilities is clear: it enables countries to respond more flexibly and decisively in the face of threats, thereby supporting broader defence objectives and national sovereignty.

While self-reliance, stockpile sufficiency, and robust R&D form the structural backbone of any nation's ammunition strategy, recent conflicts suggest that these elements alone are not enough. The dynamic tempo of high-intensity warfare exposes new vulnerabilities that demand operational foresight: the capacity to absorb unexpected surges in consumption, the resilience of supply chains under attack, the ability to integrate smart munitions with legacy stocks, and the assurance of quality and accountability even during production spikes. These operational imperatives, when addressed in tandem with self-reliance, create a framework for ammunition management that is not only smarter and faster, but also more sustainable.

Accurate Estimation of Consumption Rates and Planning for Surge Capacity

One of the most striking lessons from contemporary conflicts has been the chronic underestimation of wartime consumption rates. In Ukraine, daily artillery use exceeded pre-war planning norms by several multiples, with Russian and Ukrainian forces at times expending tens of thousands of shells in a single day. NATO countries too found their reserves depleted within weeks, underscoring the gap between linear peacetime forecasts and the reality of prolonged, high-intensity combat.[31] This highlights the need for scalable production systems that can expand rapidly in wartime. Pre-negotiated surge contracts, modular and reconfigurable manufacturing lines, and assured access to raw materials must therefore become integral to national planning. For India, embedding surge clauses in multi-year procurement contracts and creating standby capacity within both public and private sector ammunition plants will be critical to sustaining operational readiness in a future conflict.

Resilient and Secure Supply Chain

Another important factor is the resilience of supply chains. Conflicts have shown that concentrated ammunition depots and predictable resupply routes are highly vulnerable to precision strikes. Ukraine's adoption of dispersed forward stocks and mobile resupply nodes allowed it to maintain tempo even under sustained attack, while Russian logistics faltered under repeated strikes on centralised dumps. This underlines the need to move from large, static depots towards a network of smaller, hardened, and redundant storage nodes co-located with operational commands. Beyond the physical dimension, the digital backbone of logistics also demands protection. Modern inventory and movement-control systems, often reliant on real-time data, are vulnerable to cyber intrusions, spoofing, and electronic warfare. Strengthening cyber defences through hardened, partially air-gapped networks, tamper-proof authentication measures, and anomaly-detection systems is therefore essential to prevent paralysis during conflict.[32]

Integration of Smart and Legacy Ammunition Stocks

The integration of smart munitions with legacy stockpiles is equally significant. Precision-guided munitions provide unparalleled accuracy against high-value targets, but they cannot substitute for the suppressive volume of conventional shells in wars of attrition. The future battlefield will require a balanced mix of both, with doctrine and procurement calibrated accordingly. India's current approach, heavily weighted towards conventional shell stockpiling, must therefore be supplemented by investment in indigenous precision artillery rounds, loitering munitions, and guided rocket systems. At the same time, hidden obsolescence within legacy stockpiles exposed by dud rates during rapid drawdowns in Ukraine and Russia demands systematic shelf-life management. Reports on cluster munitions indicate dud rates ranging from 2 percent to over 40 percent in older inventories, underscoring the risks of legacy ammunition.[33] Digital lot-level tracking, predictive analytics, and data-driven refurbishment cycles can prevent operational failures and ensure that ammunition remains combat-worthy when most needed.

Ammunition Accountability, Quality and Safety

Finally, quality control and accountability become particularly challenging during wartime production surges. The pressure to replenish stocks quickly often leads to lapses in inspection and workmanship, as evidenced by reports of defective shells and misfiring PGMs in recent conflicts. Anticipating this, militaries must prepare contingency quality-assurance frameworks in advance. On-site inspection teams, automated testing lines, and rapid defect-investigation cells can help sustain safety and reliability during production spikes. In parallel, real-time traceability systems using technologies, such as, RFID, IoT sensors, and tamper-proof digital ledgers can provide visibility over each batch from factory to front line.[34] Such systems not only deter pilferage and misallocation but also enable targeted recalls if defects emerge, thereby preserving both safety and accountability.

These imperatives emphasise that effective ammunition management in the twenty-first century cannot be confined to questions of production capacity or stockpile depth alone. It must anticipate surge consumption, safeguard supply chains, integrate old and new munitions intelligently, and maintain rigorous accountability even under pressure. Addressing these dimensions in advance will enable countries like India to sustain combat effectiveness in prolonged conflicts while ensuring that their defence-industrial base remains both resilient and adaptive.

Case Study Insights

The case studies of the Russia-Ukraine and Israel-Hamas conflicts have been carefully selected due to their distinctive and illustrative dynamics in modern warfare, particularly highlighting diverse strategies in ammunition management. Each conflict showcases unique logistical challenges and strategic responses related to ammunition, providing a comprehensive understanding of its critical role in contemporary military operations.

The Russia-Ukraine Conflict

The Russia-Ukraine conflict, which intensified in 2014, exemplifies the strategic importance of ammunition management in a high-intensity, conventional warfare environment. This conflict has stressed the necessity of robust stockpile management, adept handling of imports and exports, and proactive domestic production of munitions. Initially, Ukraine struggled with inadequate stockpiles of outdated Soviet-era munitions. The conflict's duration and intensity necessitated the urgent refurbishment and augmentation of these stockpiles.[35] Reports indicated a significant increase in domestic production and modernisation efforts to replenish and upgrade these arsenals, highlighting the direct impact of stockpile readiness on combat effectiveness. The geopolitical ramifications of the conflict led to increased Western support, with NATO allies supplying a variety of munitions to Ukraine. This external support has been critical in offsetting the shortages and has had a profound impact on the dynamics of the conflict, illustrating how international aid can alter the strategic landscape.[36] Facing persistent threats, Ukraine accelerated its domestic production capabilities, focusing on becoming self-reliant in critical munitions. This shift not only aimed to mitigate immediate shortages but also to establish a long-term strategic buffer against future disruptions.[37] The Ukraine–Russia war has emerged as a live laboratory of innovation, where necessity drives improvisation at unprecedented speed. Cheap First-Person-View (FPV) drones, once seen as toys, have become lethal precision weapons in the hands of ordinary fighters. To counter them, crews weld makeshift "turtle shells" onto tanks, turning steel and scrap into life-saving armour. Even motorcycles, machines of a bygone era, are back, carrying supplies and troops through back roads where heavier vehicles would be spotted and destroyed. These adaptations highlight how modern wars blend high-end technology with low-cost improvisation, underscoring the need for armies worldwide to anticipate, absorb, and rapidly adapt to disruptive battlefield innovations.

The Israel-Hamas Conflict

The intermittent escalations between Israel and Hamas in Gaza provide a stark contrast, emphasising the role of advanced R&D and self-reliance in ammunition strategies in an asymmetric warfare context. Israel's strategic advantage is significantly bolstered by its focus on R&D, leading to the development of advanced technologies, such as, precision-guided munitions and the Iron Dome missile defence system. These innovations have allowed Israel to conduct highly effective defensive and offensive operations with minimal civilian impact and collateral damage.[38] To maintain operational security and flexibility, Israel invests heavily in domestic ammunition production. This approach not only supports the rapid deployment of forces in times of conflict but also ensures that the military is not overly dependent on unpredictable international supply chains.[39] The strategic deployment of various ammunition types tailored to specific tactical needs showcases Israel's capacity to maximise operational effectiveness while minimising risks.[40] This tactical adaptability is crucial in asymmetric warfare, where threat levels can vary significantly across different scenarios.

The case studies clearly demonstrate how ammunition management can dictate the pace and outcome of conflicts. In Ukraine, the rapid enhancement of ammunition stockpiles and production capabilities, supported significantly by Western allies, has had profound strategic implications. It not only bolstered Ukraine's defence against aggression but also strengthened ties with NATO countries, showcasing how logistical support can serve as a tool of diplomatic leverage and solidarity in international politics.[41] Similarly, Israel's advanced R&D in ammunition technology and its strategic deployment has not only ensured its military superiority but also enabled it to maintain a technological edge that is pivotal for its national security policy and for maintaining a deterrent posture in a volatile region.[42]

Ammunition management plays a crucial role in shaping international alliances and relations. Effective management and self-reliance in ammunition production can enhance a nation's sovereignty and reduce dependency on foreign entities, thereby shifting the dynamics of international military cooperation and aid. For instance, as countries like Ukraine move towards greater self-reliance, they may become less dependent on NATO supplies, which could alter the nature of their relationships with these countries. Conversely, nations that can produce and supply military munitions, like the US and Russia, wield significant influence over other countries dependent on their exports, using such dependencies as a means to exert political pressure or forge strategies. Moreover, the capability to independently manage ammunition logistics and production also impacts international arms control agreements and the global arms trade. Nations with advanced ammunition technologies and production capacities have a greater say in international forums concerning arms control, thereby influencing global standards and regulations. The lessons from the Ukraine war and the Israel-Hamas conflict emphasise the importance of precision-guided munitions, drone operations, and specialised equipment in modern warfare. Precision-guided munitions, in particular, have become indispensable in reducing collateral damage and increasing the effectiveness of strikes in urban and asymmetric warfare scenarios. The integration of drone technology and other specialised equipment into conventional and asymmetric warfare strategies further enhances operational effectiveness, providing military forces with versatile tools that can adapt to the evolving nature of conflict. These innovations must be supported by robust R&D and production capacities to maintain a strategic advantage on the battlefield.

These strategic implications suggest that effective ammunition management extends beyond mere operational considerations it influences broader defence policies, impacts international relations, and shapes the geopolitical landscape. Therefore, countries must consider their strategies for ammunition management within the larger context of their foreign policy and defence strategies, acknowledging that how they manage their ammunition not only determines their combat effectiveness but also their diplomatic and strategic positions on the world stage.

Challenges and Innovations in Ammunition Management

Ammunition management in modern warfare is facing a multitude of emerging challenges, particularly as the complexity of global conflicts and the technological landscape evolve. These challenges are deeply intertwined with the innovations that are currently shaping the future of ammunition logistics. One significant challenge in global ammunition logistics is the increasing sophistication of warfare technologies and the corresponding need for advanced munitions, which demand intricate manufacturing processes and rare materials.[43] As conflicts become more technology-driven, the logistics of sourcing, producing, and maintaining advanced munitions strains existing supply chains. Moreover, geopolitical tensions often restrict access to necessary materials or disrupt logistics routes, complicating the global supply chain dynamics. Ammunition supply chains in modern warfare are critical to maintaining the continuity and effectiveness of military operations. From factory production or imports to the final point of application, ensuring the reliability and resilience of these supply chains is paramount. This includes not only maintaining robust production capacities and active vendor relationships but also implementing strategies to protect supply chains from potential enemy attacks. The decentralisation of production facilities, diversification of supply routes, and use of advanced technologies for real-time monitoring and threat detection are key measures to safeguard these logistics networks. Moreover, ensuring that production capacities can be scaled quickly in response to surges in demand is vital for sustaining prolonged military engagements. Effective supply chain management not only supports operational readiness but also contributes to the overall strategic resilience of military forces.

Another pressing issue is the environmental impact of ammunition production and deployment, which has led to increased regulatory scrutiny.[44,45] The need for environmentally friendly munitions is pushing military R&D to develop less harmful alternatives that comply with international environmental standards without compromising performance. Stockpile management, logistics optimisation, and real-time data management are critical components of modern munitions management. Ensuring that stockpiles are sufficient, well-maintained, and strategically positioned is essential. This requires integrating advanced data management and operational optimisation tools, such as, statistical modelling and simulations, into military exercises and planning processes. Moreover, production capacities must be dynamic, with the ability to scale rapidly in response to increased demand during conflicts. Military planning should include simulations that realistically model munitions production and distribution logistics, enabling forces to anticipate and mitigate potential supply chain disruptions.

Addressing these challenges, several innovations in ammunition management are emerging. One prominent trend is the development of smart ammunition systems that enhance precision and reduce unnecessary collateral damage.[46] These systems use real-time data and connectivity to adjust their trajectory, targeting, and detonation characteristics dynamically. Additionally, the drive towards more sustainable munitions is leading to innovations, such as, biodegradable training ammunition and non-toxic primer formulations. These developments not only address environmental concerns but also reduce the health risks to military personnel and local populations.[47] The future of ammunition management will likely see increased integration of artificial intelligence and machine learning in logistics operations, enhancing forecasting accuracy, optimising stock levels, and streamlining supply chains. This technological integration is expected to significantly improve the responsiveness and efficiency of ammunition logistics, adapting quickly to the changing conditions on the battlefield.

Key Takeaways

The examination of ammunition management in modern warfare reveals its critical role in shaping defence policies and military strategies. Through this analysis, several key findings emerge. Firstly, ammunition management is integral to military readiness and operational effectiveness. The availability, distribution, and maintenance of ammunition directly impact a military's ability to execute missions and respond to threats swiftly and decisively. Secondly, effective ammunition management contributes to strategic stability and deterrence. Nations with robust ammunition stockpiles and efficient logistical systems project strength and resilience, deterring potential adversaries and bolstering confidence among allies.

Furthermore, ammunition management influences resource allocation and force structure, guiding defence policymakers in optimising military capabilities and enhancing operational readiness. Reflecting on these insights, it is evident that ammunition management has profound strategic implications for defence policies and military strategies. Therefore, policymakers must prioritise investments in ammunition management infrastructure, technology, and personnel to ensure national security and strategic resilience. Looking ahead, future research in the field of ammunition management and modern warfare should focus on several key areas. Firstly, there is a need for further exploration of the impact of emerging technologies, such as, additive manufacturing and artificial intelligence, on ammunition production and logistics. Additionally, research should examine the implications of evolving geopolitical dynamics, such as, shifting alliances and regional conflicts, on ammunition supply chains and strategic stability. Furthermore, studies on the integration of ammunition management with broader defence planning processes, including force posture assessments and contingency planning, can provide valuable insights into optimising military readiness and responsiveness.

In conclusion, ammunition management is a critical determinant of military effectiveness and strategic stability in modern warfare. Strategic ammunition management is a cornerstone of modern military strategy, integral not only to the success on the battlefield but also to the formulation of broader security policies and international diplomacy. As warfare continues to evolve, so too must our strategies and technologies, ensuring that future conflicts are waged smarter, faster, and more sustainable.

3

Unmanned Dominance: The Drone Revolution in Warfare

The character of warfare in the twenty-first century is being fundamentally reshaped by the rapid proliferation and employment of unmanned systems, particularly drones. Once regarded as auxiliary platforms for surveillance and reconnaissance, drones have now evolved into decisive instruments of both conventional and hybrid warfare. Their integration into modern militaries has altered the traditional balance between offense and defence by enabling cost-effective, precise, and persistent operations across multiple domains. From the deserts of the Middle East to the contested airspaces of Eastern Europe, drones have demonstrated their ability to shape outcomes on the battlefield, challenge established doctrines, and impose significant costs on adversaries. They are no longer niche assets but force multipliers that can extend the reach, lethality, and adaptability of armed forces.

The evolution of drone warfare reflects broader transformations in global security. Whereas industrial-age conflicts were defined by large formations of men and machines, and the information age emphasised networked command structures, today's conflicts are increasingly marked by autonomous and semi-autonomous systems capable of operating at scale. Unmanned Aerial Vehicles (UAVs), in particular, exemplify the convergence of multiple technologies, artificial intelligence, advanced sensors, satellite navigation, and precision-guided munitions, into a single platform that can provide persistent Intelligence, Surveillance, and Reconnaissance (ISR), carry out precision strikes, and even undertake swarm-based operations. This integration represents a paradigm shift in the way military power is conceptualised and projected.

Globally, the diffusion of drone technology has been remarkable. States that once monopolised advanced military technologies now find themselves competing with smaller nations and even non-state actors who leverage commercially available drones for tactical advantages. The United States pioneered the large-scale military use of UAVs through systems like the Predator and Reaper, which became symbols of counterterrorism operations in Afghanistan and Iraq. However, it is the more recent deployment of low-cost, expendable drones by countries, such as, Turkey, Israel, and Iran, as well as by non-state entities like the Houthis in Yemen, that highlights the democratisation of this capability. The battlefield utility of drones is no longer limited to technologically advanced militaries but is increasingly within the grasp of actors with modest resources, thereby reshaping the strategic calculus of both state and non-state competition.

The implications of this revolution in warfare are particularly significant for India. Situated in a contested neighbourhood with hostile adversaries on both its northern and western borders, India cannot ignore the disruptive potential of drones. The 2019 Abqaiq–Khurais attacks in Saudi Arabia, the 2020 Nagorno-Karabakh war, and the ongoing Russia–Ukraine conflict have all underscored how drones can bypass traditional air defences, overwhelm conventional systems, and impose asymmetrical costs. India itself has faced the menace of drones in its internal security environment, particularly in Jammu and Kashmir and along the western border, where small drones have been used for surveillance, arms drop, and narcotics smuggling. These developments point to the necessity of both harnessing drone technologies for national defence and preparing countermeasures against adversarial use.

For India, the revolution in unmanned systems must also be contextualised within the broader framework of its defence industrial base and the ambition of achieving self-reliance under the vision of *Atmanirbhar Bharat*. The Defence Acquisition Procedure (DAP) 2020, the Innovations for Defence Excellence (iDEX) initiative, and targeted policy interventions have created opportunities for start-ups and private industry to enter the drone ecosystem. Indigenous platforms, such as, the DRDO's Rustom series and private-sector loitering munitions illustrate the growing momentum in this domain. However, India still faces significant challenges in scaling production, integrating advanced technologies like swarm intelligence, and building resilient supply chains for components, such as, engines, sensors, and secure communication systems.

The emergence of drones also intersects directly with the central theme of ammunition management, which forms the broader canvas of this book. Drones are not merely platforms but also delivery mechanisms for precision-guided munitions, loitering weapons, and novel warhead designs. Their increasing use transforms the demand profile of ammunition, away from bulk stockpiles of traditional shells and rockets towards specialised, high-precision, and often expendable munitions tailored for unmanned delivery. This shift underscores the need for India to not only indigenise drone platforms but also to integrate ammunition R&D with drone warfare requirements, ensuring that the supply chain is prepared for next-generation demands.

In essence, the drone revolution is not just a technological trend but a strategic inflection point. It compels a rethinking of military doctrines, acquisition policies, and industrial strategies. For India, the stakes are especially high: drones represent both an opportunity to leapfrog technological gaps and a vulnerability if adversaries exploit them more effectively. As this chapter will demonstrate, understanding the trajectory of drone warfare, from its historical evolution to its contemporary applications and future prospects, is critical to appreciating how unmanned systems are redefining the conduct of war and what this means for India's aspiration to emerge as a secure, technologically advanced nation by 2047.

Historical Evolution of Drone Warfare

The evolution of drone warfare has been shaped by technological innovation, doctrinal experimentation, and the shifting nature of conflict. Although drones are often seen as a product of twenty-first century battlefields, their origins can be traced back to the early twentieth century when militaries first sought unmanned aerial platforms for reconnaissance and target practice. Over the decades, drones progressed from rudimentary prototypes to sophisticated combat systems, reflecting broader trends in the militarisation of technology.

The earliest conceptual attempts at drone-like systems emerged during World War I. In 1916, the British experimented with the "Aerial Target," a radio-controlled aircraft designed primarily for training anti-aircraft gunners. Around the same period, the United States developed the Kettering Bug, an early cruise missile prototype that used gyroscopic guidance to deliver explosives over a range of 40 miles.[48] These early experiments, while limited in accuracy and reliability, demonstrated the strategic imagination behind unmanned flight: the ability to project power without risking pilots.

During World War II, drone development entered a new phase with the introduction of pilotless target aircraft and guided munitions. The German V-1 "buzz bomb," technically a cruise missile, blurred the line between drones and rockets by delivering explosive payloads over long distances with rudimentary autopilot systems. The US military, meanwhile, converted warplanes, such as, the B-17 Flying Fortress into remote-controlled "drones" packed with explosives, though operational effectiveness remained questionable.[49] These innovations marked the growing recognition of unmanned systems as both training tools and offensive weapons, even if their role remained experimental.

The Cold War period accelerated drone research, primarily for reconnaissance. The United States, constrained by the risks of piloted overflights after the downing of Gary Powers' U-2 spy plane in 1960, invested heavily in unmanned reconnaissance vehicles. The Ryan Model 147 "Lightning Bug" drones, deployed extensively during the Vietnam War, provided valuable intelligence while avoiding the political costs of pilot losses.[50] By the 1980s, Israel emerged as a pioneer in operational drone warfare. Israeli forces used the Scout and Pioneer drones for real-time battlefield surveillance, electronic warfare, and target designation during the 1982 Lebanon War.[51] This marked the first large-scale, successful integration of drones into combined arms operations and underscored their utility in enhancing precision strike capabilities.

The post-Cold War era saw drones evolve from surveillance assets into armed platforms. The United States led this transformation in the late 1990s with the MQ-1 Predator, initially designed for ISR missions but later weaponised with AGM-114 Hellfire missiles. This innovation redefined drone warfare, allowing unmanned platforms to conduct precision strikes against high-value targets in counterterrorism campaigns.[52] During the wars in Afghanistan and Iraq, armed drones became symbols of a new era in warfare: persistent, precise, and capable of striking without deploying ground troops. These systems blurred the boundaries between tactical and strategic operations by enabling targeted killings that influenced both battlefield dynamics and global counterterrorism policies.

These parallel developments occurred in other parts of the world. Israel, building on its earlier successes, became a leading exporter of UAV technology.[53] China developed indigenous systems, such as, the Wing Loong and CH-series drones, offering affordable alternatives to states that could not access U.S. or Israeli platforms.[54] Turkey's Bayraktar TB2, entering service in the 2010s, demonstrated the disruptive potential of relatively inexpensive drones when effectively integrated into military strategy, as seen in Syria, Libya, and later in the Nagorno-Karabakh conflict.[55] These developments underscored a significant shift: drones were no longer niche assets of great powers but accessible tools of warfare for mid-level states and, increasingly, non-state actors. The twenty-first century has also witnessed the diversification of drone roles. Beyond ISR and targeted strikes, drones are now employed for electronic warfare, logistics, and swarm operations. The development of loitering munitions, sometimes called "suicide drones", such as, Israel's Harop or Iran's Shahed series, further expands the operational envelope.[56] These systems combine surveillance with attack capabilities in a single expendable platform, complicating traditional air defence doctrines.

Thus, the historical trajectory of drones reflects a gradual but decisive shift: from experimental curiosities in the early twentieth century to indispensable instruments of statecraft and warfare in the twenty-first. Their evolution highlights not only technological ingenuity but also the way in which strategic needs and doctrinal innovation drive military adoption. In the following sections, the analysis will move from this historical overview to an examination of global trends in drone development, focusing on case studies that illustrate the strategic impact of unmanned systems in contemporary conflicts.

Global Trends in Drone Development

The United States: From Predator to Global Dominance

The United States occupies a singular position in the history of drone warfare, having transformed unmanned aerial vehicles from experimental reconnaissance tools into decisive instruments of modern combat. The MQ-1 Predator, introduced in the mid-1990s, marked a turning point by combining long-endurance surveillance capabilities with the precision strike power of AGM-114 Hellfire missiles. This innovation allowed the US to conduct targeted killings of high-value individuals during counterterrorism operations in Afghanistan, Iraq, Pakistan, and Yemen without exposing pilots to direct risk. Over time, the Predator was succeeded by the larger MQ-9 Reaper, which offered greater payload capacity, extended range, and improved sensors, thereby entrenching drones as integral to US military operations.

Beyond these iconic platforms, the US invested in a wide array of UAVs to serve diverse operational needs. The RQ-4 Global Hawk provided high-altitude, long-endurance surveillance for strategic intelligence collection, while the stealth-oriented RQ-170 Sentinel supported sensitive missions in denied airspaces, including operations over Iran and Pakistan. The US Navy experimented with carrier-based drones, such as, the X-47B to integrate unmanned systems into naval aviation, signalling ambitions to extend drone capabilities into maritime domains. Equally significant has been the doctrinal incorporation of drones into America's broader counterinsurgency and counterterrorism strategies. Drones enabled persistent surveillance over insurgent strongholds, close coordination with special operations forces, and precise kinetic engagements that reduced the need for large troop deployments. Yet, these advantages were accompanied by strategic dilemmas. Drone strikes drew criticism for civilian casualties, questions of legality under international law, and concerns about lowering the threshold for the use of force. As such, US drone warfare became as much a subject of ethical and political debate as of military effectiveness.

Looking forward, the US continues to push the boundaries of unmanned technologies. Research into swarming drones, artificial intelligence-enabled autonomy, and loyal wingman concepts that pair UAVs with manned aircraft suggests that drones will remain central to the future of American airpower. Washington's dominance lies not only in possessing advanced platforms but also in its ability to integrate drones into multi-domain operations, making them indispensable to both strategic deterrence and tactical combat.

Israel: Innovator and Exporter of UAV Technology

Israel has long been a pioneer in the field of unmanned aerial systems, driven by its unique security environment and the constant need for technological asymmetry. From the late 1970s onward, Israel began experimenting with UAVs as tools for reconnaissance, surveillance, and electronic warfare. This culminated in the operational use of the Scout and Pioneer drones during the 1982 Lebanon War, where they provided real-time intelligence on Syrian air defences. The integration of drones into a combined arms framework proved decisive, allowing Israeli aircraft to neutralise Syrian surface-to-air missile batteries with minimal losses. This success became a model for future UAV employment worldwide and established Israel's reputation as a leading innovator in unmanned systems.

Over subsequent decades, Israel diversified its drone portfolio. The Heron and Hermes series became central to long-endurance surveillance and precision targeting, while the Harop loitering munition blurred the line between UAV and missile by enabling autonomous target engagement. These platforms were not only employed domestically in monitoring militant activity in Gaza and the West Bank but also adapted for export, making Israel one of the world's largest suppliers of UAV technology. Over fifty countries, including India, Germany, and Brazil, have acquired Israeli drones, reflecting the global appeal of platforms that combine combat reliability with advanced sensor integration.

What distinguishes Israel's drone development is the close synergy between operational demand and industrial capacity. The Israel Defence Forces (IDF) work in tandem with companies, such as, Israel Aerospace Industries (IAI) and Elbit Systems to ensure rapid adaptation of UAVs to evolving security challenges. This civil-military partnership has enabled quick transitions from prototypes to combat-ready systems, maintaining Israel's technological edge in the face of persistent asymmetric threats.

Moreover, drones have become a diplomatic instrument in Israel's foreign policy. By exporting UAVs to diverse regions, Israel has built strategic partnerships and secured influence in key markets. The ability of Israeli drones to deliver operational results in real conflicts has enhanced their credibility, while flexible export policies have given Israel an advantage over competitors constrained by stricter regulations. In effect, Israel's UAV industry serves not only its national defence needs but also its broader strategic objectives, positioning the country as both a technological innovator and a global drone hub.

China: Mass Production and Export Competitiveness

China has emerged as one of the most prolific developers and exporters of unmanned aerial vehicles, leveraging its industrial capacity and civil–military integration to close the gap with established drone powers. Unlike the United States, which emphasises high-end platforms, or Israel, which combines innovation with niche exports, China's strategy has focused on scale, affordability, and accessibility. This approach has allowed Beijing to dominate markets in the Global South, where states often face political or financial barriers to acquiring US or Israeli systems.

Central to China's drone ecosystem are the Wing Loong and CH (Cai

Hong, or "Rainbow") series, which have been exported to countries across the Middle East, Africa, and Asia. These platforms, often referred to as "Predator equivalents," provide long-endurance surveillance and precision strike capabilities at a fraction of the cost of Western systems. States, such as, Saudi Arabia, Egypt, Nigeria, and Pakistan have acquired Chinese UAVs, using them in both counterterrorism operations and regional conflicts. Their deployment in Saudi-led operations in Yemen, for instance, demonstrates both the utility and growing legitimacy of Chinese drones in contested theatres.

Domestically, China has invested heavily in research and development to diversify its UAV portfolio. Advanced stealth drones, such as, the Sharp Sword prototype, high-altitude long-endurance systems like the WZ-7 Soaring Dragon, and swarming drone experiments highlight Beijing's ambition to rival the US not only in exports but also in next-generation technologies. Civil–military fusion has been a cornerstone of this growth, with companies like AVIC (Aviation Industry Corporation of China) drawing upon the expertise of China's booming commercial drone industry, exemplified by firms, such as, DJI, to accelerate military applications.

China's drone development also reflects its broader geopolitical strategy. By supplying affordable UAVs without the restrictive end-use clauses that often accompany US sales, Beijing has positioned itself as a reliable security partner for states in Africa and the Middle East. This enhances China's diplomatic influence, particularly in regions critical to its Belt and Road Initiative. However, questions remain about the reliability, survivability, and combat effectiveness of Chinese drones compared to US or Israeli counterparts. Reports of operational shortcomings, such as, poor endurance in harsh environments and vulnerabilities to electronic warfare, suggest that China's drones, while accessible, may still lack the sophistication of high-end systems.

Nevertheless, the Chinese model underscores how scale and affordability can democratise drone warfare. By lowering the barriers to entry for states that previously could not afford advanced UAVs, China has not only disrupted global defence markets but also contributed to the wider diffusion of unmanned systems across the world. This trend has significant implications for international security, as the spread of Chinese drones alters regional balances of power and normalises the use of UAVs in both conventional and irregular conflicts.

Turkey: The Bayraktar Model and Affordable Disruption

Turkey has emerged as one of the most influential new actors in drone warfare, demonstrating how middle powers can leverage indigenous innovation to achieve outsized strategic impact. Unlike the United States or Israel, which focused on high-end technological sophistication, Turkey's approach has been to develop affordable yet effective UAVs that can be produced at scale and rapidly deployed in diverse conflict zones. The centrepiece of this strategy is the Bayraktar TB2, a medium-altitude, long-endurance drone that has become synonymous with Turkish drone diplomacy.

The TB2 combines endurance, precision strike capability, and cost-effectiveness in a way that has reshaped modern battlefields. Armed with lightweight guided munitions, it has been used extensively in Syria, Libya, and Nagorno-Karabakh, where it played a decisive role in altering the tactical balance of power. In the 2020 Nagorno-Karabakh conflict, for example, TB2 drones enabled Azerbaijani forces to neutralise Armenian armour and air defences, showcasing how a relatively inexpensive platform could achieve disproportionate battlefield outcomes. These successes elevated the TB2 to iconic status, making it a sought-after system for countries seeking affordable alternatives to US or Israeli drones.

Turkey's UAV strategy reflects its broader political and security ambitions. By exporting the TB2 to countries, such as, Ukraine, Poland, Morocco, and several African states, Ankara has extended its geopolitical reach while bolstering its defence industry. The export success of the TB2 has not only generated economic benefits but also enhanced Turkey's diplomatic influence, providing Ankara with leverage in regions ranging from Eastern Europe to North Africa.

At the same time, Turkey continues to diversify its drone portfolio. The larger Akinci UAV, capable of carrying heavier payloads and advanced sensors, represents a shift towards higher-end systems, while the Kizilelma unmanned fighter project points to ambitions of integrating UAVs into air combat roles traditionally reserved for manned aircraft. Turkey has also invested in counter-drone technologies and swarm concepts, reflecting a recognition that future conflicts will involve contested drone environments.

The "Bayraktar model" illustrates how innovation need not always mean cutting-edge sophistication. By focusing on cost-efficiency, operational reliability, and exportability, Turkey has disrupted the drone market and empowered smaller states to field capabilities that were once the preserve of great powers. This democratisation of drone warfare underscores a larger trend: the diffusion of unmanned systems is no longer driven exclusively by technological leaders but also by agile middle powers willing to experiment, deploy, and export aggressively.

To illustrate these global trends more systematically, the following table provides a comparative overview of the four principal actors, United States, Israel, China, and Turkey. Each represents a distinctive model of drone development and deployment shaped by technological priorities, export strategies, and operational experiences. The United States has emphasised high-end, precision-focused platforms integrated into multi-domain operations; Israel has combined rapid innovation with aggressive exports, turning drones into both military assets and diplomatic tools; China has pursued mass production and affordability, thereby opening access for many states in the Global South; while Turkey has adopted a disruptive middle-power model that leverages cost-effectiveness and bold operational employment.

Country	*Signature Systems*	*Core Strengths*	*Export Strategy*	*Battlefield Impact*	*Limitations*
United States	MQ-1 Predator, MQ-9 Reaper, RQ-170, Global Hawk	Advanced tech, long endurance, integration into multi-domain ops	Selective exports, strict controls	Precision strikes in Afghanistan, Iraq, Pakistan	Criticism of civilian casualties, high costs
Israel	Heron, Hermes, Harop loitering munition	Innovation, civil-military synergy	Aggressive exports to 50+ countries	Effective ISR/strike integration (Lebanon 1982, Gaza)	Limited scale compared to US/China
China	Wing Loong, CH-series, WZ-7	Mass production, affordability	Open, low-cost exports to Global South	Use in Yemen, Nigeria, Egypt	Reliability issues, electronic warfare vulnerabilities
Turkey	Bayraktar TB2, Akinci, Kizilelma (under dev.)	Cost-effectiveness, operational agility	Exports to Ukraine, Africa, Europe	Decisive impact in Nagorno-Karabakh, Syria	Limited range/ payload compared to US/China

The table highlights how these divergent approaches are not merely technical differences but reflections of broader strategic cultures. US systems, while technologically superior, remain politically constrained by export controls and public debates about ethics and legality. Israel's innovations reflect its asymmetric security environment, but its limited industrial scale constrains global dominance. China, through affordability and volume, has democratised drone warfare, though concerns about quality persist. Turkey's Bayraktar model demonstrates that even middle powers can shape battlefields and markets by prioritising reliability and accessibility over sophistication.

This comparative framing underscores that drone warfare today is no longer defined by a single technological trajectory. Instead, multiple models of development and diffusion coexist, each altering regional balances of power and contributing to the broader global proliferation of unmanned systems.

Technology Trajectory: Drone Warfare

The drone revolution is not just about wider use on the battlefield, but about the technological directions that are making these systems more lethal, reliable, and versatile. Among the most important is the growing role of artificial intelligence. In earlier conflicts, drones relied almost entirely on human pilots operating them remotely, often from thousands of miles away. Today, the balance is shifting towards systems that can "think" and act on their own in certain situations. AI and edge computing allow drones to recognise targets, adjust flight paths, and even adapt missions when communications are jammed or GPS signals are denied. This capability has already been seen in Ukraine, where drones equipped with autonomous navigation have continued to operate effectively despite heavy Russian electronic warfare efforts.[57] In essence, autonomy is turning drones from remote-controlled machines into active participants in battle.

Alongside autonomy, swarming technology is beginning to reshape how militaries think about mass and firepower. A single drone can be effective, but dozens or even hundreds of them, operating as a coordinated swarm, represent a fundamentally different challenge. Through decentralised algorithms and mesh networks, swarms can share information in real time, assign roles among themselves, and attack from multiple directions simultaneously. RAND's recent analysis shows that swarms are no longer futuristic speculation; militaries are treating them as practical tools for both offense and defence.[58] A well-coordinated swarm could overwhelm even advanced air defence systems, forcing adversaries to rethink how they allocate resources and protect high-value assets.

A third important trajectory is the shrinking of warheads to fit on smaller and cheaper drones. Loitering munitions, sometimes called "kamikaze drones", embody this trend by combining the platform and payload into one expendable system. These drones can circle above a battlefield before diving onto a target at the right moment. They have become a defining feature of the Ukraine war, where inexpensive loitering munitions have been used to knock out tanks, artillery pieces, and even radar systems worth many times their cost.[59] This inversion of traditional cost dynamics using thousands of dollars to destroy millions of dollars explains why states and non-state actors alike are turning to these weapons.

Also, equally significant is the development of "mothership" concepts and manned-unmanned teaming. Here, larger drones or even manned aircraft act as controllers, launching and coordinating smaller unmanned systems. In the United States, DARPA's LongShot project is exploring drones that can carry and fire air-to-air missiles, extending the reach of manned fighters without exposing pilots to danger. India's Combat Air Teaming System (CATS) is pursuing a similar path, envisioning "loyal wingman" drones that fly alongside the Tejas fighter jet, carrying sensors and weapons to expand its combat envelope.[60] These innovations are not only about adding firepower, but also about changing the very way air combat is imagined less a duel between pilots and more a contest between networks of manned and unmanned systems.

The final trajectory is integration across multiple domains. Drones are no longer confined to the skies. Naval drones have been used with striking effect in the Black Sea, where Ukraine has deployed them to challenge and damage Russian warships. Undersea drones are beginning to play a role in maritime surveillance, mine clearance, and even potential strike missions. On land, small quadcopters have become nearly ubiquitous in trench warfare, scouting enemy positions and dropping grenades with deadly accuracy. When these systems are linked together, *vis-à-vis*, airborne surveillance feeding data to ground units, naval drones relaying information to coastal defences, they create what analysts describe as a "kill web," where information and firepower flow seamlessly across domains.[61]

For India, these trajectories are not distant possibilities but immediate realities. In the deserts of Rajasthan, swarming drones could one day take on the role of traditional artillery, neutralising advancing armoured columns with speed and precision. In the Himalayan frontiers of Ladakh and Arunachal Pradesh, cold-resistant drones with secure satellite links have already been tested, showing how they can operate at extreme altitudes where traditional aircraft struggle. In crowded urban centres, micro-drones can scout buildings, identify threats, and reduce risks to soldiers in counterterrorism operations. At sea, India's leased MQ-9A Sea Guardian drones are already enhancing maritime surveillance, and the planned acquisition of MQ-9B drones for all three services promises to push this integration further. These examples illustrate that India cannot treat drone warfare as an optional capability. Dedicated units for autonomous systems, new doctrines for swarm employment, and closer collaboration between platform designers and ammunition developers will be essential.

Ultimately, the technological trajectory of drones' points to a future where combat power will be measured less in the number of tanks or aircraft a nation fields and more in the intelligence, adaptability, and resilience of its unmanned systems. For India, embracing this shift is not only about keeping pace with adversaries but about shaping its own role as a technologically self-reliant and strategically agile power.

India's Drone Ecosystem

India's entry into the era of unmanned aerial systems has been shaped by a combination of indigenous innovation, reliance on imports, and policy frameworks designed to stimulate domestic capacity. While the global drone revolution has advanced at a rapid pace, India's trajectory has been more gradual, reflecting both structural challenges and the opportunities created by a growing emphasis on self-reliance in defence production. The current ecosystem reflects a hybrid model in which imported systems provide immediate operational capability, indigenous projects aim to build long-term technological competence, and government policies attempt to bridge the gap between innovation and deployment.

Indigenous Developments

Indigenous drone development in India has been spearheaded by the Defence Research and Development Organisation (DRDO) and increasingly supplemented by the private sector. DRDO's Rustom series, particularly the

TAPAS-BH 201 (also known as Rustom-II), represents India's first attempt at a Medium-Altitude Long-Endurance (MALE) UAV capable of Intelligence, Surveillance, Target Acquisition, and Reconnaissance (ISTAR) roles. Although delays and performance limitations have slowed its induction, the TAPAS project demonstrates India's determination to field a homegrown platform comparable to global MALE systems.

Another key project is the Ghatak stealth UCAV, which aims to provide India with an unmanned combat platform featuring stealth characteristics and autonomous strike capabilities. Though still in developmental stages, it highlights India's ambition to integrate advanced technologies, such as, stealth shaping, precision munitions, and autonomous mission planning into its future drone arsenal. In addition, the Abhyas high-speed expendable aerial target has been developed for air defence training and evaluation, further diversifying India's drone portfolio.

Beyond DRDO, the Hindustan Aeronautics Limited (HAL) has launched the Combat Air Teaming System (CATS) program, which envisions manned-unmanned teaming operations. Under this concept, a fighter aircraft, such as, the Tejas will control multiple loyal wingman drones capable of carrying sensors and weapons. This approach aligns India with emerging trends in advanced air warfare where drones augment, rather than replace, manned platforms.

Importantly, indigenous innovation is no longer restricted to state-owned enterprises. India's startup ecosystem has begun to play a vital role, spurred by initiatives, such as, the Innovations for Defence Excellence (iDEX). Companies like *ideaForge* (supplier of surveillance drones to Indian forces), *NewSpace Research and Technologies* (focused on swarming systems), and *ZUPPA* (developing logistics drones) demonstrate the potential of private industry to complement government R&D. These firms, often born from the civil drone sector, are contributing to dual-use technologies that enhance both commercial and defence applications.

Imports and External Collaborations

Despite indigenous progress, India's current drone capability remains heavily dependent on imports. The Israeli Heron and Searcher UAVs have been the backbone of India's surveillance network for decades, deployed for monitoring borders with Pakistan and China as well as for maritime reconnaissance. These systems provided India with reliable, combat-tested platforms at a time when domestic alternatives were not yet mature.

More recently, India has pursued collaboration with the United States to acquire advanced systems. The lease of MQ-9B SeaGuardian drones for the Indian Navy has already enhanced maritime domain awareness, and negotiations are underway for the purchase of additional MQ-9B drones for the Army, Navy, and Air Force. Such acquisitions not only provide immediate capability but also reflect the strengthening of the India–US strategic partnership.

The technology transfer and joint production agreements are also becoming more prominent. Discussions with both Israel and the US have explored co-production opportunities that could allow India to integrate imported expertise into its domestic manufacturing base. Such collaborations are crucial for addressing gaps in propulsion systems, sensor technology, and secure communication links—areas where India still lags behind global leaders.

Policy and Institutional Frameworks

The evolution of India's drone ecosystem has been significantly shaped by institutional reforms and policy frameworks aimed at stimulating domestic production. The Defence Acquisition Procedure 2020 streamlined procurement for unmanned systems, encouraging private-sector participation and creating specific categories for indigenously designed and developed platforms.

The iDEX initiative has been pivotal in supporting start-ups through funding, mentorship, and integration into defence supply chains. By creating innovation challenges and partnering with the armed forces, iDEX provides a structured pathway for small firms to contribute directly to military needs. Similarly, the establishment of Defence Industrial Corridors in Tamil Nadu and Uttar Pradesh offers infrastructure and incentives for drone and aerospace companies to cluster and collaborate.

The government has also introduced a Production-Linked Incentive (PLI) scheme for drones and drone components, reflecting the recognition that civil and military drone markets are interlinked. By supporting both segments, the scheme aims to create economies of scale that can reduce costs, encourage exports, and ensure dual-use synergies. These measures are aligned with the broader vision of *Atmanirbhar Bharat*, which seeks to reduce dependence on imports and promote indigenous capacity across the defence sector.

India's drone ecosystem is marked by ambition and uneven progress. Indigenous platforms highlight technological aspirations but are yet to match the reliability of imported systems. Imports provide immediate capability but carry long-term risks of dependency. Policy frameworks are robust in design but face the challenge of effective implementation and industry uptake. Nonetheless, the interplay between these three dimensions, indigenous development, foreign procurement, and policy reform, indicates that India is moving steadily towards building a comprehensive ecosystem. This ecosystem is not only central to enhancing India's operational capabilities but also to positioning the country within the evolving global landscape of drone warfare. By harnessing indigenous talent, leveraging strategic partnerships, and aligning policy incentives, India can transform its drone sector from a patchwork of initiatives into an integrated pillar of national defence. As subsequent sections will argue, the success of this transformation will depend on addressing persistent challenges and aligning drone development with broader strategic goals, particularly the demands of ammunition supply chains and the vision of *Viksit Bharat 2047*.

Challenges for India

While India's drone ecosystem has made visible progress, several critical challenges continue to constrain its potential. These challenges are not only technological but also doctrinal and institutional, reflecting the interplay between capability development and operational preparedness. Addressing them is essential if India is to build an autonomous, resilient, and strategically relevant unmanned systems sector.

The first set of challenges lies in technology gaps. Despite advances in indigenous projects, such as, TAPAS and Ghatak, India continues to depend heavily on foreign suppliers for crucial components, including engines, advanced sensors, secure data links, and satellite navigation systems. This dependency leaves India vulnerable to supply-chain disruptions and external political pressures. For instance, export restrictions or sanctions could delay critical programmes and undermine the credibility of domestic projects. Unless these core technologies are indigenised, India's ambition of strategic self-reliance will remain incomplete.

The second challenge is the development of swarm technology and next-generation autonomy. Swarming drones, capable of overwhelming adversary defences through coordinated, semi-autonomous operations, are increasingly seen as a disruptive force multiplier. China, for example, has tested swarms of fixed-wing and quadcopter drones in operational settings, signalling significant doctrinal preparedness. In India, by contrast, swarming remains at an experimental stage, with start-ups and DRDO laboratories exploring concepts but limited battlefield integration. Without accelerated investment and doctrinal experimentation, India risks lagging behind its adversaries in this emerging domain.

The third challenge relates to counter-UAV systems. Drones have already been used by non-state actors along India's western border for arms drops and narcotics smuggling, underscoring the vulnerability of India's internal security environment. While the armed forces and paramilitary units have initiated the deployment of anti-drone systems—including radio-frequency jammers and laser-based interception—the scale of the threat far outpaces current defensive capabilities. Detection remains difficult for small, low-flying drones, and electronic warfare assets are not yet widely deployed across border areas. This creates persistent operational vulnerabilities that adversaries could exploit in both peacetime and wartime contexts.

Finally, India faces challenges at the level of the industrial ecosystem. Delays in procurement, bureaucratic bottlenecks, and uneven collaboration between public and private sectors slow the pace of innovation. While policy frameworks, such as, iDEX and the PLI scheme have generated momentum, they require more consistent funding, transparent procurement, and integration into the armed forces' long-term capability planning. Without structural reforms, India risks repeating the cycle of underutilised indigenous projects and over-reliance on imports.

These challenges can be summarised in the following table, which highlights the key issues and their broader strategic implications:

Challenge Area	*Key Issues*	*Strategic Implications*
Technology Gaps	Dependence on foreign engines, sensors, secure comms	Limits autonomy; vulnerability to sanctions/export restrictions
Swarm Technology	Early-stage R&D, lack of tested swarm doctrine	Risk of lagging behind adversaries like China
Counter-UAV Systems	Gaps in detection, EW, and kinetic interception	Border vulnerabilities; asymmetric risks from non-state actors
Industrial Ecosystem	Delays, bureaucracy, limited private-sector integration	Slows innovation; continued reliance on imports

These challenges reveal that India's drone ecosystem is at a critical juncture. While the foundations have been laid, the next decade will determine whether India can transition from a dependent consumer to an autonomous producer and innovator. Failure to address these bottlenecks could leave India vulnerable in future conflicts where drones are not optional enablers but indispensable instruments of combat power.

Relevance of Supply Chains

The revolution in unmanned warfare is not confined to platforms alone; it also reshapes the logic of ammunition production, management, and supply. Traditionally, India's ammunition system was geared towards the bulk production of artillery shells, rockets, and small arms cartridges. This approach reflected the needs of large-scale conventional warfare, where volume mattered more than precision. However, the advent of drones as both delivery platforms and autonomous strike assets has fundamentally altered this equation.

Drones demand a qualitatively different category of munitions. Instead of sheer volume, there is now an emphasis on precision, modularity, and expendability. Loitering munitions, often described as "suicide drones," are themselves a fusion of platform and payload, embodying the convergence of ammunition and delivery systems. Similarly, drones carrying lightweight precision-guided bombs or air-to-surface missiles require warheads that are compact, high-yield, and adaptable to diverse operational environments. This trend compels a shift in India's ammunition ecosystem from a model based on standardised stockpiling to one that prioritises flexibility, rapid adaptation, and integration with emerging technologies.

The growing use of drones also transforms logistical demands. In a drone-dominated environment, supply chains must cater to a mix of traditional ammunition and advanced UAV-compatible payloads. Unlike conventional artillery shells, drone-based munitions often require integration with advanced guidance systems, secure data links, and power sources. This means that future ammunition management will need to be deeply integrated with electronics, software, and aerospace engineering—fields historically outside the remit of India's ordnance factories. Building such cross-domain supply chains will be critical if India is to sustain a credible drone arsenal.

Another dimension is the strategic cost-effectiveness of drone-delivered munitions. A loitering munition costing a few tens of thousands of dollars can neutralise a tank or artillery piece worth millions. This inversion of cost dynamics underscores why adversaries increasingly invest in drones: they can impose high costs on technologically superior opponents through relatively inexpensive systems. For India, this implies that ammunition production must incorporate affordability as a strategic metric, ensuring that stockpiles are not only technologically advanced but also financially sustainable.

The dual role of drones as both consumers and creators of demand for counter-ammunition systems is equally important. As adversaries employ drones for asymmetric operations—such as, cross-border infiltration, arms drop, or swarm attacks—India's defence establishment must also procure and develop interceptors, electronic warfare payloads, and directed-energy weapons. These countermeasures, too, are a form of specialised ammunition, extending the scope of the supply chain into domains that blur the traditional boundaries of ordnance.

Finally, the integration of drones into the armed forces compels India to rethink its research and development framework for ammunition. Instead of treating platforms and munitions as separate silos, India must adopt an integrated approach in which ammunition is co-designed with delivery systems. This includes close coordination between drone developers, ammunition manufacturers, and armed forces end-users. Without such integration, India risks creating platforms that outpace its ammunition capacity, or munitions that are incompatible with its evolving drone fleet.

In this sense, drones represent more than a technological novelty; they are catalysts for restructuring the entire ammunition supply chain. They push India towards a future where ordnance is not just mass-produced but technologically smart, modular, and aligned with next-generation platforms. This integration is indispensable for realising the vision of *Viksit Bharat 2047*, where India aspires to achieve both defence self-reliance and global competitiveness.

Integrating Drone Ecosystem with Ammunition Industry

The trajectory of drone warfare demonstrates that unmanned systems are no longer auxiliary tools but central elements of modern combat power. From their modest origins as experimental reconnaissance devices, drones have evolved into precision strike platforms, loitering munitions, and swarming technologies that can decisively alter the course of conflicts. Case studies from Ukraine, Nagorno-Karabakh, and the Middle East illustrate that drones are force multipliers, capable of neutralising conventional advantages and imposing asymmetric costs on adversaries. The global landscape further reinforces this trend, with the United States, Israel, China, and Turkey each advancing distinctive models of drone development that reflect their strategic cultures and industrial capacities.

For India, the drone revolution is both an opportunity and a challenge. On the one hand, indigenous projects like TAPAS and Ghatak, supported by private start-ups and policy frameworks, such as, iDEX and the PLI scheme, showcase the potential for innovation. On the other hand, persistent gaps in critical technologies, limited doctrinal integration, and vulnerabilities to adversarial drone use highlight the unfinished nature of India's preparedness. Unless these gaps are addressed, India risks being outpaced by adversaries who are already deploying drones in hybrid and conventional contexts.

Most importantly, drones compel a rethinking of ammunition production and management. They blur the line between platforms and payloads, driving demand for precision-guided, modular, and expendable munitions. They also expand the scope of ordnance to include counter-drone interceptors, electronic warfare payloads, and directed-energy systems. This represents a fundamental shift from a model of stockpiling mass ammunition to one of developing adaptive, technology-driven supply chains.

Looking ahead, India must integrate its drone ecosystem with its ammunition industry to achieve the vision of *Viksit Bharat 2047*. This requires investing in indigenous R&D, strengthening public–private collaboration, and embedding drones into joint force doctrines. Drones are not just tools of tactical advantage but also symbols of technological sovereignty and strategic maturity. Their effective integration into India's defence posture will determine whether the country can not only safeguard its borders but also project itself as a resilient, innovative, and influential power in the evolving security order of the twenty-first century.

4

Building a Robust Ecosystem for Smart Munitions Manufacturing

Evolution of Smart Munitions in Modern Warfare

The landscape of modern warfare has undergone a profound transformation, driven by rapid advancements in military technology. Among these developments, smart munitions have emerged as a critical component of contemporary combat strategies, significantly enhancing precision, efficiency, and operational effectiveness.[62] Unlike conventional ammunition, which rely on fixed trajectories and unguided targeting, smart munitions integrates advanced guidance systems, artificial intelligence, and real-time data processing to achieve unprecedented levels of accuracy and lethality.[63] The increasing adoption of Precision-Guided Munitions (PGMs) reflects a shift from traditional attrition-based warfare to precision-based engagements, where reducing collateral damage and optimising strike efficiency are paramount.[64] This transition is particularly crucial in an era marked by geopolitical tensions, asymmetric warfare, and urban combat scenarios, where surgical precision can determine the outcome of military operations.[65] Smart munitions, through its ability to autonomously adjust flight paths, identify high-value targets, and integrate with network-centric warfare systems, is redefining the nature and scope of armed conflicts.[66] Despite these advancements, many nations, especially developing military powers, continue to rely on external sources for the procurement of high-end smart munitions.[67] This dependence raises critical concerns related to national security, economic sustainability, and technological sovereignty, particularly in times of conflict or strained international relations.[68] India, one of the largest military forces globally, finds itself at a crossroads, balancing its growing defence needs with an urgent requirement for indigenous capabilities in smart munitions development.[69] Although government-led initiatives, such as, 'Make in India,' *Atmanirbhar Bharat*, and the SRIJAN Portal aim to strengthen domestic defence production, challenges, such as, fragmented research efforts, reliance on foreign components, and slow technology transfer continue to hinder India's progress towards self-sufficiency in smart munitions manufacturing.[70] The Defence Research and Development Organisation (DRDO), alongside private defence players and state-owned enterprises, has undertaken several initiatives to bridge the technological gap in ammunition development. Programs focused on precision-guided artillery shells, air-dropped bombs, loitering munitions, and hypersonic missiles indicate India's commitment to modernising its defence capabilities.[71] However, the existing R&D ecosystem remains fragmented, limiting the country's ability to compete with global leaders in smart munitions development, such as, the United States, Russia, and China.[72]

This chapter explores the evolution, technological advancements, global landscape, and strategic importance of smart munitions. It critically examines India's defence industry, the role of key stakeholders, and the need for a robust indigenous R&D ecosystem to achieve self-reliance in smart munitions.[73] By assessing the impact of smart munitions on modern warfare, this chapter highlights the urgency of accelerating India's defence innovation to ensure strategic autonomy and enhanced military preparedness in an increasingly volatile world.[74]

Characteristics of Smart Munitions

Smart munitions, also known as PGMs, represents a significant advancement in modern military weaponry, integrating artificial intelligence (AI), advanced sensors, and sophisticated guidance systems to enhance accuracy, efficiency, and operational effectiveness in combat scenarios.[75] Unlike conventional ammunition, which follow a fixed trajectory after being fired, smart munitions incorporate guidance and control mechanisms that enable real-time trajectory adjustments, ensuring precision targeting and minimising collateral damage.[76] The defining characteristics of smart munitions include precision guidance through GPS, laser, infrared, or radar-based targeting systems autonomous targeting capabilities, leveraging AI and machine learning for real-time threat assessment;[77] reduced collateral damage, achieved through controlled detonation mechanisms[78] enhanced lethality and efficiency, with specialised warheads and advanced fusing technologies improving penetration and explosive effectiveness[79] and seamless integration with network-centric warfare, allowing coordination with Unmanned Aerial Vehicles (UAVs) and real-time data-sharing platforms for synchronised attacks.[80] These attributes make smart munitions a critical component of modern military operations, transforming combat strategies and battlefield dynamics by shifting warfare from large-scale conventional conflicts to precision-based engagements where technological superiority determines combat outcomes. With its ability to enhance operational effectiveness, reduce resource consumption, and improve mission success, smart munitions are increasingly becoming indispensable in contemporary combat environments.

Advantages of Smart Munitions in Warfare

One of the primary advantages of smart munitions is its precision strike capability. Traditional ammunition rely on unguided ballistic trajectories, often resulting in unintended destruction and civilian casualties. In contrast, smart munitions employ sophisticated guidance systems to accurately strike targets, significantly reducing collateral damage and ensuring compliance with international humanitarian laws.[81] For instance, Laser-Guided Bombs (LGBs) and GPS-guided ammunition have been successfully deployed in urban warfare, mitigating unintended destruction while neutralising enemy forces with minimal risk to civilians.[82]

Smart munitions enhance military effectiveness by reducing the number of ammunition required to neutralise a target. Traditional bombardment methods often involve saturation attacks, leading to excessive ammunition expenditure and logistical challenges. Smart munitions optimise strike capabilities by ensuring high first-hit probability, thereby conserving resources and improving operational efficiency.[83] Nations investing in smart munitions gain a strategic edge over adversaries, as precision strikes can disrupt enemy supply chains, command centres, and key installations with minimal effort.[84]

Modern battlefields are diverse, encompassing urban, mountainous, and maritime environments. Smart munitions are highly adaptable, designed to function effectively across varying combat scenarios. For example, smart artillery shells equipped with GPS and inertial navigation systems can accurately strike enemy fortifications in mountainous regions, while smart torpedoes use advanced sonar and AI-based tracking for effective naval engagements.[85]

With the advent of digital warfare and artificial intelligence, smart munitions seamlessly integrate with network-centric combat strategies. Modern military forces rely on interconnected communication networks, drones, and reconnaissance systems to gather real-time battlefield intelligence. Smart munitions can receive mid-course updates, adjust trajectories based on enemy movements, and collaborate with other defence systems for coordinated attacks.[86] This synergy enhances battlefield awareness, improving decision-making capabilities and overall mission success rates.

Although the initial investment in smart munitions development is higher than traditional ammunition, the long-term cost benefits are substantial. Conventional warfare tactics often lead to excessive ammunition wastage due to inaccurate targeting, necessitating continuous resupply and logistical support. Smart munitions mitigate these issues by ensuring precise and effective target engagement, reducing overall expenditure on ammunition stockpiling and replenishment.[87] The continuous evolution of smart munitions is driven by advancements in artificial intelligence, machine learning, and autonomous systems. Future developments are expected to enhance decision-making capabilities, integrate swarm intelligence in ammunition, and improve adaptability against evolving enemy countermeasures.[88] The emergence of hypersonic smart missiles and AI-driven target recognition further underscores the critical role of smart munitions in shaping future warfare dynamics. Finally, smart munitions represent a paradigm shift in military strategy, emphasising precision, efficiency, and strategic superiority. As defence forces worldwide modernise their arsenals, investing in indigenous research and development for smart munitions remains a crucial priority for enhancing national security and maintaining technological sovereignty.

Evolution of Conventional Ammunition to Smart Munitions

Ammunition has played a pivotal role in military warfare for centuries, evolving from rudimentary projectiles to highly sophisticated precision-guided ammunition. The transition from conventional ammunition to smart munitions has been driven by advancements in materials, electronics, AI, and automation in modern warfare. The need for enhanced accuracy, efficiency, and operational effectiveness has necessitated the shift towards smart munitions, which offer superior precision and control compared to traditional rounds.[89]

Conventional Ammunition: Limitations and Challenges

Conventional ammunition, which includes unguided bullets, artillery shells, rockets, and bombs, has historically formed the backbone of military arsenals worldwide. These ammunition primarily rely on mechanical or chemical energy to achieve target impact and destruction. However, they come with significant limitations. Conventional ammunition follows a ballistic trajectory, making accuracy dependent on factors, such as, wind, weather, and human error in aiming.[90] Due to limited targeting capabilities, unintended civilian casualties and infrastructure destruction are common in conflict zones.[91] Excessive ammunition usage is required to ensure target elimination, leading to logistical and economic burdens.[92] Despite incremental improvements, such as, enhanced propellants and aerodynamic designs, conventional ammunition remains constrained by its inherent lack of adaptability to dynamic battlefield conditions.

Emergence of Smart Munitions: Technological Advancements

The advent of PGMs marked a paradigm shift in munitions technology, setting the foundation for the development of smart munitions. Smart munitions is characterised by its ability to adjust its trajectory mid-flight using onboard sensors, guidance systems, and actuators, thereby significantly enhancing accuracy and efficiency.[93]

Key technological advancements that facilitated this transition include:

- **Electro-Optical and Infrared (EO/IR) Guidance Systems:** These systems enable munitions to lock onto targets based on heat signatures or optical recognition, reducing reliance on manual aiming.[94]
- **Inertial and GPS-Based Navigation:** Integration of Inertial Measurement Units (IMUs) and Global Positioning Systems (GPSs) allows projectiles to correct their path in real time.[95]
- **Artificial Intelligence and Machine Learning:** AI-based targeting and decision-making algorithms optimise impact precision and differentiate between hostile and non-hostile targets.[96]
- **Autonomous and Networked Warfare:** Smart munitions are now being integrated into network-centric warfare systems, enabling communication with drones, satellites, and command centres for enhanced situational awareness.[97]

Evolutionary Milestones in Smart Munitions Development

The evolution from conventional to smart munitions has been marked by key technological breakthroughs:

- **Laser-Guided Bombs – 1970s:** The first major advancement in precision-guided munitions came with the development of LGBs, which used laser designation to home in on targets.[98]
- **Global Positioning System-Guided Munitions – 1990s:** The introduction of GPS-enabled bombs, such as, the Joint Direct Attack Ammunition (JDAM), allowed greater accuracy even in adverse weather conditions.[99]
- **Autonomous and AI-Driven Munitions – 2010s-Present:** Modern developments have focused on incorporating AI to improve target identification and minimise human intervention, seen in loitering munitions and next-generation artillery shells.[100]

The ongoing research and development in smart munitions are paving the way for next-generation autonomous munitions. These include, Swarm Munitions: Coordinated smart projectiles that operate as a group, optimising attack efficiency, Hypersonic Smart Weapons: High-speed guided projectiles capable of manoeuvring at hypersonic velocities to evade enemy defences, Enhanced Cybersecurity in Munitions: Ensuring resilience against electronic warfare and hacking threats. With continuous advancements, smart munitions are expected to revolutionise military operations by enhancing strategic capabilities while reducing collateral damage and operational inefficiencies.

Global Dependence on Smart Munitions and India's Challenge

Despite the advancement in ammunition technology various nations' defence sectors are still dependent on external sources for the supply for advanced munitions, especially with respect to smart munitions. This dependence has implications for national security, economic stability and the overall readiness of the armed forces especially in case of conflict and geopolitical tensions. A self-reliant military with a strong R&D serves as a backbone of a sovereign nation especially since recent technologies have brought a paradigm shift in the nature and scope of warfare. The Defence Research and Development Organisation (DRDO) is the R&D Wing of the Ministry of Defence of India and its objective is to promote Indian industries with DRDO developed technologies so that they can become globally competitive. It addresses matters related to transfer of technology. issuing of licences, access of DRDO test facilities to industries, technology acquisition and exports of military products. Although India is trying to indigenise its defence industry through initiatives, such as, 'Make in India', *Atmanirbhar Bharat*, SRIJAN Portal, Technology Development Fund, and working on various programs, such as, precision-guided munitions for artillery systems and air-dropped bombs or the induction of Smart Anti-Airfield Weapon (SAAW), yet its current Research and Development still remains underdeveloped and fragmented. This gap inhibits India to fully explore its potential and manufacturing capabilities in smart munitions. The contemporary world scenario is characterised by regional conflicts, such as, the Russia-Ukraine conflict, Israel-Gaza conflict, and turmoil in South Asia. Therefore, it is extremely critical that India works on its R&D which will strengthen its defence and ensure political, economic and social stability in India as well as the region.

In recent years, the landscape of military technology has witnessed a significant transformation, driven by rapid advancements in smart munitions. This shift is not just a matter of technological evolution but a strategic imperative for nations aiming to enhance their defence capabilities and reduce reliance on external sources for advanced munitions. The development and deployment of smart munitions are crucial due to its ability to significantly increase precision, reduce collateral damage, and provide substantial logistical and operational advantages. As geopolitical tensions continue to rise and conflicts, such as, those in Ukraine and the Middle East persist, the importance of a nation's ability to independently produce and innovate in the field of smart munitions becomes not only a component of national security but also a determinant of its international autonomy and influence. Despite these pressing needs, India's defence sector finds itself at a crossroads. The country's dependence on foreign technology and hardware for critical defence capabilities underscores a vulnerability that could be exploited in times of international isolation or conflict. This dependency is further complicated by the rapidly changing dynamics of warfare, where the integration of artificial intelligence and autonomous systems is becoming the norm. The Defence Research and Development Organisation (DRDO) of India, despite its efforts to foster innovation through various initiatives like 'Make in India' and *Atmanirbhar Bharat*, faces significant challenges. These include fragmented research efforts, inadequate funding, and a lack of integration between research outputs and defence needs. This situation necessitates a strategic re-evaluation of India's approach to research and development in the defence sector, particularly in the area of smart munitions. Building a robust R&D ecosystem is essential not only for enhancing military readiness but also for supporting the indigenous defence industry, thus contributing to the broader economic and technological stature of the country on the global stage. The urgency of this development is amplified by the increasing instances of regional conflicts, which demand a more self-reliant and technologically empowered stance to ensure stability and peace.

Key Technological Advancements in Smart Munitions

The evolution of conventional ammunition to smart munitions has been facilitated by a series of groundbreaking technological advancements across multiple domains, including miniaturised electronics, advanced guidance systems, artificial intelligence (AI), and modern materials science. The transition from traditional unguided munitions to precision-guided smart munitions has been primarily driven by the need for increased accuracy, lethality, and efficiency in modern warfare scenarios, where minimising collateral damage and optimising target engagement are of paramount importance. One of the most significant technological breakthroughs in this domain has been the development of advanced guidance and navigation systems, such as, GPS, Inertial Navigation Systems (INS), and laser-guided technologies, which have enabled ammunition to strike designated targets with exceptional precision. These navigation systems allow for real-time target tracking and trajectory adjustments, significantly reducing the margin of error compared to traditional ballistic trajectories. The incorporation of semi-active and active laser guidance systems has further enhanced the effectiveness of smart munitions by enabling precision targeting based on reflected laser energy, thereby increasing the probability of a successful strike even in dynamic battlefield environments.[101]

Another crucial advancement in the development of smart munitions is the integration of AI and Machine Learning (ML) algorithms, which have revolutionised the way modern munitions process and respond to battlefield information. AI-driven ammunition can autonomously identify, classify, and prioritise targets based on pre-programmed threat assessments and real-time sensor data, significantly reducing reliance on human operators and enhancing operational efficiency. In, *Artificial intelligence integration in modern smart munitions: Challenges and prospects*,[102] Modern AI-driven guidance systems are capable of adaptive targeting, wherein ammunition can modify its flight path mid-course based on evolving battlefield conditions and adversary countermeasures.[103] The introduction of neural networks and deep learning models has further refined target recognition capabilities, allowing smart munitions to differentiate between military and civilian assets with unprecedented accuracy, thereby aligning with modern rules of engagement and reducing unintended collateral damage.

The advancement of Network-Centric Warfare (NCW) capabilities has also played a crucial role in the development of smart munitions. NCW emphasises the real-time integration of various battlefield assets, including Unmanned Aerial Vehicles (UAVs), satellites, and ground-based sensor systems, to create a unified combat environment that enhances situational awareness and decision-making.[104] Smart munitions have greatly benefitted from these advancements, as modern network-enabled munitions can receive updated target coordinates and threat assessments during flight through secure data links, making them more adaptable and responsive to changing battlefield scenarios.[105] Additionally, the use of secure communication protocols and encryption techniques ensures that smart munitions remains resistant to electronic warfare threats, such as, jamming and spoofing, which are increasingly being employed by adversarial forces to disrupt guided weaponry.

In parallel, advancements in microelectronics and miniaturised sensor technologies have significantly contributed to the enhanced functionality and operational efficiency of smart munitions. The miniaturisation of components, such as, accelerometers, gyroscopes, and high-speed processors has allowed for the development of highly compact yet sophisticated guidance and control systems that can be integrated into a wide range of munitions, from artillery shells to air-dropped bombs.[106] The incorporation of multi-mode sensors, including infrared, radar, and electro-optical sensors, has enabled smart munitions to operate effectively in diverse environmental conditions, including low visibility and adverse weather. The fusion of data from multiple sensors has also improved the reliability and accuracy of target acquisition systems, reducing dependency on any single guidance mechanism and enhancing overall resilience against countermeasures.[107]

Materials science has also played a pivotal role in the evolution of smart munitions, particularly through the development of advanced composite materials and nanotechnology-based enhancements. Modern munitions now incorporate high-strength, lightweight materials that not only improve aerodynamic performance but also enhance durability and resistance to extreme battlefield conditions.[108] Additionally, innovations in energetic materials have led to the creation of more efficient and stable propellants and explosives that optimise blast effects while minimising unintentional detonations. The introduction of self-healing materials and shape-memory alloys has further expanded the possibilities for smart munitions by enabling structural integrity maintenance and adaptive deformation properties that improve penetration capabilities against fortified targets.[109]

Furthermore, the integration of next-generation power sources has significantly extended the operational range and endurance of smart munitions system. Traditional batteries have been replaced by high-energy-density lithium-based power sources and even energy-harvesting technologies, which allow munitions to sustain extended flight durations and maintain electronic functionalities for prolonged periods.[110] This has been particularly crucial for loitering munitions (also known as kamikaze drones), which require sustained power to continuously survey targets before executing an attack. Additionally, advancements in solid-state energy storage systems have enhanced the reliability and safety of onboard power management, reducing the risks associated with thermal runaway and explosive failures.[111]

Overall, the technological advancements driving the development of smart munitions represent a convergence of multiple cutting-edge domains, including AI, advanced guidance systems, network-centric warfare, microelectronics, materials science, and power management. These innovations have collectively transformed the landscape of modern warfare by enabling the deployment of highly precise, autonomous, and adaptive munitions that maximise combat effectiveness while minimising unintended consequences. The continuous evolution of smart munitions is expected to further revolutionise military operations by incorporating even more sophisticated autonomous decision-making capabilities, swarm coordination mechanisms, and hypersonic propulsion technologies, thereby defining the future of strategic defence and combat engagement.[112]

Importance of Smart Munitions for Indian Army

The Indian Army, as one of the largest and most technologically evolving military forces in the world, is progressively integrating modern warfare technologies to enhance combat effectiveness, operational efficiency, and strategic deterrence. In this evolving battlefield landscape, the adoption of smart munitions, a class of PGMs that leverage advanced guidance, control, and targeting systems, has become imperative. Smart munitions significantly enhances the accuracy, lethality, and operational flexibility of the Indian Army, ensuring that military engagements are conducted with minimal collateral damage while maximising impact on adversarial targets.[113] Unlike conventional munitions, which primarily relies on unguided trajectories, smart munitions incorporates advanced navigation technologies, such as, GPS, laser guidance, infrared homing, and artificial intelligence-based target recognition, making it an indispensable asset for modern warfare scenarios.[114] The significance of smart munitions for the Indian Army extends beyond battlefield effectiveness; it also plays a pivotal role in meeting India's broader national security objectives, reducing dependency on foreign defence imports, and fostering a robust indigenous defence manufacturing ecosystem.[115]

One of the foremost advantages of smart munitions lies in its enhanced precision and accuracy, which substantially reduces the likelihood of unintended casualties and collateral damage. In contemporary warfare, especially in counter-insurgency operations, urban warfare scenarios, and cross-border conflicts, the need for targeted engagement with minimal unintended impact is paramount. For example, in border engagements along the Line of Control (LoC) with Pakistan and the Line of Actual Control (LAC) with China, the use of precision-guided artillery shells and missiles ensures that Indian Army operations are effective yet restrained, preventing unnecessary escalation while maintaining deterrence capabilities.[116] Additionally, the surgical strike doctrine and precision targeting against high-value enemy assets necessitate the deployment of smart munitions, which offers superior control over engagement outcomes. Traditional ammunition often requires multiple rounds to neutralise a single target, leading to excessive expenditure of military resources. In contrast, smart munitions are designed to achieve a one-shot, one-kill capability, thereby improving operational efficiency and reducing logistical burdens.[117]

Furthermore, smart munitions enhance strategic deterrence by providing the Indian Army with advanced force-multiplier capabilities that deter adversaries from initiating conflicts. The nations with superior precision-strike capabilities possess a distinct psychological and operational advantage over their adversaries, influencing enemy decision-making and discouraging escalation.[118] The deterrence factor is particularly relevant for India, given its security environment characterised by dual-front challenges from both Pakistan and China. Smart munitions, including guided artillery shells, precision rockets, and loitering munitions, allows the Indian Army to conduct high-impact operations with pinpoint accuracy, effectively countering enemy advances while preserving vital military assets and personnel safety.[119] The growing emphasis on NCW further underscores the importance of smart munition, as modern military engagements increasingly rely on real-time battlefield Intelligence, Surveillance, and Reconnaissance (ISR) systems to guide precision strikes. By integrating smart munitions with Unmanned Aerial Vehicles (UAVs), satellites, and electronic warfare platforms, the Indian Army can conduct rapid, data-driven, and highly effective strike operations with minimal exposure to threats.

Another key advantage of smart munitions is its role in reducing operational costs and logistical constraints associated with prolonged military engagements. Conventional munition, due to its inherent inaccuracy, often leads to excessive wastage of resources, necessitating larger stockpiles and extensive resupply chains. In contrast, smart munitions, through its high efficiency and target-specific precision, reduces the overall ammunition consumption rate, thereby lowering logistics and transportation burdens for frontline units. This advantage is particularly crucial in challenging terrains, such as, the high-altitude regions of Ladakh, the dense jungles of the Northeast, and the desert warfare environments of Rajasthan, where logistical support is often constrained. By reducing the frequency and volume of ammunition resupply missions, the Indian Army can enhance the sustainability of prolonged operations while improving troop mobility and resource optimisation.[120]

Moreover, the development and deployment of smart munitions align with India's broader strategic defence objectives and self-reliance ambitions under initiatives, such as, 'Make in India' and *Atmanirbhar Bharat* (Self-Reliant India). Historically, India has relied heavily on foreign defence imports to fulfil its military requirements, leading to strategic vulnerabilities and cost escalations. By fostering indigenous research, development, and production capabilities for smart munitions, India can significantly reduce its dependence on foreign suppliers, thereby enhancing its strategic autonomy and economic resilience.[121] The integration of domestic defence manufacturers, research institutions, such as, Defence Research and Development Organisation

(DRDO), and private sector players in smart munitions development presents an opportunity to build a robust indigenous defence ecosystem that caters not only to national requirements but also to export potential in the global arms market.[122]

The importance of smart munitions for the Indian Army cannot be overstated. Its ability to provide unparalleled precision, enhanced operational efficiency, strategic deterrence, and cost-effectiveness makes it a critical component of India's modern defence strategy. As geopolitical threats continue to evolve and warfare paradigms shift towards precision and information-driven combat, the integration of smart munitions will play a transformative role in shaping India's military preparedness and national security framework.[123] By investing in cutting-edge research and indigenous manufacturing, the Indian Army can ensure that it remains at the forefront of technological innovation, maintaining a decisive battlefield advantage while reinforcing India's position as a self-reliant defence powerhouse.

Global Landscape of Smart Munitions Development

The global landscape of smart munitions development is characterised by significant investments in research, innovation, and defence technology, driven by the strategic need for precision-guided munitions in modern warfare. Countries, such as, the United States, Russia, China, and European nations have been at the forefront of smart munitions development, integrating cutting-edge technologies, such as, AI, advanced guidance systems, and next-generation explosives to enhance battlefield effectiveness. The United States, through its Department of Defence (DoD) and agencies, such as, the Defence Advanced Research Projects Agency (DARPA), has been a pioneer in the development of smart munition, with programs focused on extended-range precision-guided munitions, enhanced lethality, and autonomous targeting systems. The US military has successfully deployed smart munitions, such as, the Excalibur guided artillery shell, the Joint Direct Attack Munitions (JDAM), and the Small Diameter Bomb (SDB), all of which leverage GPS, inertial navigation, and laser guidance to achieve pinpoint accuracy.[124] Additionally, initiatives, such as, the US Army's Extended Range Cannon Artillery (ERCA) project aim to develop advanced smart artillery shells capable of hitting targets over 70 kilometres away with extreme precision.

Russia, another global leader in smart munitions, has heavily invested in hypersonic missile technology and precision-guided munitions to strengthen its strategic and tactical capabilities. Russian defence firms, such as, the Kalashnikov Concern, Rostec, and Tactical Missiles Corporation have been instrumental in developing advanced smart munitions, including the Krasnopol laser-guided artillery shell and the Hermes precision missile system.[125] The Krasnopol shell, used extensively by the Russian military, employs a semi-active laser guidance system to engage high-value targets with accuracy beyond conventional artillery rounds. Russia's advancements in electronic warfare and artificial intelligence integration have also contributed to the development of autonomous smart munitions capable of adapting to dynamic battlefield conditions. Furthermore, the recent focus on hypersonic missile technology, exemplified by the Avangard and Tsirkon systems, demonstrates Russia's commitment to next-generation smart munitions designed to evade missile defence systems and deliver precision strikes at unprecedented speeds.[126]

China has emerged as a formidable player in smart munitions development, driven by its ambitious military modernisation programs and extensive investment in indigenous defence technologies. The Chinese military-industrial complex, led by state-owned enterprises, such as, Norinco, AVIC, and CASIC, has developed a wide range of smart munitions, including the GP155 laser-guided artillery shell, CM-501 precision-guided missile, and the YJ-18 supersonic cruise missile. China's advancements in satellite navigation, AI-driven target recognition, and autonomous decision-making have significantly enhanced the effectiveness of its smart munitions. The integration of BeiDou satellite navigation into precision-guided munitions has provided the Chinese military with an independent and highly accurate targeting capability, reducing reliance on foreign navigation systems, such as, GPS. Additionally, China has demonstrated its growing expertise in swarm intelligence and network-centric warfare, where multiple smart munitions communicate and coordinate attacks autonomously to maximise combat effectiveness.

European nations, particularly France, Germany, and the United Kingdom, have also made substantial advancements in smart munitions development, often in collaboration with leading defence firms, such as, MBDA, BAE Systems, and Rheinmetall. The development of the Brimstone missile system, the Precision Guided Kit (PGK) for artillery shells, and the AASM Hammer guided bomb exemplifies Europe's focus on high-precision, low-collateral damage smart munitions.[127] France's AASM Hammer bomb, developed by Safran, integrates multiple guidance systems, including inertial, GPS, infrared, and laser targeting, making it one of the most versatile precision-guided munitions in the world. Similarly, Germany's SMArt 155 artillery shell, co-developed by Rheinmetall and Diehl Defence, features advanced target-seeking submunitions capable of engaging armoured targets autonomously.[128] The United Kingdom's SmartSea 500 project, aimed at developing AI-powered naval munitions, highlights Europe's growing emphasis on integrating artificial intelligence into future smart munitions.[129]

Other nations, including Israel, South Korea, and India, are also making significant strides in smart munitions development. Israel, known for its cutting-edge defence technology, has developed precision-guided munitions, such as, the Spike missile family, the MPR 500 guided bomb, and the Iron Sting laser-guided mortar system.[130] South Korea's Hanwha Corporation has successfully developed and exported advanced smart artillery shells, such as, the K9 Thunder's precision-guided rounds, to multiple countries. India, while still in the early stages of smart munitions development, has made notable progress through organisations like the Defence Research and Development Organisation, which is working on guided artillery shells, long-range precision missiles, and AI-enhanced targeting systems.

Overall, the global landscape of smart munitions development is shaped by technological innovation, strategic military requirements, and geopolitical imperatives. The increasing adoption of artificial intelligence, network-centric warfare, and hypersonic technology is expected to drive the next phase of smart munitions evolution, with countries vying for superiority in precision-strike capabilities. As nations continue to invest in R&D and collaborate with private defence firms, the future of smart munitions will likely be defined by greater autonomy, enhanced lethality, and improved adaptability to complex combat environments.[131]

Current State of Ammunition Manufacturing and R&D in India

India's ammunition manufacturing industry has long been a critical component of the country's defence preparedness, evolving through a combination of public sector enterprises, private sector participation, and collaborations with foreign defence manufacturers. Historically, India's ammunition production was largely dominated by state-owned entities, such as, the Ordnance Factory Board (OFB), which was responsible for the production and supply of conventional ammunition for the Indian Armed Forces.[132] However, following structural reforms in 2021, the OFB was disbanded and reorganised into seven new Defence Public Sector Undertakings (DPSUs), each specialising in different aspects of defence manufacturing, including ammunition production.[133] These new entities, including Munitions India Limited (MIL), have taken over ammunition production, aiming to enhance efficiency, quality, and self-reliance in defence manufacturing. Despite these reforms, India's ammunition industry still faces several challenges, such as, outdated technology, dependence on imported raw materials, and limited private sector participation.[134]

The dependence on imports for critical components remains a major hurdle in achieving self-sufficiency in ammunition production. While India has made significant progress in manufacturing small and medium-calibre ammunition indigenously, it still relies on foreign suppliers for certain high-tech ammunition components, such as, PGMs, smart artillery shells, and specialised warheads.[135] The lack of indigenous research and development in smart munitions has further exacerbated this dependence, compelling India to procure advanced ammunition from countries like Russia, Israel, and the United States. The government has recognised this shortfall and has introduced multiple initiatives, such as, the 'Make in India' and *Atmanirbhar Bharat* (Self-Reliant India) programs, which emphasise the need for domestic innovation and manufacturing capabilities.[136] These initiatives have encouraged domestic defence manufacturers, including private firms like Bharat Forge, Larsen & Toubro (L&T), and Tata Advanced Systems, to enter the ammunition production domain.[137]

Furthermore, the Defence Research and Development Organisation plays a crucial role in developing indigenous ammunition technologies. DRDO, in collaboration with DPSUs and private industries, has been working on advanced ammunition projects, such as, the Smart Anti-Airfield Weapon

(SAAW), Pinaka multi-barrel rocket system, and long-range guided artillery shells.[138] However, despite these efforts, India has struggled with technology gaps, production delays, and quality control issues, which have hindered the mass production and deployment of advanced munitions.[139] The government has been pushing for increased private sector involvement and Public-Private Partnerships (PPPs) to accelerate innovation and manufacturing capabilities. Policy measures, such as, the increase in the Foreign Direct Investment (FDI) cap in the defence sector from 49 percent to 74 percent under the automatic route have further facilitated collaborations with global defence firms.[140]

Additionally, India's ammunition manufacturing ecosystem faces infrastructural and logistical challenges that impact production efficiency. Many of the legacy ammunition factories inherited from the colonial era have outdated production lines, leading to inefficiencies in manufacturing high-tech munition.[141] The lack of cutting-edge manufacturing techniques, such as, additive manufacturing, automated assembly lines, and AI-based quality control mechanisms further affects the quality and scalability of ammunition production. To address these concerns, the government has announced several modernisation programs aimed at upgrading ammunition manufacturing facilities, incorporating advanced production technologies, and fostering collaborations between research institutions and industry stakeholders.[142]

In recent years, India has made some noteworthy progress in developing indigenous smart munitions capabilities. The collaboration between DRDO and Bharat Dynamics Limited (BDL) has led to the development of advanced ammunition systems, such as, the guided Extended Range Pinaka Rockets and smart loitering munitions.[143] However, these efforts are still in their early stages, and India needs a more robust research and development ecosystem to compete with global ammunition manufacturers. The way forward involves strengthening indigenous capabilities through targeted investments in defence research, incentivising private sector participation, and forging strategic collaborations with global defence leaders.[144] The integration of cutting-edge technologies, such as, artificial intelligence, machine learning, and big data analytics in ammunition design and manufacturing can significantly enhance India's ability to produce smart munitions domestically.

Overall, while India has a well-established ammunition manufacturing sector, there is a pressing need to modernise infrastructure, reduce import dependency, and enhance indigenous R&D capabilities to achieve complete self-reliance in ammunition production. The transition from conventional ammunition manufacturing to smart munitions development requires a holistic approach involving policy reforms, technological advancements, and collaborative efforts between government agencies, private enterprises, and academic institutions. The successful implementation of these measures will be instrumental in ensuring that India not only meets its own defence requirements but also emerges as a global leader in ammunition manufacturing and exports.

The defence manufacturing ecosystem in India has evolved significantly over the years, with the DRDO, Ordnance Factories, and private sector enterprises playing crucial roles in enhancing the country's self-reliance in defence technology, including the development of smart munitions. The DRDO, established in 1958 under the Ministry of Defence, has been the primary research and development (R&D) institution responsible for spearheading technological advancements in India's defence sector. With over 50 laboratories engaged in the research of various defence-related fields, such as, aeronautics, armaments, electronics, and combat vehicles, the DRDO has played an instrumental role in developing a broad spectrum of advanced ammunition and weaponry for the Indian Armed Forces.[145] Smart munition, which integrates state-of-the-art guidance and control systems to improve accuracy, lethality, and operational efficiency, has been a key focus area in DRDO's R&D endeavours. Various programs under DRDO, such as, the development of PGMs, advanced artillery shells, and loitering munitions, highlight the organisation's commitment to strengthening India's defence capabilities. However, despite its substantial contributions, DRDO has often been criticised for delays in project execution, cost overruns, and technological dependence on foreign collaborations, which have hindered India's complete self-reliance in smart munitions production.[146]

Alongside DRDO, the Ordnance Factories, operating under the Armament Research and Development Establishment (ARDE) and the OFB, have historically been the backbone of India's ammunition manufacturing sector. The OFB, with its extensive network of over 40 factories, has been responsible for producing a wide range of conventional munition, small arms, explosives, and artillery shells.[147] While ordnance factories have demonstrated considerable expertise in manufacturing traditional munitions, their transition to smart munitions production has been relatively slow due to outdated infrastructure, lack of cutting-edge technology, and bureaucratic inefficiencies.

Recognising the limitations of the existing structure, the Government of India restructured the OFB into seven new DPSUs in 2021, aimed at modernising production processes and enhancing operational efficiency. These reforms are expected to streamline the manufacturing of advanced weaponry and promote collaboration between government-run establishments and private enterprises in smart munitions development. The introduction of smart artillery shells, programmable fuzes, and guided rockets within ordnance factories is a testament to India's commitment to enhancing the technological sophistication of its munitions.[148] Nevertheless, the need for extensive R&D investment and rapid technological adoption remains critical for India to keep pace with global advancements in smart munitions.

In recent years, the private sector has emerged as a significant player in India's defence manufacturing landscape, particularly following the liberalisation of defence production policies and the implementation of the Defence Procurement Procedure (DPP) reforms.[149] Several private defence companies, such as, Larsen & Toubro (L&T), Bharat Forge, Tata Advanced Systems, and Mahindra Defence Systems, have made substantial strides in the development and production of sophisticated military hardware, including smart munitions. The increasing involvement of the private sector has led to greater technological innovation, enhanced production efficiency, and reduced reliance on foreign imports. Notably, collaborations between Indian private firms and global defence contractors have facilitated knowledge transfer and accelerated the integration of next-generation technologies into India's defence arsenal.[150] Under the *Atmanirbhar Bharat* (Self-Reliant India) initiative, the Indian Government has actively encouraged indigenous defence production by granting incentives, easing Foreign Direct Investment (FDI) norms, and promoting public-private partnerships.[151] The establishment of defence industrial corridors in Uttar Pradesh and Tamil Nadu has further strengthened India's indigenous manufacturing capabilities by fostering innovation, research collaboration, and investment in state-of-the-art defence technologies.[152]

Despite these progressive developments, significant challenges persist in establishing a fully self-reliant R&D ecosystem for smart munition. The primary hurdles include funding constraints, limited testing facilities, dependence on foreign critical components, and insufficient collaboration between academic institutions and defence industries.[153] Additionally, while the private sector has demonstrated immense potential, its participation in defence R&D has been relatively limited compared to government-led initiatives due to the high-risk nature of investments in defence technology and long gestation periods for returns. Moving forward, a holistic approach that fosters seamless coordination between DRDO, ordnance factories, and private sector players will be imperative in ensuring India achieves self-reliance in smart munitions production. This can be achieved by enhancing technology-sharing mechanisms, increasing R&D budget allocations, expanding skill development programs, and strengthening regulatory frameworks to support indigenous defence innovations.[154] By leveraging AI, ML, advanced materials, and next-generation propulsion systems, India can accelerate the development of smart munitions that meets the operational requirements of the Indian Army and aligns with the evolving nature of modern warfare.

Strengthening R&D Ecosystem for Smart Munitions

The development of smart munitions, which integrates precision-guidance systems, advanced fuzes, AI, and next-generation explosives, has become a critical aspect of modern warfare, enhancing the operational effectiveness of armed forces worldwide. However, for India to establish itself as a self-reliant and technologically advanced military power, it is imperative to build a robust Research and Development (R&D) ecosystem that fosters innovation, accelerates indigenous manufacturing, and reduces dependency on foreign technology. The need for such an ecosystem is driven by several key factors, including national security concerns, economic considerations, technological advancements, and policy imperatives. India's defence R&D landscape has traditionally been dominated by government agencies, such as, the Defence Research and Development Organisation (DRDO) and the Ordnance Factories, but recent reforms have opened doors for increased participation from the private sector, academia, and global partnerships. To meet the evolving demands of the Indian Army and ensure that India stays ahead in the global defence technology race, a comprehensive approach to developing, sustaining, and scaling smart munitions R&D are required.[155]

One of the primary reasons for strengthening R&D in smart munitions are the strategic imperative of self-reliance in defence production. India remains one of the largest importers of defence equipment, with a significant portion of its munitions, missiles, and critical components sourced from foreign manufacturers, such as, Russia, Israel, France, and the United States.[156] This reliance poses substantial risks, including supply chain disruptions during geopolitical conflicts, increased procurement costs, and challenges in technology transfer. A strong indigenous R&D ecosystem can mitigate these risks by enabling India to develop cutting-edge weaponry tailored to its specific operational needs. The recent push under the *Atmanirbhar Bharat* (Self-Reliant India) initiative aims to reduce India's dependency on imports and promote indigenous defence manufacturing, with a specific emphasis on smart munitions, precision-guided bombs, and advanced artillery shells. A well-established R&D framework will allow India to not only develop its own smart munitions but also export high-quality defence products to allied nations, positioning itself as a global leader in defence innovation.

Another critical factor necessitating a robust R&D ecosystem is the rapid evolution of military technology and the increasing complexity of modern warfare. Contemporary battlefields are witnessing greater emphasis on precision strikes, network-centric warfare, and AI-driven targeting systems. Conventional ammunition, which relies on basic ballistics and unguided explosive mechanisms, is no longer sufficient to meet the precision, range, and lethality requirements of modern combat operations. Smart munitions, such as, sensor-fuzed munitions, loitering munitions, and guided artillery shells, offers unparalleled advantages in target accuracy, reduced collateral damage, and enhanced operational flexibility. However, the development of such advanced systems requires a multi-disciplinary approach that integrates electronics, materials science, propulsion systems, and AI-based guidance technologies. Investing in a comprehensive R&D ecosystem will ensure that Indian defence scientists and engineers have access to state-of-the-art laboratories, cutting-edge simulation tools, and world-class testing facilities, enabling them to develop next-generation smart munitions tailored to India's unique battlefield conditions.[157]

The economic benefits of strengthening India's defence R&D ecosystem are equally significant. Investing in indigenous smart munitions development can drastically reduce the financial burden associated with importing high-end defence equipment. Currently, the acquisition of foreign smart munitions systems involves not only high procurement costs but also additional expenditures on maintenance, technology licensing, and upgrades. By contrast, an efficient domestic R&D ecosystem can enable India to produce cost-effective and customised solutions, reducing long-term operational costs while fostering job creation, skill development, and technological upskilling in the defence sector. Moreover, a thriving indigenous smart munitions industry can boost India's defence exports, allowing Indian defence manufacturers to compete in the global arms market. Countries in Southeast Asia, the Middle East, and Africa, which are looking for affordable and high-quality defence solutions, present a lucrative market for India's smart munitions industry.

The establishment of a robust R&D ecosystem also requires strong policy support, institutional frameworks, and strategic collaborations. The Indian government has introduced several reforms, such as, the Defence Acquisition Procedure (DAP) 2020, the Strategic Partnership Model (SPM), and increased Foreign Direct Investment (FDI) in the defence sector, to encourage innovation and private sector participation in defence R&D. However, challenges, such as, bureaucratic delays, inadequate funding, and lack of synergy between academia, defence PSUs, and private enterprises continue to hinder the growth of indigenous R&D. To address these issues, it is essential to increase budget allocations for defence R&D, streamline procurement procedures, and enhance collaboration between DRDO, private players, and research institutions. The creation of defence innovation hubs, incubation centres, and startup accelerators can further promote the development of disruptive defence technologies, including AI-driven targeting systems, smart artillery, and autonomous weaponry.

Finally, fostering a culture of research excellence and innovation in the defence sector is crucial for ensuring long-term sustainability in smart munitions development. Encouraging university-led research, joint defence-academic programs, and skill development initiatives will ensure a steady pipeline of highly trained scientists, engineers, and defence technologists. Furthermore, establishing international collaborations with technologically advanced nations can facilitate technology transfer, joint ventures, and co-development projects, thereby accelerating the pace of innovation in India's defence R&D ecosystem.

The development of a robust and self-sufficient R&D ecosystem for smart munitions is not just a necessity but a strategic imperative for India. With evolving security threats, technological advancements, and global defence dynamics, India must prioritise investments in defence R&D, strengthen institutional frameworks, and foster a culture of innovation to achieve self-reliance and global competitiveness in smart munitions manufacturing. By leveraging government policies, industry-academia collaborations, and cutting-edge research, India can position itself as a leader in next-generation smart munitions technology, ensuring enhanced combat readiness, operational efficiency, and national security.

Priority Technology Thrust for a Smart Munitions Ecosystem

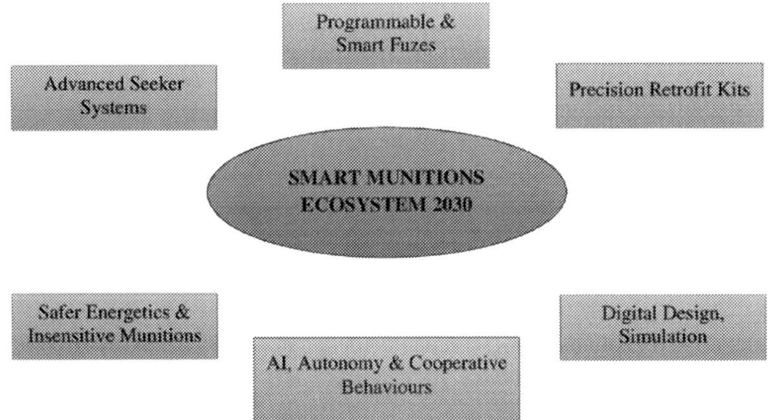

As India charts the path towards a self-reliant and globally competitive munitions industry, it is essential to identify a focused set of technology priorities that can guide investment and innovation. Rather than dispersing effort across too many fronts, concentrating on six core thrusts provides clarity, coordination, and measurable progress. The accompanying flow chart captures these thrusts in an integrated manner, underscoring how they reinforce one another to form the backbone of a smart munitions' ecosystem.

At the operational level, the development of reliable seeker systems remains fundamental. These seekers which blending optical, infrared, and radar technologies are what transform an ammunition from a simple projectile into a precision instrument capable of striking accurately even in poor visibility, electronic countermeasure environments, or cluttered terrain. Programmable and smart fuzes add a parallel layer of adaptability, allowing a single round to perform in multiple modes, airburst, delay, or contact, thereby maximising effectiveness across diverse battlefield conditions. Retrofit precision kits represent perhaps the most cost-effective short-term pathway: by converting existing artillery shells and rockets into guided weapons, India can quickly improve accuracy and reduce wastage while leveraging its current stockpiles. Safety and sustainability must accompany lethality. Insensitive munitions and greener energetics lower the risks of accidental explosions during storage or transit, reduce logistical hazards, and bring India closer to NATO and UN norms on handling and transport. Beyond hardware, artificial intelligence and autonomy are redefining the cognitive dimension of smart munitions.

Target recognition, adaptive trajectories, and limited cooperative behaviours, while retaining human oversight, can enhance speed and flexibility in contested theatres. Underpinning all of these priorities is the modernisation of design, testing, and manufacturing pipelines. Digital twins, simulation-driven prototyping, additive manufacturing, and automated quality control can shorten development cycles and enhance reliability.

Therefore, these thrusts, such as, seekers, fuzes, retrofit kits, safer energetics, AI and autonomy, and advanced manufacturing can provide a coherent technological roadmap. Their integration ensures that India's efforts go beyond incremental improvements to deliver a holistic, future-ready munitions ecosystem. By situating this roadmap within the broader framework of *Atmanirbhar Bharat* and aligning it with export opportunities, India can shift its role in the global defence market: from being seen primarily as a bulk producer of conventional ammunition to being recognised as a trusted supplier of precision-oriented, safe, and environmentally responsible smart munitions by 2030.

5

Securing Ammunition Input and Raw-Material Foundations for Self-Reliance

Introduction

A nation's readiness and autonomy for defence and its armed forces' capability for the defence relies on the manufacturing of ammunition. In addition to production of bullets, shells and missiles it is a highly industrialised process involving metallurgy, chemical engineering, electronics and advanced manufacturing techniques. Given India's large armed forces and growing regional security responsibilities, the supply of mobile, indigenous, high-quality ammunition is crucial since disruptions would be eminently embarrassing and destabilising. The geopolitical context of the country – with long border tussles, cross border terrorism and strategic rivalry in Indo Pacific region makes the need for a resilient and self-reliant defence industrial base still more redundant.[158]

India's historic ammunition manufacturing has largely remained in the state control of the Ordnance Factory Board (OFB) to promote efficiency, accountability and modernisation, which had recently been corporatised into seven Public Sector Undertakings (PSUs). This structure has worked, in a sense, to meet the basic necessities regarding the Indian Armed Forces but it has not been able to catch up with technological advancement, dynamic perceived threats, and rising smart ammunition and high technology munitions requirements. A key factor behind this impasse is the country's reliance on imports of raw materials like metals, copper and tungsten, chemicals like

RDX and HMX, and high-tech electronic components to manufacture precision guided munitions.[159]

An *Atmanirbhar Bharat Abhiyan* has recognised ammunition production as a strategic endeavour towards self-reliance on defence sector. The Defence Production and Export Promotion Policy (DPEPP) 2020 has ambitious targets for increasing indigenous content in defence production as well as reducing dependence on foreign suppliers, which provide evidence of the practice. Defensive Strategy of *Atmanirbhar Bharat* includes development of India as a global hub defence manufacturing by motivating private sector participation, FDI liberalisation and pushing innovation through research and development.[160] Despite these policy efforts, however, there is a fundamental bottleneck related to the lack of adequate domestic availability as well as inadequate processing capabilities of essential input materials.

The lack of key input material is multifaceted in nature. India has huge mineral resources, but exploiting it is hampered by environmental restrictions, obsolete mining technologies, logistical snags, and lack of investment in modern material science. In addition, the defence sector needs high purity, defence grade materials, such as, special alloys, propellants, electronic sensors and almost none of this is available in India or cannot be manufactured in the country right now either. In addition, it increases the cost of production and carries very high risks to the country security with regard to geopolitical disruptions, trade sanctions, or war.[161]

Therefore, there must be a comprehensive strategy aimed at securing and developing domestic sources of raw materials for ammunition manufacturing, which is to be self-reliant. These include building mining infrastructure, encouraging refining and processing technologies, providing incentive for the public private partnership and integration of supply chains through defence corridor and industrial clusters. Additionally, indigenous material substitutes and the propagation of sustainability in the extraction and recycling of materials present long term solutions to present constraints.

Given this context, a critical analysis of the availability of input materials for ammunition manufacturing in India is both timely and necessary. Such an inquiry must address key questions: What are the critical materials required for different types of ammunition? To what extent are these materials sourced domestically? What are the existing challenges in material procurement, processing, and integration into the defence supply chain? And most importantly, what policy, industrial, and technological interventions can pave the way for sustainable and strategic material self-sufficiency? By shedding light on this critical aspect of defence preparedness, the study contributes to the broader national goal of achieving technological and strategic autonomy.

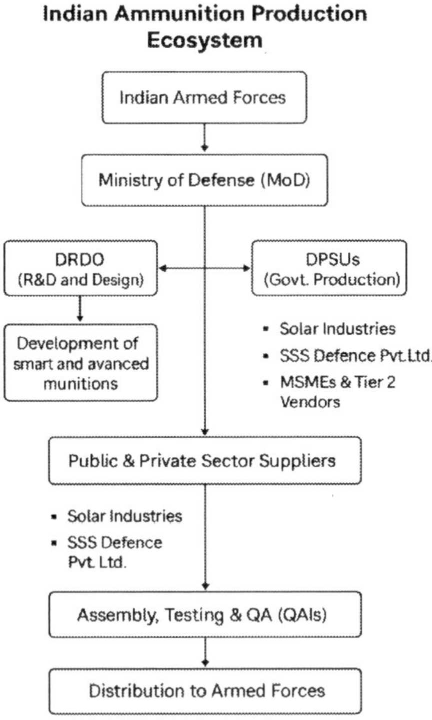

Figure 5.1: Indian Ammunition Production Ecosystem.

Overview of Ammunition Manufacturing in India

Ammunition manufacturing in India is an essential part of its defence production capability, covering a broad spectrum of munitions, such as, small arms cartridges, artillery shells, air-dropped bombs, tank ammunition, rockets, and smart or precision-guided munitions. Each category of ammunition has its unique material requirements, production technologies, and supply chain complexities, all of which influence India's defence readiness and strategic autonomy. The Small arms ammunition includes bullets used in rifles, pistols, and machine guns, ranging in calibre from 5.56 mm to 12.7 mm. These are widely used by the Indian Army, paramilitary forces, and police services. The heavy firepower in the armed forces is based on artillery ammunition in 105 mm, 130 mm and 155 mm shells. The indigenous platforms, such as, Arjun MBT and T-90 come equipped with tank and anti-tank ammunition. Aerial bombs, mortar shells and rocket propelled grenades are other important categories. However, in recent years, the interest has been pivoted to smart ammunition and guided munitions, that is, smart ammunition and guided munitions collectively consist of electronics and sensor for higher accuracy, lethality, and reduced collateral damage.[162]

Traditionally, Ordnance Factory Board (OFB), as it was then known, constituted the largest manufacturer of munitions in India; it has been restructured into seven Defence Public Sector Undertakings (DPSUs) under the Ministry of Defence. Among these, Advanced Weapons and Equipment India Limited (AWEIL) and Munitions India Limited (MIL) have been given the ammunition production responsibility. Currently, MIL is the biggest conventional ammunition producer in India and cater for all three services of the armed forces as well as of paramilitary and police forces (these DPSUs produce over 150 guns including small, medium, and high calibre rounds).[163]

Along with the public sector, some private players have also entered the aperture of ammunition manufacturing in a liberal set of defence industrial policies of the government. One of the notable ones is Solar Industries India Ltd, a Nagpur based company that fast likes by its reach in domain of high energy materials, explosives and propellants. A close ally is SSS Defence in Bengaluru, which is into small arms and ammunition designed for the Indian terrain and operational requirements. DRDO and DPSUs, these companies are getting increasingly closer to Defence Research and Development Organisation with an aim to develop next generation munitions as well as to reduce the import dependence.

The establishing of Defence Industrial Corridors (DICs) in Uttar Pradesh and Tamil Nadu is a major enabler for this transition. The purpose of these corridors is to create integrated ecosystem of defence manufacturing by providing infrastructure, policy encouragement and cluster-based development. Uttar Pradesh is being developed as key nodes around can also support ammunition and small arms manufacturing at Kanpur, Aligarh, Jhansi and Chitrakoot. DIC of Tamil Nadu is Coimbatore, Salem, Hosur and Chennai with component and special manufacturing units. It is also anticipated that these corridors will be able to indigenise critical components and input materials required in the production of ammunition.[164] Flagship initiatives, such as, 'Make in India', *Atmanirbhar Bharat Abhiyan* and the Defence

Production and Export Promotion Policy (DPEPP) 2020 further bolster India's vision of a self-reliant India in defence. The goal of these initiatives is to enhance the indigenous content in defence production from the present 60-65 percent to more than 80 percent in coming decade. This means that not only will ammunition be manufactured both domestically, but capabilities along the upstream streams of material extraction, refining, propellant chemistry, and electronic sub-systems will be developed commensurate with the demands of the resultant ammunition products. Amongst them the government has identified various types of ammunition which are included in Positive Indigenisation list, thus prohibiting their import.[165] Although such efforts have been made, inconsistencies, lack of quality control, and lowered global competitiveness are still challenges. However, the changing defence industrial landscape with increasing levels of foreign investment, private sector participation and R&D collaboration implies a positive trend towards achieving self-sufficiency in terms of ammunition manufacturing in India.

Key Input Materials for Ammunition Manufacturing

However, the manufacturing of ammunition is very laborious process and it is highly depended on the availability of the value-added input materials. Included in these materials are metals and alloys of casing and penetrators, high energy explosives and propellants for charge and propulsion, chemicals and binders for stability and performance, and more recently advanced electronics and sensors for smart or guided ammunition. Ensuring a consistent and indigenous supply of these components is fundamental to achieving self-reliance in defence manufacturing.

Metals and Alloys

Metals and alloys form the structural backbone of ammunition. Brass, an alloy of copper and zinc, is extensively used for cartridge cases due to its corrosion resistance, formability, and high ductility. India sources a significant portion of its brass from Hindustan Copper Ltd., although imports still supplement domestic production to meet defence-grade specifications.[166] Copper, valued for its excellent electrical and thermal conductivity, is crucial not only for brass but also for electric primers and fuzes in smart ammunition. Steel, particularly high-carbon and stainless variants, is used in projectile cores, bomb casings, and armour-piercing shells due to its superior mechanical strength and penetrative capability.

Tungsten, a dense and hard metal, is employed in kinetic energy penetrators and armour-piercing rounds. However, India lacks domestic tungsten reserves and relies almost entirely on imports, primarily from China and Russia, making it a strategic vulnerability.[167] Aluminium, known for its light weight and thermal resistance, is commonly used in aircraft-delivered munitions, missile casings, and pyrotechnic compositions. It also enhances the thermobaric effects of certain explosives.

The development of high-performance alloys combining the properties of two or more of these metals is also critical, especially in next-generation and smart munitions where weight, impact resistance, and thermal performance must be carefully balanced.

Propellants and Explosives

Propellants and explosives are the energetic materials responsible for launching the projectile and causing terminal effects on the target. Among the most commonly used high explosives in Indian ammunition manufacturing are RDX (Cyclotrimethylenetrinitramine) and HMX (Cyclotetramethylene-tetranitramine). RDX is widely used due to its high detonation velocity and relatively safe handling characteristics, while HMX is reserved for high-performance military applications including warheads and shaped charges. TNT (Trinitrotoluene), although older, remains a widely used explosive due to its balance between stability and explosive power. India has indigenous production facilities for RDX and TNT, although production of high-purity HMX remains limited and often depends on imports or joint ventures. Nitroglycerine (NG) and Nitrocellulose (NC) form the core of single-base, double-base, and composite propellants used in artillery and tank ammunition. Glycerol and cellulose are synthesised through nitration; these are however very stringent to the environmental and process controls. Though India is capable of producing these materials, environmental restrictions and the degradation of the infrastructure have limited output volumes and consistency.[168]

Chemicals, Stabilisers, and Binders

Chemical, stabilisers, and binders play vital roles exactly on the same level as the explosive materials in modern ammunition. Shelf life is improved, premature detonation is prevented, and performance is improved under various climatic conditions by these additives. In nitrocellulose-based propellants stabilisers are added like diphenylamine or Centralite in order to help retard degradation over time. These compounds retard the autocatalytic decomposition of energetic materials and are critical to prevent the occurrence of unsafe situations during storage and transportation.

Polymeric binders are made more flexible and the brittleness of explosives reduced by the addition of plasticizers like tributyl citrate and diethyl phthalate. Since HTPB (Hydroxyl-Terminated Polybutadiene) and GAP (Glycidyl Azide Polymer) binders have become very energetic, they are increasingly used as binders in composite propellants for missiles and rocket systems. Generally, these chemicals are being imported because there are no big facilities for large scale, defence grade production in India. Thus, they also need to be procured within the international compliance frame of the Chemical Weapons Convention (CWC), further complicating the complexity.

Electronics and Sensors for Smart Ammunition

Electronics in ammunition is indispensable with the progression of modern warfare, and the need for precision precursor strike. Miniaturised electronics enable smart ammunition, such as, guided artillery shells, loitering munitions and programmable airburst rounds to navigate, detonate and target discriminate. MEMS (Micro Electromechanical Systems) sensors, gyroscopes, accelerometers, fuzes and programmable logic controllers are core components. The precision targeting as well as the inflight trajectory correction, as well as the optimised detonation their number enhances mission effectiveness.

With the exception of inputs, such as, silicon and copper, India currently does not possess domestic production capacities for most of these advanced electronic components. But Bharat Electronics Ltd (BEL) and others have now started developing indigenous solutions; but it remains a heavily imported sector, with imports coming from the US, Israel and South Korea, among others.[169] As a part of the 'Make in India' and Defence Electronics Policy, development of a robust ecosystem for defence microelectronics is therefore a key priority.

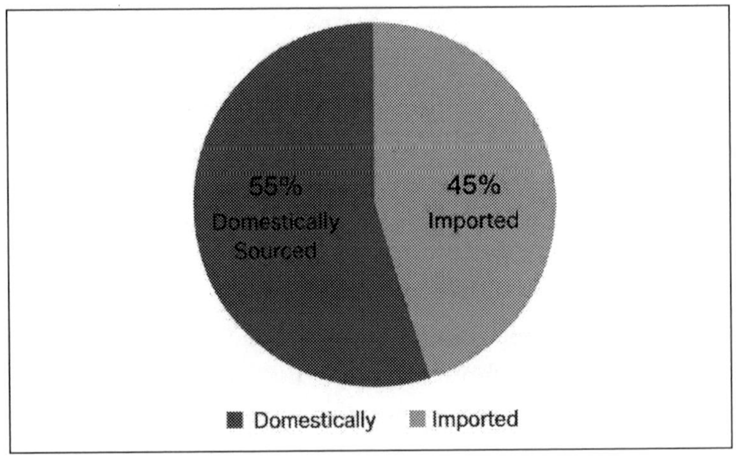

Figure 5.2: Key Input Materials in Ammunition and Their Sources

Sources and Supply Chains of Input Materials in India

A robust and resilient ammunition manufacturing industry is heavily reliant on the strength of its raw material sourcing and supply chain infrastructure. In India, the availability of input materials for ammunition, ranging from metals and explosives to electronics and chemical stabilisers, hinges on a combination of domestic mining and processing capabilities, the involvement of Micro, Small, and Medium Enterprises (MSMEs), foreign imports, and an array of regulatory and logistical frameworks. Understanding the intricacies of this supply chain is essential for charting the path toward strategic self-sufficiency in defence production.

Mining and Processing Companies

Though India is rich in natural resources, their application to defence purposes is somewhat limited because of technological, regulatory and policy constraints. Hindustan Copper Ltd (HCL) is the lead state owned enterprise engaged in copper ore mining and smelting which is a critical metal for pistol cartridges as well as critical for electronic components. Despite being the only vertically integrated copper producer in the country, HCL fulfils only a fraction of India's defence requirements, necessitating imports from countries like Chile, Zambia, and Indonesia.[170] The National Mineral Development Corporation (NMDC) plays a pivotal role in the mining of iron ore, which is essential for producing steel used in shell casings, bomb bodies, and armour-penetrating ammunition. However, the conversion of iron ore into defence-grade steel requires specialised alloying and heat treatment processes, typically carried out by select public and private sector units. The Bhabha Atomic Research Centre (BARC) is a key institution for the development of high-energy materials and rare-earth processing, especially those used in advanced munitions and smart ammunition electronics. While BARC has made substantial contributions to India's nuclear and missile programs, its capacity to scale and commercialise materials for conventional ammunition remains limited, requiring partnerships with manufacturing firms and defence PSUs.

Involvement of MSMEs and Local Industry

MSMEs form the backbone of India's industrial ecosystem and play a vital role in the defence supply chain, particularly in the supply of non-strategic components and sub-systems. These include cartridge clips, packaging materials, small mechanical parts, primers, and fuze components. Under the Defence Procurement Procedure (DPP), MSMEs have been encouraged to participate more actively in supplying to DPSUs and private ammunition manufacturers. In addition, industrial clusters around Pune, Hyderabad, Coimbatore, Kanpur, and Nagpur have emerged as hubs for component manufacturing, machining, and chemical processing. Some of these MSMEs have received DRDO technology transfers for specific defence applications, such as, thermobaric chemicals, plastic-bonded explosives, and additive manufacturing for fuze components.[171] However, MSMEs often face challenges related to access to finance, certification for defence-grade quality, and long payment cycles from large procurement agencies.

Foreign Imports and Strategic Dependencies

Despite the availability of some raw materials domestically, India remains dependent on foreign suppliers for several critical inputs. A significant portion of high-purity tungsten, copper, nickel, RDX, HMX, and propellant stabilisers is imported due to inadequate local production or quality constraints. The primary countries from which India imports defence-grade materials include China, Russia, Israel, and the United States. China is a dominant supplier of rare-earth elements and tungsten, but India's overdependence poses strategic vulnerabilities in light of ongoing border tensions. Advances in smart munitions and electronic fusing systems are provided by both Israel and Russia in the explosives, propellant formulation, large calibre shell component areas. The United States, under bilateral defence cooperation agreements, supplies a wide range of energetic materials, precision electronics, and defence chemicals.[172]

The higher cost of procurement, as well as the risks to supply chain disruption in the case of geopolitical crisis, a global pandemic or a diplomatic dispute, increases the dependency on external imports. Additionally, the import of such materials can take on long lead times, complex international licensing and export control as in the case of export control regimes, such as, Wassenaar Arrangement.

Licensing, Environmental Regulations, and Logistical Constraints

Ammunition materials are highly regulated in India for procurement and production. The Explosives Act of 1884 governs the licensing of production, transport and storage of explosives and propellants of which the Petroleum and Explosives Safety Organisation (PESO) is the supervisory agency. While all these regulations are necessary for national safety, they could also delay production timelines because bureaucracy and inspection time.

The other layer of complexity is environmental regulations, particularly those that pertain to mining and chemical processing. As an example, the nitrocellulose and nitro-glycerine are extracted and refined from hazardous waste that must be dealt under the directives of the Ministry of Environment, Forest and Climate Change (MoEFCC). The many regulatory constraints tend to discourage private participation in capacity expansion and delay it. The defence supply chain suffers from additional economic and logistical inefficiencies. There are strict security norms for the transportation of explosive materials; therefore, approved routes are restricted, there are restricted timings and a no police escort cannot be taken off. Moreover, India's rail and road infrastructure continues to be optimised for the lower priority, more time insensitive requirements of defence logistics.[173]

Key Challenges in Material Availability

India's ambition to self-reliance in defence manufacturing, specifically ammunition production, depends on which input materials are available. Although policy initiatives, structural reforms and technological progress have been made to address the lack of sources, supply and technological integration of such materials, the ecosystem supporting their sourcing, processing and integration continues to be dilapidated. Below are the key challenges that limit the availability of material in India's ammunition manufacturing value chain.

The most urgent is lack of domestic production of vital metals and explosives used in ammunition. Although India has natural reserves of iron and bauxite, as well as copper, but it does not have shown reserves or efficient extraction capability for a number of strategic materials, including tungsten, nickel, tin and rare earth metals which are vital for production of Armour piercing round, penetrators and other electronic components used in smart munitions. High purity explosives, such as, RDX, HMX and CL-20 are produced domestically by a very few defence laboratories and public sector units and are constrained by outdated equipment, exhausted processes, bottlenecks and environmental compliance. This increased reliance on import and growing shortages of supply during high demand scenarios is due to the lack of the ability to scale up production of these materials.

Another critical barrier is the lack of indigenous capacity in advanced materials Research and Development (R&D). Defence manufacturing demands materials that exhibit superior properties, such as, high melting points, thermal stability, corrosion resistance, and energy density, under extreme operational conditions. India's public sector institutions like DRDO and BARC have made progress in niche areas, but the translation of laboratory-scale innovations to industrial-scale production remains limited.[174] Furthermore, private sector involvement in defence materials R&D is minimal due to high entry barriers, long gestation periods, and limited access to testing infrastructure. There is also a lack of dedicated national centres for research in defence metallurgy, explosives chemistry, and smart materials, leading to technological dependence on foreign suppliers for high-performance alloys and precision electronics.

India continues to depend heavily on imports for several raw materials and semi-processed components, such as, tungsten carbide, beryllium, fusing systems, optical fibres, and programmable guidance modules. While global sourcing offers technological advantages, it also subjects India's ammunition supply chain to volatility in foreign exchange rates, tariff fluctuations, and supply chain markups. Additionally, the procurement of such strategic materials from foreign vendors often involves complex compliance with international regulations, export control regimes (e.g., ITAR, Wassenaar Arrangement), and licensing requirements, which further delay procurement and increase costs.[175] This import dependency also creates an imbalance in India's defence trade posture, affecting long-term sustainability and national security.

The recent global events, such as, the COVID-19 pandemic and geopolitical tensions with China, have exposed severe vulnerabilities in India's external supply chains. During the pandemic, the international movement of materials like high-grade copper, electronic sensors, and explosive precursors was significantly delayed due to lockdowns, port closures, and logistic disruptions. These delays impacted the timely production and delivery of ammunition for both training and operational readiness. Furthermore, the strategic rivalry between India and China, of which the latter is India's major supplier of rare earth materials and electronic sub-components, constitutes a serious security risk. India runs the danger of losing access to crucial materials who are hard to substitute or rapidly replaced with complementary supply from non-Indian sources.[176] Similarly, the Russia–Ukraine conflict has disrupted traditional supply lines for military-grade metals and explosives, affecting global pricing and availability.

The current defence material procurement framework in India is fragmented across various departments, PSUs, and armed service commands. The absence of a unified and digitised National Defence Material Grid results in poor forecasting, overlapping orders, and inefficient inventory management. Many ammunition manufacturers face delays due to non-availability of timely approvals, licenses, or supply chain transparency. Procurement procedures under the Defence Acquisition Procedure (DAP) are also time-consuming and often not aligned with the fast-paced demands of modern ammunition production cycles. Additionally, there is limited interoperability and coordination between public-sector production units, DRDO laboratories, and private suppliers—resulting in delayed indigenisation efforts and under-utilisation of domestic capabilities.[177]

A less visible but equally critical challenge is the shortage of specialised human resources in areas like defence metallurgy, explosives chemistry, material formulation, and defence-grade electronics. Most Indian technical institutions focus on general engineering disciplines, with limited exposure to defence-specific applications in materials science. While premier institutes like IITs, IISc, and DRDO centres offer select programs, there is a glaring gap in vocational training and mid-level technical workforce for operating and maintaining explosive manufacturing facilities, metallurgical plants, and quality testing units. This lack of skilled manpower affects not only R&D but also the quality assurance and safety of finished ammunition products (Verma *et al.*, 2021).

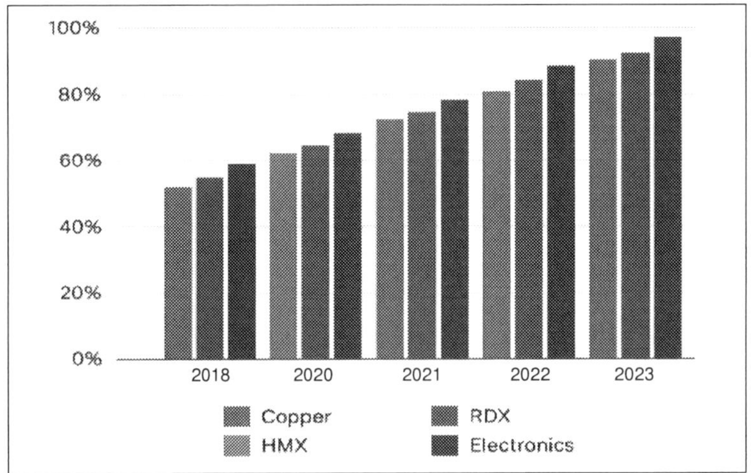

Figure 5.3: Import Dependence of Strategic Materials (2018–2023)

Global Best Practices and Comparative Insights

To strengthen its ammunition manufacturing capabilities and achieve material self-sufficiency, India can draw valuable lessons from the defence production strategies of other leading nations. Countries, such as, the United States, China, and Israel have developed robust systems for managing strategic materials, ensuring seamless integration of industrial and military objectives. Their models offer insights into how India can restructure its policy, infrastructure, and innovation ecosystem to enhance indigenous capacity in ammunition manufacturing.

United States - Defence Industrial Base and Rare-Earth Policy

The United States maintains one of the world's most advanced defence industrial bases, supported by a well-orchestrated supply chain network and a strategic focus on critical materials. Through its Defence Production Act (DPA) and National Defence Stockpile Program, the US government ensures the availability of essential raw materials, such as, rare-earth elements, titanium, beryllium, and high-performance alloys required for munitions and advanced weapon systems. The Defence Logistics Agency (DLA) plays a key role in managing inventories and coordinating with private manufacturers to maintain strategic reserves of metals and chemicals. Furthermore, the Office of Industrial Base Policy ensures that defence procurement decisions support domestic production and technological innovation.[178]

To mitigate supply chain risks, especially from China, the US has prioritised the reshoring of rare-earth mineral processing and invested in public-private partnerships to develop alternative sources from allied nations, such as, Australia and Canada. These initiatives aim to secure long-term independence in critical material supply.[179]

China – Integrated Military–Industrial Complex

China's success in defence manufacturing, particularly in material self-sufficiency, lies in its Civil-Military Integration (CMI) strategy. Under this model, Chinese defence production is deeply embedded within its national industrial and scientific framework. State-owned enterprises, such as, Norinco and China North Industries Group manage end-to-end production of ammunition and explosives, sourcing materials directly from domestic mining and chemical industries. China controls over 60 percent of the global supply of rare-earth elements, including neodymium and dysprosium, which are critical to guided missile systems and smart munitions. Through policies, such as, the Made in China 2025 plan, the government provides massive subsidies and policy support for indigenous R&D in materials science and explosives engineering.[180] Additionally, China has heavily invested in automation, artificial intelligence, and nano-materials in munitions development, creating high-performance, lightweight, and cost-efficient weapons. In particular, Indians involved in indigenisation can draw from the experience of China in top-down integration on the industry-academia-defence services.

Israel – Innovation in Material-Efficient Smart Weapons

Israel's successful innovation-driven, defence manufacturing sector is particularly relevant for resource constrained countries and can be used to develop a similar model. The development of smart ammunition using a reduced footprint of material, while maintaining lethality and precision-made history through companies, such as, Rafael Advanced Defence Systems, IMI Systems, among others. The strength of Israel's design is the ability to configure modular weapon systems using standardised components that are optimal for resource use and flexible manufacturing. Compact, fast and capable of firing a large number of shells or rockets, Israeli firms manufacture high impact munitions with minimal reliance on strategic metals using innovations in microelectronics, MEMS based sensors and lightweight composite materials.[181]

On the other hand, Israel's defence system of R&D is an ecosystem that is characterised by close collaboration between the military, the universities, and the startups. SIBAT (International Defence Cooperation Directorate) helps the government agencies, such as, government agencies to promote the indigenous technology and facilitating the global partnership. This can be emulated by India too, by making stronger DRDO, IIT, and private industry linkages.

Policy Frameworks India Can Adopt

India stands to gain by selectively adapting policy frameworks from these nations:

- From the US, India could adopt strategic stockpiling of rare and essential materials and establish a Defence Materials Authority akin to the DLA.
- China's civil-military integration model can inspire India to establish defence-focused industrial clusters with dedicated material supply lines.
- Israel's innovation incubation and modular design philosophy could guide India's R&D model towards agility and cost-efficiency.

Additionally, India can also examine bilateral resource sharing and international research collaboration for diversifying sourcing and improve its strategic material supply chain. A globally competitive and self-reliant ammunition production ecosystem can be built with the correct combination of policy, investment and institutional coordination in India.

Recent Developments and Indian Initiatives

In the backdrop of many years of defence material self-sufficiency challenges and global supply chain vulnerabilities, India has evolved several strategic policies and initiatives that promote growth of indigenous defence manufacturing ecosystem. All of these measures converge with the national vision of *Atmanirbhar Bharat* (Self-Reliant India), for the reduction in import dependency, improvement in industrial capability, and increase in export of defence products including ammunition and other related materials.

The Defence Production and Export Promotion Policy (DPEPP) 2020 is a comprehensive policy for indigenous defence production. According to the policy, annual turnover of INR 1.75 lakh crore and export revenues of INR 35,000 crore in defence manufacturing should be achieved by 2025. The MoD focuses 3 criteria on DPEPP: development of critical technologies, decrease of import dependency on strategic materials, and expansion of domestic capacity through innovation and infrastructure investment.[182] It also establishes the mechanisms for the indigenisation of imported parts, classification of items for local production on the Positive Indigenisation List and has mechanisms for supporting the startups and MSMEs in ammunition components development, raw materials and explosives development.

Within the last few years, the Defence Research and Development Organisation (DRDO) has partnered with both public and private industry players to speed up production of ammunition and smart munition payloads. Specially under the Strategic Partnership Model, Indian private firms are being given the nod to partner with DRDO, and foreign OEMs (Original Equipment Manufacturers) for the co-development and manufacture of high technology defence products. It resulted in Transfer of Technologies (ToT) for high energy materials, propellant systems, electronic fusing, metal alloys, to companies including Solar Industries, SSS Defence and Bharat forge. Apart from that, DRDO also provides handholding while testing prototypes, licensing and quality standardisation.

The Defence Testing Infrastructure Scheme (DTIS), announced in 2020, is taken as the groundwork of a good quality assurance system. Under the public private partnership, DTIS would spend an allocation of INR 400 crore to set up state of the art testing facilities for defence equipment and materials. These facilities are especially useful for the qualification of the performance and safety of ammunition materials, such as, explosives, stabilisers, metals, and fusing systems. In DTIS program the testing infrastructure is being set up at various key defence manufacturing clusters which are reducing the dependency on limited number of government labs, and shortening the product validation cycles.[183]

The Technology Development Fund (TDF), administered by DRDO, is designed to finance the development of defence technologies by Indian startups, MSMEs, and academia. TDF supports projects with high-risk, high-reward potential in the fields of energetic materials, composite metallurgy, pyrotechnics, and defence electronics. Through TDF, several indigenous materials and components used in ammunition, such as, thermobaric explosives, lead-free primers, and composite casings, are currently under development. The initiative encourages innovation and ensures that small-scale developers can contribute meaningfully to defence self-reliance without being hindered by financial constraints.[184] These policy interventions and programmatic developments underscore a paradigm shift in India's defence production strategy, moving from a state-controlled to a collaborative, innovation-driven ecosystem focused on building long-term resilience in material sourcing and ammunition manufacturing.

Recommendations and the Way Forward

To achieve long-term self-reliance in ammunition manufacturing, India must address the foundational gaps in its material availability and production ecosystem. While significant progress has been made through recent policies and institutional reforms, sustainable and scalable development demands a multi-dimensional approach. The following recommendations outline strategic interventions aimed at building a robust domestic ecosystem for input materials, fostering innovation, and enhancing national defence preparedness.

The first and foremost priority is to expand and modernise domestic mining and refining capabilities for key input materials, such as, copper, tungsten, nickel, aluminium, and rare-earth elements. India must move beyond ore extraction to value-added processing, which is essential for producing defence-grade raw materials. Existing public sector companies such as Hindustan Copper Ltd., NMDC, and IREL should be provided with policy incentives and technology upgradation support to increase output and reduce wastage. At the same time, private players should be encouraged to invest in rare-earth separation plants, metal purification, and high-performance alloy processing through tax incentives and simplified environmental clearances.[185]

To reduce technology gaps and foster innovation, India should actively promote Public-Private Partnerships (PPPs) and international Joint Ventures (JVs) in ammunition material development. DRDO and defence PSUs can collaborate with domestic private companies in areas, such as, explosives chemistry, fusing systems, and microelectronics through co-development and co-production models. Additionally, JVs with countries like Israel, France, South Korea, and Japan can help acquire technologies for high-purity energetic materials, advanced binders, and precision guidance components. These collaborations should focus on long-term technology transfer, localisation of supply chains, and export-oriented production to maximise strategic and economic benefits.[186]

India should establish a centralised mechanism for strategic material stockpiling, especially for high-dependency and high-cost materials like RDX, HMX, tungsten, rare-earth magnets, and high-purity metals. These stockpiles should be managed under a proposed National Defence Material Authority, akin to the US Defence Logistics Agency. Such facilities can ensure buffer reserves during conflicts, supply chain disruptions, or emergency procurement delays. Geographic diversification of warehouses and integration with defence industrial corridors (e.g., UP and TN DICs) will enhance logistical efficiency and inventory security.[187]

The Targeted R&D support must be extended to academic institutions, start-ups, and industry for developing next-generation energetic materials, eco-friendly propellants, lead-free primers, programmable fuzes, and miniaturised smart components. Special emphasis should be placed on dual-use materials that can be repurposed for both military and civilian applications. Programs under Technology Development Fund (TDF) and IMPRINT should be scaled up and aligned with global trends in smart ammunition and nanomaterial-based explosives. Establishing Centres of Excellence in Defence Materials at premier institutes, such as, IITs, IISc, and NITs will foster interdisciplinary innovation and practical applications.

A unified and digital National Defence Material Grid (NDMG) should be established to centralise procurement, inventory management, and inter-agency coordination. This platform would provide real-time insights into the availability, consumption patterns, and projected demand of critical input materials across all defence units. The NDMG should link stakeholders across the value chain, from raw material suppliers and manufacturing units to logistics providers and quality control agencies, ensuring supply chain transparency, reduced redundancy, and better planning. It can also serve as a single-window system for licensing, tenders, and compliance tracking.[188]

In order to create a workforce capable of grooming a future ready defence metallurgy, materials science, explosives engineering and defence electronics, India must invest in human capital development in these areas. It can be put into place through the introduction of specialised diploma and postgraduate programmes, short term certification and on-the-job training modules in collaboration with DRDO, academia and industry. IIT Madras, IISc

Bengaluru, DIAT Pune can very well establish niche programs in high performance materials and safety engineering at institutions like it. Moreover, Industrial Training Institutes (ITIs) located near the defence industrial corridors could incorporate such special modules as propellant handling, quality testing, and material safety protocols.[189]

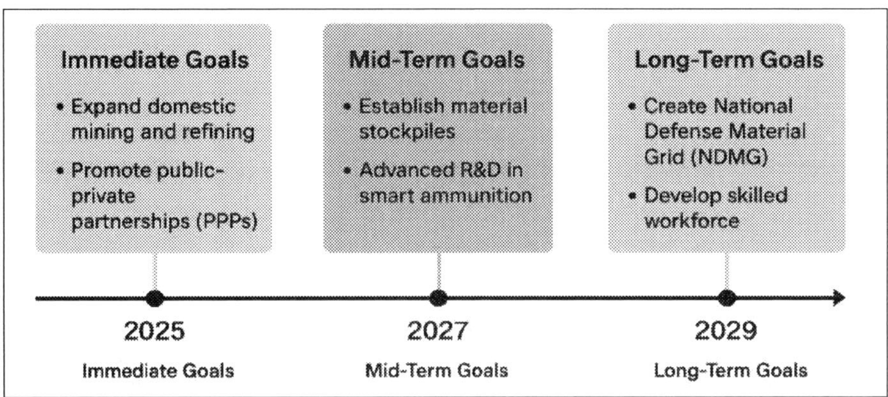

Figure 5.4: Roadmap for Material Self-Reliance in Defence Manufacturing (2025–2030)

Conclusion

India's efforts for self-reliance in ammunition manufacture are at a cusp, influenced by its in-house and outside realities. The country has, in many ways, been commendable in developing a 'pull' from within, with indigenisation of weapon platforms and extending private sector presence. However, critical input materials availability continues to remain a fundamental bottleneck. Vulnerability of India's defence supply chain lies in its dependence on imports to supply strategic metals, high energy explosives, such as, RDX and HMX, and smart components, such as, microelectronics and sensors making India vulnerable for defence procurement. These material constraints are however, strategic constraints, rather than just logistical constraints. However, on the occasion of geopolitical unpredictable disturbances, trade embargoes, or global supply recessions (like COVID 19 and ongoing conflicts), India's capability to fulfil the operational requisite of its armed forces can get severely curtailed. First of all, the dispersed nature of the domestic material ecosystem is joined by insufficient R&D capability for defence grade materials and a shortfall in mining and refining infrastructure that carries along with-it systemic delays as well as increases in costs and restricted innovation. In this respect, achieving self-sufficiency in ammunition materials is not a goal, but a strategic necessity. It enables the country to function with full operational independence, shield themselves from these supply chain shocks, and reduce their need for foreign vendors for this critical wartime resource. Besides, an auto-reliant defence material ecosystem can serve as a spur for industrial growth, employment generation and export competitiveness, thereby ensuring both India's national security and economic resilience in general.

Therefore, there is a critical imperative for a consolidated national endeavour by the public and private sectors, as well as academia, scientific institutions and strategic partners. This strategy should include all the elements of developing a NDMG, the establishment of indigenous facilities for mining and advanced refining, R&D support in energetics material and smart munition devised, and structured skill development programs. India's concept of *Atmanirbhar Bharat* in defence manufacturing will always be incomplete without material sovereignty. By empowering India's ammunition manufacturing capabilities, this will also provide a robust and resilient material ecosystem for India to strengthen its position as a global defence manufacturing hub of the future.

6

Leveraging Geopolitical Synergies to Secure Ammunition Supply Chains

Introduction

A leading industry, the global ammunition manufacturing industry is important to support the national defence capabilities and also contributes greatly to economies of various countries. In today's geopolitical tectonics, the importance of aviation industry's strategic is growing, especially in the global arms industry, including ammunition, the turnover in which nowadays amounts to over $100 billion a year.[190] Ammunition manufacturing strategic partnerships live among the frontiers of the industrial partnerships; they are determinative alliances that bond the geopolitical interests with the resiliency of the supply chains. In times of political unrest or war, having these partnerships allows countries to pool resources, exchange knowledge, and secure supply, particularly, of key materials.[191] Also, as Wheeler points out, such alliances are critical to offsetting the balance of power and keeping the region stable in violent geopolitical backdrops.[192]

The purposes of this review are to study the effects of geopolitical factors on the ammunition manufacturing and strategic partnerships. This will also explore the economic and security benefits of such an alliance in differing cases from all over the globe. The review also aims to evaluate the landscape of the future of these partnerships, identifying trends and suggesting policies and strategies that will strengthen global supply chain resiliency for policymakers and industry leaders. Thus, in this review, we will take a closer look at the intricate interrelationship of geopolitical interests and strategic partnerships as they are important actors in ensuring and promoting the national and regional security of the state and region around the world.[193]

Geopolitical Landscape and Ammunition Manufacturing

The geopolitical dynamics of global powers and defences are highly interwoven within the ammunition manufacture development circle. Control and access to ammunition production has become a key element of national security strategies of the nations for achieving military self-sufficiency and strategic dominance.

Overview of Key Global Players and Alliances

Being amongst the key players in the global ammunition market, there are leaders like United States, Russia, China and several European nations. For instance, the United States has long provided its leadership by making massive investment in R&D, while also encouraging alliance with NATO countries that are strong in technological and logistical aspects of ammunition supply chain. In contrast, Russia leverages its vast natural resources and established military-industrial complex to supply ammunition not only domestically but also to allies in Eastern Europe and Asia, reinforcing its geopolitical influence.[194] China's recent expansions in ammunition manufacturing capabilities are part of its broader "Military-Civil Fusion" strategy, designed to elevate its standing in global arms trade and counterbalance the influence of Western alliances.[195] Additionally, European countries like France and Germany play critical roles, often balancing between aligning with US strategies and fostering independent defence capabilities within the EU framework.[196]

Geopolitical Tensions and Their Impact on Ammunition Supply Chains

Geopolitical tensions significantly influence the stability and security of ammunition supply chains. For example, the ongoing conflicts in the Middle East and Ukraine have demonstrated how regional instabilities can lead to increased demand for ammunition, prompting nations to reassess their supply chain vulnerabilities and seek more robust partnerships.[197] The US-China trade war and its rising sanctions have heightened the risks of overspending and oversensitive on the supply of critical military components of foreign sources, and urged more domestic production and more diversified international sources.[198] The tensions do not only impact members of the direct participants but also the global network of suppliers and manufacturers involved in supporting them. In the latest turn of events, countries are realising that they have to maintain a balance between domestic production capabilities and international partnerships to maintain a steady and secure supply for the domestic industry, especially in crises.[199]

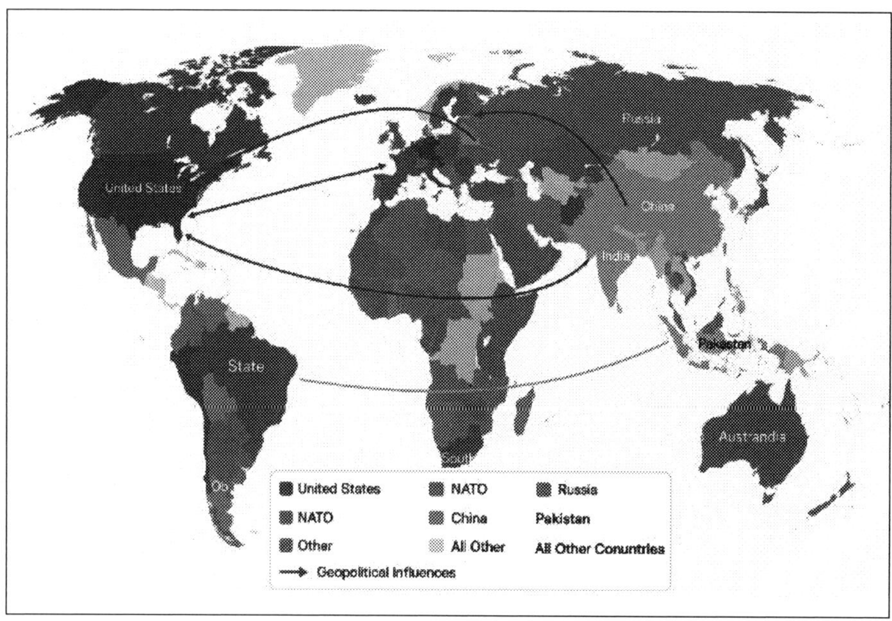

Figure 6.1: Map of Major Ammunition Manufacturing Alliances and Their Geopolitical Influences

The second part of the review focuses particularly on the extent to which ammunition manufacturing is affected by geopolitical dynamics. Nations and alliances in the attempt of securing their ammunition supply chains against disruption are evolving strategies as global tensions develop. By adopting this, the risks are mitigated and it also guarantees that the reliable and efficient production and distribution networks supporting national and regional defence strategies are used.

Strategic Partnerships: Case Studies

USA and Allies: A Model of Collaboration

Making ammunition for use around the world is an old and well-worn path the United States has employed with great success to promote its global influence as well as the security of its allies. Key agreements, such as, the US-Japan Mutual Defence Assistance Agreement and the NATO Standardisation Agreements (STANAG) have been instrumental in standardising military equipment and protocols across allied nations, thus ensuring interoperability and swift collective response capabilities.[200] The outcomes of these agreements include enhanced joint military readiness, improved logistic efficiencies, and reduced costs through economies of scale. For instance, the shared development and procurement programs have enabled the production of standardised ammunition types like the 5.56 × 45mm NATO cartridge, used by over 30 countries, thus significantly reducing the logistical challenges during joint operations.[201] The collaborative efforts under these agreements have markedly improved regional security. For example, the European Deterrence Initiative, strengthened by US-EU ammunition supply agreements, has bolstered the defence posture against potential aggressors by ensuring a steady supply of ammunition to frontline states.[202] These partnerships also enhance supply chain resilience, as seen during the 2022 global supply chain crisis, where diversified production and stockpiling strategies minimised disruptions.[203]

Russia and Eastern Bloc: Integration of Supply Chains

Russia's approach to strategic partnerships in ammunition manufacturing is deeply rooted in its historical ties with Eastern Bloc countries, leveraging these relationships to foster a robust military-industrial complex. Historically, the Soviet Union established extensive military-industrial ties with Eastern Bloc nations, which have evolved today into complex interdependencies in ammunition production and supply. Modern implications of these partnerships are evident in joint military exercises and operations, where logistical synchronisation of ammunition supplies plays a critical role.[204]

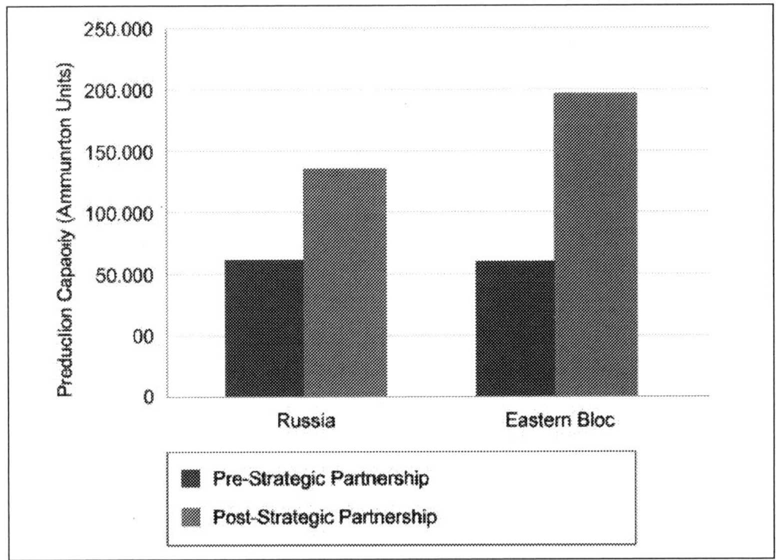

Figure 6.2: Comparative Analysis of Pre- and Post-Strategic Partnership Production Capacities

Emerging Markets: India, Brazil, and South Africa

Although some emerging markets like India, Brazil and South Africa are still in a state of developing their own strategic ammunition partnerships, they are investing in this sector as a means to increase their defence capabilities and integrate more deeply into the global supply chain. Unique opportunities and challenges in the strategic partnerships exist for these countries. This includes access to advanced technology and markets, which can promote local industries development and technological innovations.[205] Yet, political instability, regulatory hurdles, and sizable investment in infrastructure hamper the establishment as well as make such partnerships successful.[206]

Technological Innovations and Their Role in Strategic Partnerships

In the world of ammunition manufacturing, technology is increasingly making the landscape ever more about increasing production capacity as well as securing sensitive data, improving operations. These technological advancements are often leveraged strategically by the partnerships to keep them on the competitive edge and help in national security.

Advances in Manufacturing Technologies

The manufacture of ammunition has undergone recent and significant changes particularly with regard to automation and precision engineering. One can find automated assembly lines facilitated by robotics and AI, increasing their production rate and high quality and consistency production. For example, the digital twinning technology, which helps create virtual replicas of physical systems, allows manufacturers to run and optimise ammunition manufacturing processes without actually manufacturing, saving material and operations run.[207]

Another area in which additive manufacturing, or 3D printing, has impacted production is complex ammunition components where rapid prototyping and just in time production of parts is feasible. For instance, this technology is highly useful in strategic partnerships that require bespoke designs to be made in response to changes in the battlefield environment.

Cybersecurity in Ammunition Manufacturing

In the present day, with the growth of technological advances in ammunition manufacturing, cybersecurity is a critical deterrent against potential issues that surround these assets. Due to the nature of strategic partnerships, the focus is now on establishing robust cybersecurity measures to ensure intellectual property and sensitive production data from cyber threats. Securing data communication and operation within the supply chain entail normal practices of advanced encryption techniques and intrusion detection systems.

The manufacturing plants have added the Internet of Things (IoTs) devices for them to become a part of the Internet of Things, and that has increased the surface area of attacks on the surface, thus emphasising the need for partnerships to put in place a comprehensive cybersecurity strategy to achieve security and defend against other attacks. For instance, real-time monitoring systems can monitor for and neutralise possible security breaches before they can cause harm to production.

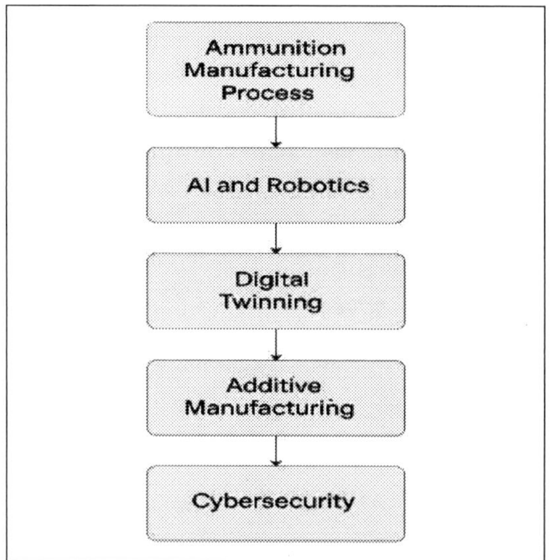

Figure 6.3: Flowchart of Technology Integration in Ammunition Manufacturing

Economic and Industrial Impacts of Strategic Partnerships

Apart from enhancing military capabilities, forming of strategic partnerships in the manufacturing of ammunition generates important economic and industrial benefits. These alliances can improve the economy of scale, technology transfer and amount of employment of the participating countries to great extent which, in turn, impacts the local economy of participating countries greatly.

Cost-Benefit Analysis of Strategic Partnerships

There is strong economic rationale to enter strategic partnerships with manufacturers of ammunition. Their alliances allow them to share R&D costs, give access to new markets, as well as share manufacturing facilities. It's not surprising that countries who partner for these projects often see up to a 20 percent decrease in production costs, produced by smoother processes and collaboration of technological advancements between countries.[208] In addition, the sharing of resources may have an effect of reducing the cycles of innovation allowing those parties involved to have a better competitive edge at the global level as stated in a Global Economic Defence Review, 2025.[209]

Impact on Local Economies and Employment

Transformative partnerships for local economies are possible. For example, the workforce demand of joint venture facilities results in job creation and workforce development in regions where ammunition manufacturing plants are located. As per Economic Development Board,[210] the setting up of a US-Poland ammunition plant led to a 15 percent rise in the number of local employments in the manufacturing industry within the first three years of operation. These facilities often act as development hubs for further economic growth by promoting the development of the logistics, housing and the retail related ancillary industries.

Case Study: Economic Impact of a Strategic Partnership in a Developing Country

Collaboration of India and Israel is a pertinent example of the economic impact of strategic partnerships in developing countries. Under this partnership, the two countries worked together in co-development and co-production of advanced defence technologies, including ammunition. The collaboration proved to be fruitful in the sense that several manufacturing units in India were set up, hence providing a boost to the country's defence industry.

Besides, transferring critical technology to India, the partnership also played a significant role in building a local supplier base that is vital to a country's pursuit of self-reliance in ammunition manufacturing. According to Sharma and Kaur,[211] training and development programs of Israel complemented the direct investment, and consequently increased the skill set of the local workforce. Economic analysis demonstrates that during the first five years of this strategic partnership, India gained approximately $500 million contribution to its GDP from which almost half of it is from exports.[212] In these case studies and analyses, it is demonstrated that there are significant economic benefits in strategic partnerships of ammunition manufacturing. Such alliances thus not only strengthen countries' defence capabilities but also can lead to substantial economic growth through fostering collaboration between them.

Challenges and Barriers to Effective Partnerships

Despite the benefits of strategic partnership in ammunition manufacturing, the partnerships have a number of challenges and barriers that will hinder their effectiveness and durability. Politic risks, legal and regulatory aspects, and logistical and personnel aspects are the main hurdles which must be treaded carefully.

The Political risks are a large stumbling block to real strategic partnerships where political stability cannot be guaranteed. Government and policy change can radically change terms of partnership or lead to its dissolution, leaving one partner with a choice. For example, changing of government may lead to changed protectionist policy stance, restricting foreign collaboration or favouring domestic production over joint venture.[213] In addition, political instability can lead to changes in the defence policy that are unpredictable and have the potential of disrupting the continuity and reliability of partnership agreements.

There are many difficulties in developing and sustaining international strategic partnership, one of which is major differences in the legal and regulatory frameworks between countries. It is essential to care for the details of compliance with ideas about international trade laws, regulations on the arms control, as well as export restrictions in order not to cause serious legal problems damaging the partnership. For instance, the International Traffic in Arms Regulations (ITARs) in the United States governs the export of defence related material and puts onerous controls on such materials that requires partners to comply with time consuming and costly compliance procedure.[214] Moreover, standards and practices integration across divergent legal systems can be arduous. Logistics and operating costs can be worsened if partners need to harmonise their operations in order to meet the highest standards of their partnering countries.

It's no exaggeration to say that running a strategic partnership in the manufacture of ammunition is no picnic. There exist important issues related to the partnership that include the supply chain coordination and quality control among different sites of production, as well as the synchronisation of production schedules. Inconsistencies in the quality of the product can be attributable to divergent manufacturing standards and practices and this can have detrimental effects on the reliability of the ammunition and the partners involved.[215] The other logistical hurdle is for transportation of the ammunition and related materials across international borders while complying with security and regulatory considerations. Collection and timely deliveries of goods and managing inventory in dispersed geographical locations needs sophisticated supply chain solutions that can contribute quite high to the costs if not delicately managed.[216]

Future of Strategic Partnerships in Ammunition Manufacturing

The future of strategic partnerships in the ammunition manufacturing realm appears to be on the verge of being completely adaptive and evolving. These alliances are brought up by technology advancements, geopolitical shifts together with the manifest insatiable appetence for economic efficiency. In this chapter, we discuss predictions and emerging trends in addition to roles of international legislations and agreements in this strategic endeavour.

Predictions and Emerging Trends

The need for enhanced interoperability and mutual benefits of shared technological innovation in the manufacture of ammunition would seemingly lead to increased participation in multinational strategic partnership for ammunition manufacturing over the next decade. Prominently, digital platforms and big data analytics are being widely used by companies to manage their complex supply chains efficiently and promptly respond to the market and geopolitical change.[217] Additionally, there is a new emphasis on sustainability and environmental factors when manufacturing ammunition. This is a trend that will probably lead to strategic partnerships that endeavour not only at producing more efficiently but more with smaller environment impact as well. Some examples would be nontoxic materials and propellants and the recycling of ammunition part.[218]

Role of International Regulations and Agreements

And international regulations and agreements will still have a hand in how the framework in which these strategic partnerships will operate is shaped. Without these regulations, the global peace and security would not exist and the weapons and the ammunition will proliferate and become untransparent. Such regulations include the Arms Trade Treaty (ATT) and various UN sanctions that bind countries to adhere to specific standards and reporting mechanisms which influence strategic partnership forming and maintaining.[219] In addition, trade tensions and geopolitical conflicts will lead to more focus on complying with the international laws to avoid such risks associated with cross border transfers of military goods. This compliance is not only legal, but it also provides for a basis of trust and reliability in international partners.

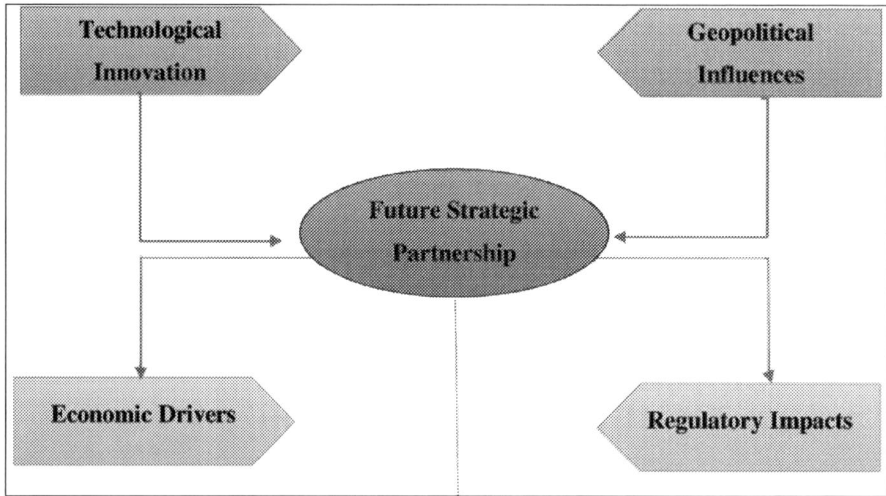

Figure 6.4: Predictive Model of Future Strategic Partnership Trends in Ammunition Manufacturing

Recommendations for Strengthening Strategic Partnerships

The importance of strategic partnerships in the manufacture of ammunition has been exposed during their exploration in granting not only advantages through development of military strength but also the generation of economic and scientific advancements among participating nations. A panel of geopolitical, technological and regulatory factors determine the nature and results of these partnerships. Nations that wish to capitalise on technology, production capacity and market reach have found that strategic partnerships are critical for that task. Interoperability amongst allied forces, economic growth through job creation and technological innovation and increase in the resilience of global supply chains for disruptions have been facilitated by them. Yet, these partnerships are not without challenges as well, ranging from political instability, differences in legal systems as well as the difficulties involved in logistics, which hampers their efficiency and sustainability.

The strengthening of strategic partnerships in ammunition manufacturing will require nations to build alliances that are both resilient and adaptive. A Clear and transparent communication among partners is essential to align objectives and avoid mistrust, while harmonising regulatory standards can ease the burdens of compliance and facilitate smoother collaboration. Shared investment in research and development should be prioritised, not only to reduce costs but also to accelerate innovation and ensure that new technologies are integrated across partner states. Finally, partnerships must be framed with flexibility, allowing them to evolve in response to shifting geopolitical, economic, and technological landscapes.

Way Ahead: Model for India

India's pursuit of ammunition self-reliance is increasingly shaped by vulnerabilities in critical raw materials, niche technologies, and fragile global supply chains. Recent conflicts in Ukraine, Gaza, and the Caucasus have shown how sanctions, trade disruptions, and shortages of inputs can directly degrade operational readiness. As the world's second-largest arms importer, India cannot afford such fragility. To address this, a dedicated Strategic Partnerships for Ammunition Resilience Consortium (SPARC) could serve as the institutional anchor for securing critical materials, co-developing smart munitions, upgrading production processes, and diversifying export markets across the Global South.

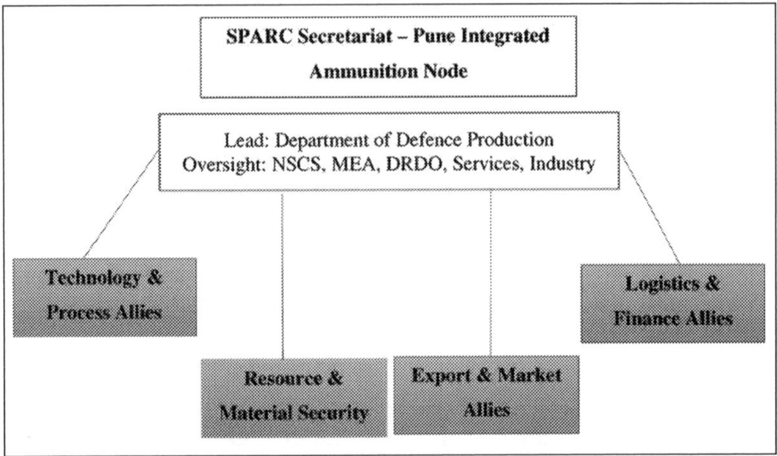

The SPARC model rests on four functional pillars of international cooperation. First, technology and process allies, such as, France and Israel could provide precision fuzes, insensitive munitions, and process safety, while Japan, South Korea, and the Nordics contribute in robotics, MEMS sensors, additive manufacturing, and AI-driven quality assurance. Second, resource and material security allies like Australia, Vietnam, Indonesia, Central Asia, and Africa could supply tungsten, copper, rare earths, antimony, cotton linters, and cobalt—inputs vital for energetics and propellants. Third, export and market allies across ASEAN, Africa, the Middle East, and Latin America could absorb India's ammunition output, deepening defence-industrial ties while providing scale and resilience. Finally, logistics and finance allies, such as, the UAE, Oman, and partners in the International North–South Transport Corridor can underpin supply chain continuity, with Japanese and European DFIs supporting green financing for energetics parks.

The Governance would be centralised under the Department of Defence Production, with a SPARC Secretariat located at the Pune Integrated Ammunition Node, overseen by NSCS, MEA, DRDO, services, and industry representatives. Instruments, such as, joint ventures, co-development agreements, material offtake MoUs, and escrow arrangements for IP would ensure alignment of interests and protection of strategic autonomy. Financing could draw on blended capital from NIIF, EXIM, and SIDBI, complemented by partner export credit agencies and outcome-based payments linked to performance indicators, such as, defect reduction, shelf-life assurance, and export growth. Risk mitigation would demand ITAR-free baselines for each munition type, caps on geographic supply concentration, and joint-IP frameworks to avoid lock-in.

A phased roadmap would establish the Secretariat within 30 days, secure MoUs with Australia, Vietnam, Israel, and France within 60 days, and launch pilot production lines for insensitive munitions and smart fuzes within six months. By the end of the first year, an export coalition with ASEAN and Africa could be operationalised under MEA-led diplomacy. The strategic payoff is substantial: India would hold ninety-day reserves of critical inputs, operate dual-sourced supply chains, maintain an ITAR-free smart munitions portfolio by 2030, and by 2047 emerge as a trusted ammunition hub for the Global South.

7

Harnessing AI for Optimising Ammunition Supply Chains

Introduction

The ammunition supply chain is a complex logistical framework that is critical to defence operations and the security of a nation. The factor that sets it apart from the general supply chain is the sensitivity nature of ammunition, therefore from production to distribution, it is requires high precision, secure handling, and rapid adaptation to changing operational demands. There is no space for failure in ammunition supply chains as it risks not only military readiness but its operational effectiveness as well. India's ammunition logistics rely mostly on traditional supply chains which face issues, such as, logistical delays, inaccurate forecasting of demands and requirements, etc. These inaccuracies might lead to overstocking in some cases and inadequate supply of few products on the other hand which further compromises military operability and its readiness. It is against this backdrop that the emerging technologies, such as, Artificial Intelligence and Machine Learning come into the forefront especially because of its ability to address contemporary challenges as it helps streamline the entire process of ammunition supply chains from forecasting to procuring to distributing it efficiently.

In order to address these issues, this study examines research questions such as, the primary logistical and institutional challenges in India's ammunition supply chain and the role of AI in enhancing the efficiency, accuracy and resilience of ammunition supply chains. Second, the study explores the application of AI across critical stages *vis-à-vis* demand forecasting, inventory management, transportation and its maintenance. This chapter also discusses prospects and challenges to incorporate AI in Ammunition supply chain. Furthermore, it assesses how global defence supply chains have integrated AI within their military infrastructure and what India can learn from them. These questions will provide a foundation to comprehensively understanding the ammunition supply chain landscape by examining both conventional gaps and AI-driven solutions. The primary objective of the research is to examine the current ammunition supply chain infrastructure, highlight existing gaps and propose actionable recommendations for the integration of AI in defence sector. This research is crucial not only for the defence sector but also supply chain management professionals in to ensure the efficaciousness of the current supply chain systems with the dynamic demands of the contemporary warfare.

Leveraging Ammunition Supply Chain with AI

The Supply Chain Management, according to the World Bank refers to "the coordination of activities needed to provide a final product or service. It starts with procuring the raw materials and ends with delivering the final product or any service to the end customer."[220] In addition to this, SCM also includes the recycling or the remanufacturing of the product.[221] It is important to note that managing a supply chain is more than just the contractor and a borrower. It also entails managing and monitoring the dependence of suppliers and even sub-contractors. Therefore, the longer the supply chain, greater is the risk of disruptions.[222] The contemporary world is a globalised one and many organisations are dependent on a global supply base but the physical distance makes it challenging, that is why a lot of sectors are incorporating information technology for coordination and smooth conduct of business. Additionally, the suppliers and the borrowers have to also consider geopolitical disruptions, such as, COVID-19 or conflicts, such as, Russia-Ukraine War as they significantly affect the efficiency and preparedness of a country. In India, traditional defence logistics suffers from various constraints, such as, underdeveloped digital infrastructure, bureaucratic fragmentation especially when it comes to ammunition production and distribution as highlighted by operational shortfall and audit concerns. Most literature are now suggesting that AI could address these challenges by real-time monitoring and data-driven decision making.

The Niti Aayog[223] in its '*National Strategy for Artificial Intelligence #AIFORALL*' refers to AI as the 'ability of the machines to perform cognitive tasks like thinking, perceiving, learning, problem solving and decision making.' The Niti Aayog highlights five sectors that can benefit from AI include healthcare, agriculture, education, smart cities and infrastructure, and smart mobility and transportation'.[224] AI performs its task using two methods, *vis-à-vis*, Machine Learning and Deep Learning. Machine learning or ML gains knowledge from training data and then predicts or recognises patterns in data. Deep Learning or DL on the other hand, is a subset of ML which uses Artificial Neural Networks (ANNs). Deep learning systems have the ability to excel at complicated tasks and might even be able to generate new works of art etc.[225] AI is an umbrella term which includes Machine learning, robotics, expert systems, vision processing etc.[226]

The report by Accenture, *Responsible AI: From principles to practice*[227] highlights four pillars of Responsible AI, *vis-à-vis* Organisational, Operational, Technical and Reputational. For AI to work effectively in any sector it is important that the working ecosystem facilitates human and machine collaboration by focusing on upskilling. Additionally, it is important that there is a system of governance which boosts AI and lastly incorporating AI in any sector should broadly coincide with its ethical guidelines and expected standards. In modern warfare logistics form an important part of the process especially with respect to supply, transport etc. While AI has a lot of benefits for military but it is primarily used for surveillance via drones primarily, or sometimes even to sort through private and public data to flag any suspicious suppliers.[228]

The Scholars around the world are divided over the incorporation of AI in Defence Supply Chains. One perspective pushes for the apt utilisation of AI as it not only bolsters intelligence analysis but also reinforces the resilience of defence supply chain by streamlining the logistics. AI ensures robust cyber security infrastructure wherein network traffic is continuously monitored to protect against cyber threats.[229] On similar lines, Col Lacroix[230] posits that AI can help revolutionise supply chain management in Army logistics as it can perform multifarious tasks, such as, analyse enormous data and predict patterns and trends; and second, adaptive logistics as it accesses data from systems across various army source systems. While this integration of AI is beneficial but it has drawbacks as well, such as, AI creates a false sense of security, budget constraints, vulnerability to cyberattacks, job displacement and ethical decision making. Therefore, adopting a comprehensive approach is the need of the hour.

Hooda[231] iterates the key requirements for effective incorporation of AI. First being Quality Data which is the primary requirement when it comes to using AI for military applications but he emphasises that this data has to be 'cleansed and transformed' in a way that data is specific to the operating environment of the armed force. Second, with respect to the AI, all three services have to be networked with each other so that it bolsters interoperability in any military requirements. Third, is the security because of the AI systems have to be used in military then they should be secure form any cyber threats and attacks. Lastly, all these requirements require expertise, computing power and adopting a strict ethical guideline to keep us ahead than our adversaries.

Sellers[232] provides four ways of AI being leveraged in defence supply chains. First, predictive analysis to help in forecasting demand for supplies by analysing historical data. Second, AI-powered autonomous systems can help avoid risk to human personnel and in some cases also deliver important resources. Third, is to minimise disruptions and help leadership to make more informed decisions. Lastly, joint collaboration is the key to build resilience and revolutionise logistics in defence supply chains.

Also, several global powers have integrated AI in their logistics and supply chain frameworks. For instance, Defence Advanced Research Projects Agency of the United States announced an investment of about $2 billion to research on AI which was collectively called as its "AI Next" campaign.[233] In a recent interview, Matt Turek, deputy director of DARPA's Innovation Office, stated that AI and machine learning are being used in around 70 percent of DARPA's programs and that an important objective of DARPA is to make AI credible for the Defence department.[234] Recently, the US Air force recently integrated artificial intelligence and machine learning for predictive maintenance – Predictive Analytics and Decision Assistant (PANDA) codeveloped with C3 AI. This has led to analyse bulk of data to 'increase the operational reliability or weapon systems'.[235] These are few examples wherein AI integration in aligned with the government approach of transparency standards and infrastructure readiness. China on the other hand has adopted a state-driven model through its "New Generation Artificial Intelligence Development Plan," which aims to become a global AI leader by 2030.[236] The PLA is actively exploring AI for autonomous systems, logistics automation, and real-time battlefield management and a recent example of it is the usage of Llama 13B large language model from Meta to construct a military focused AI tool.[237] These examples suggest that AI integration is dependent on strategic coherence, cross-sectoral collaboration in addition to technological advancement. It is important to note that while a lot of research has been done on integrating AI in defence supply chains, scholars note a dearth of literature focused specifically on Ammunition Supply Chain Optimisation through AI. Therefore, with this chapter, the objective is to address that gap and contextualise AI integration with India's ammunition logistics.

Quantitative Assessment of Ammunition Logistics in India

India's ammunition supply chain has faced operational inefficiencies and this can be evidenced by data-driven examination of three aspects *vis-à-vis* inventory levels, procurement timelines, and wastage rates. Despite increased allocation in defence modernisation and procurement, logistical gaps critically affect India's operational readiness. According to the 2024 CAG Report No. 10,[238] the inefficiencies within the propellant manufacturing and distribution network is a significant bottleneck in the ammunition production ecosystem. India's four propellant factories have consistently failed to meet deadlines when they were to meet annual targets by January to support timely supply to six ammunition filling factories, The Comptroller and Auditor General (CAG) observed delays in propellant issuance in 67 percent of instances by January and 43 percent by March which further affected the filling schedule and timely delivery of ammunition to the Armed Forces. Furthermore, production of three ammunition and one rocket which collectively amounted to ₹ 1,053 crore, was delayed due to a propellant shortfall worth ₹ 276 crore from sister factories. Additionally, audit reports flagged systemic issues which included ₹ 27.82 crore worth of unused propellant. In fact, the five propellants valued at ₹ 21.61 crore and one ammunition worth ₹ 77 crore was also rejected due to quality concerns. It was during the same period that 214 accidents involving four types of ammunition were reported by the Army. Such accidents could be attributed to many defects to deviations in the moisture content of propellants, which further highlight the need for quality assurance in the early stages of the ammunition supply chain.[239] It is notable that these inventory shortfalls are not only a wartime concern but they also tend to impact peacetime training and preparedness as it forces the Army to ration its usage.

The second indicator of logistic inefficiency include the delay in procurement and production of ammunition, which manifests as outstanding orders and slow replenishment. Even after the corporatisation of the OFBs, there has been a backlog of 25,911 production warrants, out of which 3,425 warrants have been pending for over 10 years. This has further led to outstanding expenditures which exceed more than ₹ 1,902 crore. Therefore, it can be asserted that these delays and backlogs highlight a systemic failure to complete production orders within the normal cycle of six months which affects the entire structure of ammunition supply chain.[240]

Lastly, persistent wastage rates and quality-related losses also undermine the efficiency of India's ammunition logistics ecosystem, despite many organisational reforms. For instance, a critical blending machine remained non-operational for over three years at a major ordnance factory, which led to 99.75 metric tonnes of propellant (valued at ₹ 11.24 crore) becoming unusable (CAG, 2024, p. 3). Another case is that of an Ordnance Factory Badmal wherein 98,574 units of a key component which were valued at ₹ 11.08 crore deteriorated beyond usability, while 29,961 units worth ₹ 3.37 crore were on the verge of obsolescence.[241]

All these findings underscore a supply chain that can be characterised by fragmented process which is inherently reactive when it comes to crisis management, and affected by substantial resource inefficiencies. Therefore, addressing these structural deficiencies could be positively impacted by adoption of predictive, data-driven technologies, such as, artificial intelligence, which enhance forecasting accuracy and procurement cycles. AI helps traditional supply chain mechanisms to embed real-time quality assurance in order to transform India's ammunition supply chain into a more resilient and responsive system.

AI in Ammunition Supply Chain Optimisation

Application in Demand Forecasting

The application of AI has significant scope in Ammunition supply chain optimisation. Primarily it can be used in demand forecasting as it can help in predicting the demand for a particular type of ammunition and prevent overstocking and understocking as it leads to financial inaccuracies and storage issues on one hand and could compromise operational readiness in the other. Time-series analysis and neural networks can help identify patterns and forecast future needs. The Incorporation of AI can be effective in demand forecasting for munitions. For instance, AI could help analyse historical consumption data, operational patterns, or even external factors and can forecast ammunition requirements far more accurately than legacy methods. Improved forecasts could enable the military to stock the right types and quantities of ammunition, which would reduce both stockouts and excess inventory. In fact, there was a study that was done by Indian Army researchers which illustrated that AI-based demand forecasting dramatically lowers prediction errors.[242] In this study, machine learning models were trained on five years of ammunition consumption data for a set of inventory items and the AI models' demand forecasts were compared to traditional moving-average forecasts for various time horizons. The results are summarised in the table below.

Table 7.1: Forecast Accuracy Improvement with AI vs. Traditional Methods

Forecast Horizon	*Legacy Forecast Error (MAE)*	*AI Forecast Error (MAE)*	*Error Reduction*
Weekly Demand	7.39	4.74	35.9%
Monthly Demand	87.07	73.30	15.8%
Quarterlv Demand	294.10	82.93	71.8%
Yearly Demand	711.00	500.50	29.6%

MAE = Mean Absolute Error. Lower values indicate better forecasting performance. Compiled by Author.[243]

The data highlights significant quantitative advantages that AI-driven forecasting offers, especially in in medium and long-term planning. Reducing forecast errors means better inventory management, minimised stockouts, reduced overstocking, and optimised procurement schedules. All these improvements can improve the efficiency of India's ammunition supply chain by laying a foundation for a more responsive, and cost-effective military logistics system.

Stock Optimisation and Inventory Management

AI-driven models could also help in stock optimisation and inventory management as it can provide real-time data on stock-levels across various locations on a fingertip which in turn helps in allocating adequate allocation of resources. In addition to this, predictive maintenance has also helped reducing any delays. It can also forecast maintenance intervals and can detect malfunctions etc. AI could also be used in route optimisation by taking into consideration both speed and safety of the cargo. AI has the ability to analyse and predict the best route for transporting ammunition by considering variables, such as, traffic patterns and security threats as it would boost flexibility in transport operations by providing alternative route in real time. It is true that the emergence of AI has brought up the risk of cyber-security threats but logistics in defence must be fortified in a way to prevent any unauthorised access and data breach. In this context, AI can even detect threats and contains the impact of any such attack. Therefore, AI has transformative potential but with this it has challenges as well.

Transportation and Maintenance

The logistics of transporting and maintaining ammunition is another major challenge after stock optimisation. As it is already known, ammunition is a high-risk cargo which requires secure handling, real time monitoring and controlled environments for transit and storage. Most of the transportation infrastructure in India comprises railhead depots, road corridors, warehouses for storage which are part of obsolete systems that are mostly limited. The supply disruption often arises as a result of bureaucratic lag, infrastructure constraints and absence of coordination between military logistic agencies and civilian authorities.[244]

AI-enabled route optimisation and autonomous logistics have the potential to streamline ammunition transportation as AI systems can examine multiple variables simultaneously, such as, terrain complexity, weather patterns or any threat perception. These systems can dynamically respond to evolving circumstances which further enhance responsiveness of the supply chains.[245] Incorporating blockchain and GPS can help end-to-end tracking and route authentication which can help reduce ambush, pilferage or miscommunication. Therefore, integrating AI in this part of the process can enable secure and traceable delivery, however, materialising this potential also requires robust digitisation of transport nodes and transport pipelines.

Similarly, integrating AI in predictive maintenance can help maintain safety of logistics equipment as traditional models usually operate on fixed schedules which do not align with the unpredictability and mission-specific defence supply chains. Predictive analytics can anticipate machinery wear and tear, change in temperature or any component failure. For instance, the adoption of PANDA system by the US can help reduce lifecycle costs of defence equipment and optimise repair cycles.[246] Deploying similar models can help India to counter risks like obsolete infrastructure and quality control.

Challenges and Prospects

The prospects provided by implementing AI in defence supply chains are compelling but it faces several constraints especially for India. Firstly, as AI works on data that is provided hence, data quality and availability is a major challenge. In the case of defence supply chains data like inventory levels, consumption rates, delivery timelines may be siloed, inconsistent and are not fully digitised. The defence logistic system for long has been thesis-based and spread across different system-heads like separate records for ordnance depots. The data gaps also exist globally wherein data has been seen insufficient for some strategic materials hindering the risk assessments.[247] Hence, implementing AI requires robust data pipelines, sensors for real time tracking, integration across the three-force logistics, cleaning and consolidating of the data. Hence, it becomes an arduous task in terms of cost and complexity.

The second challenge to the use of AI is organisational and cultural barriers. The defence organisations need to change their traditional thought and must adapt to trust and effectively use AI. The resistance to AI would be present in logistic personnel and bureaucratic inertia. As a recent example, Israel's state comptroller stated that despite having high-tech talent the absence of a long-term AI strategy and lack of coordination has led to slow implementation of AI projects in their government.[248] In similar lines, Indian defence establishment will need to clear top-down directives in order to mandate AI integration and usage in supply chain logistics. Also, training programs to upskill the personnel in AI tools is an essential part of the Human-AI team for the same.

The third challenge can be seen in technical limitations. While integration of AI is widely accepted, the developing and deploying of AI models for the supply chain would require skilled data scientists and engineers as well as reliable infrastructure. Moreover, defence data is a sensitive matter, therefore the solutions put forth are often developed in–house or carefully vetted partners. Hence, the government initiatives with AI readiness and specific expertise in defence logistics would be needed.[249] Additionally, technical challenges like customising commercial AI to match the unique demands of ammunition logistics as in irregular demands, safety requirements or classified aspects should be treated carefully.

Fourthly, relying on AI for critical ammunition supply decisions for instance like missions or operations taken up by the government would increase the concerns around reliability and security. With cyber warfare and cyber security as a paramount issue, an AI system which controls ammunition supplies could be targeted by adversaries which would lead to data breaches or manipulation.

Furthermore, ethically the percentage of autonomy to be granted to AI is still questionable. The redistribution of ammunition or classifying a supplier as a high-risk to the nation is traditionally a human judgement task, such decisions if given to AI would need transparency and ability to audit its own decisions. This field is in itself under-developed but active research is ongoing. Also, the increased reliance on AI would raise questions on its accountability. Hence, for the current situation of AI usage in ammunition supply chains, security and ethical concerns remain a major constraint.

Lastly, the investment and integration efforts pose a serious challenge. The contemporary world has seen the rise of information technology but still a lot of organisations work on outdated systems, therefore integrating AI systems to the already existing systems would require substantial system upgrades and upfront fundings. For instance, India's existing inventory management system is complex and integrating AI into it requires overhauling of legacy systems and allowing interoperability with AI modules. Such activities require avoidance of disrupting ongoing operations and smooth transition too.

Tackling these challenges would require significant investment in infrastructure, personnel training and data management systems. Helo and Hao[250] iterate various ways to tackle this. First, there is a need for a clear AI strategy and well-informed top management. Second, any sector that wants to incorporate AI in their framework require two things *vis-à-vis* robust technological infrastructure and collected data. Third, AI-related technologies are generally expensive and skilled experts also charge hefty amount for their service.

In order to adopt AI in Indian military, Lt Gen. Hooda[251] recommends changes at the level of Chief Defence Staff and Integrated Defence Staff.

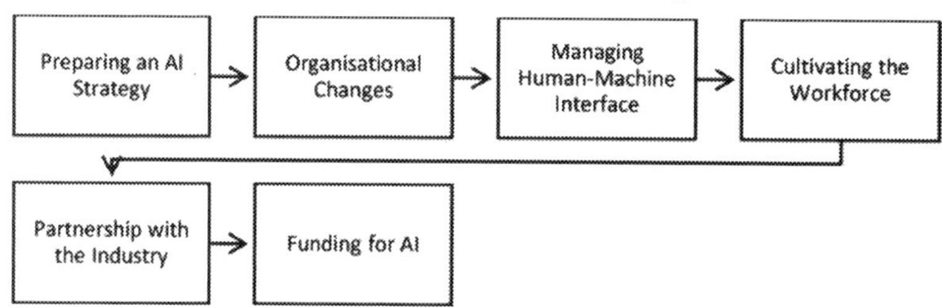

The roadmap or framework of an AI strategy should look into the objectives it aims to fulfil and its scale of application. He recommends changes in the organisational structure *vis-à-vis* setting up of Directorate of Artificial Intelligence at HQ IDS which is categorised into policy section, data section and acquisition section. Another important issue to look into is the level of autonomy to be given to AI since humans form an integral part of decision-making process in defence related matters. This is why Defence Advanced Research Projects Agency is looking into model of 'Explainable Artificial Intelligence' which aims to come up with an explainable model for the user with respect to the decision made by the AI.[252] Other recommendation includes upskilling the work force and collaboration with civilian industries and analysing what applications could be if use in military, for instance, image recognition, robotics etc. Lastly, funding forms an important part of incorporating AI as China is investing big in this sector.[253] China aims to be 'world's primary leader in AI with multiple AI technology innovation and personnel training centre'.[254]

AI-driven autonomous vehicles are a groundbreaking opportunity in ammunition logistics as it can help in transport of supplies without any human intervention. With this feature these AVs can be used in conflict-prone areas and hazardous environments and simultaneously reduce harm to defence personnel. Since, these vehicles are equipped with AI, therefore, they can adapt to real-time conditions, optimise routes and therefore bolster reliability and safety of ammunition supply chains.

Furthermore, integration of blockchain with AI is another promising development to ensure security and transparency of ammunition logistics. The decentralised structure of the block chain can track sensitive information and reduce the risk of unauthorised access and as a result provide a transparent framework for managing and verifying shipments wherein all stakeholders can track origin, condition and current location in real time. Predictive analysis also helps in making real-time decisions as it identifies trends and forecast demands but above all investment in AI technologies is key to all to transforming this emerging technology and utilising it as a strategic advantage. Nations around the world are developing AI driven technologies and investing in new innovations.

For instance, India launched its first national strategy for AI in 2018 which was then followed by creation of Defence AI Council and Defence AI

Project Agency which was recommended by the task force that was set up by the Department of Defence Production under the chairmanship of N. Chandrasekaran. All DRDO laboratories now have AI technology groups in order to introduce AI features in the products, such as, Centre for Artificial Intelligence and Robotics in Bangalore, DRDO Young Scientist Laboratory etc. In fact, Rs. 100 crore per year have been set aside for the AI projects for the armed forces for five years. With respect to defence, India even released a list of 75 AI products in 2022 categorised under AI Platform Automation, Autonomous/Unmanned/Robotic Systems, Block Chain based Automation, C4ISR Systems, Cyber security etc.[255]

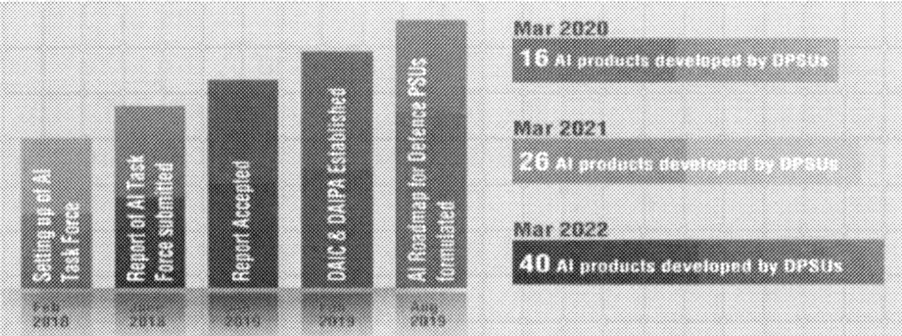

Source: 'AiDef' 2022: The New Age of Defence Presenting AI Preparedness of the Country in Defence, Department of Defence Production, Ministry of Defence India.

All the branches of military have incorporated AI and few instance of this include, first, establishing Quantum Lab at Military College, Mhow by the Indian Army.[256] Second instance is that of a three-day AI workshop organised at INS Valsura in 'Artificial Intelligence for the Future Fleet'.[257] Another instance of incorporating AI in the armed forces constitute the establishment of Unit for Digitisation Automation by the Indian Air Force.[258,259]

Another important factor is ammunition quality and the compliance with regulatory standards for operational effectiveness. Supply chains are inherently exposed to disruption like cyberattacks, natural disasters and geopolitical conflicts but AI systems can affirmatively detect it and in some cases even develop contingency plans by working on various simulation scenarios. The future of ammunition supply management lies in seamless integration of emerging technologies as this ensures end to-end traceability, reduced costs and security. In the near future AI-driven technologies might also aid in environmentally responsible practices. A collaborative approach is the need of the hour where stakeholders, such as, the government, private sectors and research institutions together can build robust frameworks for efficacious supply chains.

Ammunition Supply Chains Insights from Country Case Studies

United States

The United States has implemented several initiatives to secure its ammunition supply chains, focusing on risk mitigation and industrial base modernisation. The Joint Munitions Command (JMC) developed a comprehensive risk model to identify and address vulnerabilities in munitions supply chains. This model played a critical role in ensuring supply continuity, particularly during industrial disruptions, such as, the 2017 explosion at the Lake City Army Ammunition Plant, which significantly impacted production.[260] The model allows the US Army to predict and mitigate supply chain disruptions in real-time, ensuring that ammunition stockpiles remain resilient against logistical bottlenecks. The modernisation of ammunition manufacturing has been one of the key focuses on the US government and as a result the government has established production facilities, such as, the 155 mm artillery shells in Texas in collaboration with the defence contractors. These facilities employ AI based quality control and predictive maintenance to enhance their production efficiency to keep up with the increased demands especially in light of the Russia-Ukraine conflict.[261]

NATO

NATO focuses on standardising military cooperation between member nations to enhance security throughout the ammunition supply chain. Through the Multinational Precision-Guided Munitions Initiative of 2016 NATO member states from eight nations combine their resources to buy and store munitions at reduced costs while maintaining united warfare capabilities.[262] The Multinational Precision-Guided Munitions Initiative originated from the Libya conflict (2011) because participating nations used up their precision ammunition but other nations had excess supplies despite not being compatible. NATO creates a shared munitions system which allows for dynamic distribution of items to meet operational requirements.

The Ukraine war-related ammunition shortages prompted NATO to pursue a massive expansion project to build up procurement programs while boosting manufacturing capabilities. The alliance made public a € 2.4 billion investment to create ammunition including artillery shells together with anti-tank weapons and air-defence missiles.[263] Through this procurement framework NATO member states can joint purchase high-priority munitions with pre-established agreements that prevent emergency acquisition delays. In case of a crisis NATO uses collective planning with strategic reserve management as its supply chain security approach to maintain sufficient supplies for its forces.

Israel

Israel's approach to secure ammunition supply chain have been shaped by historical challenges, particularly the 1973 Yom Kippur War, when its munitions stockpiles were nearly depleted. It was this crisis that resulted in the start of Operation Nickel Grass, a US-led strategic airlift operation delivering over 22,325 tonnes of ammunition and military supplies to Israel, and thereby allowing the nation to maintain its military operations.[264] This crisis underscored the need of pre-positioning supplies and keeping close logistical ties with allied countries.

Israel and the United States created the pre-positioned US-owned ammunition stockpile, War Reserve Stockpile Ammunition-Israel (WRSA-I), on Israeli territory so that it could avoid future supply shortages, therefore, this reserve lets Israel quickly access vital weapons during war, so simplifying resupply procedures.[265] WRSA-I proved crucial in several conflicts including the 2006 Lebanon War and the 2014 Gaza conflict, when Israel removed weapons from the stockpile to support protracted military operations. Israel's model emphasises the importance of strategically forward-deployed reserves as they can reduce supply chain vulnerabilities and guarantee quick response capacity.

These case studies highlight different strategies for securing ammunition supply chains from the United States' risk modelling and industrial modernisation to NATO's multinational cooperation and pooled procurement and Israel's reliance on pre-positioned stockpiles and allied logistics support. Each of these methods emphasise strategic significance of technological investments, and flexible logistics planning in order to lower supply chain interruptions' risks. It is this strategic foresight serve as a blueprint for contemporary defence systems trying to improve ammunition security in a time of changing geopolitical risks.

Applications of AI in Ammunition Supply Chains

Advanced technologies, such as, AI can significantly enhance forecasting and logistics optimisation as the predictive analytics systems of AI help military logisticians to accurately forecast ammunition demands by analysing historical usage, training schedule assessments and evaluating intelligence on contemporary conflicts.

The improved inventory management produces decisions which prevent both supply deficits and inventory excesses. Lockheed Martin alongside other defence contracting companies use artificial intelligence to predict part and munitions requirements through their supply chain management solutions leading to better inventory control and excess stock reduction.[266] By training algorithms on years of consumption data and operational scenarios, militaries can anticipate needs for different ammunition types (from small arms to missiles) under various conditions. Notably, data-driven logistics have shown their value in recent conflicts: Ukraine, with Western support, has used predictive models to position ammunition and other supplies in advance, in stark contrast to Russia's more reactive approach.[267] These AI-informed forecasts ensure troops have the ammo they need before crises hit, and help planners efficiently allocate production and transportation resources.

Second, AI tools can optimise the sourcing of raw materials and components by analysing supplier performance, lead times, and market conditions. Machine learning algorithms quickly identify patterns in supply chain data – for instance, flagging if a particular supplier consistently delivers late or if a certain critical material is trending scarce or expensive. The US Department of Defence notes that AI can enhance procurement by processing vast amounts of data in real time to select the best suppliers and schedule orders optimally.[268] This is especially valuable for ammunition, where global supply of key inputs (like certain chemicals or microchips in smart munitions) might be tight. AI systems can recommend placing orders earlier or diversifying sources for at-risk components. They can also streamline the contract management process by predicting price fluctuations and suggesting when to buy in bulk. Overall, AI-enabled procurement reduces costs and helps avoid bottlenecks by staying ahead of supply disruptions.

Third, optimising the movement of heavy and hazardous ammunition is a complex puzzle that AI is well-suited to tackle. AI algorithms can dynamically route shipments of munitions, taking into account factors like transit times, weather, and threats. For instance, an AI system could analyse real-time data to suggest rerouting a convoy to avoid a newly identified risk or to prioritise which depot should send supplies to a unit based on distance and stock levels. Militaries are working on predictive logistics models that decide "what gets moved, where, and when" in anticipation of needs rather than in reaction.[269] This approach uses AI to coordinate transportation assets (trucks, cargo planes, ships) more efficiently.

Fourth, the machinery that manufactures ammunition and the equipment that stores or transports it (e.g., production lines, depot climate control, trucks) all benefit from predictive maintenance enabled by AI. By monitoring sensor data (temperature, vibration, etc.) from these systems, AI can predict failures before they happen. For example, the US Army is implementing AI-based predictive maintenance tools to anticipate when critical equipment will fail, allowing repairs or part replacements in advance.[270] In the context of ammunition, this concept also extends to munition health monitoring – AI can analyse data from smart sensors on stored missiles or artillery shells to predict degradation. One study even applied machine learning to an Army stockpile reliability program to better predict shelf-life of mortar shells.[271] By detecting problems early (e.g., a batch of propellant starting to destabilise or a factory machine getting out of calibration), such systems prevent costly downtime and ensure consistent output and quality. This is aligned with the military's broader move towards Condition-Based Maintenance Plus (CBM+) to keep its supply chain infrastructure running at peak efficiency.[272]

In addition to the above, AI significantly aid in identifying supply chain risks and enhancing resilience. Sophisticated algorithms can continuously scan supply chain databases (like JMC's Industrial Base tool) and external data (geopolitical news, financial reports of suppliers, etc.) to flag vulnerabilities. For instance, an AI might detect that a key chemical used in propellants is sourced from only one country and identify that as a strategic risk, prompting efforts to find alternate suppliers. As ammunition logistics become digitised (through IoT sensors, warehouse management systems, etc.), protecting these networks from cyberattack is vital. AI plays a dual role here. On one hand, AI-powered cybersecurity systems monitor networks for anomalies, detecting and countering hacking attempts in real time. They can identify unusual patterns (for example, an unauthorised data access in a depot inventory system) faster than human analysts.[273] On the other hand, the increasing use of AI itself introduces new cyber considerations, adversaries might attempt to trick logistics AIs with false data or target the algorithms. Therefore, robust cybersecurity (often AI-enabled) must be layered in to protect the integrity of supply chain data and the functionality of logistic AI tools. The Pentagon emphasises that AI must be integrated responsibly, with resilience against adversarial interference as a priority.[274]

The integration of AI into ammunition supply chains significantly enhances efficiency, security, and sustainability by ensuring precise forecasting of demand, preventing stock shortages and reducing excess inventory. AI provides real-time tracking of munitions by optimising delivery routes, and identifying potential risks, such as, supply chain bottlenecks.[275] Predictive maintenance powered by AI reduces equipment failures in storage depots, transportation vehicles, and manufacturing facilities, ensuring uninterrupted production and supply chain functionality. Beyond operational efficiency, AI contributes to sustainability and lifecycle management by ensuring the proper rotation of stockpiles, preventing munitions degradation, and reducing unnecessary disposal costs. As AI continues to advance, its application in ammunition logistics will significantly improve cost savings, security, and strategic adaptability, ensuring that defence forces remain well-equipped and responsive in any operational environment.

Recommendations for Strengthening the Ammunition Supply Chains

A comprehensive policy framework is imperative for the ammunition supply chain to be resilient as it would ensure protection from any global disruptions and geopolitical volatility. Defence supply chains are extremely crucial for security of any nation therefore; its robustness should be made a strategic priority. For instance, National Policy on Defence Supply Chain Security can be formed into a Comprehensive National Policy wherein the key focus should be Supply Chain Security Framework, Monitoring & Risk Assessment, and Tri-Sectoral Strategic Framework. Partnerships or Agreements in between government agencies, industry and international agencies. The government should encourage such initiatives to mitigate the vulnerabilities in production, procurement, and logistics. Furthermore, regular assessment of geopolitical threats and market fluctuations due to which supply chain risks occur should be monitored. Lastly, the Tri-sectoral framework should include formalised partnerships between government agencies, stakeholders of the industry and international partners to bolster supply chain resilience. The government should roll out such initiatives and policy measures that reduce dependency on imports and technology gaps. It should focus on diversified imports and ensure that the supply chains are secure from any external threat. Therefore, it is important for us to establish national reserves of critical raw materials and consistently work on supplier diversification to reduce dependencies.

Supply chain risks can be mitigated if the ammunition components are domestically produced as that can help the government keep an oversight on the entire supply chain. In fact, in time of need, one can even provide incentives to bolster domestic manufacturing capabilities, such as, subsidies, access to low-interest loans or tax breaks. Favourable policies can help the private manufacturers to focus their efforts on R&D and develop technologies that tailored to our needs. Also, a targeted financial and infrastructural aid should be provided to MSMEs and SMEs which specialise in Niche manufacturing. Furthermore, to promote innovation, a defence ecosystem can be established which would contain defence-focused clusters or corridors so as to facilitate collaboration between academic, industry and government agencies. Lastly, the government can also simplify the regulatory process or probably have a single window to reduce bureaucratic hurdles for defence manufacturers and start-ups.

Traditional procurement practices in defence sector were by and large focused on minimising the expense but the government can now look into reforming the procurement policies and base it on factors, such as, supply chain, resilience, quality and reliability. Transparency in contracts can help foster trust and accountability between the suppliers and government and it would further help in streamlining decision making. It is pertinent that the strategy involves implementing of local sourcing mandates and with long-term contracts with suppliers for stability and capacity building. Furthermore, performance-based metrics can help to ensure better quality standards.

Incorporate sustainable practices by rewarding suppliers that adopt green technologies so as to reduce any operational footprint. For instance, the initiatives should focus on Recycling and reuse system to recover valuable material like brass and steel from ammunition that has been used to reduce waste and conserving resources. Additionally, green manufacturing standards can be adopted across production process and investments can be prioritised to create biodegradable alternatives so that the carbon footprint of the military equipment can be minimised.

To address the emerging challenges in the present world dynamic, forming regional alliances with neighbouring and resource-rich nations can assure access to critical materials. This strategic partnership will help in seamless working of R&D that is simpler access to new technology, scholarly works, and research for advanced materials used in ammunition, such as, nano-composites. Moreover, it will create new opportunities within the academic field as specialised training modules would be formed for the workforce.

Continuous investment in AI research which is tailored to defence requirements of a nation is pertinent for a robust supply chain framework. Government must allocate funds to develop algorithms for supply chain optimisation, simulation, and anomaly detection in the munition's context. A key aspect of this is the development of digital twin models, which allow planners to stress-test AI tools in a virtual environment, ensuring their reliability before implementation. Additionally, modernising IT infrastructure is crucial, adopting cloud computing, deploying IoT sensors at scale, and integrating AI-driven data analytics can significantly enhance logistics efficiency. For example, the Organic Industrial Base modernisation plans in the US embed advanced data systems in factories, improving real-time supply chain visibility. Expanding secure 5G networks on military bases will enable real-time data transmission from storage facilities to AI hubs, ensuring seamless communication and automated decision-making.

The vision for future ammunition supply chains is a fully integrated AI-driven logistics network, where multiple AI systems communicate seamlessly be it handling procurement, transport, depot management, or battlefield resupply. But to reach this milestone, it is important that defence organisations set incremental targets, such as, automating 50 percent of inventory decisions and deploying AI-assisted autonomous resupply vehicles. The adoption of AI in military logistics must align with strategic objectives, ethical standards, and legal frameworks. Defence organisations should establish clear policies on AI's role in decision-making, ensuring that human oversight remains integral to all critical logistics operations. Compliance with international laws of war and ethical AI principles must be prioritised to prevent unintended consequences, such as, biased decision-making or unintended stockpile misallocations. Moreover, AI should be leveraged not only for supply chain security but also for countering adversary logistics capabilities. By predicting and disrupting enemy supply chain vulnerabilities, AI can serve as a force multiplier in future conflicts. Building resilience is another key factor—

militaries should assume that AI-driven logistics systems will be actively targeted in contested environments, necessitating redundant pathways and fallback manual methods in case of cyberattacks or signal disruptions. Additionally, stockpiling critical AI hardware, such as, processing chips and secure servers, should be considered to reduce reliance on foreign suppliers.

Therefore, a coordinated approach which focuses on prioritising domestic production, innovation, transparency is the need of the hour as it would not only enhance national security but result in growth and make India self-reliant.

Conclusion

The application of AI in ammunition supply chain is an underexplored area which requires further research and substantial investment. Its exploration in optimisation of ammunition supply chain is a transformative potential as it can address long-standing inefficiencies and further will help in creating a futuristic logistics approach. The above-mentioned data analysis shows that AI integration notably improves forecasting trends, accuracy, optimises inventory levels, less wastage, quality control, identifying anomalies and accelerates the procurement timelines for a nation. In an era of hybrid conflicts and rapid mobilisations, a responsive and agile logistics becomes a decisive factor in determining superiority. Hence, AI integrated systems can create proactive logistics and resilient system.

Despite its transformative potential, nations are still cautious of adopting it because of sensitivity of defence logistics and continuous cyber threats around the world. Globally, nations around the world are working to incorporate AI but it necessitates robust framework which supports development of AI technologies and ensuring resilient cybersecurity measures as well. Although India has adopted AI but it is still a long road ahead especially since it lags behind countries like US, Israel, Russia and China. Therefore, India must invest in research, infrastructure and collaborations. India needs to invest its innovative spirit to position itself as a global leader in defence landscape. Therefore, a few recommendations for AI integration in Ammunition Supply Chain Optimisation are, first, prioritising an AI ecosystem which is tailored to the defence landscape of a country. This could be done through innovation centres, AI defence labs etc. Second, fostering a public-private partnership which is aligned with national security objectives. Lastly, developing skilled workforce is a necessity, therefore, boosting R&D and innovation be strategically advantageous. In conclusion, AI should be not be seen as a standalone innovation, rather a critical enabler of faster and resilient ammunition supply ecosystem which is capable of meeting current operational demands and resolves future challenges in accordance with conflictual landscapes.

8

LEVERAGING INDUSTRY 4.0 TO MODERNISE AMMUNITION FACTORIES

Introduction

India's defence manufacturing sector has transitioned from legacy systems to the adoption of the fourth Industrial revolution in manufacturing. Industry 4.0 incorporates advanced technologies, such as, Artificial Intelligence, Big Data Analytics, Internet of Things which leads to formation of 'smart factories.' Historically, India has relied on Ordnance Factory Board (OFB) which dated back to the 18th century in order to supply arms and ammunition but the performance of OFBs was criticised for its inefficiencies and obsolete practices. This led to major reforms in India's defence manufacturing wherein the government dissolved the OFB and reorganised its manufacturing factories into seven new Defence Public Sector Undertakings (DPSUs) with a renewed focus on innovation and efficiency. This chapter analyses the India's current legacy ammunition production system and discussed key Industry 4.0 technologies and their relevance in defence manufacturing. It further explores the strategic advantages of defence modernisation and a shift from self-reliance to increased export potential. The chapter aims to present a strategic outlook on transforming India's ammunition factories to smart factories of the future.

Legacy Ammunition Production in India: OFB and the DPSU Transition

The Ordnance Factory, a department under the Ministry of Defence was the one of the world's largest and oldest defence production organisations. It constituted 41 OFBs and supplied arms, ammunition and explosives etc to the Indian Army. Over the years, various issues were identified in the OFB system, such as, production shortfalls, cost overruns and quality issues.[276] Lt Gen VK Saxena summarised the 'OFB Blues' due to issues, such as, "Huge shortfalls in production targets, Delayed deliveries, Poor processes, Poor quality, Lack of technological advancements, Unfulfilled promises and Issues related to work culture, mind set and attitudes."[277] The CAG Report No. 15 of 2019 highlighted evidences, such as, the OFBs only achieved 49 percent targets and its exports decreased by 39 percent in 2017-18 from 2016-17. Additionally, OFB could not fill Army's requirement of electronic fuze due to lack of material and infrastructure. Even the e-procurement system failed to capture duplicity in email, phone numbers of invalid PAN IDs. Lastly, defective ammunition and "injudicious procurement of shell filling machine" were some of the major flaws associated with the OFBs.[278]

The Various committees examined the restructuring of OFB vis-à-vis the T K Nair Committee (2000) which suggested the conversion of the OFB to Ordnance Factory Corporation Limited; Vijay Kelkar Committee (2004) which suggested that the status of '*Navratna*' be accorded to OFB which would push it to be more accountable and responsible; and lastly, Vice Admiral Raman Puri Committee (2015) which recommended the OFB to be divided into few specialised segments.[279,280] All this culminated in 2019, when Ministry of Defence proposed the Corporatisation of the OFB into a 100 percent Government owned PSU in order to provide "functional and financial autonomy and managerial flexibility so as to enable the organisation to grow at a faster pace and play a greater role in defence preparedness of the country while also adequately safeguarding the interests of the workers."[281] In 2021, the Government of India officially converted OFB to a 100 percent Govt. owned corporate entities which started business from October 1, 2021.

Industry 4.0 Technologies and Their Relevance for Defence Manufacturing

The modernising ammunition factories in India are embracing Industry 4.0 technologies, a mix of digital and automation tools which will enable smart, connected and efficient manufacturing. Marked with internet of things, artificial intelligence, big data analytics and robotics, India can pave the way for a new era of manufacturing excellence.[285,286]

DPSU	*Headquarters*	*Product Domain*
Munitions India Limited (MIL)	Khadki, Pune	Small Arms Ammunition, Medium and Large Caliber Ammunition, RCL & Tank Ammunition, Mortar Bomb, Pinaka, Explosives and Propellants
Armoured Vehicles Nigam Limited (AVNL)	Avadi, Chennai	Armoured vehicles
Advanced Weapons and Equipment India Limited (AWE India)	Kanpur	Small Arms and Artillery Guns
Troop Comforts Limited (TCL)	Kanpur	Advanced clothing for extreme conditions
Yantra India Limited (YIL)	Nagpur	Military grade components – forgings, castings etc.
India Optel Limited (IOL)	Dehradun	Opto-electronic devices
Gliders India Limited (GIL)	Kanpur	Parachutes

Source: Compiled by the Author from Press Information Bureau, India,[282] MIL,[283] TCL[284]

IoT is referred to as smart objects or interrelated devices which collect and exchange data in real time. In the case of ammunition factory, IoT would mean an array of sensors on production machines, assembly lines and storage depots. These networked sensors will continuously monitor in real time visibility which will help in operations, equipment health and environmental conditions. IoT helps in predictive maintenance which could utilise data to highlight quality defects or predict machine filters in advance. It is along these lines that the Indian Defence Secy Giridhar Aramane announced the implementation of Industry 4.0/ QA 4.0 to boost defence manufacturing.[287] This was further highlighted at the National Quality Conclave 2025 which "underscored the need to transition from legacy QA models to predictive, data-driven, and automated systems".[288] This conclave introduced "Industry 4.0/QA 4.0 Roadmap, developed jointly by DGQA and industry partners. It includes deployment of smart technologies like Internet of Things-enabled test benches, automated data capture, digital dashboards, and AI-powered analytics—aimed at reducing human error, enhancing efficiency, and enabling continuous quality monitoring across defence product life-cycles" (ibid 2025).

Artificial Intelligence is another significant keystone in Industry 4.0. AI emulates human cognitive functions and makes decision autonomously based on extensive data sets.[289] With respect to ammunition manufacturing it could be used for quality inspection and it could help India achieve the 'Zero Defect Zero Effect' (ZED) needed for munitions reliability.[290,291] AI-driven analytics can optimise the production process by acting upon bottlenecks and keeping constant check on machine performance. Furthermore, Industry 4.0 also incorporates Robotics and Automation which revolutionises several processes. For instance, it is primarily important for tasks which are repetitive but dangerous for humans. This might include filling explosives or assembling detonators etc. Modern robots can collaborate and work alongside humans which helps augmenting round-the-clock operation which could increase output and meet surge demands. Bharat Dynamics Limited is constantly upgrading its manufacturing processes by incorporating Robotics operated workshops to further push *Atmanirbhar Bharat* Initiative.[292] Similarly, Adani Defence and Aerospace recently inaugurated the largest ammunition and missiles complex in Asia which will employ advanced automation and leverage modern machinery.[293]

For legacy Indian factories, digital twin technology is another pivotal technology that can act as a bridge between legacy systems and Industry 4.0. A digital twin is "an exact digital replica or representation of the entity (physical twin) and includes the properties, condition, and behaviour of the real-life object through models and data."[294] Digital twins are different from Simulations in matters of scale or applicability of real-time data etc. While simulations just examine any one process, a digital twin can study multiple processes simultaneously with respect to any equipment. The digital twin can help diagnose the wear and tear of any part and can even identify bottlenecks and quality issues in advance when it comes to factory. Adopting digital twin technology can push India's ammunition factories to a paradigm wherein data and continuous simulations can constantly enhance supply and quality. Lastly, Industry 4.0 also incorporates Big Data and Analytics which primarily constitutes "large data sets collected at every stage of production from devices and operators".[295] In terms of smart ammunition, data is extremely important and can be made available from each operation or test result or even supply delivery. This helps in situating trends and patterns which otherwise humans would overlook. The entire process from data mining to AI driven analysis is based on data which can further improve quality or even aid in supply chain optimisation. Establishing robust data infrastructures can result in more informed operations and would align with a defence production ecosystem that is technology-driven. Therefore, Industry 4.0 technologies aim to overcome the limitations of the OFB-era and push India to new production methods which position India at par with global best practices.

Roadmap for Transition: From Legacy Systems to Smart Ammunition Factories

The transition from legacy ammunition factories to Smart Ammunition requires a comprehensive roadmap as it not just involves buying new machines or software rather upgradation in infrastructure, workforce skills and digital integration.

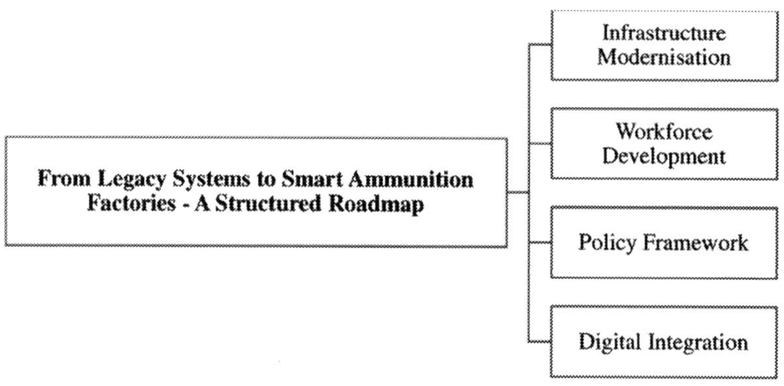

Source: Illustrated by the Author

The first phase for the transformation is infrastructure modernisation. OFB factories obsolete equipment which affected quality and efficiency. Therefore, a through audit of the existing machinery should be conducted so that critical issues, such as, unsafe or outdated equipment can be identified. The need of the hour today is to invest in state-of-the-art production lines which include advanced presses, automated filling machines for explosives, modern equipment with digital controls etc. Additionally, smart ammunition factories should install digital infrastructure, such as, sensor networks, IoT gateways as IoT-enabled facilities can monitor dashboards in real time and also help in data collection. Further, introducing robotics and Additive manufacturing for handling hazardous, labour-intensive operation and a local solution could be printed for an imported machine should also be prioritised as it can reduce downtime. The long-term objective of this phase is to have at least partial automation for ammunition production line so that India can have fully automated 'dark' or 'lights out' manufacturing for some processes.[296]

The second phase in this structured roadmap is Workforce development because any ammunition factory is only as good as the people running it. Although the OFB workforce might be experienced but they might lack the skills for advanced digital technologies. It is to note that while workforce retraining is important but it does not necessarily mean radical reforms in education as different goals can be set based goals and resources of the organisation.[297] Technical institutes and organisations, such as, National Skill Development Corporation can also collaborate with DPSUs to upskill their existing workforce. Equally important is to address the human factors as most workers believe that new technologies would replace human workforce completely in the near future. It is important to clearly communicate to the workforce that automation is a means to augment their role and not replace it. Employees who acquire new skills could be encouraged with reskilling incentives or retention bonus etc. Lastly, DPSUs should look into hiring young professionals who are well versed in digital technologies and fields like AI and cybersecurity. India needs an innovative mindset which can be sustained through workshops, hackathons etc.

The third phase is the Policy framework. Upgrading legacy systems to smart ammunition factories requires quite a substantial investment and therefore, the government should play a significant role in this. One way of doing this could be granting low-interest loans for capital equipment or providing tax incentives to companies investing I Industry 4.0 technologies. A similar fund like the Technology Development Fund under DRDO could be announced for modernisation projects with the DPSUs. Moreover, the government must ensure strategic policy alignment with defence modernisation and self-reliance initiatives. Lastly, Policy framework should also encourage collaboration between DPSUs and private sector by facilitating joint ventures and technology partnerships.

The final phase of this framework is Digital Integration wherein all new technologies are integrated together into a digital ecosystem which links all aspects, such as, factory-floor systems, such as, IoT enable networks with resource planning and product lifecycle management. One of the major challenges for smart ammunition factories is when different machines and software do not communicate, therefore digital integration is key as it allows seamless flow of information. Such integration would also require secure data centres both on-site and cloud to store and process data. Another way to achieve this is by having centralised analytics platforms with apt firewalls which have aggregated data. Such a framework can enable cross-learning and cross-checking across various factories dealing in same products. While digital integration in pertinent, this also calls for stringent and secure cybersecurity measures, such as, a specialised defence industrial control system which could assist DPSUs. Lastly, in case smart systems fail, the factories should have fall back modes so that they continue essential production of critical components despite failure.

Therefore, this transition from legacy systems to smart ammunition factories should be approached in phased manner. Initially, pilot implementations could be carried out successfully and then it should be rolled out. This would help tackle challenges in real time and adapt to form a better framework.

Challenges and Risks in Modernisation

The major challenge for factories after becoming digitally connected is cyber-attacks. A smart ammunition factory's security breach would be through hacking into its production systems ranging from intellectual property theft to sabotaging machine instructions to cause defects or accidents. Thus, data/ cybersecurity related risks should be mitigated with robust measures, such as, firewalls, intrusion detection, regular audits and training for personnel. The DPSUs should collaborate with specialised agencies like CERT. Also, with increased data-sharing clear protocols are needed with proper defence security standards. Hence, a zero-trust security model should be implemented.

With the increased usage of new machinery, digital systems, and training programs for the modernisation requires a massive financial outlay. The industry 4.0 technologies, such as, advanced robotics, AI systems, digital twin software, are expensive to implement especially at large scale. DPSUs are government-owned entities having budget constraints and competing priorities, hence high costs and funding is huge risk as it would stall the process or could lead to partial implementation.[298]

Another major challenge is to integrate legacy systems with new digital ones. The older machines struggle to readily connect to IoT networks in modern formats. Also, there can be compatibility issues between different generations of control systems. Furthermore, each factory needs a customised integration solution due to the absence of standardisation and conversion of outdated machines into more modern ones requires careful engineering.

Human expertise is another factor as existing technical staff would be unfamiliar with new Information Technology-Operational Technology convergence. Therefore, to address the issue DPSUs must hire consultants and systems integrators with industrial digital transformation experience. Some analogous cases in other industries like Indian automative, pharma have incorporated modern technologies. This challenge is surmountable but requires a systematic combining the old and new.

There could be a weaning phase with new systems going online, during which time learning curves could cause output to be interrupted or quality to decline. This leads to manage the crucial military supply during changeover. Also, until new systems are stable, both the systems old and new, need to be run in parallel hence making it resource-intensive. Additionally, quality assurance organisation will be more vigilant as people adjust to new machines. Although, the DGQA conclave's emphasis on preventing unwanted delays while modernising testing procedures is addressed. A robust QA 4.0 approach will help ensure that even if the processes and systems change the output meets specs.

Lastly, external dependencies in the form of foreign technology like advanced robotics, semiconductor chips for sensors, specialised software may need to be licensed or imported. Similarly geopolitical factors could also affect these movement, for instance, if restrictions are posed on export of machinery or shortages of global chip persists than adoption of industry 4.0 will be slow. To mitigate, India needs to focus on indigenise or have multiple sources for critical tech inputs. Although, the India's FDI policy now allows 74 percent and even to 100 percent for niche technology to be transferred[299] but over reliance should be avoided. A delicate balance of leveraging global technology while securing it under domestic control will build local capability in industrial automation tech reducing dependency.

All in all, the challenges of modernising India's ammunition industry are formidable but not insurmountable. India can navigate these pitfalls by integrating cybersecurity from first day, setting aside modernisation budget, piloting integration and running extensive change management programs. With the industry 4.0 in play persistence and adaptability will be key.

Conclusion

India's quest to modernise its ammunition industries from legacy institutions into smart Industry 4.0 enabled industry is a critical measure at the intersection of national security and technological advancement. This chapter examines the transition from old Ordnance Factory Board System to the new DPSUs provides a structural opportunity to infuse modern technology and practices into defence manufacturing. The industry 4.0 technologies, IoT, AI, robotics, digital twins, and big data analytics offers powerful tools to enhance production efficiency and quality in the field of ammunition manufacturing. The adoption of these tech is a strategic imperative for India to achieve self-reliance in armaments ensures reliable supply chains in the face of global uncertainties and to emerge as a defence exporter and regional power. Although the current ammunition production faces systemic issues of inefficiency but addressing them through emphasis on upgradation of physical assets, reskilling the workforce, reforming policies to support innovation and integration of digital systems will yield positive results both in quality and output. With more advanced technology new challenges will emerge. The cybersecurity threats, upskilling of workforce, adequate funding and also change in the organisational culture will require a robust ecosystem to be created. To conclude, modernising India's ammunition industry is a long-term plan but a necessary endeavour. The shift will represent intelligence, connectivity and agility in the defence production

9

Transforming Defence Corridors into Engines of Self-Reliance

Introduction

The vision of *Viksit Bharat 2047* represents India's aspiration to emerge as a fully developed nation by its 100th year of independence. Central to this vision is the strengthening of national security, economic independence, and strategic autonomy. In this regard, the defence sector assumes critical importance as it not only safeguards sovereignty but also drives technological innovation, industrial growth, and employment generation. Over the years, India's reliance on defence imports has been a significant concern, impacting both strategic flexibility and economic resilience. To address these vulnerabilities, the Government of India has launched several initiatives under the broader framework of *Atmanirbhar Bharat* (self-reliant India), with Defence Industrial Corridors (DICs) emerging as pivotal engines for achieving self-reliance and catalysing the broader national development agenda.[300]

The Defence corridors are dedicated zones designed to foster an ecosystem of research, manufacturing, testing, and export in the defence and aerospace sectors. By concentrating resources, infrastructure, and policy support, these corridors aim to attract investments, boost indigenous production, integrate Micro, Small, and Medium Enterprises (MSMEs) into global supply chains, and facilitate technology transfer. The Uttar Pradesh Defence Industrial Corridor (UPDIC) and Tamil Nadu Defence Industrial Corridor (TNDIC) are the two primary examples currently operational, strategically leveraging the respective regional advantages of skilled workforce, academic institutions, industrial base, and logistical connectivity.[301] The establishment of defence corridors is not an isolated intervention. Still, it is synchronised with broader policy instruments like the Defence Acquisition Procedure (DAP) 2020, the Defence Production and Export Promotion Policy (DPEPP) 2020, and strategic programs, such as, Innovations for Defence Excellence (iDEX).[302] These initiatives collectively aim to create a vibrant defence manufacturing ecosystem where startups, MSMEs, and large players co-exist and collaborate. The expected outcomes include not only enhanced domestic capabilities but also positioning India as an export hub for defence equipment and technologies. Globally, the model of defence corridors is inspired by successful examples in countries like the United States, the United Kingdom, and France, where cluster-based development has significantly enhanced competitiveness and innovation in the defence sector.[303] India's approach is unique in its integration of socio-economic goals, such as, employment generation, regional industrialisation, and the upliftment of tier-2 and tier-3 cities. Thus, defence corridors in India are not merely industrial hubs but are envisaged as strategic enablers that can bridge the gap between national security imperatives and economic development goals.

As India advances towards 2047, ensuring that defence corridors fulfil their intended role will require overcoming several challenges, including infrastructural bottlenecks, regulatory hurdles, technology gaps, and investment constraints. Nevertheless, with strategic interventions, robust public-private partnerships, focused R&D initiatives, and global collaborations, defence corridors hold the potential to become dynamic engines of self-reliance, contributing substantially to India's vision of becoming a developed, secure, and prosperous nation. This chapter systematically explores the evolution, strategic contributions, challenges, and future prospects of India's defence corridors in shaping *Viksit Bharat 2047*.

Evolution of India's Defence Industrial Base and the Role of Corridors

Historical Overview of India's Defence Manufacturing

India's defence manufacturing landscape has evolved through several distinct phases, reflecting shifts in geopolitical realities, economic priorities, and technological capabilities. In the post-independence era, the Indian leadership recognised the critical need for a robust defence industrial base to safeguard national sovereignty. However, the initial strategy emphasised self-sufficiency through state-led production, resulting in the establishment of major Public Sector Undertakings (PSUs), such as, Hindustan Aeronautics Limited (HAL), Bharat Electronics Limited (BEL), and Ordnance Factory Board (OFB).[304] Despite these early efforts, the growth of indigenous capability was hampered by technological dependence on foreign suppliers, bureaucratic inefficiencies, and limited R&D investment. During the Cold War period, India's defence industry was predominantly shaped by strategic alignments, particularly with the Soviet Union, leading to substantial imports of military hardware and licensed production agreements. While this partnership enabled India to build critical platforms, such as, fighter jets, submarines, and armoured vehicles, it often restricted full technology transfer, thereby constraining the development of an independent technological.[305] Indigenous innovation remained limited, and the private sector was largely excluded from defence manufacturing activities, reinforcing the dominance of PSUs. The economic liberalisation of the 1990s did not immediately translate into reforms in the defence sector. It was only after the Kargil conflict of 1999 that a major introspection of India's defence preparedness occurred, leading to key policy shifts. The establishment of the Defence Research and Development Organisation (DRDO) was strengthened, and the private sector was gradually allowed to participate in select defence projects.[306] However, systemic challenges, such as, fragmented procurement processes, delays in project execution, and quality control issues persisted.

Recognising these critical gaps, the 21st century witnessed a series of transformative initiatives aimed at revitalising India's defence manufacturing capabilities. Notable milestones included the Defence Procurement Procedure (DPP) 2002, subsequent iterations culminating in the Defence Acquisition Procedure (DAP) 2020, and the formal recognition of private players as eligible participants in defence production (Banerjee *et al.*, 2023). Policy frameworks, such as, the 'Make in India' campaign, the Strategic Partnership Model, and the Defence Production and Export Promotion Policy (DPEPP) 2020 marked a paradigm shift towards fostering indigenous manufacturing, promoting exports, and building a globally competitive defence ecosystem. The establishment of defence industrial corridors in Uttar Pradesh and Tamil Nadu reflects the latest phase of this evolution, focusing on creating specialised zones that synergise manufacturing, research, and innovation. These corridors aim to overcome the historical limitations of dispersed efforts by building concentrated, well-supported ecosystems that integrate large firms, MSMEs, start-ups, and academia. The emphasis is not merely on manufacturing but on developing full-spectrum capabilities, including design, testing, and export competitiveness, thereby positioning defence manufacturing as a central pillar of India's vision for strategic self-reliance and economic resilience by 2047.[307]

Need for Indigenous Defence Capabilities

The imperative for building indigenous defence capabilities in India is deeply rooted in the nation's historical experiences, strategic vulnerabilities, and aspirations for geopolitical autonomy. For decades, India's dependence on external suppliers for critical defence technologies and platforms has posed significant risks to national security, particularly during periods of geopolitical tension when timely access to military equipment became uncertain. This overreliance on imports has not only strained the national exchequer but also limited India's ability to exercise independent strategic choices, especially in high-stakes regional conflicts.[308] Indigenous defence capabilities are essential for ensuring self-sufficiency in times of conflict, reducing susceptibility to supply chain disruptions, and fostering rapid innovation tailored to India's unique operational environments. Global experience demonstrates that countries with robust domestic defence industries, such as, the United States, Russia, and China, possess a strategic edge through technological superiority and reduced external dependency.[309] For India, achieving similar resilience requires not only manufacturing competence but also indigenous design, development, and testing capabilities across land, air, sea, space, and cyber domains. Economically, the development of indigenous defence capabilities offers significant advantages. Defence manufacturing stimulates high-value industrial activities, drives technological spillovers into civilian sectors, and creates substantial employment opportunities. According to recent estimates, every investment of INR 100 crore in defence manufacturing can potentially generate 1,500–2,000 direct and indirect jobs, thereby contributing to inclusive economic growth.[310] Moreover, a thriving defence ecosystem can position India as a credible exporter in the global arms market, reducing the balance of payments deficit and enhancing diplomatic leverage through defence diplomacy.

Strategically, indigenous capabilities enable the customisation of equipment and systems to India's specific operational needs, such as, high-altitude warfare, desert combat, and maritime security in the Indian Ocean Region (IOR). Imported systems, while often technologically advanced, may not always be optimised for these unique environments, necessitating expensive retrofitting and adaptation. Indigenous solutions, developed through close interaction between the armed forces, Defence Public Sector Undertakings (DPSUs), private industry, and research institutions, ensure better operational effectiveness and lifecycle cost efficiency.[311] Furthermore, indigenous defence development fosters a culture of innovation and builds critical Intellectual Property (IP) assets that strengthen India's knowledge economy. The strategic importance of emerging technologies, such as, Artificial Intelligence (AI), robotics, quantum computing, and directed-energy weapons underscores the need for domestic research and industrial ecosystems capable of pioneering next-generation defence solutions.[312] Without indigenous expertise, India risks technological obsolescence and strategic irrelevance in an era of rapid military technological evolution. Recent policy shifts, including the prioritisation of indigenous procurement under the Defence Acquisition Procedure (DAP) 2020 and the notification of positive indigenisation lists banning imports of specific defence items, underscore a clear commitment to fostering self-reliance. Defence corridors, defence start-up programs like iDEX, and enhanced public-private partnerships are structured interventions to accelerate this transition towards indigenous capabilities.[313]

Concept and Genesis of Defence Corridors in India

The idea of establishing defence corridors in India stems from a strategic recognition of the need to create concentrated ecosystems that can drive indigenous defence manufacturing, foster innovation, and facilitate exports. Inspired by the global success of cluster-based industrial models, the Government of India conceptualised defence corridors as dedicated zones where firms involved in defence and aerospace sectors could operate synergistically, benefitting from common infrastructure, policy incentives, and proximity to research and training institutions.[314] These corridors are envisioned not merely as production hubs but as integrated ecosystems facilitating research, design, development, and testing of defence equipment, thereby building full-spectrum capabilities domestically. The genesis of this initiative can be traced back to the broader strategic framework of *Atmanirbhar Bharat* and 'Make in India' campaigns, both of which emphasise self-reliance across critical sectors, with defence being a priority area. Recognising that mere policy announcements were insufficient without a strong manufacturing backbone, the idea of spatial concentration through corridors emerged as a practical solution to harness regional industrial strengths, encourage private sector participation, and attract Foreign Direct Investment (FDI) into the defence sector.[315] In 2018, two Defence Industrial Corridors were formally announced, the Uttar Pradesh Defence Industrial Corridor (UPDIC) and the Tamil Nadu Defence Industrial Corridor (TNDIC). These locations were selected based on a combination of factors, including existing industrial base, availability of skilled manpower, proximity to Defence Public Sector Undertakings (DPSUs) and ordnance factories, and the potential to develop supporting infrastructure, such as, testing facilities and logistics networks. The UPDIC connects key nodes like Aligarh, Agra, Jhansi, Chitrakoot, Kanpur, and Lucknow, while the TNDIC links Chennai, Coimbatore, Hosur, Salem, and Tiruchirappalli, creating geographically integrated defence manufacturing belts.

The corridors are designed to offer a range of advantages to participating entities. These include plug-and-play industrial facilities, tax incentives, streamlined regulatory processes, ready access to testing and certification centres, and active support for research collaborations with academic and scientific institutions. Furthermore, the state governments of Uttar Pradesh and Tamil Nadu have instituted specific policies to incentivise further investments, including land banks, subsidies, and Special Purpose Vehicles (SPVs) for project execution.[316] The strategic intent behind the creation of defence corridors is multifaceted. On one hand, they are expected to enhance India's defence production capacity, reduce dependence on imports, and promote export competitiveness. On the other hand, they serve the broader objective of regional economic development by fostering ancillary industries, generating employment, and integrating MSMEs into global supply chains.[317] In operational terms, the defence corridors represent a shift from fragmented industrial growth to a more coordinated approach where scale, specialisation, and synergy drive efficiency and innovation. By clustering industries, research labs, and training centres within a defined geographical area, the corridors aim to replicate the success of defence innovation hubs seen in countries like the United States (Silicon Valley for defence tech startups) and France (Toulouse aerospace cluster), tailored to the Indian context. The Defence Corridors initiative is also complemented by broader enablers, such as, the Defence Testing Infrastructure Scheme (DTIS), Innovations for Defence Excellence (iDEX), and liberalisation of the FDI regime in the defence sector up to 74 percent through the automatic route. These measures collectively seek to lower entry barriers, enhance competitiveness, and drive the transition from a buyers to a builder's ecosystem for India's armed forces.[318]

Key Defence Corridors

India's defence industrialisation strategy has been significantly reinforced by the establishment of two major Defence Industrial Corridors, the Uttar Pradesh Defence Industrial Corridor (UPDIC) and the Tamil Nadu Defence Industrial Corridor (TNDIC). These corridors are designed to serve as catalysts for indigenous manufacturing, innovation, and exports, strengthening India's ambition to emerge as a major defence producer globally. Each corridor leverages its regional industrial ecosystem, policy support, and infrastructure to promote investment, skill development, and R&D activities essential for self-reliance in defence production.[319] The Uttar Pradesh Defence Industrial Corridor, announced during the 2018 Uttar Pradesh Investors Summit, strategically connects six nodes: Aligarh, Agra, Kanpur, Chitrakoot, Jhansi, and Lucknow. This corridor capitalises on Uttar Pradesh's strong manufacturing base, large labour pool, and the presence of academic and research institutions to create a robust ecosystem for defence manufacturing. The UPDIC is being developed with targeted investments exceeding INR 20,000 crore, aiming to attract defence OEMs (Original Equipment Manufacturers), MSMEs, and start-ups into a seamless industrial cluster.[320] Notable projects include the establishment of BrahMos missile manufacturing units in Lucknow and a Defence Testing Infrastructure at Kanpur. The state government has proactively facilitated land acquisition, introduced investor-friendly policies, and established single-window clearances to expedite project execution.[321] Moreover, collaborations with institutions like IIT Kanpur and HAL are reinforcing research and advanced skill development in defence technologies across the UP corridor. The Tamil Nadu Defence Industrial Corridor, announced in 2019, encompasses five key nodes: Chennai, Coimbatore, Hosur, Salem, and Tiruchirappalli. Tamil Nadu has a historically strong presence in the automobile, electronics, and heavy engineering industries, making it a natural choice for developing an aerospace and defence manufacturing cluster. The TNDIC is projected to mobilise investments worth over INR 10,000 crore, supported by the Tamil Nadu Defence Industrial Policy and initiatives like Aerospace Research Parks and Centres of Excellence.[322] Global defence majors, such as, Lockheed Martin and Boeing already have significant manufacturing footprints in the state, creating opportunities for local vendors and MSMEs to integrate into global supply chains. The corridor emphasises advanced manufacturing technologies, such as, composites, avionics, precision machining, and simulation-based design, positioning Tamil Nadu as a hub for high-end defence production.

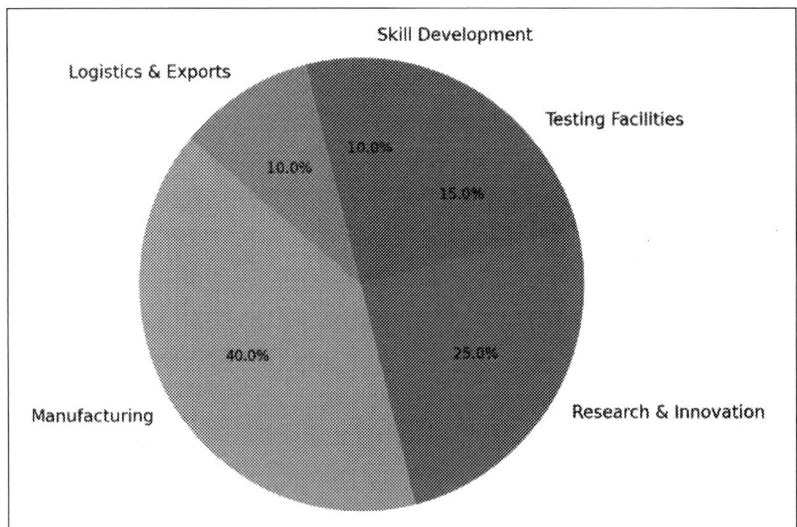

Figure 9.1: Focus Areas in Indian Defence Corridors

Both corridors focus on integrating private players with DPSUs and DRDO laboratories, thereby promoting innovation-led growth rather than traditional license-based manufacturing. They also provide common facilities, such as, testing ranges, prototyping centres, certification labs, and design incubators, essential for reducing entry barriers for startups and MSMEs.[323] A key differentiator of India's defence corridors compared to earlier industrial models is their integrated approach, combining policy support, infrastructure development, skill enhancement, and financial incentives into a cohesive ecosystem. The role of state governments has been pivotal in the success of these corridors. Both Uttar Pradesh and Tamil Nadu have established dedicated corridor management agencies, organised investor outreach programs, and entered into MoUs with industry associations and educational institutions to create a comprehensive industrial network. The corridors are also designed to complement national-level initiatives like the Defence Testing Infrastructure Scheme (DTIS), Innovations for Defence Excellence (iDEX), and the liberalised FDI regime to maximise synergy between policy and practice.[324] In addition to direct manufacturing, the corridors aim to foster ancillary services like logistics, Maintenance, Repair, and Overhaul (MRO), boosting the entire defence value chain. The development of these corridors reflects a strategic vision where India not only meets its internal defence requirements indigenously but also emerges as a credible exporter of defence products to friendly foreign countries, aligning with the broader goal of achieving *Viksit Bharat 2047*. Through sustained efforts, transparent policy execution, and public-private collaboration, the Uttar Pradesh and Tamil Nadu Defence Corridors are poised to transform India's defence industrial landscape.

Strategic Contributions of Defence Corridors to Self-Reliance

Infrastructure Development and Industrial Clusters

Infrastructure development forms the backbone of successful defence corridors, providing the essential physical and institutional framework necessary to stimulate industrial growth, foster innovation, and attract both domestic and international investments. In the context of India's defence corridors, significant emphasis has been placed on creating integrated industrial clusters with state-of-the-art infrastructure, including dedicated manufacturing zones, logistics hubs, research and development centres, testing facilities, and training institutes.[325] These clusters are designed not only to house production facilities but also to offer a complete ecosystem that supports design, prototyping, validation, and scaling of defence products. One of the fundamental objectives behind the creation of industrial clusters within the Uttar Pradesh and Tamil Nadu Defence Corridors is to maximise operational efficiency by geographically concentrating suppliers, service providers, and manufacturers. This proximity facilitates knowledge transfer, reduces transaction costs, accelerates innovation cycles, and promotes competition and collaboration simultaneously.[326] Industrial clustering also supports the development of specialised supply chains, where tiered vendors provide critical components, sub-assemblies, and maintenance services, essential for sophisticated defence systems, such as, missiles, aircraft, and armoured vehicles. In terms of physical infrastructure, both corridors are witnessing the development of multi-modal connectivity through highways, dedicated freight corridors, and air and sea linkages to ensure seamless transportation of raw materials and finished goods. For instance, nodes in Uttar Pradesh, such as, Kanpur and Jhansi, are being linked with expressways and logistics parks, while Tamil Nadu's nodes, like Hosur and Coimbatore, are leveraging their proximity to Chennai Port and international airports to facilitate global trade.[327] Power, water, and digital infrastructure are also being upgraded to meet the high-reliability demands of defence manufacturing.

Beyond physical infrastructure, the corridors are investing heavily in institutional infrastructure, such as, Centres of Excellence (CoE) in areas like aerospace engineering, AI for defence, and materials science. These CoE, often established in collaboration with premier institutions like IITs, DRDO labs, and industry partners, are intended to create innovation hotspots where new technologies can be developed and rapidly transitioned to manufacturing.[328] Moreover, specialised skill development centres have been set up to train technicians, engineers, and managers in advanced manufacturing processes, quality control standards, and defence-specific regulatory compliance. The concept of "smart industrial clusters" is also being introduced, wherein clusters are designed using Industry 4.0 principles, such as, IoT-enabled smart factories, digital twins for design optimisation, and blockchain-based supply chain management for security and transparency.[329] This approach aims to ensure that India's defence corridors are future-ready and globally competitive in terms of technology adoption. Furthermore, the development of industrial clusters within defence corridors aligns with India's broader strategy of regional economic development. By situating high-value manufacturing clusters in less industrialised areas, the corridors contribute to balanced regional growth, generate local employment, and stimulate ancillary industries like logistics, hospitality, and education. Clustering also encourages MSMEs to scale up through linkages with large anchor firms, thus democratising access to the defence sector's opportunities.[330]

Public-Private Partnerships and MSME Empowerment

Public-Private Partnerships (PPPs) and the empowerment of Micro, Small, and Medium Enterprises (MSMEs) are vital pillars in the architecture of India's defence industrial growth, especially within the context of defence corridors. Recognising that achieving technological sovereignty and supply chain resilience cannot be accomplished solely through Public Sector Undertakings (PSUs), the Indian government has strategically reoriented its defence industrial policy to facilitate active private sector engagement. This paradigm shift aims to leverage the innovation potential, agility, and cost competitiveness of the private sector, particularly MSMEs, which constitute the backbone of India's manufacturing economy.[331] Public-Private Partnerships have been encouraged through multiple policy mechanisms, including the Strategic Partnership Model, the Innovations for Defence Excellence (iDEX) program, and offset policies that mandate foreign vendors to invest in Indian industries. These initiatives create avenues for private players to collaborate with defence PSUs, the Defence Research and Development Organisation (DRDO), and the armed forces in co-development, co-production, and testing of defence products.[332] Within the defence corridors, PPP models have facilitated the development of common testing facilities, R&D centres, and manufacturing hubs, reducing the high capital entry barriers that typically deter private investment in the defence sector. MSMEs, which often operate with limited resources, stand to benefit significantly from the structured ecosystem being built in the Uttar Pradesh and Tamil Nadu defence corridors. By clustering MSMEs alongside large defence manufacturers and research institutions, the corridors promote technology transfer, mentorship, and supply chain integration, enabling smaller firms to move up the value chain from low-end components to high-value assemblies and even complete systems.[333] Access to government-sponsored Centres of Excellence (CoEs), subsidised land and utilities, financial incentives, and streamlined procurement policies are critical enablers for MSME participation in defence production.

Furthermore, initiatives, such as, the Defence Testing Infrastructure Scheme (DTIS) and the Technology Development Fund (TDF) have lowered the barriers for MSMEs to innovate and validate their products without the prohibitive costs of setting up standalone facilities. Through targeted capacity-building programs, skill development initiatives, and support for quality certifications like AS9100 and ISO standards, MSMEs are being systematically prepared to meet the stringent demands of defence manufacturing.[334] The empowerment of MSMEs also aligns with broader economic goals. Defence corridors are not just manufacturing zones; they are instruments for regional development and employment generation. MSMEs, with their ability to absorb large numbers of semi-skilled and skilled workers, play a crucial role in achieving these objectives. Studies have shown that MSME-led growth within defence corridors can significantly contribute to regional economic resilience and help bridge urban-rural industrial disparities.[335]

Research, Innovation, and Technology Transfer

The Research, innovation, and technology transfer are pivotal components of the strategy to transform India's defence corridors into dynamic engines of self-reliance and global competitiveness. Without indigenous research capabilities and the seamless transition of innovations from laboratories to production lines, the ambition of building a robust defence manufacturing ecosystem would remain unfulfilled. In recognition of this, recent policy measures and institutional initiatives have strongly emphasised strengthening India's defence R&D ecosystem, fostering innovation among start-ups and MSMEs, and creating frameworks for effective technology transfer from research institutions to industry.[336] The historical model of state-driven defence R&D, largely concentrated within organisations like DRDO, is now being complemented by broader participation from private enterprises, startups, and academic institutions. Programs, such as, Innovations for Defence Excellence (iDEX) have played a transformative role in democratising defence innovation by funding small firms and startups for the development of disruptive technologies in areas like Artificial Intelligence (AI), autonomous systems, quantum communication, and cybersecurity (Saxena *et al.*, 2023). Through defence corridors, such initiatives are gaining momentum by providing a physical and financial ecosystem where innovators have access to testing facilities, prototyping centres, and mentorship from established defence companies and public sector undertakings.

The establishment of Centres of Excellence (CoE) within the Uttar Pradesh and Tamil Nadu Defence Corridors serves as a critical infrastructure for research and technology incubation. These CoE, often developed in collaboration with premier institutions, such as, IITs and IISc, focus on frontier technologies ranging from advanced materials and avionics to next-generation propulsion systems and stealth technologies.[337] By connecting academia with industry, the corridors aim to create a virtuous cycle where academic research feeds into industrial innovation, leading to the development of indigenous, high-value defence products. Technology transfer remains a crucial, though challenging, dimension. India's approach is gradually shifting from mere licensed production based on foreign designs to true technology absorption, customisation, and further innovation. Programs like the Transfer of Technology (ToT) initiatives under DRDO, coupled with policy incentives for industries that adopt and indigenise advanced technologies, are promoting a culture of ownership over critical technologies.[338] Defence corridors act as facilitators by providing platforms where ToT processes can be streamlined, monitored, and scaled through standardised protocols and shared infrastructure. Moreover, research collaborations through PPP models are becoming more prevalent within the corridors. Leading private players are now investing in joint R&D projects with public institutions and startups, ensuring that innovative solutions are rapidly prototyped, validated, and transitioned into mass production. For example, the integration of additive manufacturing (3D printing) for rapid prototyping of critical parts and components has gained significant traction, reducing development timelines and costs substantially.[339]

Employment Generation and Skill Development

The establishment of defence industrial corridors in India represents not only a strategic move towards self-reliance in defence production but also a significant opportunity for large-scale employment generation and skill development. Defence manufacturing is a high-value, technology-intensive sector that demands a wide range of skills across engineering, manufacturing, R&D, quality control, logistics, and project management domains. Consequently, the Uttar Pradesh and Tamil Nadu Defence Corridors are being positioned as engines for creating direct and indirect employment opportunities while simultaneously nurturing a skilled workforce aligned with the future needs of the defence and aerospace sectors.[340] The corridors are expected to generate employment across multiple layers. Direct employment opportunities arise in defence manufacturing units, R&D centres, testing facilities, and industrial parks. Indirect employment is stimulated through ancillary industries, logistics services, maintenance, repair, and overhaul (MRO) operations, as well as retail and hospitality sectors supporting the industrial workforce. Studies estimate that for every direct job created in the defence manufacturing sector, approximately three to four indirect jobs are generated across the value chain, indicating the tremendous multiplier effect on regional economies.[341] Skill development is a critical component to ensure that the manpower generated is employable in technologically advanced and quality-sensitive defence industries. In recognition of this, the government, in collaboration with industry associations and educational institutions, has launched several skilling initiatives tailored specifically to the defence sector. Programs under the Skill India Mission, in partnership with state-specific initiatives like the Uttar Pradesh Defence Industrial Corridor Skill Development Programme and the Tamil Nadu Aerospace and Defence Skill Sector Council, are being implemented to train technicians, engineers, and managers in critical areas, such as, CNC machining, composite material handling, avionics systems, and systems integration.[342]

The corridors are also fostering collaboration with premier institutes like IIT Kanpur, IIT Madras, and various National Skill Training Institutes (NSTIs) to establish CoE and Industrial Training Institutes (ITIs) with specialised curricula. These institutions focus on emerging areas like artificial intelligence for defence applications, cybersecurity, drone technologies, advanced welding techniques, and precision manufacturing. Additionally, apprenticeship models are being promoted within the corridors, enabling students and young professionals to gain hands-on experience in live defence projects and production environments.[343] Recognising that the future of defence manufacturing will be shaped by Industry 4.0 technologies, skill development programs are increasingly emphasising digital competencies, such as, Computer-Aided Design (CAD), digital twins, additive manufacturing (3D printing), and Internet of Things (IoTs) integrations. This forward-looking approach ensures that the Indian workforce is future-ready and capable of meeting global standards of defence manufacturing excellence.[344] Furthermore, the empowerment of women through targeted skilling and employment programs in the defence corridors is gaining momentum. Initiatives are being designed to encourage greater female participation in precision manufacturing, avionics assembly, quality assurance, and administrative roles within defence companies, contributing to the broader goals of inclusivity and gender diversity in the manufacturing sector.[345]

Exports, Foreign Direct Investment (FDI), and Global Positioning

The defence corridors of India are not only intended to fulfil domestic requirements but are also strategically aimed at positioning India as a major exporter of defence equipment and a preferred destination for Foreign Direct Investment (FDI) in the defence sector. Recognising that defence manufacturing has traditionally been a highly closed and regulated sector globally, India has progressively liberalised its policies, modernised its industrial capacities, and fostered a globally competitive environment to enhance its share in the international defence market.[346] The development of Uttar Pradesh and Tamil Nadu Defence Corridors plays a critical role in this transformation by offering integrated infrastructure, incentives, and facilitative frameworks that make India an attractive hub for manufacturing and exports. Over the past few years, India's defence exports have shown a significant upward trajectory, with exports rising from INR 1,521 crore in 2016-17 to over INR 16,000 crore in 2022-23, indicating a tenfold growth.[347] This surge is largely attributed to policy initiatives, such as, the Defence Production and Export Promotion Policy (DPEPP) 2020, the simplification of export authorisations, and the creation of a list of defence items open for industry-wide production and export. The defence corridors are designed to capitalise on this momentum by hosting export-oriented manufacturing units that can meet the demands of friendly foreign nations for systems, such as, patrol vessels, surveillance equipment, artillery guns, drones, and communication systems (Figure 9.2).

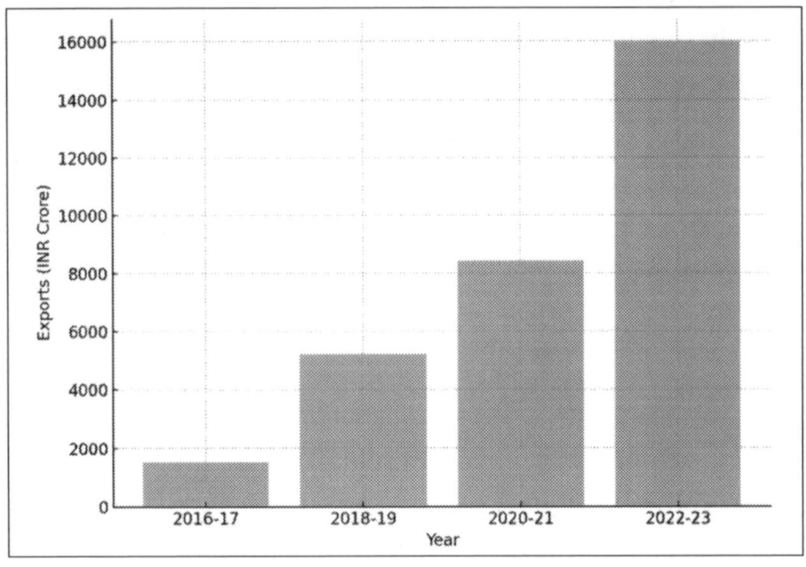

Figure 9.2: Growth of India's Defence Exports (2016–2023)

Foreign Direct Investment has been another focus area for boosting India's global positioning in defence manufacturing. The government's decision to allow up to 74 percent FDI through the automatic route and up to 100 percent through the government route for defence production has been a significant policy shift to attract foreign OEMs (Original Equipment Manufacturers) and encourage joint ventures.[348] Defence corridors offer a ready ecosystem with land, logistics, skilled manpower, and proximity to key markets, thus serving as ideal locations for international companies to set up manufacturing bases or technology partnerships. The defence corridors are actively engaging with global defence majors through roadshows, investor summits, and industry dialogues to showcase the investment potential and operational benefits of the corridors. Companies, such as, Lockheed Martin, Boeing, Saab, and Rafael have shown interest in collaborating with Indian firms and expanding their supply chains to include Indian MSMEs located within the corridors.[349] These collaborations not only bring in much-needed capital but also technology, best practices in manufacturing, quality assurance standards, and access to global markets. Building a global positioning strategy also involves branding Indian defence products as reliable, affordable, and technologically advanced. The corridors play a role in ensuring that Indian products meet international quality certifications and performance standards, which are critical factors for export competitiveness. Initiatives like setting up testing and certification centres within the corridors reduce the time and cost involved in validation, thus facilitating quicker access to global markets.[350]

Challenges and Strategic Interventions for Optimisation

Infrastructural and Logistical Bottlenecks

While the establishment of defence corridors in Uttar Pradesh and Tamil Nadu marks a significant leap towards building a self-reliant and globally competitive defence manufacturing base, several infrastructural and logistical bottlenecks continue to impede the realisation of their full potential. Robust and efficient infrastructure is critical for the smooth functioning of industrial ecosystems, particularly in sectors like defence manufacturing, where precision, reliability, and just-in-time supply chains are essential. However, ground-level realities indicate that gaps remain between policy vision and implementation on the infrastructure and logistics fronts.[351] One of the foremost challenges is the delay in land acquisition and development. However, states have earmarked land banks for industrial development, and procedural delays related to land transfer, compensation disputes, and environmental clearances often stall project execution timelines. In some nodes of the Uttar Pradesh Defence Industrial Corridor, issues, such as, fragmented landholdings, opposition from local stakeholders, and cumbersome regulatory processes have slowed the pace of infrastructure creation.[352] Such delays not only discourage private sector participation but also escalate project costs, making investments less attractive for MSMEs and foreign collaborators. Another critical bottleneck is the uneven quality of transport and logistics infrastructure. Although major cities within the corridors are well-connected through national highways and expressways, last-mile connectivity to designated industrial nodes often remains inadequate. Poor internal road networks, absence of dedicated freight corridors, limited rail connectivity, and lack of proximity to functional air cargo terminals and seaports increase lead times and logistics costs.[353] This is a serious handicap for defence manufacturing, where timely procurement of components and delivery of finished products are crucial for meeting contractual obligations, especially for exports.

The power and water supply reliability also present challenges. Defence manufacturing requires an uninterrupted, high-quality power supply for operating CNC machines, metallurgy units, and avionics assembly lines. In many designated nodes, power infrastructure upgrades are still in progress, leading to occasional outages that disrupt production schedules. Similarly, the availability of industrial-grade water, crucial for manufacturing processes like cooling, chemical treatment, and fabrication, is often inconsistent, necessitating additional investments in private water procurement and treatment facilities.[354] Logistics infrastructure for handling high-value, sensitive defence cargo is still underdeveloped. The absence of specialised warehousing facilities, bonded logistics parks, temperature-controlled storage, and secure transit solutions impedes the seamless movement of defence goods. Furthermore, customs clearance procedures, particularly for dual-use items or sensitive technologies, remain complex and time-consuming, which adds to operational inefficiencies and affects India's competitiveness in global defence markets.[355] Digital infrastructure, an increasingly critical enabler for smart manufacturing and supply chain management, also requires strengthening. While some pilot initiatives in Industry 4.0 technologies have been launched, large-scale implementation of IoT-enabled logistics, real-time tracking systems, and digital twin models for inventory management is still at a nascent stage. Without such capabilities, Indian defence manufacturers risk falling behind global benchmarks for efficiency, traceability, and security.[356] Another overlooked aspect is the lack of Common Facility Centres (CFCs) for testing, quality certification, and component validation. MSMEs, in particular, face difficulties accessing expensive testing infrastructure, leading to delays in product development cycles. While government initiatives like the Defence Testing Infrastructure Scheme (DTIS) aim to bridge this gap, the pace of operationalising these facilities within the corridors needs acceleration to meet growing industrial demands.[357]

Technological Gaps and R&D Constraints

The vision of transforming India into a self-reliant defence manufacturing powerhouse hinges critically on its ability to bridge existing technological gaps and overcome longstanding Research and Development (R&D) constraints. Despite notable progress in select domains, such as, missile systems, space technologies, and nuclear capabilities, India continues to face significant challenges in achieving technological parity with leading global defence manufacturers. These gaps are particularly pronounced in high-end areas, such as, advanced materials, aero-engines, radar technologies, cyber warfare systems, underwater platforms, and electronic warfare.[358] One of the major technological limitations lies in India's limited indigenous capabilities in designing and producing critical subsystems and components. While India has achieved success in platform-level manufacturing, such as, assembling fighter jets, submarines, and tanks, the indigenous content in core technologies like propulsion systems, stealth coatings, high-thrust engines, and precision guidance mechanisms remains low.[359] As a result, a significant proportion of India's defence production continues to rely on imported components, which not only increases costs but also exposes the country to external vulnerabilities during geopolitical crises. R&D constraints further exacerbate technological gaps. Public sector organisations like the Defence Research and Development Organisation (DRDO) have historically been the primary drivers of defence R&D. However, the traditional model has often been criticised for bureaucratic inertia, project delays, insufficient collaboration with industry, and a limited focus on commercialisation of technologies.[360] Private sector involvement in defence R&D has only recently begun gaining traction through initiatives like Innovations for Defence Excellence (iDEX). However, systemic challenges related to funding, risk-sharing, and IP ownership still deter many startups and SMEs from engaging deeply in defence research. Moreover, India's defence R&D spending, estimated at around 0.09 percent of GDP, lags significantly behind countries like the United States, China, Israel, and South Korea, where defence innovation is a national priority backed by substantial government and private sector investment.[361] The relatively low allocation of resources to blue-sky research—fundamental, high-risk, high-reward innovation projects—limits India's ability to achieve technological breakthroughs and self-sufficiency in next-generation warfare domains, such as, quantum technologies, hypersonic, and directed energy weapons.

Another constraint is the weak link between academia, research institutions, and industry. In contrast to countries with robust defence innovation ecosystems, where universities play a critical role in developing dual-use technologies and spinning off start-ups, Indian academia has only a limited footprint in defence R&D initiatives. Although programs like the Technology Development Fund (TDF) and Defence Research and Development Organisation's academia interface schemes have been launched, these efforts need significant scaling up and better integration with the private sector to achieve meaningful impact.[362] Technology transfer mechanisms within India also remain suboptimal. Although DRDO and other public labs have developed numerous technologies, the processes for transferring these technologies to industry, especially MSMEs, are often slow, opaque, and fraught with bureaucratic hurdles. The absence of mature frameworks for licensing, collaborative development, and IP co-creation further delays the commercialisation and mass production of defence innovations.[363] Finally, human resource constraints pose another major challenge. India's defence R&D sector suffers from a shortage of highly specialised talent in critical areas, such as, aerospace engineering, materials science, robotics, AI, and cybersecurity. The limited availability of skilled researchers, coupled with better opportunities abroad, contributes to a brain drain, further weakening the domestic innovation pipeline.[364]

Regulatory Hurdles and Ease of Doing Business

The effectiveness of India's defence corridors in catalysing indigenous manufacturing and strategic self-reliance is intricately linked to the regulatory ecosystem governing defence production, investment, procurement, and exports. Although several progressive reforms have been introduced over the past decade to enhance the ease of doing business in the defence sector, persistent regulatory hurdles continue to impede seamless operations, deter private and foreign investments, and slow down the full-scale operationalisation of the defence industrial corridors.[365] One of the fundamental challenges arises from the complexity and opacity of defence procurement procedures. Despite the introduction of the Defence Acquisition Procedure (DAP) 2020, which aimed to simplify processes and promote indigenous manufacturing through initiatives like Make-I, Make-II, and Buy Indian–IDDM categories, procedural delays and bureaucratic inefficiencies remain significant concerns.[366] The multi-layered approval structures, lengthy technical evaluation processes, and rigid compliance requirements often result in procurement timelines extending over several years, affecting business predictability and discouraging smaller private players and startups from participating actively. Licensing requirements for defence manufacturing also present hurdles. While the licensing regime has been rationalised under the Industries (Development and Regulation) Act, 1951, and the list of defence products requiring industrial licenses has been pruned, ambiguities remain regarding dual-use items and sensitive technologies. This lack of clarity complicates licensing procedures, creating compliance burdens for MSMEs that may not have the institutional capacity to navigate regulatory complexities.[367] Export controls and compliance mechanisms constitute another layer of regulatory challenge. Although the government has created the SCOMET (Special Chemicals, Organisms, Materials, Equipment and Technologies) list to regulate exports, overlapping jurisdictional oversight between the Directorate General of Foreign Trade (DGFT), the Ministry of Defence, and other agencies often leads to delays and confusion for exporters. Moreover, the absence of a single-window export clearance system for defence products hampers India's ability to respond quickly to international market opportunities.[368]

The Foreign Direct Investment (FDI) policies in the defence sector have been liberalised up to 74 percent through the automatic route. However, regulatory uncertainties surrounding security clearances, end-use monitoring, and offset obligations continue to create apprehensions among potential investors. Foreign OEMs seek regulatory predictability and streamlined investment approval frameworks, which are still evolving within the defence corridors.[369] State-level regulatory issues add another dimension to the challenge. Land acquisition processes, environmental clearances, building approvals, and labour compliances, though expedited in theory through single-window systems established by Uttar Pradesh and Tamil Nadu Governments, often face delays at the implementation level. Procedural bottlenecks in registering new industrial units, securing utilities, and availing incentives under state policies undermine the investor confidence that the defence corridors seek to build.[370] Efforts to improve the ease of doing business in the defence sector are underway. Initiatives, such as, the Defence Investor Cell at the Ministry of Defence, online application portals for licensing and export authorisation, and digitisation of procurement workflows represent positive steps towards greater transparency and efficiency. However, industry feedback suggests that there is considerable room for further improvement, especially in terms of grievance redressal, time-bound processing of applications, and reduction of subjective interpretations of regulations.[371]

Financial Challenges and Investment Gaps

The successful realisation of India's defence industrial corridors and the broader goal of achieving strategic autonomy critically depend on sustained financial investments across infrastructure development, Research and Development (R&D), manufacturing capabilities, and skill-building initiatives. However, persistent financial challenges and investment gaps continue to act as significant barriers to unlocking the full potential of the Uttar Pradesh and Tamil Nadu defence corridors. Addressing these economic issues is essential to attract greater participation from private industries, MSMEs, startups, and foreign collaborators.[372] One of the primary financial constraints is the high capital intensity associated with defence manufacturing. Establishing facilities for precision engineering, aerospace component production, avionics integration, and advanced testing requires substantial upfront investments, often beyond the risk appetite or capability of MSMEs and startups. Unlike traditional sectors where asset-light models can succeed, defence manufacturing necessitates heavy investments in specialised machinery, certifications, and compliance infrastructure, which many private firms, especially smaller ones, find difficult to mobilise.[373] Access to affordable and timely finance remains a major bottleneck. While schemes like the Defence Testing Infrastructure Scheme (DTIS) and Technology Development Fund (TDF) offer some funding support, the quantum of financial assistance remains limited relative to sectoral needs. Additionally, private banks and financial institutions often view defence projects as high-risk due to long gestation periods, regulatory uncertainties, and limited exit options. As a result, loan disbursals to defence-sector MSMEs and startups remain low, forcing many to either delay projects or operate at sub-optimal capacities.[374]

The Venture capital and private equity funding in the Indian defence sector are still at a nascent stage. Unlike industries, such as, fintech or health tech, where startups attract robust early-stage investments, defence startups face difficulties in securing seed or growth capital. Investors often cite regulatory risks, limited market scalability within India, and the absence of a mature Mergers and Acquisitions (M&A) ecosystem in the defence industry as deterrents.[375] This creates a vicious cycle where promising innovations struggle to scale, and the overall pipeline of investible defence technologies remains shallow. Foreign Direct Investment (FDI) flows, despite liberalisation up to 74 percent under the automatic route, have not yet reached their full potential. International Original Equipment Manufacturers (OEMs) remain cautious about making large greenfield investments in Indian corridors due to concerns related to security clearances, ownership restrictions in sensitive areas, intellectual property protection, and delays in procurement finalisations. While joint ventures and technology transfer agreements are increasing, significant capital inflows to build independent manufacturing facilities remain limited.[376] Furthermore, fiscal incentives at the state and central levels, though generous on paper, often face challenges in timely disbursement, procedural complexities, and a lack of awareness among investors. Industrial policies specific to defence corridors promise land subsidies, capital grants, tax waivers, and interest subsidies. However, industry feedback indicates that bureaucratic hurdles in availing these incentives dilute their intended impact.[377]

Future Prospects and Conclusion

The defence industrial corridors in Uttar Pradesh and Tamil Nadu represent a transformative shift in India's strategic and economic planning, aiming to build a robust, self-reliant, and globally competitive defence manufacturing ecosystem. As India charts its path towards *Viksit Bharat 2047*, these corridors are poised to serve as critical engines not only for indigenous defence production but also for regional development, employment generation, and technological innovation. The prospects of India's defence corridors are closely tied to their ability to integrate seamlessly with national strategic objectives, attract substantial private and foreign investment, nurture a skilled workforce, and create a vibrant ecosystem of research, innovation, and export competitiveness. In the coming decades, the success of the defence corridors will depend on strengthening public-private partnerships, expanding the participation of MSMEs and startups, and embedding cutting-edge technologies, such as, artificial intelligence, robotics, advanced materials, and quantum computing into the core of manufacturing processes. Establishing Centres of Excellence (CoE) focused on emerging technologies, facilitating co-development programs with foreign defence majors, and fostering a dynamic innovation culture among Indian industries and academia will be essential steps in maintaining a technological edge. The global defence market presents an unprecedented opportunity for India. By leveraging the capabilities being built in the corridors, India can expand its footprint as a trusted supplier of high-quality defence products to friendly nations, thereby enhancing strategic influence and contributing to global security architectures. However, tapping into international markets will require meeting stringent quality standards, offering competitive pricing, ensuring timely delivery, and building robust after-sales support systems. Future growth also demands policy stability, streamlined regulatory frameworks, enhanced ease of doing business, and transparent procurement mechanisms. The government must prioritise creating a single-window system for clearances, accelerating the disbursement of incentives, and promoting regulatory certainty to attract sustained, long-term investments. Additionally, investment in digital and physical infrastructure — including smart logistics hubs, specialised industrial parks, testing facilities, and bonded warehouses — must keep pace with the expanding industrial footprint of the corridors.

The Human capital development remains a cornerstone of future prospects. Tailoring skilling programs to industry needs, incentivising R&D fellowships, and facilitating international exposure for young professionals will ensure a steady supply of competent and specialised talent capable of driving innovation in the defence sector. Building attractive career paths in defence technology fields will also help reduce brain drain and channel India's demographic dividend into strategic industries. Finally, the success of India's defence corridors must be measured not merely by the volume of production or the value of exports but by their ability to catalyse a culture of innovation, strategic autonomy, and national pride. These corridors symbolise India's ambition to transition from a major importer to a major producer and exporter of defence systems, marking a decisive step towards safeguarding sovereignty through economic and technological strength.

10

Reimagining Ammunition Quality Assurance for Modern Manufacturing

Introduction

The reliability of ammunition has always been the unseen backbone of military effectiveness. While weapon platforms attract attention for their intricacy, their performance is only as dependable upon the quality of the ammunition they fire. The modern warfare, defined by high tempo operations, precision engagements, and diverse combat environments, ammunition quality assurance emerges as a strategic determinant of operational success. A defective round can cause material losses and undermine the confidence of soldiers, jeopardising not only the outcome of a mission but also the credibility of entire weapon systems. The global militaries are increasingly recognising that quality assurance is no longer a matter of routine inspection at the factory level but an integrated process spanning the entire lifecycle of ammunition, from design, production, storage, transport, and eventual disposal. The advancements in materials, embedded electronic devices, and smart munitions have raised both the opportunities and risks associated with quality assurance.

For India, the challenge is particularly acute. From the humid tropics of Northeast to the sub-zero heights of Ladakh, Indian Army must ensure reliability across a vast and varied inventory deployed in some of the most demanding environments in the world. At the same time, the quality assurance system must grapple with structural issues, such as, outdated infrastructure, dependence on state-run factories, and an increasingly complex mix of indigenous and imported ammunition. The report by the Comptroller and Auditor General 2015 and incident of the Pulgaon Central Ammunition

Depot fire in 2016 highlights how deficiencies in quality assurance can lead to tragic loss of life, financial damage, and erosion of confidence in critical systems.[378]

This chapter reimagines ammunition quality assurance not as a bureaucratic process but as a strategic capability that is essential for India's military readiness and self-reliance. It traces the global evolution of quality assurance practices and situates the Indian system within this broader context. It then critically analyses the institutional architecture and challenges facing India. Afterward, it suggests a transformed framework that leverages advanced testing technologies, digitalisation, supply chain integration, and independent oversight. Drawing upon the comparative case studies of both success and failure, the chapter demonstrates why ammunition quality assurance must be treated as a pillar of defence modernisation and as an enabler of India's *Atmanirbhar Bharat* ambitions.

Quality Assurance and the Changing Character of Warfare

The character of contemporary warfare has shifted from platform-centric contests to tightly coupled systems where sensors, networks, launchers, and munitions operate as one. In such a system, a munition is not a consumable afterthought but the decisive element that converts information into effect.[379] This shift elevates ammunition quality assurance from a back-end factory practice to a front-line determinant of operational credibility. Precision engagements, dispersed operations, and accelerated decision cycles mean tolerance for failure has narrowed dramatically. Failures that were once localised, such as, a dud round, now cascade across networks, degrade tempo, and erode deterrence.

The modern ammunition embody advances in materials science, micro-electronics, energetic chemistry, and software governance. The electronic fuzes, safety-and-arming devices, smart seekers, and modular propelling charges introduce new failure modes that visual inspection cannot detect.[380] Consequently, prominent militaries have transitioned from inspection-heavy, end-of-line testing to lifecycle assurance that prioritises for quality at the outset, implements statistical control in manufacture, surveys stocks in storage, and monitors performance in the field.[381] In practice, this means building reliability in rather than attempting to inspect it in after the production.

Two main vectors drive this evolution. The first is complexity, reflected in increased part counts, stricter tolerances, and software-defined behaviours that expand the range of potential defects. The second is environmental dispersion, as ammunition move through extreme temperatures, altitude cycles, shock and vibration, humidity, and salt-fog. Ageing of propellants and explosives alters burn characteristics and sensitivity, while packaging and handling introduce latent damage that only manifests at firing.[382] A quality assurance regime adequate for legacy shells is insufficient for multi-domain operations where the same inventory must be safe at Siachen and reliable in the Northeast's humidity.[383]

Technologically, quality assurance has become data-rich and non-destructive. Digital radiography, computed tomography, ultrasonic phased arrays, acoustic emission, and laser-induced breakdown spectroscopy allow internal defect detection without compromising rounds. High-speed imaging and instrumented firing capture transient events, such as, pressure rise, setback forces, projectile yaw, and recoil dynamics to link defects with ballistic signatures. On the process side, statistical process control and attributes sampling plans manage variability at scale, while reliability growth methods track defect discovery and corrective action across design iterations. Environmental stress screening pushes early-life failures out of field inventories. These techniques, already embedded in NATO Standardisation Agreements, are increasingly paired with digital threads that retain traceable histories for every lot and, where feasible, every round.[384]

Quality has also broadened beyond physical conformance to assured function under mission conditions. For insensitive munitions, quality includes predictable response to hazards, such as, cook-off, bullet impact, and fragment attack so that storage and transport remain safe even under accident conditions. For smart rounds, it includes firmware integrity, anti-tamper protections, and counterfeit-avoidance in micro-electronics supply chains. These domains draw on standards culture, such as, ISO 9001 for quality management systems and ISO 31000 for risk management, but also intersect with security governance.[385,386] As supply chains globalise, traceability and serialisation become essential to isolate defective lots, investigate root causes, and meet export-market due diligence.

This reframing of quality assurance aligns directly with India's self-reliance goals. Defence corridors create production capacity, but credibility in domestic service and export markets depends on demonstrable, standards-driven quality.

International buyers and offset partners evaluate not only price and performance but also process maturity, including certified management systems, independent oversight, calibrated metrology, accredited test houses, and transparent non-conformance handling. Without these, corridors risk becoming throughput channels rather than trust-producing ecosystems. Embedding shared quality assurance infrastructure, such as, proof ranges, climatic test facilities, explosives laboratories, calibration centres, and digital conformity assessment within the Uttar Pradesh and Tamil Nadu corridors would allow smaller manufacturers to meet prime-contractor and export requirements at lower transaction costs, while giving the Services confidence in multi-vendor sourcing.[387]

A lifecycle view also changes institutional roles. The user Service is not only the receiver of finished goods but a co-designer of quality through clear, testable Staff Qualitative Requirements, participation in design reviews, and surveillance sampling from depots that feeds reliability data back to producers. The quality assurance authority's remit expands from gatekeeping to systems assurance, auditing supplier process capability, qualifying special processes, and enforcing lot genealogy so that investigations can move from symptom to cause with speed. Manufacturers, whether Defence Public Sector Undertakings or private firms, must shift from inspection departments to quality-by-design organisations using Six Sigma for chronic defects and design for manufacturability for new lines.[388] This culture reduces rework and write-offs, improves safety, and shortens cycle times. The stakes are strategic. India seeks to field larger volumes of precision fires and to become a net defence exporter. Both require that ammunition be not only produced at scale but provably reliable. Accidents, such as, the Central Ammunition Depot Pulgaon tragedy illustrate the costs of inadequate surveillance and storage governance, while best-practice militaries show that integrating advanced non-destructive testing, digital traceability, and independent oversight reduces defect rates and sustains confidence.[389] In short, quality assurance is strategy. It converts industrial policy into combat credibility and export competitiveness.

India's Ammunition QA Landscape

The scale of India's armed forces and the legacy of its defence industrial base both are reflected in its ammunition quality assurance system. It is a complex arrangement involving the Directorate General of Quality Assurance (DGQA), the restructured Defence Public Sector Undertakings (DPSUs), and the Indian

Army as the end-user. Together, these actors manage inspection, testing, and acceptance of ammunition across a spectrum that ranges from small-arms cartridges to artillery shells, rockets, and smart munitions. While the framework is extensive, its effectiveness has often been called into question by reports of defective stocks, accidents, and inefficiencies in procurement and storage.[390]

Institutional Roles

The DGQA functions as the nodal authority under the Department of Defence Production, Ministry of Defence. Its mandate is to provide second-party assurance across all defence stores, including ammunition. This involves inspections during production, evaluation of imported lots, liaison with suppliers, and technical advice to the services.[391] The manufacturing function, historically carried out by the Ordnance Factory Board, now lies with seven DPSUs created through corporatisation in 2021. These entities produce the bulk of India's conventional ammunition, implementing internal quality controls before delivery. The Army, as the user, supplements this process with acceptance trials, depot-level surveillance, and defect reporting from the field.[392]

On paper, this multi-layered arrangement ensures checks at every stage. In practice, overlapping jurisdictions and dated procedures have led to systemic gaps. The DGQA's dependence on the same DPSUs it oversees raises questions of impartiality. Corporatisation has opened space for private manufacturers, but the integration of their quality systems into the national framework remains limited. Meanwhile, the Army's acceptance process is reactive, often identifying defects only after delivery. This architecture therefore tends to identify faults late, rather than prevent them upstream.

Procurement and Supply Chain Complexity

India sources ammunition both domestically and through imports. Indigenous production covers a wide range of calibres but struggles to keep pace with modern requirements in smart munitions and precision-guided systems. Imports fill these gaps but introduce heterogeneity in standards, documentation, and testing requirements. The supply chain is further complicated by environmental stresses across diverse operational theatres and by the need for long-term storage under challenging conditions. As Lee notes, quality in such contexts is inseparable from logistics, since packaging, handling, and stock rotation determine whether munitions remain reliable at the point of use.[393]

Corporatisation of the Ordnance Factory Board was intended to address inefficiencies, but it has also created transitional challenges. DPSUs must now operate as commercial entities, balancing cost, output, and innovation while meeting stringent military requirements. For quality assurance, this means moving away from compliance-driven processes towards globally benchmarked systems of risk management, traceability, and supplier qualification.

Testing and Standards

India employs a range of testing methods, including non-destructive testing, ballistic trials, chemical analysis, and acceptance sampling. These align with Joint Services Specifications (JSSs) and defence standards produced by the Directorate of Standardisation. For imported items, NATO Standardisation Agreements (STANAGs) and ISO references are often applied. However, as Metz and Johnson (2001) observe, such testing regimes are only as effective as the technologies and data systems that underpin them. Much of India's infrastructure relies on ageing equipment and manual inspection, limiting the ability to detect subtle or latent defects.[394]

Analytical Frameworks Applied

When evaluated against established quality management theories, India's current system shows both strengths and gaps. Total Quality Management (TQM) emphasises continuous improvement, process orientation, and empowerment of employees. Applied to ammunition, this would imply that suppliers, manufacturers, inspectors, and soldiers all contribute to a culture of quality.[395] In reality, India's QA remains compartmentalised, with feedback loops between the Army, DGQA, and DPSUs often weak or delayed. Six Sigma, with its structured methodology for defect reduction, highlights another shortfall. The DMAIC cycle—Define, Measure, Analyse, Improve, Control—requires robust data collection and statistical analysis.[396,397] While the DGQA gathers defect data, the lack of integrated digital platforms means patterns are not always analysed in a way that drives systemic process improvement.

The ISO 9000 family of standards sets global benchmarks for management systems, supplier qualification, and conformity assessment.[398] Many defence firms worldwide adopt ISO 9001 certification to reassure buyers of their process maturity. In India, only select DPSUs and private players have achieved such certifications, and integration with military oversight remains patchy.[399] Without harmonisation, India risks operating parallel regimes that do not translate into export credibility.

Finally, risk management frameworks, such as, ISO 31000 emphasise proactive identification and mitigation of hazards (Bitzinger, 2015). In ammunition terms, this means anticipating deterioration in propellants, monitoring temperature and humidity in storage, and introducing predictive analytics to detect failure risks. India's system, however, remains largely reactive, with failures often highlighted only after accidents or user complaints.

Deficiencies in the quality regime have been underlined by incidents, such as, accidents linked to faulty ammunition, reports of unsafe stockpiles, and operational disruptions due to unreliable supplies.[400] At the same time, the push for *Atmanirbhar Bharat* and increased defence exports places new demands on credibility. Buyers and partners will not only assess India's capacity to produce but also its ability to demonstrate internationally recognised quality assurance. India's ammunition QA landscape presents a paradox. The institutional framework is comprehensive, yet its outputs are inconsistent. Theories of quality management suggest pathways for reform: embedding continuous improvement, statistical rigour, compliance with international standards, and risk-based monitoring. However, bridging the gap between theory and practice requires investment in infrastructure, integration of digital platforms, and above all a cultural shift that treats quality as a shared responsibility rather than a box-ticking exercise.

Towards a Transformed QA Paradigm

The limitations of India's existing ammunition quality assurance system highlight the need for a decisive transformation. Incremental improvements will not suffice in an environment where munitions are becoming increasingly sophisticated, where operational theatres impose extreme demands, and where the credibility of India's defence exports depends on demonstrable reliability. What is required is not merely stronger inspection but a new paradigm of quality assurance that is proactive, technology-driven, and institutionally accountable?

A reimagined framework for ammunition quality assurance must rest on several interrelated principles. First, quality must be controlled across the entire lifecycle of a munition, from design to production, storage, transportation, and eventual disposal. The failures rarely originate at the point of use, they are often the cumulative result of upstream flaws. Second, quality must be risk-informed, with a systematic identification and through mitigation of potential hazards before they manifest as faults. Third, transparency and accountability should be institutionalised, with clear lines of responsibility, documented protocols, and independent scrutiny. Fourth, technology must be leveraged to increase accuracy, efficiency, and speed in both inspection and analysis. Finally, the framework must prioritise reliability under diverse conditions, ensuring that ammunition meets the same performance standard whether stored in desert depots, mountain bunkers, or forward bases in humid regions.

Advanced Testing and Inspection Technologies

The adoption of cutting-edge Non-Destructive Testing (NDT) techniques is essential. Digital radiography, ultrasonic phased arrays, and computed tomography can reveal internal defects that traditional inspection would miss. Laser-induced breakdown spectroscopy enables rapid compositional analysis of energetic materials, while high-speed imaging captures transient ballistic behaviour. The integration of robotics and automation into inspection lines reduces human error, increases throughput, and ensures repeatability. Real-time sensors embedded in packaging or storage facilities can provide continuous data on environmental conditions, feeding into predictive maintenance models.[401]

Integrated Supply Chain Management

Quality must extend beyond the factory floor into the entire supply chain. This requires stringent supplier qualification, regular audits, and continuous monitoring of raw material quality. Serialisation and traceability allow every lot of ammunition to be tracked across its lifecycle, enabling rapid isolation of defective batches and investigation of root causes. Just-in-time inventory systems, combined with digital dashboards, can reduce overstocking and minimise the risks of degradation during long-term storage. An integrated supply chain framework would also create interoperability between DPSUs, private firms, and the Services, ensuring that standards are uniform and consistently enforced.[402]

Digitalisation and Data Management

The digital transformation of quality assurance processes can provide the backbone of the new paradigm. Centralised digital platforms can collect, store, and analyse quality data from multiple nodes, factories, depots, field units, creating a continuous flow of information. Artificial intelligence and machine learning can detect patterns in defect data, predict emerging risks, and suggest corrective measures before failures occur. Blockchain can secure the integrity of quality records, ensuring that tampering or falsification is impossible. Digital twins of ammunition types could be created to simulate degradation under different storage and operational conditions, guiding both preventive maintenance and user awareness.[403]

Independent Oversight and Governance

A transformed system cannot rely solely on self-regulation by manufacturers or shared oversight by DGQA and the Services. Independent oversight, through a strengthened QA authority or a new statutory body, is necessary to ensure impartiality. Such a body could conduct audits, certify facilities, and enforce compliance with national and international standards. Clear accountability mechanisms, including transparent reporting of failures and corrective action, would reinforce trust within the armed forces and among potential export partners. Regular public reporting, without compromising security, could also demonstrate India's commitment to transparency in defence production.

Enhanced Training and Skill Development

Quality assurance is only as effective as the workforce that implements it. The transformation must therefore invest heavily in training at multiple levels. Inspectors and technicians require hands-on familiarity with advanced NDT tools and statistical methods. Engineers and managers must be trained in quality-by-design, Six Sigma, and risk management methodologies. Soldiers and depot personnel need awareness training on handling, surveillance, and reporting. Continuous professional development programs, in partnership with technical universities and defence R&D institutions, can ensure that personnel remain up to date with evolving technologies and standards.[404]

Implementation Strategy

Transformation of such scale must be phased and carefully managed. Pilot projects could be initiated at selected DPSU facilities, integrating advanced

NDT, digital traceability, and AI-based defect prediction. Successful pilots would then inform phased rollouts across other facilities and depots. Adequate funding must be earmarked for modern infrastructure, software systems, and workforce training. Stakeholder engagement is crucial; the Army, DGQA, DPSUs, and private firms must participate in shaping new procedures to ensure buy-in. Change management strategies must anticipate institutional resistance and communicate the long-term benefits of reform for safety, efficiency, and operational effectiveness.

The benefits of the transformed framework would be substantial. Ammunition reliability and safety would improve significantly, reducing accidents and malfunctions. Operational effectiveness would rise as soldiers gain confidence in their weapons and logistics systems face fewer disruptions. Waste and rework would decline, generating long-term cost savings. The credibility of India's defence industry would also grow, reinforcing its capacity to meet the twin goals of self-reliance and export competitiveness. Most importantly, a transformed quality assurance paradigm would create a culture of accountability and continuous improvement, ensuring that quality is not an afterthought but an embedded principle of defence manufacturing.

Lessons from Experience

The case for transforming India's ammunition quality assurance system becomes sharper when viewed through concrete examples of success and failure. Comparative experiences illustrate not only what can go wrong when quality is neglected but also what can be achieved when advanced technologies, independent oversight, and lifecycle monitoring are embedded into practice.

Success in Global Context: The United States Army

The United States Army provides a compelling illustration of how systemic transformation can elevate ammunition reliability. Facing rising complexity in munitions during the 1990s and 2000s, the Army undertook a comprehensive overhaul of its quality assurance regime. Key measures included the adoption of advanced non-destructive testing technologies, such as, digital radiography, computed tomography, and automated inspection systems. These tools allowed for early detection of internal defects that manual inspections could not identify. Lifecycle quality management became institutionalised, with rigorous surveillance of stocks in storage, real-time data capture during firing trials, and traceability systems linking every batch to its raw material sources.[405]

The presence of an independent oversight was another crucial feature. The Defence Contract Management Agency (DCMA) conducted audits, certified suppliers, and ensured that production facilities adhered to international standards. This separation of roles created accountability and avoided conflicts of interest between manufacturers and inspectors. Most importantly, the US Army leveraged digitalisation, integrating data from depots, laboratories, and operational units into central platforms that supported predictive analytics. By combining advanced technologies, robust governance, and continuous feedback, defect rates declined and confidence in ammunition reliability increased significantly.[406]

This example directly validates various pillars of the framework proposed for India. The emphasis on advanced testing demonstrates how crucial it is to invest in state-of-the-art inspection technologies. While the presence of an independent oversight agency demonstrates the value of impartial governance, lifecycle surveillance and digitisation highlight the role of data-driven prediction systems. India can draw clear lessons from this case, particularly, in terms of adopting digital platforms and institutionalising the external audits to reinforce trust and confidence in its ammunition supply chain.

Failure in Domestic Context: The Pulgaon Tragedy

The 2016 fire at the Central Ammunition Depot (CAD) in Pulgaon, Maharashtra, stands as a sobering reminder of the consequences of inadequate quality assurance. The incident, which resulted in significant loss of life and destruction of large quantities of ammunition, was traced to deficiencies in storage protocols, inspection lapses, and the deterioration of ageing stocks. Investigations pointed to weaknesses in surveillance mechanisms, insufficient monitoring of environmental conditions, and gaps in accountability for defective batches.

This tragedy underscores the dangers of reactive rather than proactive quality assurance. The absence of predictive monitoring allowed defective or unstable ammunition to remain in circulation until it caused catastrophic failure. Weak feedback loops meant that lessons from earlier accidents were not fully integrated into systemic reforms. Moreover, the lack of independent oversight created ambiguity in responsibility, delaying corrective measures.

When viewed against the proposed framework, the Pulgaon fire highlights exactly what India must avoid. It illustrates the need for real-time monitoring systems in storage, digital traceability to identify vulnerable lots, and robust training for personnel handling sensitive stocks. Most importantly, it demonstrates why accountability must be enforced through transparent mechanisms and independent governance. The lessons from Pulgaon should serve as a catalyst for reform, reminding policymakers and practitioners that the costs of neglecting quality are measured not only in material losses but in human lives.[407]

Bridging Lessons to Reform

These experiences present a clear trajectory wherein the reforms in the US Army demonstrate that proactive, technology-driven, and independent quality assurance produces tangible improvements in reliability and trust. The Pulgaon tragedy on the other hand, reveals the human and strategic costs of outdated practices and fragmented oversight. For India the lesson is clear that it should incorporate global practices while addressing domestic challenges to ensure quality assurance. Quality Assurance is a bridge between industrial capacity and strategic autonomy as it would align the ammunition ecosystem if India with international standards by incorporating advanced testing technologies, digitalisation, supply chain integration, independent audits, and comprehensive training.

Conclusion

The ammunition reliability is more than a technical matter, it is a matter of military credibility, soldier's safety, and national strategy. This chapter has argued that in modern warfare, where precision and swiftness define success, ammunition quality assurance should be reimagined as a strategic capability rather than a routine procedural function. The global evolution of quality assurance shows a clear shift from reactive, end-of-line inspection to proactive, lifecycle management. This change is underpinned by advanced testing technologies, data-driven analysis, and independent oversight. India's current system, though institutionally comprehensive, has struggled to keep pace with these changes in adapting to these developments. The involvement of multiple agencies, the legacy of state-run production structures, and the limited integration of digital platforms have produced a system that identifies faults late rather than preventing them in the first place. The theories of quality management like Total Quality Management, Six Sigma, and ISO frameworks emphasise methods towards improvement, however, their application in India has been partial and inconsistent. The Pulgaon fire reveals the risk of maintaining outdated practices, while similar incidents, such as, the United States Army's reforms demonstrate the tangible benefits of adopting a modern, lifecycle-based assurance.

The proposed framework outlined in this chapter seeks to address these challenges comprehensively. India can move towards a system that not only ensures safety and reliability but also builds trust among soldiers, policymakers, and international partners through the implementation of advanced testing technologies, integrating supply chains through traceability and serialisation, leveraging digital platforms for predictive analysis, establishing independent oversight, and investing in skill development. This Implementation must be phased, inclusive, and adequately resourced, but the long-term gains in terms of reliability, safety, and efficiency over time justify the investment. Most importantly, a transformed ammunition quality assurance system has implications beyond immediate operational needs. It is central to India's ambitions of self-reliance in defence production and its aspiration to emerge as a credible exporter of advanced military hardware. Without demonstrable reliability and compliance with international standards, India's growing defence corridors risk producing volume without trust. By contrast, a quality system aligned with global best practices will reinforce *Atmanirbhar Bharat* and also position India as a responsible and competitive player in the international defence market. In essence, quality assurance is a strategy. It is the invisible but indispensable bridge that connects industrial capacity to combat effectiveness and export credibility. For India, reimagining ammunition quality assurance is not simply about preventing accidents or reducing number of defects. But it's about building a defence ecosystem that soldiers trust, partners respect, and adversaries recognise as reliable and resilient.

11

Munitions Without Missions: A Growing Dilemma in India's Ammunition Manufacturing

The Paradox of Ammunition Self-Reliance

The pursuit of self-reliance in defence manufacturing has become one of the central pillars of India's strategic vision for the twenty-first century. Ammunition, the lifeblood of any military force, lies at the heart of this ambition. Unlike platforms, such as, aircraft or tanks, ammunition is both consumable and perishable; it must be replenished continuously, produced in bulk, and tailored to the evolving demands of the battlefield. In this context, India's ongoing efforts to indigenise ammunition production reflect not only a desire to reduce dependence on imports but also a larger aspiration to build resilience in times of conflict. Yet, a paradox has emerged. While India is in the process of expanding its ammunition manufacturing capacity and encouraging private sector participation, the system has begun to reveal imbalances. Seeing the zeal among private players and the huge potential India possesses, there may arise a situation in the future where ammunition could be produced in surplus to operational requirements, and at the same time, these companies may find it difficult to secure markets for their products in the global arena either due to an international oversupply or export restrictions rooted in geopolitics. Therefore, this dilemma, which exemplifies what can be described as the "Munitions Without Missions" syndrome, must be addressed proactively before it escalates. It is a condition where industrial enthusiasm, policy incentives, and corporate investments are not matched by corresponding demand signals, deployment strategies or procurement coherence.

This dilemma matters because ammunition is not a neutral commodity. Unlike consumer goods, it cannot simply be stockpiled indefinitely or diverted to alternative uses. It is tied intimately to doctrines, missions, and theatres of operation. Producing the wrong kind of ammunition, or producing it without assured end use, not only wastes resources but also creates distortions in the defence ecosystem. It undermines industry confidence, burdens logistics infrastructure, and risks leaving the armed forces with the illusion of strength rather than operational readiness. The roots of this problem are complex. They lie in the legacy of a centralised and monopolised system of production, the structural constraints of India's procurement culture, and the uncertainties of forecasting future conflicts. They also reflect the tensions of transition, between state-owned ordnance traditions and the entry of private players, between the drive for rapid indigenisation and the realities of global technology denial regimes, and between the ambition of *Atmanirbharta* and the lack of a national ammunition roadmap.

This chapter examines the contours of the "Munitions Without Missions" dilemma. It begins by tracing the historical evolution of India's ammunition manufacturing ecosystem, before moving into the contemporary challenges of overproduction, fragmentation, and export bottlenecks. It then unpacks the consequences of this syndrome for industry, armed forces, and policy, followed by an analysis of the structural drivers that perpetuate the problem. Finally, the chapter outlines possible pathways towards aligning industrial capacity with strategic need, proposing reforms in technology development, procurement culture, and institutional architecture. By doing so, the discussion sets the tone for the book's broader argument: that ammunition is not merely a technical or industrial issue but a strategic one. Getting it right is not only a matter of efficiency, rather a prerequisite for India's credibility as a military power and for the fulfilment of its long-term vision of *Viksit Bharat 2047*.

Historical Evolution of Ammunition Manufacturing in India

The challenges confronting India's ammunition ecosystem today cannot be understood in isolation from their historical roots. Ammunition manufacturing in India has evolved through distinct but interconnected phases: the colonial legacy of ordnance factories established for imperial needs, the post-independence expansion of the Ordnance Factory Board and its monopoly over supply, the successes and failures of this system during periods of war, and the eventual pressures for reform that culminated in corporatisation. Alongside this trajectory, the gradual entry of private industry and the persistence of structural constraints have shaped an ecosystem that is at once expansive in scale yet uneven in capability. Tracing this evolution provides the necessary context to appreciate how the present "Munitions Without Missions" dilemma emerged, and why aligning production with strategy remains such a complex task.

The origins of India's ammunition manufacturing system lie in the strategic imperatives of the British Empire. From the late eighteenth century onwards, the East India Company and later the British Crown recognised the necessity of sustaining localised production of arms and ammunition to maintain control over the vast subcontinent. Importing ammunition from Britain was costly, slow, and vulnerable to disruptions in sea lanes, especially during periods of European conflict.[408] Establishing ordnance factories in India was therefore less about empowering indigenous capability and more about ensuring the uninterrupted supply of munitions for imperial campaigns.[409]

Among the earliest of these facilities was the Gun and Shell Factory at Cossipore, founded in 1801, which became a key supplier of artillery ammunition for the British Indian Army.[410] This was followed by the establishment of the Rifle Factory at Ishapore in 1901 and the Ammunition Factory at Dum Dum in 1846, which gained notoriety for the "Dum Dum bullet," a controversial expanding round that drew international criticism and led to revisions in the Hague Conventions on the laws of war.[411] These factories were technologically dependent on Britain, relying on imported designs, machinery, and technical expertise. Indian workers staffed the shop floors, but strategic decisions and research remained firmly under British control. The colonial ordnance system was not intended to foster a comprehensive industrial ecosystem. Instead, it functioned as an appendage of the empire's global supply chain. Innovation was minimal, restricted to modifications in ammunition types that suited the demands of colonial policing and imperial warfare. Moreover, the system entrenched a culture of centralised control and bureaucratic rigidity, traits that would persist in India's defence production long after independence. By the time India gained freedom in 1947, the country inherited 18 such factories scattered across different regions. They were assets in terms of basic capacity but carried the burden of a legacy that prioritised continuity of supply over technological advancement. This colonial inheritance shaped the DNA of India's post-independence ammunition industry: a system focused on maintaining quantity and reliability rather than pursuing innovation or adaptability to emerging forms of warfare.

Expansion and Role of the Ordnance Factory Board

After independence, the network of 18 ordnance factories inherited from the British was consolidated and gradually expanded under the Government of India. Recognising the strategic vulnerability exposed by colonial dependence on foreign supplies, Indian leaders viewed ammunition production as a sovereign function that could not be left to the vagaries of international markets. In 1979, these factories were formally grouped under the Ordnance Factory Board (OFB), headquartered in Kolkata, to bring them under unified administrative control. By the early twenty-first century, the OFB had grown to encompass 41 factories producing a wide range of ammunition, explosives, small arms, artillery shells, rockets, and ancillary components.

The OFB's mandate was both ambitious and restrictive. On the one hand, it sought to ensure that India would never face crippling shortages of ammunition in wartime, a fear rooted in the supply constraints of the colonial period. On the other hand, its monopoly status meant that the armed forces had little choice but to rely on its output, regardless of quality or timeliness. Over time, this created a system geared more towards meeting annual production targets than innovating or adapting to changing battlefield requirements. The organisation often operated in a siloed manner, with limited integration between research, production, and user feedback.

Despite its limitations, the OFB played an important role in sustaining India's military readiness during crucial moments. During the wars of 1965 and 1971, when international embargoes curtailed the flow of defence supplies, the ordnance factories were able to maintain steady output of conventional ammunition. Similarly, during the 1999 Kargil conflict, the OFB's production lines were pressed into extended shifts to meet urgent requirements. These contributions underscored the value of having a domestic ammunition base. Yet, the inefficiencies of the OFB were also laid bare during these same conflicts. The armed forces repeatedly flagged issues of defective ammunition, poor reliability, and long delays in delivery. Parliamentary Standing Committees and reports by the Comptroller and Auditor General (CAG) throughout the

1990s and 2000s documented cases where ammunition stocks had to be written off due to substandard quality or expired shelf life. Such findings not only raised questions about the effectiveness of the OFB but also highlighted the risks of over-centralisation in defence production.

By the 2010s, consensus began to emerge that while the OFB had served as the backbone of India's ammunition manufacturing, it was ill-suited to meet the demands of a modernising military. Its bureaucratic culture, lack of competitive incentives, and dependence on obsolete production methods created a structural drag on efficiency. The very monopoly that once guaranteed self-sufficiency had now become a bottleneck, setting the stage for calls to reform and restructure the institution.

The performance of India's ammunition manufacturing system has historically been tested most severely during wartime. Each major conflict since independence has revealed both the strengths and the weaknesses of the ordnance system, underscoring the paradox that has long characterised India's ammunition base.

During the 1965 and 1971 wars, the ordnance factories played a crucial role in ensuring the availability of ammunition despite international embargoes. In 1965, following the outbreak of hostilities with Pakistan, India faced restrictions on external supplies of both arms and ammunition. The ordnance factories were compelled to ramp up production rapidly, often working in extended shifts, to keep the armed forces supplied. While this demonstrated the value of having an indigenous production base, it also highlighted the system's limits. Much of the ammunition produced was based on outdated designs, with limited accuracy and high maintenance requirements in the field.

The 1971 war, fought on two fronts, once again tested India's ammunition reserves. In this instance, the ordnance factories managed to sustain the war effort, particularly in conventional artillery shells and small arms ammunition. The war underscored that India could not afford to depend entirely on external suppliers, but it also reinforced the need for continuous modernisation of production facilities. The lessons of 1971 gave a temporary sense of confidence in the adequacy of the ordnance system, delaying deeper structural reforms.

It was during the 1999 Kargil conflict that the deficiencies of India's ammunition ecosystem came into stark relief. The high-intensity, high-altitude fighting demanded large volumes of precision artillery shells and specialised ammunition that the OFB was ill-prepared to supply at short notice. India was forced to resort to emergency imports from countries, such as, South Africa and Israel, revealing a dangerous vulnerability at a time of active conflict. The Kargil Review Committee's findings were unequivocal: India's defence production system, particularly in ammunition, was not aligned with the operational realities of modern warfare.

The wars also revealed recurring quality concerns. Several CAG reports from the 2000s highlighted that defective ammunition supplied by the OFB not only reduced combat effectiveness but also caused avoidable accidents in training and operational zones. Instances of misfires, premature explosions, and shelf-life inconsistencies created deep mistrust between the armed forces and the production agencies. Even when volumes were sufficient, reliability was often in doubt, undermining the very purpose of indigenisation.

All in all, these episodes show a dual reality. India's ammunition manufacturing system provided a degree of resilience during critical wars, proving the importance of indigenous capability. Yet, it consistently failed to keep pace with the qualitative and technological demands of modern battlefields, leaving gaps that had to be filled by costly and time-sensitive imports. This tension between volume and quality would become a defining feature of the ammunition dilemma that persists into the present.

Calls for Reform and Structural Critiques

By the early 2000s, it had become evident that India's ammunition manufacturing system required significant restructuring. While the ordnance factories had served as a dependable source of supply during earlier wars, their inefficiencies, outdated processes, and limited capacity for innovation had drawn sustained criticism from policymakers, auditors, and the armed forces alike. A chorus of reform voices began to emerge, each highlighting a different dimension of the structural malaise.

One of the earliest and most authoritative calls came from the Kargil Review Committee (1999), which underscored the dangers of India's reliance on an ossified and centralised production system. The committee's report emphasised that future conflicts would require rapid replenishment of ammunition and greater technological sophistication—requirements that the Ordnance Factory Board was ill-equipped to meet. The report also highlighted the urgent need to diversify suppliers and encourage private sector participation in order to reduce bottlenecks.

The Comptroller and Auditor General (CAG) issued a series of critical reports through the 2000s and 2010s. These exposed recurring deficiencies, such as, defective ammunition consignments, delays in production, and frequent accidents during handling and training. For example, a 2017 CAG report revealed that more than 20 percent of ammunition produced by the OFB over a certain period had quality defects, leading to both wastage and safety hazards. Such findings eroded the credibility of the system and reinforced the armed forces' scepticism about depending solely on domestic production. Parliamentary Standing Committees on Defence also joined in the critique. Their reports repeatedly flagged the slow pace of indigenisation in ammunition, the lack of modernisation in filling and fusing technologies, and the persistence of an archaic procurement culture focused on cost (the L1 system) rather than capability. These committees stressed that unless structural reforms were introduced, India would continue to face shortages during crises and depend on emergency imports, thereby undermining its strategic autonomy.

Scholars and analysts added further depth to these critiques. Defence economists, such as, Laxman Behera and institutes like the Institute for Defence Studies and Analyses (IDSA) highlighted how the monopoly structure of the OFB created disincentives for efficiency. With assured orders and little competition, the OFB had few incentives to improve processes or innovate. This contrasted with global practices, where a mix of state-led and private-sector-led ecosystems ensured dynamism and technological advancement.

By the mid-2010s, there was broad consensus among policymakers, the armed forces, and think tanks that the *status quo* was untenable. The question was no longer whether reform was necessary, but how deep and disruptive it should be. While incremental measures were attempted, such as, limited outsourcing to private firms, the persistence of quality and timeliness issues meant that more fundamental restructuring was inevitable. This set the stage for the eventual corporatisation of the OFB in 2021, a move that aimed to overhaul the system at its foundations.

Corporatisation of OFB and Creation of DPSUs

The decision to corporatise the OFB in 2021 marked the most significant restructuring of India's ammunition manufacturing system since independence. The move was driven by a growing recognition that incremental reforms had failed to address chronic inefficiencies, and that only a structural overhaul could align the ammunition ecosystem with the requirements of modern warfare. On 1 October 2021, the OFB was officially dissolved, and its 41 factories were reorganised into seven Defence Public Sector Undertakings (DPSUs), each tasked with specific domains of production. Among them, Munitions India Limited (MIL) was designated as the principal entity responsible for ammunition and explosives, while other DPSUs, such as, Armoured Vehicles Nigam Limited and Advanced Weapons and Equipment India Limited took on complementary roles. The corporatisation aimed to replace the departmental structure of the OFB, which was embedded in bureaucratic procedures, with corporate-style governance that emphasised efficiency, accountability, and competitiveness.

The rationale for corporatisation was multi-fold. First, it was intended to make ammunition production more responsive to the armed forces, by introducing commercial accountability in place of guaranteed supply contracts. Second, it sought to encourage technological innovation, by enabling the new DPSUs to enter into joint ventures and partnerships with private industry, both domestic and foreign. Third, corporatisation was expected to open pathways for export expansion, positioning India not only as a self-reliant producer but also as a supplier of cost-effective ammunition to friendly nations.

The transition, however, was not without challenges. Employees' unions initially resisted corporatisation, fearing job insecurity and the loss of state protections. Critics also questioned whether corporatisation alone could overcome deeper structural problems, such as, dependence on imported raw materials, slow procurement procedures, and limited R&D in advanced munitions. In addition, legacy issues of quality assurance and delayed deliveries continued to plague some production lines even after the formal restructuring.

Nevertheless, the corporatisation of the OFB represented a paradigm shift. By transforming a bureaucratic monopoly into specialised corporate entities, the reform created the possibility of greater synergy with the private sector and more competitive practices within India's ammunition ecosystem. While its long-term success will depend on how effectively these new DPSUs adapt to global standards of innovation, quality, and supply chain resilience, corporatisation was a clear acknowledgment that the old model had run its course. It also signalled a broader policy shift under the *Atmanirbhar Bharat* framework, which increasingly views defence production not only as a security imperative but also as an engine of industrial growth and strategic influence.

Emergence of Private Sector Participation

Alongside the state-led structures of the Ordnance Factory Board and its successor entities, the private sector has gradually emerged as a player in India's ammunition manufacturing landscape. This shift was neither immediate nor easy. For decades after independence, ammunition production was considered too sensitive to be entrusted to private industry, and participation remained minimal. It was only in the 2000s, as the limitations of the OFB became more apparent, that policymakers began cautiously opening doors for private firms.

The earliest entrants were companies with prior experience in explosives and related industries. Solar Industries India Limited, for instance, leveraged its expertise in commercial explosives for mining to venture into defence-grade propellants and warhead filling. Economic Explosives Limited (EEL), a subsidiary of Solar, became a notable supplier of high-energy explosives and sub-systems. Similarly, Premier Explosives Limited and Sandeep Metalcraft made inroads into specialised niches, such as, solid propellants, fuzes, and shell components. Over time, these companies demonstrated not only technical competence but also export potential, with some managing to secure contracts in markets across Africa, Southeast Asia, and the Middle East.

Yet, the private sector's role has remained constrained by structural barriers. Access to critical technologies, such as, advanced energetic materials (RDX, HMX, CL-20), precision fuzes, and automated filling systems, has largely been monopolised by state entities like the Defence Research and Development Organisation (DRDO) and the newly created DPSUs. Technology denial regimes under international frameworks, such as, the Missile Technology Control Regime (MTCR) and the Wassenaar Arrangement have further restricted India's ability to import and indigenise certain categories of inputs. As a result, private firms often found themselves relegated to producing shell bodies, packing materials, or lower-end components, with limited opportunities to integrate into the higher-value segments of the ammunition value chain.

Another constraint has been the lack of consistent and predictable demand. Private manufacturers have repeatedly highlighted that orders are sporadic, routed primarily through DPSUs, and often subject to delays in payment. Without assured volumes or long-term contracts, it has been difficult for firms to justify large investments in advanced manufacturing facilities. This has created a vicious cycle: the state hesitates to trust private firms with critical technologies due to limited scale, while private firms cannot build scale without predictable state support.

Despite these challenges, the private sector has introduced a degree of dynamism and innovation into India's ammunition ecosystem. Startups and mid-sized firms, in particular, have been more agile in experimenting with technologies, such as, drone-deployed munitions, smart fuzes and modular charges. Government initiatives, such as, the Innovations for Defence Excellence (iDEX) programme have further encouraged this trend by providing funding and incubation support to smaller firms with disruptive ideas.

The emergence of private players, therefore, represents both a challenge and an opportunity. While they remain constrained by structural barriers, their growing competence signals the possibility of a more diversified and competitive ammunition ecosystem in the future. If adequately integrated into national planning and supported through policy reforms, these firms could help break the monopoly-driven inertia that has long plagued India's ammunition sector.

Continuing Constraints and the Present Paradox

Despite corporatisation and the gradual entry of private firms, India's ammunition manufacturing ecosystem continues to grapple with fundamental constraints that have carried over from earlier decades. These constraints reveal why the system, though extensive in scale, remains misaligned with operational requirements, leading to the paradox of "Munitions Without Missions". One of the most pressing issues is import dependence for critical inputs. India still relies heavily on foreign suppliers for advanced energetic materials, such as, RDX, HMX, and CL-20 substitutes, as well as for specialised metals like tungsten used in armour-piercing rounds. Denial regimes under multilateral frameworks restrict easy access to these inputs, making supply chains vulnerable to geopolitical shocks. Without indigenisation of raw materials, ammunition production lines remain incomplete, producing shells and casings without the matching filling or fuzes needed to render them battle-ready.

A second constraint is procurement and testing culture. The Defence Acquisition Procedure (DAP) continues to emphasise the lowest-cost bidder (the L1 system), which discourages innovation and rewards incrementalism. Quality assurance remains concentrated in the Directorate General of Quality

Assurance (DGQA), whose testing protocols are often criticised as archaic and time-consuming. Long trial cycles and rigid procedures delay time-to-field, meaning that ammunition often enters service well after its intended operational window.

Third, there is a lack of ecosystem-level integration. DRDO, DPSUs, and private firms operate in silos, with little synchronisation in design, testing, and production. For instance, casing manufacturers often have no visibility into when or where their products will be filled or tested, creating fragmented supply lines and idle stockpiles. The absence of a national ammunition roadmap compounds this problem, with no central agency responsible for forecasting long-term demand or aligning capacity with evolving doctrines.

Finally, the system faces a credibility gap with the armed forces. Years of defective supplies, shelf-life issues, and slippages in delivery schedules have created deep mistrust. Even as production capacity has expanded, users remain sceptical of the reliability and combat-worthiness of domestically produced ammunition. This mistrust, in turn, fuels reliance on emergency imports during crises, perpetuating the very dependence that self-reliance was meant to eliminate.

The outcome of these constraints is a paradox. India today possesses a large and diverse ammunition manufacturing base spanning public sector units, mushrooming private firms and startups yet this base is often disconnected from actual missions. Unsynchronised production pipelines and missed export opportunities illustrate a syndrome where manufacturing capacity grows without a matching operational anchor. It is this paradox that forms the backdrop for the present chapter, and which continues to raise fundamental questions about how India can align industrial enthusiasm with strategic coherence.

The Emerging Dilemma

The phrase "Munitions Without Missions" captures a distinctive problem facing India's defence production landscape today. Unlike the chronic inefficiencies of the Ordnance Factory Board which were rooted in monopoly, bureaucratic inertia and outdated technology, this dilemma is born out of a very different context. It emerges not from scarcity or incapacity, but from a possible expansion of production capacity that is poorly aligned with actual missions, doctrines, and operational requirements. In practice, the syndrome refers to a situation where ammunition is produced in large volumes without a clear assurance of use. Factories may produce shell bodies, explosives, and sub-components in anticipation of bulk orders or export opportunities, yet these outputs can remain idle if they are not integrated into complete, certified systems ready for deployment. The result is an ecosystem where industrial activity is vibrant on paper, but much of it fails to translate into usable combat capability.

This syndrome reflects a paradox of India's self-reliance journey. On the one hand, reforms and private sector participation have energised production, creating a sense of momentum towards *Atmanirbharta*. On the other hand, the absence of a coordinated national plan has meant that enthusiasm has outpaced coherence. Manufacturing capacity, instead of serving as a foundation for resilience, risks becoming a source of inefficiency when it does not feed directly into military missions or export contracts. In essence, "Munitions Without Missions" is not merely an industrial issue but a strategic misalignment. It signifies that the relationship between production and doctrine, between what is made and what is needed, has not been clearly articulated. Without correcting this misalignment, India risks building stockpiles that look impressive in numbers yet contribute little to operational readiness or strategic credibility.

One of the clearest manifestations of the "Munitions Without Missions" dilemma lies in the overproduction of artillery ammunition, most notably the 155 mm shells. Following the corporatisation of the Ordnance Factory Board and the government's push to involve the private sector, multiple firms both public and private expanded their manufacturing capacity in anticipation of sustained demand. Yantra India Limited (YIL), Nibe Ltd, Goodluck Defence, Bharat Forge Ltd, Sunita Tools Ltd, and Balu Forge have either established or are in the process of establishing facilities to produce 155 mm empty shell bodies. In contrast, Munitions India Limited (MIL) and private firms, such as, Economic Explosives Ltd, SMPP Ltd, Adani Defence Systems & Technologies Ltd (ADSTL) and Reliance Defence are investing in end-to-end capability to manufacture complete 155 mm shells. Crucially, none of these investments are backed by assured orders. When peacetime training consumption, War Wastage Reserve (WWR) norms, surge rate requirements and realistic export prospects are analysed and war-gamed together, planned capacity may exceed actual demand exposing firms to serious financial risk from surplus inventories and idle plants.

Also, while this surge reflected a renewed industrial confidence, it is not matched by corresponding orders for the other components required to make the shells operational. Ammunition is not a single product but a carefully integrated system comprising the shell body, high explosive filling, propellant charges and fuzes. The expansion of capacity in shell casings far outpaced that of bi-modular charges, modern fuzing systems and safe filling facilities. The consequence visualised would be warehouses filled with unfinished ammunition shells waiting for critical sub-systems not produced in adequate numbers.

The overproduction of 155mm shells is particularly problematic because of their sensitivity to global demand cycles. Several countries already have well-established suppliers, and India's attempts to push into the export market are hampered by a lack of globally certified complete rounds. Domestically, the armed forces cannot absorb the excess volumes, as procurement is tied to operational doctrines and training requirements rather than industrial availability. Thus, the mismatch between capacity and demand can create idle stockpiles that may generate costs without adding to operational capability. This example highlights the deeper risk of overproduction without mission-linked planning. Instead of strengthening self-reliance, unchecked industrial expansion can lock resources into products that do not meet immediate needs, erode industry confidence when inventories remain unsold, and expose the limitations of pursuing scale without coherence. The 155 mm shell surplus is therefore not just an industrial problem but a strategic warning of how enthusiasm for indigenisation can become detached from real requirements. This is precisely the "Munitions Without Missions" dilemma, and it should be addressed proactively at this nascent stage through calibrated procurement signals, export regulation and coordinated capacity planning.

A second dimension of the "Munitions Without Missions" dilemma is the fragmentation of production pipelines. Ammunition manufacturing is inherently a multi-stage process, requiring coordination between producers of shell casings, explosive fillers, propellant charges, and fuzes. In India, however, these stages often operate in isolation from one another, with limited visibility or synchronisation across the supply chain. The result is a pattern where components are produced in significant quantities but remain idle because complementary parts are not available in sufficient numbers. For example, a private firm may produce thousands of shell casings, while fuze manufacturers work on separate schedules with no assurance of integration.

Similarly, filling units may face delays in receiving casings or propellants, leaving their facilities underutilised. This lack of synchronisation leads to rendering the ammunition unusable due to mismatch in components, creating bottlenecks that undermine both efficiency and readiness.

Such fragmentation reflects the absence of a central coordinating mechanism. Unlike in countries where a dedicated ammunition authority forecasts demand and oversees integration, India's ecosystem remains disjointed. Public sector undertakings, private firms, and the armed forces operate on separate timelines, with procurement cycles often dictated by bureaucratic processes rather than mission requirements. Without end-to-end visibility, manufacturers cannot plan production schedules effectively, and users cannot rely on timely availability of complete rounds. The consequences of fragmented pipelines go beyond inefficiency. They erode trust between stakeholders, as producers feel their investments are wasted, while the armed forces remain sceptical of the reliability of domestic supply. Over time, this disjointedness risks entrenching a vicious cycle where industrial growth fails to deliver operational capability, reinforcing dependence on imports during crises. Unless the production chain is integrated into a seamless pipeline from design to deployment, India's ammunition self-reliance will remain partial and vulnerable.

The dilemma of "Munitions Without Missions" is further compounded by the difficulties India has faced in translating its expanded production capacity into sustainable export opportunities. Many private firms entered the defence sector with the expectation that international demand, particularly from countries in Africa, Southeast Asia, and conflict zones like Ukraine, would provide a steady outlet for surplus ammunition. Encouraged by policy rhetoric around defence exports, companies invested in new production lines and scaled up their operations in anticipation of these markets. However, global buyers typically demand fully integrated, certified ammunition systems rather than individual components. While Indian firms have succeeded in manufacturing shell bodies, propellants, and explosives, their ability to deliver complete rounds with internationally validated fuzes, fillings, and quality assurance remains limited. As a result, much of the stock produced with export ambitions has been left unsold. International procurement processes are also time-sensitive; buyers require rapid delivery during crises, but India's approval mechanisms and certification procedures have often been too slow to respond effectively.

Another hurdle lies in price and precision competitiveness. Established global players, particularly from countries like Israel, Russia, and South Korea, dominate the markets India seeks to enter. Their products often combine proven battlefield performance with competitive pricing, making it difficult for relatively new Indian entrants to secure contracts. Even when India does win export orders, they tend to be for limited quantities or lower-end categories of ammunition, leaving more advanced segments untapped. The failure to realise anticipated export gains has placed significant strain on the domestic industry. Firms that had expanded capacity with an eye on foreign markets now face unsold inventories and financial stress, undermining their ability to reinvest in innovation. For the state, this outcome has meant a missed opportunity to leverage ammunition exports as a tool of defence diplomacy, particularly with countries in the Global South that could benefit from cost-effective alternatives to Western suppliers. In this sense, the export shortfall is not just an economic setback but a strategic one. India's ambition to emerge as a reliable ammunition supplier and strengthen its geopolitical influence has been hampered by the very misalignment that defines the "Munitions Without Missions" syndrome: a manufacturing base that produces in quantity but struggles to meet the qualitative and procedural requirements of real-world markets.

A fundamental driver of the "Munitions Without Missions" dilemma is the absence of a centralised, forward-looking ammunition roadmap for India. Unlike other major military powers, which publish detailed five- or ten-year projections of ammunition requirements, India lacks a unified framework that links industrial capacity with operational planning. As a result, production often expands in response to short-term procurement requirements, political announcements or corporate enthusiasm, rather than to carefully assessed strategic needs. In countries, such as, the United States, the Department of Defense maintains long-term munitions strategies that outline projected requirements, priority categories, and investment pathways. Similarly, Russia operates a centralised system where production plans are tightly integrated with military doctrine, ensuring that every investment in capacity is tied to a defined operational role. India, by contrast, has no equivalent authority tasked with forecasting national ammunition needs, synchronising production pipelines, and aligning capacity with doctrine.

The absence of such a roadmap has led to duplication of investment and misallocation of resources. Multiple firms have set up parallel lines for the same category of ammunition, such as, 155 mm shells, even as critical gaps remain in fuzes, smart munitions, and advanced propellants. In some cases, resources continue to be devoted to categories of ammunition whose relevance on modern battlefields is declining, such as, traditional cluster munitions. Without strategic forecasting, the ecosystem risks perpetuating cycles of both shortage and surplus. This gap also undermines industry confidence. Private firms are hesitant to commit to high-value investments in research, development, and advanced manufacturing when they lack visibility into long-term demand. For public sector undertakings, the absence of coordinated guidance results in disjointed production priorities and stockpiles that do not align with user requirements. For the armed forces, it creates uncertainty about whether critical categories of ammunition will be available in adequate numbers during crises.

In effect, the lack of a national ammunition roadmap transforms indigenisation into a reactive rather than proactive exercise. Instead of serving as the backbone of strategic autonomy, production becomes vulnerable to duplication, obsolescence, and missed opportunities. Addressing this gap is therefore essential if India is to move beyond symbolic self-reliance towards genuine mission-oriented preparedness.

Why This Matters and How to Realign?

Multidimensional Consequences

The dilemma of "Munitions Without Missions" matters because its consequences cut across operational, economic and credibility domains, each reinforcing the other in ways that weaken India's defence preparedness. At the operational level, ammunition that is produced but not fully integrated into certified, battle-ready systems creates a dangerous illusion of strength. Stockpiles of shell bodies without fuzes or charges may appear substantial on paper, but in wartime they cannot deliver the firepower required by frontline units. This disconnect between numbers and utility risks leaving the armed forces underprepared in precisely the moments when reliable ammunition is most critical. The economic costs are equally significant. Ammunition production involves heavy investment in infrastructure, specialised machinery, and skilled labour. When outputs remain idle or unsold because production outpaces demand, those investments are effectively squandered, imposing financial strain on both public-sector undertakings and private firms. Micro, small, and medium enterprises are especially vulnerable, as they often lack the financial buffers to absorb prolonged periods of uncertainty. Over a period of time, the accumulation of idle stock and lost revenue discourages innovation and reduces the willingness of industry to reinvest in future capacity. Finally, the dilemma erodes credibility at both domestic and international levels. Within India, the armed forces grow sceptical of new production capacity when they perceive that it does not translate into reliable operational capability. This scepticism undermines trust and reinforces the temptation to fall back on imports during crises. Internationally, India's ambitions to emerge as a dependable defence supplier are weakened when export commitments cannot be met or when products fail to match certification and performance standards demanded by global buyers. Each unrealised order or delayed delivery chips away at the perception of India as a reliable partner in defence production.

Therefore, these operational, economic, and credibility consequences show that the dilemma is not simply about surplus capacity. It represents a structural risk that can undermine both India's self-reliance narrative and its ability to project itself as a credible military power in the region and beyond.

Moving Towards Realignment

Addressing the dilemma of "Munitions Without Missions" requires more than incremental fixes; it calls for a fundamental realignment of production with mission requirements. The goal must be to transform ammunition manufacturing from a fragmented, supply-driven process into a coordinated, demand-driven ecosystem that delivers complete, usable systems to the armed forces and credible products to global markets.

A first step is the adoption of a mission-linked production philosophy. Instead of pursuing output for its own sake, the focus must shift from "Make for Stock" to "Make for Mission." Every production run should be tied to clearly defined requirements, whether for active war reserves, training cycles, or export contracts. This approach ensures that capacity is not wasted on items with no assured utility and that investments are directed toward categories with real operational value.

Second, there is an urgent need to establish synchronised production pipelines. Shell casings, fuzes, propellants, and fillings cannot be produced in isolation; they must be coordinated within an integrated cycle that guarantees end-to-end readiness. Synchronisation would not only reduce idle inventories but also allow for more efficient use of raw materials, testing facilities, and quality assurance mechanisms. Co-location of complementary facilities, whether in the form of ammunition industrial clusters or dedicated defence corridors, can help create this integration.

The creation of a National Ammunition Authority (NAA) would provide the institutional framework needed to oversee such realignment. Tasked with forecasting demand over five- to ten-year horizons, the NAA could centralise planning, prevent duplication of capacities, and ensure that production lines are calibrated to operational doctrines. By coordinating inputs from the armed forces, DPSUs, private firms, and research agencies, such an authority would fill the critical gap that currently leaves the ecosystem disjointed.

Regular demand–supply audits should also form part of the new architecture. These audits would provide visibility into how much ammunition of each category is required, how much is being produced, and where gaps or surpluses exist. Transparent data would enable better decision-making, reassure industry about demand patterns, and give the armed forces confidence that their needs are being systematically addressed.

Finally, the establishment of ammunition clusters can anchor this vision. By co-locating design, production, filling, fuze assembly, and testing facilities within integrated ecosystems, India can move from isolated production lines to holistic supply chains. Such clusters would not only improve efficiency and reduce costs but also create synergies between public and private players, fostering innovation and competitiveness in a sector that has long been weighed down by fragmentation.

Conclusion: Strategic Payoff

The dilemma of "Munitions Without Missions" reveals itself as more than a production imbalance; it is a structural challenge that tests the very foundations of India's defence preparedness and its ambition for self-reliance. Historical legacies of monopoly and inefficiency have now given way to a new paradox—an ecosystem that produces in quantity but not always in alignment with missions, doctrine, or strategic demand. If left unchecked, this syndrome risks turning the promise of *Atmanirbharta* into a hollow achievement, where capacity exists on paper but combat power remains uncertain. Realignment offers a path forward. By tying production directly to mission requirements, synchronising pipelines across shell, fuze, charge, and filling lines, and instituting mechanisms, such as, a National Ammunition Authority and regular demand–supply audits, India can ensure that its manufacturing base translates into genuine combat capability. The development of ammunition clusters and the integration of public and private efforts add further coherence to a system long burdened by fragmentation. The payoff of such reforms is not merely industrial efficiency but strategic credibility. For the armed forces, mission-linked production restores confidence in domestic supply. For industry, it provides stability and encourages innovation in advanced technologies. For India's partners, it signals reliability, enhancing the country's stature as a defence exporter and a net security provider. Ultimately, aligning ammunition production with strategy transforms indigenisation into true strategic autonomy, laying a durable foundation for the vision of *Viksit Bharat 2047*. In this sense, resolving the dilemma of "Munitions Without Missions" is not just about fixing supply chains or avoiding wastage. It is about ensuring that every unit of ammunition produced strengthens national security, supports industrial growth, and advances India's standing as a credible and resilient power in the twenty-first century.

12

INTEGRATED AMMUNITION NODES: A STRATEGIC FRAMEWORK FOR R&D AND MANUFACTURING

Introduction

Ammunition constitutes the indispensable foundation of military power, serving as the critical element that transforms platforms into instruments of combat effectiveness. No matter how advanced a nation's aircraft, tanks, or artillery systems may be, their operational credibility is ultimately determined by the assured availability of reliable, defect-free, and technologically advanced munitions. In the contemporary security environment, ammunition is no longer a peripheral commodity but the decisive determinant of combat readiness, deterrence credibility, and strategic autonomy. The ongoing Russia–Ukraine conflict has vividly underscored this reality, as both nations' ability to sustain long-term operations has hinged upon resilient, scalable, and responsive ammunition supply chains. For India, which faces the twin imperatives of preparing for high-intensity conventional conflict and managing long-term strategic competition, the question of ammunition sufficiency has assumed existential significance.

While the country has made remarkable progress in indigenising defence platforms ranging from missile systems and rocket artillery to armoured vehicles its ammunition ecosystem remains an underdeveloped and fragile link. The corporatisation of the Ordnance Factory Board (OFB) into Munitions India Limited (MIL) in 2021 was a significant institutional reform, yet the transformation remains incomplete. Legacy production methods, dependence on critical imports, fragmented Research and Development (R&D), limited private sector integration, and recurring quality concerns continue to undermine India's ammunition preparedness. These structural shortcomings not only compromise operational readiness but also constrain India's aspiration to emerge as a credible global defence supplier under the vision of *Viksit Bharat 2047*.

This chapter argues that incremental fixes will not suffice. What is required is a systemic and transformative approach that restructures India's ammunition ecosystem into a cohesive, resilient, and technologically advanced grid. To achieve this, the chapter introduces the concept of Integrated Ammunition Nodes (IANs) which is a national framework of interconnected hubs where R&D, prototyping, production, testing, and lifecycle management converge seamlessly. Anchored around Pune, Hyderabad, and Jabalpur, these nodes will serve as the design centre, innovation engine, and industrial backbone respectively, creating a unified ammunition ecosystem. The purpose of this chapter is to present the rationale, framework, implementation roadmap, governance mechanisms, and risk-mitigation strategies for establishing IANs. By embedding innovation, ensuring supply chain sovereignty and integrating users with industry and academia, the IAN framework seeks to transform ammunition from a recurring vulnerability into a strategic advantage for India as it moves towards its centenary as a modern republic in 2047.

Historical and Contemporary Context

The contemporary challenges of India's ammunition ecosystem can only be understood by tracing its evolution across historical, institutional, and technological phases. Ammunition production in India was born out of colonial imperatives, when the British established ordnance factories not as centres of innovation but as logistical appendages of empire. These facilities were designed to deliver volume rather than quality, producing time-tested calibres needed for imperial policing and continental wars. When India gained independence in 1947, it inherited an extensive ordnance factory network, which provided the comfort of basic production capacity but lacked the dynamism required for innovation. This legacy of continuity over adaptability became deeply ingrained in the institutional culture, shaping ammunition manufacturing for decades to come. Even the corporatisation of the Ordnance Factory Board into Munitions India Limited in 2021, though a step forward in granting autonomy and accountability, has not yet overturned the structural inertia of the system.

The difficulty has never been the absence of research or scientific talent. Laboratories of the Defence Research and Development Organisation, such as, the Armament Research and Development Establishment and the High Energy Materials Research Laboratory, have developed a range of explosives, propellants, and fuzes. The challenge lies in bridging the gap between laboratory prototypes and production-ready solutions. Technology transfer remains cumbersome, scaling up is inconsistent, and innovations often fail to reach the armed forces in time. The result is a widening chasm between the promise of indigenous research and the practical needs of soldiers on the frontlines.

At the same time, India's dependence on imports for critical raw materials continues to expose systemic vulnerabilities. Inputs, such as, nitrocellulose, RDX and HMX derivatives, tungsten, and specialised alloys are sourced externally, creating chokepoints that can be exploited during crises. The Russia–Ukraine conflict demonstrated that ammunition stockpiles in modern wars are consumed at a scale far beyond peacetime planning, leaving import-dependent nations scrambling for supplies. India faces a similar risk: in any prolonged conflict, access to these critical materials could become uncertain, undermining both readiness and sovereignty.

The role of the private sector has emerged as an important corrective but remains limited in scope. Companies, such as, Solar Industries, Bharat Forge, and Larsen & Toubro have demonstrated competence in propellants, shell bodies, and subsystems, yet they continue to operate on the periphery. Procurement contracts remain short-term, demand projections opaque, and intellectual property frameworks ambiguous. As a result, private industry finds little incentive to make long-horizon investments in advanced ammunition technologies, while micro and small enterprises are confined to low-value component supply rather than integrated system design. Perhaps the most critical gap lies in the weak feedback loop between users and producers. The Army, Navy, and Air Force frequently encounter defects or limitations in ammunition during field use, yet these operational experiences are rarely absorbed into the production cycle in a systematic manner. Quality concerns that surfaced during the OFB era persist today, reinforcing scepticism about reliability and slowing the pace at which new battlefield requirements, such as, precision-guided artillery shells or counter-drone munitions, can be met.

Similarly, the slow pace of manufacturing modernisation is equally significant. Many facilities continue to rely on legacy machinery, batch-based assembly lines, and manual quality assurance checks. Adoption of automation, additive manufacturing, predictive analytics, or digital twins remains minimal, leading to inefficiencies, high wastage, and shelf-life uncertainties. The cumulative effect is an ecosystem that is extensive in scale but fragile in performance, which is capable of sustaining routine requirements but ill-equipped to support high-intensity or prolonged conflicts.

This combination of colonial legacies, research–production disjunctions, import dependencies, limited private participation, weak user integration, and slow technological modernisation defines the contemporary landscape of India's ammunition sector. The experience of past decades makes clear that piecemeal reforms cannot address these structural challenges. What is required is not incremental adjustment but a paradigm shift, one that embeds research, production, and user feedback within a cohesive national framework and transforms ammunition from a liability into a strategic strength.

Concept of Integrated Ammunition Nodes

The weaknesses of India's ammunition ecosystem, when viewed against contemporary security demands, point to the need for a systemic redesign rather than piecemeal repair. Ammunition today is not a consumable accessory but a decisive enabler of military effectiveness, and therefore the architecture of its production must mirror its strategic importance. The concept of Integrated Ammunition Nodes (IANs) emerges from this recognition. It is an attempt to move beyond isolated factories, fragmented research, and episodic user feedback towards a tightly interlinked national grid where research, design, production, testing, and lifecycle management operate in a seamless loop.

The essence of IANs lies in breaking down institutional siloes. In the present arrangement, laboratories, such as, ARDE and HEMRL continue to innovate, but their outputs are often stalled at the stage of industrial scaling. MIL factories, for their part, are equipped to manufacture at volume but remain locked into legacy calibres and processes. Private firms and MSMEs, though agile, are confined to component-level participation without visibility into long-term demand. The armed forces, the ultimate users of ammunition, are often spectators rather than participants in the R&D and production cycle. IANs seek to dissolve these barriers by creating geographic clusters where these actors are co-located physically or digitally networked, enabling iterative design and rapid responsiveness to emerging needs.

A second imperative behind the IAN model is operational resilience. India's dependence on imported precursors, such as, nitrocellulose or high explosives leaves the system vulnerable in times of crisis. By building clusters dedicated to indigenous production of critical inputs, from energetics to alloys, IANs would insulate the supply chain against external shocks. This is not merely about substituting imports but about ensuring sovereignty over the most essential elements of national defence.

The global shift towards precision and smart munitions has left many industrial ecosystems struggling to adapt. India, still burdened by a "legacy overhang," risks being trapped in the production of outdated calibres. The IAN framework is designed to embed emerging technologies—digital twins for predictive shelf-life management, additive manufacturing for complex shell geometries, ruggedised electronics for seekers and fuzes—directly into the production system. This would allow India not to inch forward incrementally but to leapfrog into the smart munitions' era.

Finally, IANs are conceived as an engine of economic and diplomatic influence. The global ammunition market is expanding, with rising demand for both conventional and smart systems. India's defence exports, though growing in platforms, remain negligible in ammunition. By aligning production with NATO and UN standards and offering co-production kits to friendly nations in Asia, Africa, and Latin America, IANs can position India as a trusted, non-aligned supplier. In this sense, the model is not only about meeting domestic requirements but also about expanding India's strategic footprint abroad.

Thus, the IAN framework represents a paradigm shift: from fragmented production to integrated ecosystems, from import vulnerability to supply chain sovereignty, from legacy stockpiles to smart munitions and from a domestic focus to global competitiveness. It is a doctrine as much as it is an industrial plan—an attempt to transform ammunition into both a cornerstone of national security and an instrument of strategic diplomacy.

A mature node is far more than a single factory or laboratory, it is a convergence hub where the full ammunition lifecycle spanning from discovery to deployment is embedded within the same operational ecosystem. In practice a mature node co-locates high-end research and innovation (DRDO laboratories, IITs, DIAT and similar institutes working on propellants, high-energy materials, smart fuses and additive manufacturing) with large-scale industrial manufacturing (public enterprises, such as, Munitions India Limited supported by private partners like Bharat Forge, L&T and Tata Advanced Systems) so prototypes can be scaled rapidly into certified production. Moreover, the node institutionalises a continuous user-feedback loop with the end users. Representatives from the Army, Air Force and Navy (and bodies, such as, the Army Design Bureau and CQA-Ammunition) are embedded in development and trials to ensure design decisions map directly to battlefield needs. Additionally, a mature node also rests on secure supply-chain foundations which are reliable, preferably indigenous sources of brass, copper, propellant precursors (nitrocellulose), explosives (RDX/HMX), tungsten and other critical inputs. It is pertinent that it is supported by resilient logistics and national material grids. Finally, integrated testing and certification facilities (instrumented ranges, proof establishments and accredited QA labs) ensure that designs can be validated quickly under operationally relevant conditions and moved into service with confidence. By clustering R&D, manufacturing, testing, and user feedback within a single ecosystem, mature nodes significantly shorten design-to-deployment cycles, enhance self-reliance through indigenous sourcing, and drive innovation via Industry 4.0 and AI-enabled systems. They foster enduring collaboration among academia, industry, and the armed forces, translating research outcomes into battlefield capability. International parallels, such as, the US Defence Innovation Unit and Israel's Talpiot–Elbit ecosystem, demonstrate how concentrated clusters can catalyse rapid technological breakthroughs. For India, developing mature nodes at Pune, Hyderabad, and Jabalpur which integrate MIL, DRDO, and private partners, and are supported by enabling policy frameworks, digital infrastructure, and export alignment with NATO/UN standards can transform ammunition manufacturing into a self-reliant, innovation-led enterprise central to national security.

The functional design of the Integrated Ammunition Nodes is summarised in the table below, highlighting how the Tri-Node framework translates this mature-node concept into coordinated regional ecosystems anchored at Pune, Hyderabad, and Jabalpur.

Node (Role)	*Existing Assets*	*Core Functions*	*Expected Outcomes*
Pune*(Design - Integrate - Qualify)*	• PSU-BEL, MIL factories (AFK, HEF, OF Dehu Road); • Private Industry (Bharat Forge, Nibe); • Academia (DIAT, AIT, IIT Bombay); • Quality Assurance (CQA Ammunition & CQA Military Explosives); • DRDO (HEMRL & ARDE); • User (CME, Artillery, Mechanised Infantry & Armoured Schools) • Nearby ranges & SME cluster; • Proximity to Mumbai airports and port	Smart-munitions R&D; Fuse/ seeker integration; Digital twins; User trials; TNPO HQ	Faster design '! field cycles; integrated final assembly; export
Hyderabad *(Energetics & Electronics)*	• DRDO (DRDL & RCI); - PSU (BDL & ECIL);- Private (Premier Explosives); • User (MCME)-SME propellant/ electronics cluster; • Chennai: IIT Madras, electronics manufacturing; • Bengaluru: major defence/aero R&D, avionics & electronics firms, IISc and high-tech SMEs	Propellant & explosive R&D (IM & green energetics); Ruggedised fuse/seeker electronics	Indigenous energetics supply; Hardened fuse subsystems; Strong SME supply chain
Jabalpur *(Metals, Cases & Propellants)*	• PSU (OF Khamaria, Varangaon, Bhandara, Chanda, Katni & OF Itarsi); • Private (Solar explosives) • Proof: Central Proof Establishment Itarsi, CPR Khamaria, CQA Wpns Jabalpur; • Academia (IIT Indore); • User (CMM, Infantry School, AAD College)	CNC & AM for casings/liners; Propellant production & QA; Proofing; scale metal forging & heat-treat	Stable metal & propellant backbone

Integrated Ammunition Nodes: A National Grid for Smart Munitions

The Integrated Ammunition Nodes (IANs) concept translates into an operational architecture through a hub-and-node model in which each geographic centre plays a distinct but interdependent role within a unified national grid. The model positions Pune as the central design–integration–qualification hub, Hyderabad as the energetics and electronics innovation engine, and Jabalpur as the metallurgy and propellant backbone. At the apex of coordination sits the Tri-Node Program Office (TNPO), which synchronises outputs, harmonises standards, and manages the product lifecycle across nodes. The deliberately triangular geometry of this arrangement *vis-à-vis* brain, engine, and spine ensures that innovation, industrial capacity, and user requirements converge rapidly into fieldable, export-quality munitions rather than travelling along disconnected, time-consuming pathways.

Pune's role as the central hub is both strategic and practical. The city already hosts a dense constellation of relevant assets: multiple Munitions India Limited (MIL) factories with legacy competencies in ammunition assembly and precision machining; DRDO establishments with expertise in systems integration; CQA Ammunition at Khadki and CQA Military Explosives at Aundh, academic partners, such as, DIAT and proximity to premier institutions like IIT Bombay; and nearby firing ranges and training schools that facilitate immediate user trials. In the IAN model, Pune becomes the design–integrate–qualify centre where fuze and seeker modules developed elsewhere are harmonised with shell bodies and propellant lots, assembled into integrated rounds, and subjected to rigorous hardware-in-the-loop (HIL) and software-in-the-loop (SIL) validation. Pune's integration lines would host capabilities that are difficult to decentralise: real-time telemetry capture during trials, X-ray CT and non-destructive testing of filled rounds, digital twin simulations for shelf-life and environmental stress testing, and smart assembly cells for rapid configuration of precision-guided kits. By concentrating these systems in one node, Pune reduces iteration times between design changes and operational verification, enabling same-season user-informed refinements that shorten the design-to-deploy cycle from years to months.

Hyderabad's contribution centres on energetics and electronics include the chemical and electronic heart of modern munitions. The city's established DRDO laboratories (ARDE, DRDL, RCI), state-owned enterprises, and an increasingly capable private SME ecosystem create a favourable milieu for developing insensitive munitions, environmentally safer propellant chemistries, and ruggedised fuze/seeker electronics. Within IANs, Hyderabad should host pilot-scale energetic formulation lines that comply with Insensitive Munitions (IM) protocols, shock and vibration hardening chambers, and electromagnetic compatibility (EMC) testbeds. Crucially, Hyderabad becomes the incubator for green energetics and novel grain geometries that balance performance with safety and environmental footprint; parallel electronics hardening centres ensure that seekers and fuzes survive the extreme acceleration, temperature, and electromagnetic stresses of modern battlefields. Close coupling between Hyderabad's pilot lines and Pune's integration labs allows newly validated energetic formulations and electronic subassemblies to be evaluated in end-to-end systems rapidly, accelerating maturation and de-risking scale-up.

Jabalpur provides the industrial steel spine that underpins the entire model. Its centuries-old ordnance ecosystem comprising the shell casing production, propellant manufacturing expertise, and proof ranges is uniquely placed to serve as the nation's metallurgy and propellant backbone. The IAN approach requires Jabalpur to modernise these competencies with CNC machining, hybrid additive manufacturing (AM) for complex liners and sabots, advanced heat-treatment furnaces for high-strength alloys, and digitised QC processes, such as, micro-CT scanning of propellant grains and in-line burn-rate monitoring. Jabalpur's Central Proof Establishment becomes a real-time proofing and lot-acceptance node that feeds empirical ballistic and proof data into the TNPO-managed digital spine. By elevating Jabalpur from a volume-focused production centre to a materials innovation hub, the IAN framework secures continuity of supply for precision shell bodies, stabilised propellant lots, and validated alloy compositions that meet both operational and export standards.

Most importantly, the coordination across nodes is not merely administrative, rather it is technical and data-driven. The TNPO, seated conceptually at the triangle's centre, enforces a single Product-Lifecycle Management (PLM) schema and a shared Manufacturing Execution System (MES). Each component, such as, propellant lot, fuze serial, casing batch is assigned a serialised digital identity that persists through production, integration, testing, and depot storage. This genealogy enables instantaneous root-cause analysis for defects, predictive shelf-life analytics using digital twins, and harmonised Cp/Cpk capability tracking across production lines. The TNPO also manages the Bill of Materials (BoMs) dictionary, coordinates export certification, adjudicates joint-IP arrangements, and synchronises user-in-the-loop trial schedules so that operational feedback is embedded into iterative design sprints rather than processed as belated corrective actions.

Practical linkages between nodes are therefore designed around predictable, high-frequency exchanges. Hyderabad ships fuel and fuze subassemblies to Pune on an accelerated cadence once a design has passed pilot trials; Jabalpur delivers serialised shell bodies and validated propellant lots timed for integration windows; Pune performs the final assembly, HIL/SIL validation, and user trial coordination. This pipeline reduces inventory degeneration and avoids the historical lag where research outputs idle for months waiting for production slots or procurements. It also enables modular co-production arrangements with external partners: for exports, India can offer co-production kits in which shell bodies and propellants are supplied from Jabalpur while partner nations perform final integration with locally sourced subassemblies, providing strategic leverage and industrial diplomacy.

The hub-and-node model also provides clear pathways for private sector and MSME participation. Rather than confining industry to peripheral supplier roles, IANs create defined integration points where private firms can own and operate pilot production lines (especially in Hyderabad) or supply AM components and specialised machining services for Jabalpur and Pune. Long-term procurement envelopes and co-funded R&D incentives encourage these investments; joint IP frameworks and revenue-sharing mechanisms de-risk collaboration with DRDO and MIL. Academic institutions are woven into this fabric through directed research chairs and doctoral programmes that align curricula to IAN needs, ensuring a steady talent pipeline.

Finally, the model incorporates a built-in export and standards strategy. Harmonised QA metrics, validated via the TNPO's shared data spine, allow batches to be certified against STANAG, UN IATG, and ISO norms. Defence diplomacy then leverages the nodes as demonstrable evidence of India's ability to supply reliable, quality-assured munitions serving as vital credibility requirement for global markets.

In operational terms, the hub-and-node model transforms ammunition production from a sequential, siloed process into a parallel, feedback-rich ecosystem: research matures in pilot lanes, materials are validated in instrumented proofing trails, and systems are integrated and tested in a user-informed loop, all under the orchestration of a central program office and a digital backbone that guarantees traceability, predictability, and speed. This model is not merely a reorganisation of capacity; it is an architectural shift that aligns industrial capability, scientific innovation, and operational necessity into a coherent national instrument for ammunition sovereignty and strategic influence.

Implementation Roadmap

Translating the Integrated Ammunition Nodes (IANs) concept into reality requires a phased, well-resourced, and policy-backed programme that aligns political will, institutional incentives, and industrial capacity. The first and most important enabler is policy: a National Ammunition Mission (NAM) must be constituted with a mission-mode mandate and cross-ministerial authority. NAM should set clear, time-bound targets for domestic production, R&D maturity, and export readiness for 2030, 2035 and 2047; it should be ring-fenced with multi-year financing so that ammunition modernisation does not get displaced by competing platform purchases. To incentivise private investment, the mission must include long-term procurement guarantees (10–15-year offtake frameworks for critical sub-systems), tax and R&D credits for capital expenditure on pilot lines and additive-manufacturing cells, and matching grants for joint DRDO–industry demonstrators. Procurement rules should be simplified with a 'fast-track' corridor for innovations validated within the IANs, allowing prototypes that pass HIL/SIL and pilot proofing to be fast-tracked into limited series buys and operational trials without being trapped in slow, file-driven tenders.

Institutional integration is the second pillar. The Tri-Node Program Office (TNPO) must be established in Pune as the executive coordinating body with statutory authority to manage a single product backlog, harmonise Bills of Materials, approve test schedules across nodes, and arbitrate IP and revenue-sharing arrangements. TNPO should have a compact, empowered governance board comprising representatives from MIL, DRDO, Quality Assurance (Ammunition), Army Design Bureau, and nominated private sector partners; it must also include an independent technical advisory panel drawn from academia and international experts to provide technology roadmaps. Practically, TNPO will implement a unified PLM/MES architecture and a single Cp/Cpk reporting regime so that capability indices are comparable across factories, labs, and private pilot lines.

On infrastructure, each node requires targeted capital works that convert legacy assets into modern, networked facilities. Pune needs investment in integration lines, X-ray CT and NDT suites for filled rounds, instrumented ranges with real-time telemetry, and a Shelf-Life Digital Twin centre that aggregates depot exposure data. Hyderabad requires IM-compliant pilot energetic lines, electronics hardening chambers (shock, vibration, EMI/EMC), and small-batch production cells certified to host green energetics scale-ups.

Jabalpur must prioritise CNC retrofits, hybrid AM cells for complex casings and sabots, advanced heat-treatment furnaces, and digitised propellant QA including micro-CT and in-line burn-rate monitoring. Each node should include secure testbeds and safety-rated containment systems to meet modern environmental and occupational health norms. Importantly, these upgrades must be designed for modular expansion so that pilot successes can be scaled without wholesale plant rebuilds.

Moreover, it is the human capital that converts machines into capability. IANs should be accompanied by a coordinated academic and skilling programme: specialised MTech and PhD tracks at DIAT, IITs, and select NITs in energetics, additive manufacturing, materials science, and embedded systems; ammunition chairs tied to IAN project portfolios; and modular certification for factory technicians to transition into Industry 4.0 roles. Structured exchange programmes should rotate DRDO scientists, MIL engineers, and private sector technologists across nodes for 6–12-month stints to build common practices and create 'field-tested' integrators. User integration must be formalised through a 'User-in-the-Loop' protocol that embeds serving and retired officers into development sprints and trial planning, ensuring operational requirements shape acceptance criteria from the outset.

Global outreach and standards harmonisation complete the implementation picture. TNPO should stand up an Export Certification Cell to align processes with STANAG, UN IATG, and ISO quality norms, while offering co-production packages for partner nations: India supplies validated shell bodies and propellant lots, while co-producers perform final assembly or integrate mission-specific subassemblies. Defence diplomacy must leverage exhibitions and bilateral exchanges to showcase certified IAN outputs, positioning India as a reliable, non-aligned supplier of smart munitions.

A realistic phased timeline organises these components. Phase 1 (0–3 years) establishes NAM and TNPO, funds critical pilot upgrades (digital twins in Pune, IM pilot line in Hyderabad, CNC retrofits in Jabalpur), and launches specialised academic programmes. Phase 2 (3–7 years) focuses on full node integration starting from routine flow of serialised propellant lots and fuze subassemblies into Pune's integration lines, first export-ready smart rounds, and domestic production starts for key inputs (e.g., nitrocellulose). Phase 3 (7–15 years) scales mass production, matures the digital backbone for predictive QA, and expands export co-production agreements. Phase 4 (by 2047) envisages supply-chain sovereignty across energetics, metals and electronics, a mature export portfolio, and India's recognition as a global hub for smart munitions.

Governance and Quality Assurance

The success of the Integrated Ammunition Nodes (IANs) rests not only on infrastructure or policy but on the creation of a governance and quality assurance framework that is transparent, reliable, and trusted by both domestic users and international partners. Ammunition is fundamentally unforgiving; even a single defect can compromise soldier safety, degrade operational readiness, and damage India's export credibility. For this reason, governance and Quality Assurance (QA) cannot be treated as afterthoughts but must form the very backbone of the IAN system.

At the centre of this architecture is the Tri-Node Program Office (TNPO), which functions as the nerve centre of coordination. More than an administrative secretariat, the TNPO must be endowed with executive authority to manage project backlogs, approve test schedules, enforce compliance with standards, and arbitrate intellectual property and revenue-sharing disputes. Its composition should include representatives from Munitions India Limited (MIL), DRDO, the Army Design Bureau, the Controllerate of Quality Assurance (CQA–Ammunition), private industry, and academia. This diversity ensures that decisions are technically grounded, operationally relevant, and commercially viable. By functioning as a single point of accountability, the TNPO eliminates duplication of efforts and harmonises the outputs of Pune, Hyderabad, and Jabalpur into a unified national portfolio.

Quality assurance within IANs must also be reimagined from reactive inspection to proactive, embedded monitoring. Historically, QA has relied heavily on after-the-fact sampling and inspection regimes, which are both time-consuming and prone to overlooking latent defects. In the IAN framework, QA must be embedded at every stage of the production cycle, using Industry 4.0 technologies, such as, IoT sensors, process analytics, and real-time dashboards. Each propellant batch, shell casing, fuze, or explosive fill should be linked to a digital identity that records its genealogy across the supply chain, from raw material sourcing in Jabalpur, to electronics hardening in Hyderabad, to integration in Pune. Such traceability enables rapid root-cause analysis in case of failures, strengthens accountability, and supports predictive analytics for shelf-life management.

Additionally, the harmonisation of QA standards across different institutions is also important. MIL factories, DRDO labs, private vendors, and MSMEs must adhere to a unified taxonomy of defects and a common set of process capability indices, allowing performance to be benchmarked objectively across the ecosystem. This harmonisation would be reinforced by embedding CQA officers and technical specialists within each node, ensuring that quality is assured concurrently rather than verified retrospectively. A shared Product Lifecycle Management (PLM) and Manufacturing Execution System (MES), overseen by the TNPO, would provide the digital backbone needed to sustain this harmonisation across geographically dispersed sites.

Another critical element is the integration of user feedback into the QA loop. Ammunition defects are often discovered only in operational contexts, and in the past such findings have taken months or even years to filter back to production units. IANs must institutionalise a feedback repository where frontline units can submit defect reports, range trial data, and accident investigations directly into the TNPO system. By linking QA metrics to actual field performance rather than to factory-level throughput alone, the IAN framework ensures that quality is judged by its ultimate purpose: reliability in combat.

Finally, governance must also extend to export standards. If India is to emerge as a credible global supplier of ammunition, its QA systems must be robust enough to satisfy international norms, such as, NATO's STANAG standards, the UN's International Ammunition Technical Guidelines, and ISO certifications. Establishing a dedicated export certification cell within Pune, staffed with experts in international standards, would help clear export-ready batches and instil confidence in foreign buyers. In this way, QA becomes both a guarantor of national security and a passport to international credibility.

The governance and quality assurance within the IAN model are not isolated administrative functions but the very foundation of the system's credibility. By embedding QA in real time, harmonising standards, ensuring traceability through digital tools, and integrating user and export requirements, the IANs can transform ammunition from one of India's most persistent vulnerabilities into one of its most reliable strengths.

Risks and Mitigation

While the Integrated Ammunition Nodes (IANs) framework presents a transformative vision, its implementation is not without systemic risks. Anticipating these risks and embedding mitigation measures into the design is essential if the initiative is to avoid the fate of earlier reforms that faltered under institutional inertia or resource shortfalls. The first and perhaps most entrenched risk is bureaucratic inertia. Defence industrial reforms in India have historically been slowed by overlapping jurisdictions, prolonged decision-making, and turf battles between ministries, PSUs, and research organisations. The corporatisation of the Ordnance Factory Board itself revealed how even well-intentioned reforms can be diluted if not supported by empowered governance. The mitigation lies in creating the National Ammunition Mission (NAM) with statutory authority, cross-ministerial reach, and a mission director vested with decision-making powers comparable to leaders of India's atomic or space programmes. Only such empowered leadership can cut through procedural bottlenecks and maintain reform momentum.

A second risk arises from friction between state-run enterprises and the private sector. Munitions India Limited (MIL), as the successor to the OFB, continues to carry a legacy of insularity and monopolistic attitudes. Without structural safeguards, there is a danger that private industry will be relegated to subcontractor roles, stifling innovation and deterring investment. To counter this, MIL must be positioned as a system integrator rather than a monopolistic producer, with clear frameworks for outsourcing, joint intellectual property ownership, and equitable revenue sharing. Cluster-based partnerships, for instance, private SMEs embedded within Hyderabad's energetics ecosystem or startups collaborating with Pune's integration hub can also reduce friction by creating shared stakes in success.

Input material vulnerabilities constitute another persistent risk. India remains dependent on imports for nitrocellulose, tungsten, copper alloys, and specialty chemicals. In a crisis or under sanctions, these dependencies could cripple the supply chain. Mitigation measures must include establishing domestic nitrocellulose plants under Make in India, strategic stockpiles of critical minerals, and recycling initiatives to recover metals from obsolete ammunition. This diversification would cushion shocks and reduce the risk of supply paralysis.

Technological lag is also a major challenge. Global battlefields are rapidly shifting towards smart munitions, loitering drones, and AI-enabled targeting. If IANs become preoccupied with merely modernising legacy lines, India risks falling behind. Mitigation here requires embedding cutting-edge technologies, such as, digital twins, additive manufacturing, predictive analytics into the IAN framework from the outset. Dedicated future labs within Pune should be tasked with looking beyond the immediate horizon towards 2040–2050 warfare trends, ensuring the ecosystem evolves in tandem with global shifts.

Ammunition defects or premature explosions can undermine user confidence and damage India's credibility in export markets. The solution lies in predictive QA, redundant testing protocols for export batches, and independent accident investigation boards that provide transparent audits. Finally, funding constraints remain a structural risk, as ammunition programmes often lose out to high-visibility platforms, such as, aircraft or ships. Securing ring-fenced financing under NAM, complemented by public–private co-financing models with long-term government buyback guarantees, will be vital to maintain continuity. These risks highlight that the IAN framework cannot be pursued as an engineering exercise alone; it must be underpinned by empowered governance, resilient supply chains, sustained technology infusion, and secure financing. By embedding these safeguards into its very design, India can ensure that the IAN vision moves from aspiration to enduring reality.

Conclusion

Ammunition remains the most indispensable yet historically neglected element of India's defence preparedness. Despite advances in platforms and systems, the country has struggled with recurring quality concerns, import dependencies, and fragmented institutional arrangements. The IANs framework offers a decisive departure from this trajectory by reimagining ammunition not as a consumable afterthought but as the lifeblood of combat power and a strategic asset in its own right. By weaving together research, industrial capacity, user feedback, and digital traceability into a single ecosystem, IANs promise to convert one of India's persistent vulnerabilities into a foundation of operational credibility.

At the heart of this framework lies a deliberate distribution of roles: Pune as the central hub for design, integration, and qualification; Hyderabad as the innovation engine for energetics and electronics; and Jabalpur as the metallurgy and propellant backbone. Coordinated through the Tri-Node Program Office and supported by the National Ammunition Mission, these nodes together form a national ammunition grid that is resilient, technologically advanced, and export-ready. Such an ecosystem would not only strengthen India's defence forces but also position the country as a reliable global supplier of smart munitions, enhancing its economic strength and diplomatic leverage. The road to achieving this vision, however, is fraught with risks spanning from bureaucratic inertia and funding constraints to input material dependencies and technological lag. Yet these risks are not insurmountable. With empowered governance, ring-fenced financing, proactive private participation, and sustained technology infusion, the IAN model can overcome structural hurdles and ensure that India's armed forces are never handicapped by ammunition shortages or defects.

As India approaches its centenary in 2047, the creation of IANs can stand as a defining reform. It will mark the transition of India from a nation that once inherited colonial ordnance factories to a global hub of smart munitions and resilient supply chains. More importantly, it will embed ammunition as a cornerstone of strategic autonomy, ensuring that India's military strength, economic ambition, and diplomatic credibility are underpinned by technological sovereignty and industrial self-reliance.

13

Building an Agile Ammunition Acquisition System for Rapid Technological Integration

Introduction

For the better part of the last decade, defence procurement processes worldwide have come under increasing scrutiny for being unwieldy and conducted at an excruciatingly slow pace. One the key underlying factors has been the overdependence on defence procurement manuals. These manuals were expected to provide a common platform and ensure that the process is quick and efficient. Regrettably, these manuals have now become straitjackets with almost no room for manoeuvring and discretion, resulting in huge acquisition delays. The delays in acquisition, particularly in countries like India, where modernisation is now an imperative driven by morphing security threats, has finally caught the attention of policymakers. This reality was indirectly admitted in a 2023 report by the Ministry of Defence, which acknowledged that over-dependence on defence manuals, had played a part in not finalising contracts for vital defence supplies, like fighter jets, submarines, and missile systems. This lag led to a capability brief. The armed forces have been caught in a bind between procedural rigor, on the one hand, and the compulsions of national defence, on the other. Defence procurement manuals have traditionally played a vital role in limiting corruption and promoting transparency and accountability at multiple levels of procurement. Inadvertently, though, this red tape leads to bottlenecks at every stage of the procurement lifecycle, ranging from the issue of RFPs (Request for Proposals) up to the final award of contracts. As the procedures of procurement got super complex and intricate, delays became inevitable, especially when the defence officials needed to adhere to every little thing mentioned in the procurement manuals, fearing that they would not be discretionarily exercised, and this may demand audits/investigations.[412]

For instance, in the case of India, there was a delay of over ten years in the procurement of Rafale fighter jets. Although it was a high-priority buy to replace the MiG-21s, the rigid insistence of strict adherence to policies and procedures set in procurement manuals had hindered negotiations and the end acquisition. Consequently, the delay in its acquisition affects national security, leading to public criticism and a few legal challenges, rendering the entire process even more unwieldy.[413] And an equally important aspect of the quandary is how fast technology evolves in defence.

Technological Obsolescence

The procurement cycle for a particular piece of equipment is often completed just when the technology has already become obsolete. Such a fast-paced environment is seldom genial to procurement manuals. Similarly, although Unmanned Aerial Vehicle (UAV) technologies have advanced very rapidly in recent years, procurement procedures do not similarly respond to the speed of these changes, and they continue in a heavy-handed bureaucratic way established for conventional weapons systems. The US and Israel are much faster, following a policy of flexibility in procurement; by holding the upper hand, these countries can compete with several other states that have been using manuals to process their acquisitions, which explains why so many have fallen behind with respect to critical defence capabilities.[414] Moreover, defence procurement manuals mandate layers of redundant review, approval, and re-approval before decisions are ultimately reached. This merely further encumbers the process with more bureaucratic layers. In addition, many defence procurement organisations do not have trained and qualified staff to operate in the new, rather sophisticated procurement segment. In practice, this leads to the problem worsening due to a lack of explicit guidance about what kind of situations should be considered discretionary. So, oversight is important and imperative to ensure some accountability, but it slows down the decision-making process when you have so many levels of it. One such case was the purchase of submarines by the UK Ministry of Defence, which suffered delays over several years caused by a misapplication of procurement regulations and an overly long review process. Consequently, cost overruns and delayed project timelines started weakening the UK's naval defence capabilities.[415]

In 2022, the Indian government started a number of efforts to lessen the red tape of defence procurement. The intent of the reforms was to cut down on the number of decision-making layers and establish further independence in procurement operations. The manuals of the defence procurement still control the operational manner, which compels officials to exercise compliance rather than efficiency.[416] By contrast, other countries with flexible procurement systems in place, such as, Israel and South Korea, can procure their weapons much more quickly and efficiently. For example, the Israel Defence Ministry uses a so-called "fast-track" procurement procedure when it comes to urgently needed equipment, which enables defence officials to bypass the traditional bureaucratic rules of play while maintaining accountability through post-procurement audits. In the past, this has allowed Israel to acquire state-of-the-art technologies quickly in order to preserve its regional qualitative military superiority. On the other hand, South Korea has implemented a digital procurement platform with real-time updates and full visibility, meaning that around 5000 man-years of manual documentation are eliminated for each defence procurement.[417]

Historical Insights and Current Landscape of Defence Procurement

In India the procurement has always been generically under the purview of the Ministry of Defence (MoD) through its apex body, the Defence Acquisition Council (DAC), and its manufacturing arm, Department of Defence Production (DDP). The DAC, set up in 2001 to speed up the acquisition process and standardise it across the board for all three services, was meant to empower the armed forces with modern weapons in a timely manner. The DAC was to make policies, procedures, and guidelines on how procurement business was to be conducted in such a way that efficiency was achieved, as well as create transparency, increase control on corruption, and prevent misuse of funds. That was some reaction to recurring criticism that India's defence procurement is archaic and ridden with delays.[418] The most significant reform under the DAC umbrella is the adoption of the Defence Procurement Procedure (DPP) and later DAP in 2020. The larger aim of the DAP was to boost self-reliance in defence production as part of the 'Make in India' program, with an objective aimed at cutting down on India's dependence on foreign arms suppliers. Nonetheless, we have not been able to fulfil its intended objectives effectively and efficiently because of an overly bureaucratic structure and heavy reliance on the procurement manuals. It has long been seen as a matter of concern amongst the procurement officers who found that these guidelines were extremely stringent and did not cater to the needs of military-specific or infrastructure.[419]

Nations like the United States have modernised their procurement agencies to handle the complex nature of defence procurement today. The Under Secretary of Defense for Acquisition, Technology, and Logistics founded the Defence Acquisition University to train their personnel to gain expertise on effectively running through this process. Likewise, Israel has adopted a very flexible acquisition model, designed to work with operational needs rather than be strictly procedural, allowing for quick acquisitions, particularly in high-tech fields, such as, missile defence and cybersecurity. A unique example is the US Federal Procurement Data System, which could be a model for relook into own procurement rules.[420]

Two key drivers have historically been shaping defence procurement policies worldwide, namely, the increasing complexity of military technologies and the rising demand for transparency in governmental transactions. Historically, defence procurement policies were *ad hoc* and personal initiatives between governments and military manufacturers that often overlook how compromising policy development can undermine effectiveness. However, as military technology improved and governments sought greater accountability, more formal procurement processes were introduced over time to ensure fairness, transparency, and consistency in the acquisition process.

Defence Procurement Procedure (DPP) was introduced for the first time in 2002 in India. Since then, the DPP has been revised a number of times to address new challenges in procurement, such as, increased emphasis on domestic defence manufacturing and speedier acquisition cycles. This was a major overhaul in 2020 when the DPP was replaced by the Defence Acquisition Procedure (DAP), which focused on indigenisation and the private sector's role under the "Make in India" initiative. The DAP targeted the expansion of joint ventures and associations with external defence developers to promote local defence manufacturing.[421] Though the DAP was a forward-looking document in terms of defence procurement, it did not remove some of the basic issues, like reliance on procedural manuals that often lead to delays. The interminably long approval cycle and insistence on precise procedural ways have resulted in major hold-ups, especially when trying to procure urgently needed equipment. The purchase of basic fighter jets, which are important to the security of this country, is one case in point and has been held up a number due to procedural glitches. The delays have renewed calls to reform the DAP to allow greater leeway in procurement, especially when immediate purchase is needed for reasons of national security.[422]

In the United States, defence procurement is governed by the Federal Acquisition Regulation (FAR). On one hand, FAR has broad coverage because it provides everything for acquisition, yet far enough is flexible that one can act quickly in an emergency. The UK followed suit with its 2021 Defence and Security Industrial Strategy (DSIS), emphasising technological innovation and agility in defence procurement. They implemented these reforms of how the defence acquisition process works to try and find a middle ground between transparency with the public as well as getting equipment into the hands of troops faster.[423]

A Double-Edged Sword

One of the most daunting challenges in defence procurement that's faced today is reliance on procurement manuals. On one hand, these manuals provide the necessary structure and guidance to ensure transparency and fairness in the acquisition process. At the same time, their strict enforcement can also cause major delays if officials follow them too literally, worried about accusations of impropriety if they skip any step in the process. The DAP is essentially emblematic of this problem in India. These dictate the terms of procurement in no uncertain terms but typically leave little room for creativity or discretion. That has led to critical acquisitions like helicopters, submarines, and missile systems getting delayed, which is key to the country's defensive posture. Though these guidebooks are intended to lessen corruption, their rigorous adherence leads to a phenomenon of "analysis paralysis". Here, officials are more concerned about the ticking the boxes rather than securing timely and efficient results.[424]

Similar is the For example, the UK's Type 26 Global Combat Ship program was delayed by years because of bureaucratic and box-ticking reasons pushing modern frigates past their use-by dates to replace aging ships that were plagued with problems. For example, due to an overly bureaucratic procurement process, the United States is seeing years of delay in many defence programs, especially in advanced cybersecurity technology acquisition. However, in these instances, the manuals meant to make the process more efficient have become hurdles to procurement being done quickly and effectively.[425] Over-dependence on manuals also stifles innovation in defence procurement. The pace of technology is moving swiftly, and defence acquisition today needs to stay nimble to counter the rate of advancement. In practice, though, the discipline of following policies by the book boxes procurement officials out of more flexible approaches or new technologies that don't fit neatly in old templates. More importantly, this is evident in the cybersecurity and artificial intelligence landscape, where technological innovations outpace the procurement cycle. This means that defence agencies are stuck with antiquated systems, which threatens national security. In recognition of this growing challenge, some countries are starting to reform. In Israel, an example of this is the "fast-track" procurement system implemented to quickly acquire high-importance resources, which allows officials to skip many of the phases of manuals without a transparent post-procurement audit.[426]

Way Ahead for Agile Acquisition System

Evaluation of Current Reforms

Most countries around the world have admitted inefficiencies in defence procurement systems and reformed them as a remedy to realise delays, bureaucratic bottlenecks that have plagued the process for ages, and reliance on inflexible procurement manuals. As said before, in India, the DAP (Defence Acquisition Procedure) reformed in 2020 tries to deal with some of the deep-rooted problems found in its ancestor, DPP (Defence Procurement Procedure). The DAP contained promotional items for a simplified form of procurement, greater flexibility, and encouraging domestic defence manufacturing and the "Make in India" campaign. However, despite such reforms, defence procurement in India still remains slow, with the acquisition of fighter jets or submarines stuck due to a bureaucratic maze.[427] In the United States, a second major defence procurement reform was instituted by the Department of Defence (DoD) in 2020 with its Adaptive Acquisition Framework (AAF) launch. The AAF is meant to allow program managers to tailor their acquisition strategy on a project-by-project basis. To streamline the burdensome procurement process, and enable a more agile information operations capability (e.g., in cyberspace, Artificial Intelligence (AI), or space defence) by the US military, this reform was intended for faster cycle times such that technology sectors are not passing it by.[428] Also, in 2021, the UK's Ministry of Defence unveiled the Defence and Security Industrial Strategy (DSIS) to cut foreign broadcasting suppliers and support domestic defence technology development. Along with an increased focus on defence industry agility, the DSIS highlights specific areas in which such measures are required more immediately, especially concerning large-scale, long-term projects, such as, building naval vessels and acquiring fighter jets. However, with these reforms still come delays in major defence projects stemming from bureaucratic oversight and an absence of continued coordination among various government bodies.[429] These changes, which are a step in the right direction, have been inconsistently applied. In India, DAP is not seen as an in-depth reform by many players who feel that procedural intricacies and rigidities still exist. These reforms have been quite ineffective, partially due to a lack of trained procurement officers as well as insufficient technological integration.

Policy Reforms Needed

The root cause of the continued delays and inefficiencies in defence procurement will not be fixed by changes to acquisition policy at any level. Procurement processes must be more flexible to accommodate the rapidly changing military requirements. This could include the implementation of layered procurement, which means that a tier is designated for each procurement acquisition and is proliferated in urgency, cost, and complexity. For experts, high-priority acquisitions, such as, critical military equipment that is required for immediate operational use should be facilitated through a streamlined procedure with minimum bureaucratic inhibitions. The less urgent purchases, by contrast, can continue to go through the standard purchasing process in more detail. A tiered approach would help to prevent unnecessary procedural steps from hindering the timeliness of critical acquisitions.[430] Another important suggestion is to promote the use of technology in procurement. In many defence procurement systems, manual documentation and paper-based approvals remain cumbersome, resulting in delays and errors. A completely digitised procurement system would enable real-time procurement stages to be tracked, leading to a drastic reduction in the time spent waiting for approvals and increased transparency. There could also be improved assessments of bids using AI and data analytics in procurement decision-making to help with a lower rate of disputes and delays.[431] More autonomy should be given to the procurement officers. Hundreds of small unnecessary delays exist as many defence procurement agencies force officers to take their decisions high up the approval chain. Allowing greater autonomy to procurement personnel and implementing checks and balances can help streamline the procurement process without forsaking accountability. Reduced accountability, along with increased cooperation among the agency, defence contractors, and the military, is crucial to improving outcomes in procurement. By doing so, any bottleneck in the process can be identified early and resolved before it results in major delays. An integrated approach will also play in ensuring the equipment procured is best suited to the operational needs of the armed forces and defence contractors penalised for late deliveries.

Alternative Procurement Methods

To address the persistent delays in defence procurement, exploring alternative procurement methods that enable flexibility and efficiency while maintaining accountability and transparency is crucial. These methods offer ways to mitigate the constraints of a rigid RFP-based system, aligning acquisition practices with the rapidly changing technological landscape. One promising approach is Challenge-Based Procurement, which invites suppliers to meet defined objectives rather than providing strict specifications. By focusing on outcomes, challenge-based procurement encourages innovation and faster response times, as seen in the United Kingdom's defence industry, where this approach has successfully accelerated projects requiring novel solutions.[432] Agile Procurement is another method that brings an iterative, adaptable approach to acquisitions, allowing feedback and adjustments throughout the procurement process. This model is beneficial for acquiring technology-intensive systems that evolve quickly, as demonstrated by the United States Department of defence's application of agile methods for cybersecurity and AI projects. Direct Contracting with Innovation Hubs enables direct engagement with research and technology centres specialising in defence solutions, facilitating access to cutting-edge innovations without lengthy competitive bidding. South Korea's defence sector has leveraged this approach, fostering partnerships with technology hubs to ensure rapid, relevant acquisition cycles.[433] Additionally, Framework Agreements allow defence organisations to pre-approve suppliers for repeated procurement needs, saving time by eliminating repetitive contracting processes. In Israel, framework agreements have streamlined the acquisition of critical military supplies, reducing paperwork and accelerating procurement timelines for recurring needs. Modular procurement divides large acquisition projects into manageable components, enabling phased implementation. This approach mitigates risks and allows for quicker updates to specific modules as technology evolves, which has proven successful in the European Union's collaborative defence procurement projects. Finally, Outcome-Based Procurement emphasises contracting for the desired results rather than prescribing the exact methods, thus giving suppliers the flexibility to meet operational needs in innovative ways. This approach has been effective in the United States Adaptive Acquisition Framework, were program managers contract for capabilities, allowing technology suppliers greater leeway to innovate.[434]

Technology-Based Procurement for Ammunition

While alternative procurement methods, such as, challenge-based, agile, or outcome-based acquisition offer useful pathways, they remain generic in design. Ammunition acquisition, which is marked by rapid technological change and operational urgency, demands a more tailored approach. It is in this context that the idea of Technology-Based Procurement (TBP) becomes relevant. Unlike the conventional model driven by rigid Qualitative Requirements (QRs), TBP shifts the focus towards innovation, modularity, and adaptability. It prioritises capability outcomes, such as, enhanced precision, longer range, or improved shelf life rather than narrow technical specifications. By doing so, TBP creates the flexibility to integrate emerging technologies into procurement cycles without waiting for lengthy approvals or rewriting entire manuals.

The strength of TBP lies in its ability to use Technology Readiness Levels (TRLs) as decision gates in the acquisition process. Instead of treating procurement as a one-time event, TRLs provide a phased approach: early-stage technologies receive R&D support, mid-stage prototypes undergo controlled testing, and mature systems that have already been validated in operational environments are fast-tracked into procurement. This structured staging ensures that innovation is encouraged while risk is contained, and only those technologies with proven readiness move into mass production. The detailed TRL framework and progression from TRL 1 to TRL 9 can also be visualised in the following figure, which illustrates the staged maturity of technologies under the TRL framework as applied to ammunition. Applied to ammunition, TBP would mean procurement strategies explicitly tailored to integrate smart munitions, advanced energetics, modular warheads, additive manufacturing, and sensor-enabled inventory management. Instead of being locked into decades-old specifications, the armed forces can benefit from iterative upgrades that keep pace with the battlefield. Indigenous development becomes central in this model, since public–private partnerships, industry–academia linkages, and targeted technology-transfer agreements create an ecosystem that sustains both innovation and self-reliance. Moreover, lifecycle considerations are built into the procurement logic: modular designs enable future upgrades, environmentally safe disposal reduces long-term risks, and AI-enabled monitoring systems extend the safe shelf life of stockpiles.

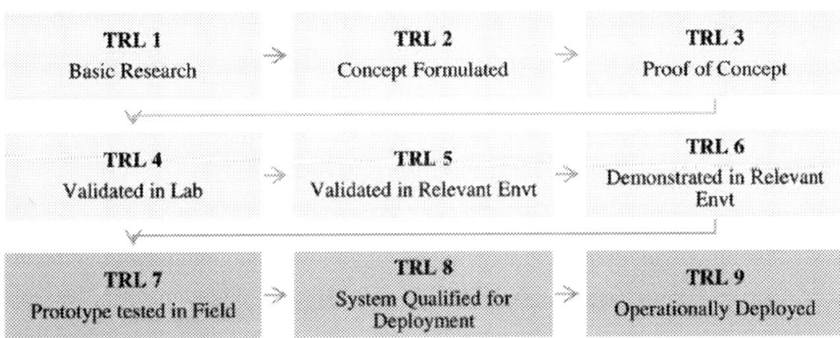

Challenges to TBP are inevitable, such as, high R&D costs, risks of technological obsolescence, dependence on foreign suppliers for critical inputs, bureaucratic inertia, and cyber vulnerabilities within digital procurement systems. However, these can be mitigated through blended funding models that share risks between the state and industry, modular architectures that allow incremental upgrades, conditional technology transfer agreements that embed localisation targets, simplified fast-track approvals with post-procurement audits, and strict supply-chain cybersecurity standards. If implemented effectively, TBP can overcome the weaknesses of both the rigid QR-based system and the overly generic alternative procurement models by providing a mechanism that is simultaneously innovative, transparent, and responsive to operational needs.

In comparative terms, QR-based procurement tends to freeze requirements at the start of the process, locking the armed forces into specifications that may already be outdated by the time contracts are finalised. TBP, by contrast, evolves with the technology cycle. It shortens procurement timelines, encourages domestic R&D, enables modular upgrades, and reduces import dependence. The most viable path ahead is likely to be a hybrid system, where broad QRs establish baseline needs while TBP provides the flexibility to integrate emerging technologies. In practice, India is already experimenting with this approach in areas, such as, guided 155 mm artillery shells developed by IIT Madras and Munitions India Ltd, loitering munitions designed by private startups, and modular systems like the Pinaka rocket family that has moved through successive iterations. These initiatives illustrate how TRL-based decision-making and flexible procurement contracts can fast-track innovation without compromising accountability. Ultimately, TBP has the potential to transform ammunition procurement in India. By shifting from rigid specifications to capability-focused, innovation-driven acquisitions, it ensures that the armed forces receive equipment aligned with the pace of technological change. It also supports the vision of *Atmanirbhar Bharat* by embedding self-reliance into the very fabric of procurement, incentivising indigenous research, and creating a resilient domestic ecosystem. If adopted systematically and integrated with existing reforms, TBP could ensure that India's ammunition ecosystem remains future-ready, operationally relevant, and strategically autonomous.

Future Implications

The future of defence procurement will be contingent on how seamlessly the government and defence agencies are capable of transitioning from the former to the ever-evolving threat sceneries. To the extent that technological progress is now potentially faster than traditional procurement cycles allow for. A nation doing so risks sacrificing military readiness. Incorporating AI, cybersecurity, and autonomous systems into defence operations would involve even more rapid procurement processes. A dynamic and evolving threat landscape alongside newer threats in the form of cyberattacks, space warfare, and hybrid warfare are making the geopolitical scenario more unpredictable than ever, and these collectively are challenging national security in new ways. The defence procurement process needs to evolve, especially in the case of rapid acquisitions, where threats that were not anticipated emerge as reality. Vital will implement "fast-track" procurement systems, which are used in

Israel and South Korea, to ensure that armed forces can stay equipped to handle these challenges. Further, the new dawn of defence procurement will see an increase in a public-private hybrid model for defence production going forward. It is imperative for government to capitalise on private industry partners because defence technologies are becoming specialised and sophisticated. Last, defence procurement reforms must keep sustainability and resilience in mind. Defence procurement systems must be efficient and adaptable to changing global security dynamics, whether driven by supply chain disruption or geopolitical tensions. This will mean a more diversified and adaptive form of defence procurement that prioritises forging long-term partnerships and nurturing innovation in the domestic defence industry.

Conclusion

The delays in defence procurement makes it amply clear that reforms are urgently required to meet these challenges. Defence procurement is a crucial process to ensure military preparedness and national security, but in many countries, the current system is characterised by inefficiencies, bureaucratic bottlenecks, and inadequate flexibility. In all of these scenarios, what was originally envisaged as a beneficial compliance mechanism has, in effect, turned out to be an impediment at times, to timely procurement due to the rigid adherence to the procurement manuals. As a result, numerous countries have spent decades trying to update any or all of their military technology in the midst of an era that stands on a time scale defined by rapid advances. While many reforms seem to be implemented for an optimal procurement process, the over-arching procedural manuals continue to blur and hinder the procurement of essential weapons. The same problems can be found in other countries, such as, the United States and the UK, where bureaucratic complexities and excessive oversight are holding up procurement. More than an inconvenience, these delays have dire consequences for our national security. Slowed acquisition processes could lead to the armed forces being without the equipment necessary to address new threats in a world were security changes from day-to-day, making it more unstable. There have been efforts to reform defence procurement, which has been, in some instances, more successful than others. Such delays may be due to the cumbersome rigid acquisition frameworks and can easily be overcome by introducing more flexible acquisition frameworks like the US Adaptive Acquisition Framework or Israel's fast-track procurement system. Defence procurement auditors This operational necessity first, procedure second approach is a model that also allows defence agencies to remain flexible in the face of evolving circumstances while backstopping accountability with audits done after the fact. This chapter points out the advantages of technology incorporation towards more efficiency and transparency in the procurement process, like what South Korea has done to digitise its procurement system.

Along this line, implementation determines success from the current round of reforms. Procedural rigidity and procedural flexibility should be introduced as metrics-longer-term efforts to build a beachhead of modularity within these relatively standardised systems. Devolving greater autonomy to procurement officers in combination with innovative technologies like artificial intelligence and data analytics could supply a path forward, facilitating faster, more well-informed decision-making without compromising transparency. Over time, defence procurement must change due to the rapidly changing nature of technology and the challenges related to warfare today. In many areas, such as, cybersecurity, space defence, and unmanned systems, innovation is happening so quickly that traditional procurement cycles cannot keep up. Government will have to be less risk-aversive and more willing to experiment if they want cutting-edge capabilities in the hands of their military. The ultimate aim of defence procurement reforms should be that the pendulum swings towards accountability with a touch of agility, enjoying the protection against unnecessary delays from being motivated by national security. Sensible, effectively tailored defence procurement reform is the only way that a country can ensure its defence buying system will rise to those twenty first century challenges.

14

Way Forward: Ten Missions, Metrics, and Transformation Plan

Introduction: From Vision to Execution

The pursuit of *Viksit Bharat 2047* in the field of ammunition manufacturing is not merely a technological or industrial ambition rather a strategic necessity that will determine India's national security and defence preparedness in the coming decades. Ammunition has historically been the invisible backbone of military power. While it has been less visible than tanks, ships, or aircraft, yet it has been decisive in shaping combat outcomes. However, India's experience has demonstrated that despite all the significant progress in indigenous defence production, the systemic challenges still undermine efficiency, innovation, and strategic autonomy. The paradoxical dilemmas of overstocked yet underperforming ammunition, quality concerns, delays in absorption of foreign technologies in real time, and critical supply chains vulnerabilities highlight the lack of a long-term and a mission-oriented approach. Therefore, the future must rest on a comprehensively designed framework which goes beyond just incremental reforms or short-term crisis responses. The need of the hour is a mission-driven transformation plan that provides coherence to otherwise disparate efforts and aligns them with measurable objectives. This framework would ensure that ammunition manufacturing is not just considered a narrow industrial process but a part of a larger national security architecture which could integrate the roles of the Army, defence PSUs, private industry, and academia. The need of the hour is for India to produce not just more ammunition, but the right ammunition which is fit for future scenarios. Therefore, the focus should be on prioritising relevance and quality rather than quantity.

As the previous chapters have highlighted, the global battlefield is being reshaped by disruptive technologies, such as, drones, precision-guided munitions, and AI-enabled targeting. For India, this creates a dual challenge of rectifying existing inefficiencies in legacy ammunition systems, and leapfrogging into the era of smart, adaptive, and export-competitive munitions in span of just a few years. Therefore, the transformation from vision to execution, in terms of ammunition ecosystem, requires firm policy choices in addition to inculcating culture of institutional integration, technological innovation, and strategic foresight.

This chapter outlines the missions, metrics, and transformation plan that presents a roadmap to guide India's ammunition ecosystem towards 2047. By defining clear missions, identifying measurable indicators of success, and presenting a phased roadmap, it seeks to provide a coherent template for action that connects today's dilemmas with tomorrow's opportunities. This concluding chapter bridges the gap between the aspirational imagination of *Scenario 2050* and the practical imperatives of defence self-reliance, ensuring that ammunition production becomes a cornerstone of India's emergence as a secure and resilient power.

Defining Missions

A transformation plan for India's ammunition ecosystem must be based on well-defined missions that provide direction, coherence, and purpose to policy and institutional reforms as without such guiding missions, the reforms will continue to be fragmented and limited in scope. Missions focus on aligning multiple stakeholders, such as, the armed forces, the state, the private sector, and academia towards common objectives of fulfilling the vision of *Viksit Bharat 2047* by simultaneously addressing India's legacy dilemmas and prepare the country for disruptive trends in modern warfare.

Mission 1: Establishing Ammunition Incubation and Innovation Hubs

In the present scenario, research and development activities are fragmented and often lack synergy with operational realities, therefore, even the private industry and academia contribute significantly to R&D but in silos, with again minimal institutional linkages to the armed forces. It is because of these reasons that the pace of innovation and the relevance of technological outcomes remain limited. Therefore, a promising model would be to create Ammunition

Incubation Hubs which are anchored in existing Army training establishments as these hubs could leverage the expertise and core competencies of institutions, such as, the School of Artillery (for artillery ammunition and UAV integration), the Armoured Corps Centre and School (for tank ammunition), the Mechanised Infantry Centre and School (for BMP ammunition), the Army Air Defence College (for Air defence ammunition and missiles), the Infantry School (for small arms and infantry ammunition), and the College of Military Engineering (for mines and demolition stores), Military College of Materials Management (MCMM) for propellants and explosives and Military College of Electronics and Mechanical Engineering (MCEME) for missiles electronics. By having research wings within such training institutions, India could establish laboratories where the armed forces, scientists, and industry practitioners collaborate in real time and incubate niche technologies, promote indigenous solutions, and ensure faster adaptation of innovations into operational contexts. In fact, they could also serve as knowledge export centres in the coming years, positioning India as a thought leader in ammunition R&D. Veterans with deep technical expertise can serve as adjunct mentors, channelling decades of institutional knowledge into new research and development. Army colleges of instruction, already established as centres of excellence with robust infrastructure, experienced faculty, ranges, workshops, and laboratories, provide ideal environments for concept testing under realistic conditions. The Army has to assume an active role in innovation by embedding incubation hubs rather than just being passive end-user of technology. In the long run, this model would ensure a sustained research culture within training establishments, similar to the TRADOC schools seed initiatives of the US Army which transition seamlessly into DARPA and industry pipelines.

Mission 2: Institutional Integration with Mission Centric Planning

One of the major drawbacks in India's ammunition ecosystem is the structural disconnect between the manufacturer and the end-user. Despite being the largest consumer of munitions, the Indian Army has only a limited role in shaping their design, manufacture, and quality assurance and its involvement is usually restricted to drafting General Staff Qualitative Requirements (GSQRs) and Requests for Proposals (RFPs). In fact, even this involvement is often based on secondary data rather than frontline realities. With the exception of the conduct of trials, the Army's role largely recedes after the RFP stage is complete. It is left out of crucial stages, such as, raw material evaluation or design iteration, prototyping, and systemic failure analysis. This diminished role of the Army in this process results in decreased performance during operational needs, shelf-life problems and a weak feedback results in stretched timelines for indigenous equipment. The final outcome is inefficiency, wastage risk of lagging behind in next-gen technology, such as, AI-enabled munitions and precision-guided munitions.

This disconnect is further compounded by the current structure of production and procurement. The Department of Defence Production (DDP), DRDO and corporatised Munitions India Limited, and an expanding set of private players oversee the Research, manufacturing, and exports. While it is true that the entry of private industry will diversify supply, especially in calibres like 155 mm shells and small arms ammunition, but it also creates risks. Without sustained orders, any company can face financial strain and collapse under surplus capacity.

Even globally due to ongoing conflicts, the market is flooded with artillery shells and conventional rounds. Such conflicts diminish export opportunities and simultaneously sanctions and geopolitical challenges result in further barriers. Therefore, it is important to note that India today stands at an inflection point with initiatives, such as, *Atmanirbhar Bharat* and *Viksit Bharat 2047*. India has gained unprecedented manufacturing capacity but India still needs to align this to its operational needs and long-term planning so that it does not fall to what may be called a "Munitions Without Missions" syndrome.

In order to escape this pitfall, India should stop relying on a quantity-based model of ammunition production and switch to a capability-based one. Unplanned production should also be replaced by mission-driven planning that only manufactures what is needed in the present and future war fighting requirements. War Wastage Reserve (WWR) standards built in a world of import reliance must be re-adjusted with the help of scenario-based consumption models based on Ukrainian and Armenian-Azerbaijani experience where accuracy, expediency, and minimal collateral damage were more decisive than quantity. Procurement procedures also need to change: open-ended indents and repetitive bulk purchases should be substituted by capped, mission-related procurement, staggered deliveries, validated forecasts and built-in performance indicators. Speculative capacity should not be encouraged to be created by private players where they do not have an obligation to either fulfil an order or an export guarantee. Rather, they should be encouraged to diversify into related markets like mining explosives, non-lethal ammunition, or precision forgings in case they are hit by changes in defence demand.

A key enabler of this approach would be an Integrated Ammunition Management Cell under the Ministry of Defence which would be a crucial facilitator. This body would include the Army, DPSUs, private manufacturers, DRDO, and quality assurance organisations to oversee the full ammunition lifecycle from production and fielding to shelf-life monitoring, revalidation, and disposal. By using digital twins, AI-driven logistics, and predictive analytics, stockpiles could be classified into three categories *vis-à-vis* Tier 1 (ready use), Tier 2 (war reserve), and Tier 3 (for export, donation, or disposal). Such a system would minimise obsolescence, and prevent overproduction. Exporting ammunition should not be considered as a means of clearing surpluses, rather as a regulated buffer. It is time that India prioritises production and export of smart munitions but only after ensuring its domestic readiness.

The Positive Indigenisation List (PIL) adds another layer of complexity as it promotes domestic sourcing by incorporating items, such as, small arms ammunition, 155 mm projectiles, rockets, smart fuzes, and loitering munitions. But without precise demand mapping, it runs the risks of deepening the surplus problem. For instance, several suppliers might produce 155 mm shells simultaneously just because they are on the indigenisation list but it might result into surplus stocks. Similarly, is the case with some of the small arms calibre ammunition, which run the risk of being phased out. Therefore, in order to counter such distortions, PIL should directly be linked into mission-linked production planning. In fact, before any item is included in the PIL, the Ministry of Defence must confirm the service demand for at least 5 to 10 years. Additionally, these items must be ranked according to their criticality and volume so that there is no speculative stockpiling. Lastly, the entire implementation must be monitored by a PIL Review Board comprising Army HQ, DMA, MoD Acquisition to avoid any dead stock ammunition.

Mission 3: Securing Supply Chain Resilience

No transformation plan can succeed without addressing the vulnerabilities of India's ammunition supply chain. Therefore, the third mission is to have a secure and resilient supply chain. Critical raw materials, such as, antimony, toluene, and specialised steels is heavily import-dependent which exposes India to geopolitical shocks and price volatility. The 2022–23 disruptions in global supply chains, exacerbated by the Russia–Ukraine war, underscored the risks of overdependence on concentrated sources of supply. The third mission, therefore, must be the establishment of a National Policy on Defence Supply Chain Security. This policy should rest on a tri-sectoral framework that brings together the government, private industry, and academia to strengthen resilience. Its key pillars would include diversifying sources of imports, negotiating long-term supply contracts with resource-rich partners in Africa and Central Asia, creating national stockpiles of critical raw materials and investing in domestic substitutes through advanced R&D. Recycling and re-use of materials, such as, brass and steel should also be institutionalised. Fulfilling this mission will ensure that India's ammunition factories are functional even during crises which would reduce India's strategic vulnerability.

Mission 4: Technological Modernisation and Smart Munitions Ecosystem

India's ammunition ecosystem needs to undergo a technological leap in order to remain relevant in the 21st-century conflicts as recent conflicts, such as, Nagorno-Karabakh or Ukraine show the growing dominance of smart munitions, AI-enabled targeting, and drone-delivered ordnance. Much of India's current production infrastructure still revolves around legacy technologies, therefore, the fourth mission is to focus on technological modernisation by embedding next-generation technologies into every stage of the ammunition lifecycle. This includes the adoption of AI in demand forecasting and supply chain optimisation, 3D printing for rapid prototyping and small-batch production, and nanotechnology for more powerful explosives and propellants. Additionally, to enhance efficiency and reduce costs Industry 4.0 tools, such as, predictive maintenance, digital twins, and secure data platforms must be integrated into ammunition factories. India can enhance its combat capabilities and create a niche in global defence markets by encouraging dual-use technologies and ensuring that advances in materials science and additive manufacturing are adapted to the defence sector.

Mission 5: Enhancing Export Competitiveness and Defence Diplomacy

For India, it is important to position itself as a trusted supplier of ammunition to the global market, especially for the Global South. While India has made progress in exporting major platforms, such as, naval vessels and aircraft, its ammunition exports still remain modest. This is primarily due to the perception of uneven quality, limited production capacities, and a lack of aggressive export promotion. To correct this imbalance, it is important that India adopts a dedicated ammunition export strategy. One way could be incentivising private players to manufacture at scale for external markets, offering competitive financing and training packages to client states and then securing long-term contracts with strategic partners in Southeast Asia, Africa, and the West Asia. Moreover, exports should be viewed more than just economic gains and looked at as important tenets of defence diplomacy which could help India strengthen influence and build durable partnerships. This could help India to enhance its economic base and geopolitical reach by evolving the ammunition exports as a cornerstone of India's foreign policy by 2047.

Mission 6: Creating Integrated Ammunition Nodes as a National Grid

India's ammunition sector must move beyond fragmented factories, siloed R&D, and slow technology adoption towards a unified, resilient, and innovation-driven system. The Integrated Ammunition Nodes (IANs) framework provides this transformation by creating interconnected hubs where research, design, production, testing, and lifecycle management converge. Anchored around Pune (design and integration), Hyderabad (energetics and electronics), and Jabalpur (metallurgy and propellants), these nodes would function as a cohesive grid, closing the gap between laboratory prototypes, industrial scaling, and battlefield deployment. Central to this mission is a Tri-Node Program Office (TNPO) with executive authority and a shared digital backbone. Each lot of propellant, casing, or fuze would carry a serialised digital identity, enabling traceability, predictive shelf-life management and rapid defect analysis. By embedding Industry 4.0 tools, digital twins, additive manufacturing, automated quality assurance, directly into the nodes, India can shorten design-to-deployment cycles, reduce failure rates and align ammunition output with operational requirements. This architecture would also secure supply chain sovereignty by localising critical inputs like nitrocellulose and energetics, while fast-tracking indigenous innovation into production.

The IAN mission goes beyond meeting domestic demand; it positions India as a credible global supplier of smart munitions. Harmonised standards, export certification at the TNPO, and modular co-production kits would make Indian ammunition competitive in international markets. By 2047, IANs can turn ammunition from a recurring vulnerability into a strategic advantage—providing the armed forces with assured, defect-free supplies while enhancing India's economic strength and diplomatic leverage.

Mission 7: Integrating Self-Reliance with Strategic Stockpiling

India's ammunition sector has entered a new era. Under *Atmanirbhar Bharat* and *Viksit Bharat 2047*, corporatised ordnance factories and private industry will have the ability to produce a wide range of munitions, from small arms ammunition to 155 mm shells, rockets, loitering systems, and even smart, guided rounds. This unparalleled manufacturing capacity may create a paradox: while India will be able to produce ammunition on demand, its stockpiling practices would remain anchored in the legacy War Wastage Reserve (WWR) model designed for an era of import dependence. The challenge would not just be to produce ammunition, but to decide how much should be held in peacetime, how inventories should be managed, and how industries can remain viable without the cushion of massive standing orders.

The WWR concept originated at a time when India faced limited domestic capability and long lead times for imports. Maintaining reserves sufficient for 40 days of combat was seen as essential insurance. But in the future, with responsive industrial base, applying the same logic across all calibres may become counterproductive. This may create bloated inventories that may strain storage facilities, increase revalidation costs, and consume financial resources that could be directed towards modernisation or R&D. Ammunition is perishable; holding large surpluses guarantees waste. Also, While the future will inevitably shift towards a balanced mix of live and simulated training, this transition will slow the turnover of older vintage ammunition, resulting in the build-up of stockpiles, a counterproductive trend that poses additional challenges of safety, storage, and obsolescence.

Beyond logistics, overstocking also distorts industrial signals. Bulk peacetime orders for categories with modest real demand encourage firms to expand capacity unnecessarily. When consumption does not match these projections, production lines fall idle, leading to financial stress or even exit from the sector. This cycle undermines the very private sector base India seeks to strengthen.

A new approach is needed, one that shifts from bulk holding to capacity assurance. A tiered system of reserves offers a practical path forward. Tier I munitions (high-demand items, such as, 155 mm shells and tank ammunition) should retain traditional WWR levels. Tier II categories (moderate-use items) may be held in reduced stocks, supplemented by surge agreements with industry. Tier III (low-use ammunition) should be produced on demand, with only token holdings maintained. This model allows India to retain strategic depth where it matters, while avoiding wasteful accumulation of munitions with little battlefield utility. Technology must be the backbone of this transition. A real-time, digital ammunition management system, linking the Army, DPSUs, and private manufacturers can monitor holdings, track shelf-life, and predict replenishment requirements using AI-based analytics. Such a system would allow planners to know not just what exists in depots, but how long it will remain usable, and when industry must step in to replenish stocks. Surge-production protocols, backed by pre-negotiated standby contracts, can ensure that industry scales quickly in emergencies without needing to keep lines continuously busy in peacetime.

The industrial dimension of this mission is crucial. Without steady government orders, private firms face a "survival gap." To bridge this, India must adopt models of assured demand without bulk peacetime orders. Framework contracts and viability-gap financing can compensate firms modestly for maintaining capacity, safety infrastructure, and skilled manpower, while guaranteeing them priority access to orders in crises. Diversification into adjacent markets, such as, paramilitary and police ammunition, mining explosives, cartridge cases, or non-lethal rounds should be encouraged, reducing dependence on the Army as the sole buyer. Export promotion under government-to-government frameworks can also absorb excess capacity, provided it does not compromise domestic readiness. To keep innovation alive, the Ministry of Defence should institutionalise an Ammunition Modernisation Fund. This fund would place recurring, small-scale orders for smart fuses, programmable rounds, and R&D-driven niche munitions, ensuring production lines remain active and technologically current even when bulk orders are absent. Together with Ammunition Innovation Clusters linking

DRDO, IITs, and private industry, this would embed research continuity into the production cycle.

Mission 8: Powering Energetics Self-Sufficiency

India's strategic autonomy in ammunition manufacturing depends on sovereign capabilities in propellants and High Explosives (HEs). This mission establishes resilient, environmentally responsible capacities for nitrocellulose-based propellants and the RDX/HMX/TNT family of explosives through an integrated ecosystem linking feedstock security, advanced process engineering, process safety management (PSM) and environmental safeguards.

The mission unfolds across four phases. Phase A (0–24 months) stabilises feedstock supplies, initiates safety retrofits in legacy plants, and pilots digital twins for nitrocellulose processing. Phase B (2–6 years) commissions modular nitrocellulose and indigenous RDX lines with solvent recovery systems conforming to environmental norms. Phase C (6–12 years) establishes two to three Integrated Ammunition Nodes (IANs) with centralised quality assurance, achieving over 70 percent feedstock domestication. By 2047 (Phase D), the ecosystem matures into a globally competitive enterprise producing Insensitive Munitions (IM) and advanced composite propellants with circular waste practices. India's existing facilities—Ordnance Factory Itarsi, Cordite Factory Aruvankadu, High Explosives Factory Khadki, and Ordnance Factories at Bhandara, Chanda, and Varangaon—provide a strong institutional base requiring targeted modernisation. The private sector, led by Solar Industries, Premier Explosives, and GOCL/IDL, can accelerate capacity creation through public–private partnerships.

The proposed Anchor MIL + Private Consortium (AMPC) model ensures rapid capacity enhancement through risk-sharing arrangements. Munitions India Limited (MIL) provides land, infrastructure, and security, while private consortia install modular production units within secure Special Purpose Vehicles (SPVs). Centralised quality assurance, feedstock pooling, and emergency surge clauses ensure operational readiness. Governance rests with the National Authority for Ammunition and Industry (NAAI), supported by a Propellants and Energetics Safety Board (PESB) and a MIL–Private Coordination Cell (MPCC).

Key performance indicators include reducing single-source dependency below 10 percent within three years, achieving PSM compliance scores above 90 percent within eighteen months, and reducing production rejects by 30 percent through digital-twin optimisation within the first year. Shared Environmental Health and Safety (EHS) funds, community advisory panels, and monitoring dashboards institutionalise accountability around production zones. Implementation begins within ninety days with pilot AMPC projects at Itarsi and Aruvankadu, a national feedstock audit, rapid PSM gap assessment, and digital-twin pilot initiation. By 2047, India will operate a sovereign, digitally intelligent, export-compliant energetics ecosystem anchored in safety, environmental integrity and technological excellence.

Mission 9: Integrating MSMEs into the Ammunition Manufacturing Ecosystem

India's ammunition production base must evolve from a limited, state-centred model into a distributed industrial network driven by Micro, Small and Medium Enterprises (MSMEs). Presently, fewer than two hundred firms contribute meaningfully to ammunition manufacture, leaving critical sub-systems dependent on a few large suppliers. Integrating MSMEs can expand depth, flexibility, and surge potential while aligning the sector with *Atmanirbhar Bharat* and *Viksit Bharat 2047*. The aim is to achieve by 2047 a self-reliant, export-ready ecosystem in which certified MSMEs supply precision components, energetics sub-systems, and digital assemblies forming at least 70 percent of the value chain.

This integration requires three complementary reforms. First, the creation of *Ammunition MSME Clusters* in existing defence corridors, each anchored to a lead production unit and supported by shared testing and safety infrastructure. These clusters will localise component manufacturing, reduce logistics costs, and strengthen compliance. Second, a graded *Defence Quality Certification* regime must allow MSMEs to meet reliability standards through modular audits, digital inspection trails, and periodic validation of lot performance. Third, procurement rules must guarantee market access through micro-vendor sourcing mandates and long-term framework contracts that assure demand without maintaining unviable peacetime inventories. Technology and finance will enable this transition. A unified *Digital Vendor Grid* should link accredited MSMEs to design data, order flows, and predictive quality analytics, ensuring traceability and rapid fault isolation. Financial instruments, such as, modernisation grants, credit-guarantee schemes, and export incentives must bridge capital gaps and accelerate Industry 4.0 adoption. Structured mentorship from DRDO and DPSUs can raise technological readiness, while co-development agreements with private primes can channel innovation directly into production.

By 2030, at least five operational clusters and 250 accredited MSMEs should be embedded in the ammunition supply chain. By 2040, MSMEs should contribute half of component value across priority calibres, supported by real-time digital oversight. By 2047, India should field a fully distributed, innovation-driven network capable of surge production, export compliance, and near-complete indigenisation of ammunition sub-systems.

Mission 10: Procuring the System – A Gun Ammunition Strategy

India must move procurement beyond transactional, lowest-price bidding to a system-centric model where the weapon and its ammunition are procured, validated and sustained as an integrated capability. The critical shortcoming today is that separate tenders for guns and rounds sever the feedback loop that improves accuracy, safety and durability. It is important to note that chamber geometry, rifling, propellant profile, fuse timing and fire-control software are interdependent and must be treated as a single design ensemble. Mission 10 therefore mandates Government-Owned, Vendor-Neutral Interface Control Documents (ICDs) that fix boundary conditions, such as, dimensions, pressure/time envelopes, messaging protocols while allowing suppliers to innovate internally. Conformance to these open standards becomes the qualifying condition for competition, enabling interoperability, repeatable testing and through-life learning.

Demand stability will be created by an Assured Long-Term Ammunition Ordering Model (ALTOM): multi-year Family Framework Agreements (7–10 years) per ammunition family, Capacity Reservation Contracts that underwrite verified base capacity with take-or-pay floors and auditable surge options, and a rolling three-year Annual Ordering Plan that provides firm and indicative visibility. For selected system families, an ALTOM-PLUS System-House layer will place end-to-end responsibility with a prime contractor for platform-level outcomes, such as, barrel life, dispersion, fuse integration and sustainment while preserving contestability through a dual-path rule that reserves a defined share of annual volume for other ICD-conformant suppliers.

Quality assurance and test regimes will be overhauled to emphasise process integrity and data linkage rather than purely end-of-line inspection. Plants achieving capability benchmarks may self-certify routine parameters under Statistical Process Control, while independent and defence QA resources concentrate on critical safety attributes, such as, pressure performance, insensitive-munitions compliance and fuse functioning. Every production lot will carry a unique digital identifier and an electronic certificate of conformance, and lot genealogy from raw inputs to process parameters, proof trials and field returns will feed a transparent merit algorithm used for annual share allocation. Digital twins for both platform and ammunition, coupled through shot records (muzzle velocity, chamber pressure, fuse settings), will support predictive maintenance, optimal issue policy and faster qualification cycles. Financial mechanisms *vis-à-vis* capacity reservation fees, indexed pricing to commodities, surge premia and time-limited value-sharing on verified process improvements will make investments serviceable and reduce risk for lenders, while capped export windows with pre-emption safeguards will keep lines active without compromising domestic readiness.

Therefore, MSME inclusion is a compulsory design element: primes must embed minimum MSME value content, ensured 90-day payment cycles, and facilitate accredited cluster participation in precision machining, electronics sub-assemblies and energetics ancillaries. Sovereign anchors, such as, state facilities and shared proof ranges will provide critical infrastructure, line leases and government-furnished energetics, where strategic control is needed. Governance will rest with an Ammunition Manufacturing Cluster Council to maintain a National Capacity Registry, run quarterly surge drills and arbitrate merit reallocations, and an Integrated Ammunition Node Programme Office to steward ICDs, convene open-test days and manage digital traceability. Implemented in sequenced pilots (artillery and small-arms families; one System-House trial) within six months, and scaled across fuses, rockets and propellants over 18–36 months, the regime aims for two or more qualified sources per critical nature, OTIF and quality thresholds that materially reduce defects and proof turnaround, living lot genealogies linking factory parameters to field performance, and a domestic industry capable of delivering verified, exportable gun–ammunition systems. Mission 10 thus converts procurement into an instrument of capability: setting standards, assuring demand, rewarding performance and sustaining competition so that India buys outcome rather than price.

In all, these missions give India a single, integrated way of working that corresponds to the operating environment described across this book: a battlespace that is faster, more precise, and increasingly shaped by unmanned systems, and recent conflicts that have underscored surge consumption, attacks on depots, and the decisive role of reliability. Re-centring the user within requirements, design, testing, and acceptance addresses the problem of "munitions without missions" and shortens the path from field feedback to production change. Locating innovation alongside Army training establishments creates an end-to-end loop from laboratory to range to line, while the production mix shifts from legacy volume to munitions that are precise, programmable, upgradable, and safe by design. In this conception, quality assurance is not a back-end ritual but part of deterrence itself: transparent, continuous, and tied to performance in troop trials.

The foundations that support this shift are equally clear. Inputs and routes are treated as strategic assets through diversified sourcing, prudent reserves, substitution and recycling, and structured international partnerships that align materials, processes, markets, logistics, and finance. Defence corridors specialise so capacity grows with discipline—heavy energetics and machining concentrated where they are strongest, seekers, electronics, and additive manufacturing where those ecosystems exist. Factories operate as digital enterprises that see their own health, anticipate failures, and surge without disruption; procurement frameworks reward performance and timeliness rather than paperwork; and exports are pursued as durable security relationships that combine reliable supply with training and support.

Metrics for Success

Strategic visions and ambitious missions are only as effective as their ability to translate into measurable progress. Without metrics, policy goals risk remaining aspirational and disconnected from ground realities. In the context of ammunition manufacturing, where outcomes must be tangible, verifiable, and directly linked to operational readiness, the establishment of clear and quantifiable metrics is indispensable. Metrics not only provide a benchmark for assessing success but also create accountability among stakeholders, ensuring that the journey to *Viksit Bharat 2047* is guided by evidence-based evaluation rather than rhetoric.

Metrics, however, cannot be generic or superficial. They must be designed to capture the multi-dimensional nature of India's ammunition ecosystem: institutional participation, innovation output, supply chain resilience, technological modernisation, and export competitiveness. Each mission outlined in the preceding section must therefore be accompanied by a set of indicators that allow for periodic monitoring, mid-course corrections, and long-term assessments. These indicators must also be time-bound, progressively ambitious, and aligned with both national security requirements and global benchmarks.

Incubation and Innovation Hubs

Innovation outcomes are best measured not by inputs, such as, funding alone but by tangible results. By 2035, at least seven Ammunition Incubation Hubs should be fully functional, anchored to Army training establishments. Success should be evaluated through the number of patents filed, the percentage of prototypes transitioned into production, and the share of R&D projects involving tri-sectoral collaboration (Army–academia–industry). An additional metric could be the reduction in lead-time for the development and induction of new ammunition technologies.

Institutional Integration

The success of institutional integration should be measured by the degree of direct involvement of Army across the ammunition lifecycle. By 2027, a Central Coordinating Authority on Ammunition under the Vice Chief of Army Staff should be operational. This authority's effectiveness can be tracked through annual audits of Army participation in R&D committees, procurement boards, and export clearance processes. A key metric here would be 100 percent user representation in decision-making structures by 2030.

Supply Chain Resilience

Supply chain resilience requires metrics that capture both diversification and self-sufficiency. By 2035, India should indigenise at least 60 percent of critical raw materials, such as, antimony, toluene, and brass, while securing long-term import contracts for the remainder through diversified partnerships. By

2047, the target should be raised to 90 percent self-reliance. Secondary metrics include the number of strategic reserves maintained (measured in months of assured supply) and the diversification index of supplier countries.

Technological Modernisation and Smart Ammunition

The metric of success for technological modernisation is the proportion of smart and precision-guided munitions in India's overall ammunition output. By 2035, at least 50 percent of production should consist of smart ammunition, rising to 80 percent by 2047. Additional benchmarks include the percentage of factories adopting Industry 4.0 practices (e.g., digital twins, predictive maintenance), the proportion of R&D expenditure dedicated to next-generation technologies, and reductions in the time-to-market for indigenous ammunition designs.

Export Competitiveness and Defence Diplomacy

Export competitiveness must be measured both quantitatively and qualitatively. By 2035, India should achieve at least USD 5 billion in annual ammunition exports, with the figure rising to USD 12 billion by 2047. Beyond financial measures, metrics should capture export diversification, including the number of countries served, the repeat-customer ratio, and the incorporation of ammunition exports into broader defence cooperation agreements. These indicators will ensure that exports contribute not only to revenue but also to India's strategic influence.

Integrated Ammunition Nodes

The success of the IAN framework must be measured by its ability to compress design-to-deployment timelines, embed full digital traceability, and achieve supply chain sovereignty in critical inputs. By 2030, at least 70 percent of ammunition lots produced at Pune, Hyderabad, and Jabalpur should carry serialised digital identities linked to predictive shelf-life analytics, while the average cycle time from prototype approval to limited series production should be reduced by 40 percent from the 2025 baseline. By 2035, no less than 60 percent of energetics and metallurgical inputs should be sourced domestically, and at least three export-certified product lines should be validated under NATO or UN standards. Ultimately, by 2047, the IAN grid must ensure that all ammunition lots are digitally tracked end-to-end, that failure rates are reduced by 60 percent compared to legacy baselines and that India emerges as a credible global supplier of smart munitions with assured surge capacity.

Energetics Self-Sufficiency

India's sovereignty in ammunition manufacturing depends on control over propellants and high explosives. By 2030, single-source dependency for critical energetics feedstocks should fall below 10 percent, with Process Safety Management (PSM) compliance scores exceeding 90 percent within eighteen months of mission launch. Production rejects should be reduced by 30 percent through digital-twin deployment within the first year. By 2035, at least two to three Integrated Ammunition Nodes under the Anchor MIL + Private Consortium (AMPC) model should be operational, achieving over 70 percent domestic sourcing of energetics inputs. By 2047, insensitive munitions (IM) should comprise at least 60 percent of total explosives output, closed-loop solvent recovery systems should achieve 95 percent recycling rates, and India should establish itself as an export-compliant energetics supplier with at least two product families certified to NATO or equivalent international standards.

MSME Integration into Ammunition Manufacturing

The transformation from state-centric to distributed manufacturing requires measurable MSME participation. By 2030, at least 250 MSMEs should be accredited under the graded Defence Quality Certification regime, contributing 30 percent of the ammunition value chain, with five operational Ammunition MSME Clusters established. By 2035, the Digital Vendor Grid should onboard at least 200 certified MSMEs, with 40 percent accessing modernisation grants or credit-guarantee schemes and 15 percent engaged in co-development agreements. By 2047, MSMEs should contribute 70 percent of the value chain, with MSME-manufactured sub-systems featuring in at least 50 percent of India's ammunition exports. The ultimate measure is a fully distributed, innovation-driven network capable of surge production, real-time digital oversight, and near-complete indigenisation of ammunition sub-systems.

System-Centric Procurement and Integrated Gun-Ammunition Strategy

System-centric procurement replaces fragmented tenders with integrated capability outcomes. Sequenced pilots should begin within six months covering artillery and small-arms families. By 2030, Government-Owned Interface Control Documents (ICDs) should govern at least five ammunition families, with at least three Family Framework Agreements spanning 7–10 years covering 40 percent of procurement value. Digital twins for gun-ammunition systems should enable shot-level traceability, while plants achieving Statistical Process Control benchmarks gain self-certification authority. By 2035, 100 percent of production lots should carry unique digital identifiers with full genealogy traceability, reducing proof turnaround times by 40 percent and defect rates by 30 percent, with two or more qualified sources per critical nature. MSME value content should reach 25 percent by 2030 with payment cycles not exceeding 90 days. By 2047, three or more qualified sources per nature should be operational under a dual-path rule ensuring contestability, living lot genealogies should link all factory parameters to field performance, MSME payment cycles should be reduced to 60 days with 40 percent value content, and India should field verified, exportable gun-ammunition systems with surge capacity under the ALTOM-PLUS System-House model.

To convert indicators into decisions, measurement must be owned and reviewed at fixed intervals. The Central Coordinating Authority on Ammunition should publish a quarterly scorecard covering all mission metrics, with a red- amber- green threshold for each indicator and a short note on corrective actions. An annual review chaired by the Vice Chief of Army Staff should consolidate results, document lessons from troop trials and field performance, and approve target resets for the following year. Independent validation through DTIS facilities and accredited third-party labs should be used for quality and safety metrics to preserve credibility. A 2025 baseline should be established for each indicator using common methods and data sources: production and defect data from factories; UID/FEFO scans and lot-health records from depots; field reliability from troop trials; supplier and stockpile data from the supply chain registry; and export volumes from the defence trade database. With baselines, governance, and safeguards in place, the metrics now guide sequencing. Early institutional and supply-chain targets (authority stood up, hubs notified, stockpile days achieved, dual-sourcing enforced) unlock the deeper technological and industrial shifts (smart-munition share, digital-twin coverage, NAQI levels) that the Transformation Plan schedules through 2030, 2040, and 2047.

Missions-to-Metrics Matrix

The table below consolidates these indicators into a comprehensive framework:

Mission	*Key Metric*	*Target 2030-35*	*Target 2047*
Incubation & Innovation Hubs	No. of hubs operational; patents filed; prototypes inducted	7 hubs functional by 2035	Innovation-to-induction cycle reduced by 40%
Institutional Integration	Army representation in R&D, manufacturing, procurement, exports	Central Authority opera-tional by 2027; 100% user representation by 2030 Integrated Ammunition Management Cell under the Ministry of Defence by 2026	Annual integrated review system To include the Army, DPSUs, private manufacturers, DRDO and quality assurance organisations
Supply Chain Resilience	% of critical raw materials indigenised; stockpile size; supplier diversity	60% indigenisation; national reserves of key inputs	90% indigenisation; fully diversified imports
Technological Modernisation	% of smart munitions in production; Industry 4.0 adoption	50% of output as smart ammo; predictive maintenance in all factories	80% of output as smart ammo; universal digital twin adoption
Export Competitiveness	Export value; diversifica-tion; repeat customers	USD 5B annually; exports to 25+ countries	USD 12B annually; exports embedded in long-term defence diplomacy
Integrated Ammunition Nodes	Design-to-deployment cycle time; % of lots digitally traceable; % of critical inputs indigenised; no. of export-certified lines	40% reduction in design-to-deploy time; 70% digital traceability of lots; 60% domestic sourcing of critical inputs; 3 export-certified lines by 2035	100% digital traceability; dud rates reduced by 60%; 90% domestic sourcing.
Energetics Self-Sufficiency	Single-source dependency; PSM compliance; % energetics inputs indigenised; reject rate; AMPC nodes operational	<10% single-source dependency by 2030; >90% PSM compliance; 70% domestic sourcing; 30% reject reduction; 2-3 AMPC nodes by 2035	90% feedstock domestication; 60% IM output; 95% solvent recovery; 2+ NATO-certified product lines
MSME Integration	No. of accredited MSMEs; % value chain contribution; operational clusters; Digital Vendor Grid adoption	250 MSMEs by 2030; 30% value chain; 5 clusters; 200 on Digital Grid by 2035; 15% in co-development	70% value chain from MSMEs; MSME components in 50% exports; surge-capable distributed network
System-Centric Procurement	ICDs established; qualified sources per nature; % under framework agreements; digital traceability; MSME content	5 ICD families by 2030; 2+ sources per nature by 2035; 40% under ALTOM; 100% digital traceability; 25% MSME content; d”90-day payments	3+ sources per nature; 90% ALTOM adherence; living lot genealogies; 40% MSME content; 60-day payments; exportable systems

The framework of missions and metrics shows that India's ammunition transformation must go beyond broad aspirations. It requires clear and measurable goals that can be tracked over time. These indicators provide a way to monitor progress, identify weaknesses, and adjust strategies when needed. They also create accountability by offering a common benchmark against which the work of the Army, industry, policymakers, and research institutions can be assessed. The sequencing of these goals is critical. Some outcomes, such as, setting up a Central Coordinating Authority or establishing incubation hubs, need to be achieved early to create the foundation for later, more ambitious targets. Only with such early milestones in place can India move towards long-term achievements like producing the majority of its ammunition as smart munitions or reaching multi-billion-dollar export levels. In this sense, the metrics serve as progressive steps, ensuring that short-term reforms contribute meaningfully to the larger vision of 2047. By placing measurable outcomes at the centre of its strategy, India can build a phased transformation plan that connects vision with execution. The next step is to outline this roadmap in practical terms, identifying what must be done in the short, medium, and long term to ensure that the country's ammunition ecosystem is both resilient and future-ready.

Transformation Plan

The transformation of India's ammunition ecosystem cannot be achieved through isolated reforms or *ad hoc* adjustments. It requires a structured and sequenced plan that aligns missions and metrics with realistic timelines. Such a phased approach ensures that immediate priorities are met without losing sight of long-term objectives. The transformation plan for *Viksit Bharat 2047* can be broadly divided into three stages: short-term (2025–2030), medium-term (2030–2040), and long-term (2040–2047). Each stage builds upon the progress of the previous one, creating a cumulative pathway toward a resilient, technologically advanced, and globally competitive ammunition ecosystem.

Short-Term Phase (2025–2030)

The immediate priority for this phase is to lay the institutional and infrastructural foundations that will support later advancements. The establishment of a Central Coordinating Authority on Ammunition under the Vice Chief of Army Staff must be completed within this period. This body should consolidate oversight over research, manufacturing, procurement, and exports, thereby reducing the current fragmentation in the ecosystem. Simultaneously, Ammunition Incubation Hubs should be launched within key training establishments, such as, the School of Artillery, Army Air Defence, Armoured, Mechanised Infantry, Infantry Schools. These hubs will foster collaboration between the Army, academia, and private industry while generating a pipeline of indigenous innovations.

In parallel, the short-term plan must focus on strengthening supply chain security. This includes mapping vulnerabilities, initiating the creation of national stockpiles of critical raw materials, and securing initial partnerships with resource-rich countries. AMPC pilot projects should be launched at facilities, such as, Ordnance Factory Itarsi and Cordite Factory Aruvankadu within ninety days to reduce single-source dependency in propellants and explosives. Process Safety Management compliance audits across legacy plants must be completed within eighteen months, while digital-twin deployments demonstrate reject rate reductions within the first year. The early adoption of Industry 4.0 practices, such as, predictive maintenance and digital tracking in select factories, should also begin at this stage to demonstrate proof of concept.

MSME integration must commence during this period through the establishment of at least two Ammunition MSME Clusters within defence corridors, supported by the rollout of graded Defence Quality Certification protocols and the Digital Vendor Grid framework. Procurement reform should be initiated through sequenced pilots covering artillery and small-arms families within six months, developing Government-Owned Interface Control Documents (ICDs) for initial ammunition families and piloting the first Family Framework Agreement to provide industry with long-term demand visibility.

Medium-Term Phase (2030–2040)

The medium-term phase will focus on scaling up reforms and embedding technological modernisation across the ecosystem. By this time, all planned Ammunition Incubation Hubs should be fully operational and producing measurable outputs in the form of patents, prototypes, and inducted systems. Supply chain resilience should advance to a stage where at least 60 percent of critical raw materials are indigenised, with the remainder secured through diversified international agreements. The energetics ecosystem should mature significantly during this phase, with two to three Integrated Ammunition Nodes operational under the AMPC model by 2035, achieving over 70 percent domestic sourcing of propellants and explosives feedstock.

This period should also witness the wider adoption of smart ammunition in operational inventories. By 2035, at least half of all new ammunition production should consist of guided or precision-enabled systems. To support this, the integration of artificial intelligence, 3D printing, and nanotechnology into production processes must become standard practice. Defence corridors, already established in states, such as, Uttar Pradesh and Tamil Nadu, should evolve into robust industrial ecosystems by this phase, hosting both public and private sector actors and enabling cost-efficient, large-scale production. MSME participation should expand rapidly, with at least 250 accredited firms contributing 30 percent of the ammunition value chain by 2030, rising to 50 percent by 2040 through five operational clusters and comprehensive digital integration.

On the policy front, procurement practices should undergo a full-scale overhaul to move beyond legacy manuals and bureaucratic procedures. Transparent, quality-focused, and resilience-oriented procurement methodologies must replace cost-minimisation as the sole driver. System-centric procurement should become standard practice, with ICDs governing at least five ammunition families, three multi-year framework agreements covering 40 percent of procurement value, and digital traceability implemented for 100 percent of production lots by 2035, ensuring at least two qualified sources per critical ammunition nature. Export promotion efforts should also intensify, with India aiming for at least USD 5 billion in annual ammunition exports by 2035.

Long-Term Phase (2040–2047)

The final phase is where India must consolidate its position as a global leader in ammunition manufacturing and supply chain resilience. By this stage, the majority of the country's ammunition output should consist of smart munitions, with at least 80 percent of production falling into this category. Industry 4.0 tools, such as, digital twins, advanced robotics, and cyber-secure manufacturing systems should be universally deployed across production facilities.

In terms of supply chain resilience, India should aim to achieve near-complete self-sufficiency, with 90 percent of critical raw materials sourced domestically or through secure, long-term partnerships. The country should also develop recycling-based resource recovery systems for brass, steel, and other inputs, ensuring sustainability. The MSME network should become fully mature, contributing 70 percent of the ammunition value chain with components featured in at least 50 percent of exports, supported by real-time digital oversight and surge-production capabilities that enable rapid scaling during contingencies.

Procurement should deliver integrated system outcomes, with three or more qualified sources per critical nature maintained through dual-path rules, living lot genealogies linking all factory parameters to field performance, and verified exportable gun-ammunition systems operating under the System-House model with significant MSME value content and streamlined payment cycles. Exports should reach a scale of USD 12 billion annually, with ammunition sales integrated into broader defence and strategic cooperation frameworks, especially with countries in the Global South. By 2047, India's ammunition ecosystem should not only be self-reliant but also globally competitive, technologically advanced, and strategically aligned with the nation's role as a net security provider. The transformation plan thus envisions a gradual but decisive transition from dependence to leadership, ensuring that the lessons of past inefficiencies are replaced by a future defined by resilience, innovation, and strategic foresight.

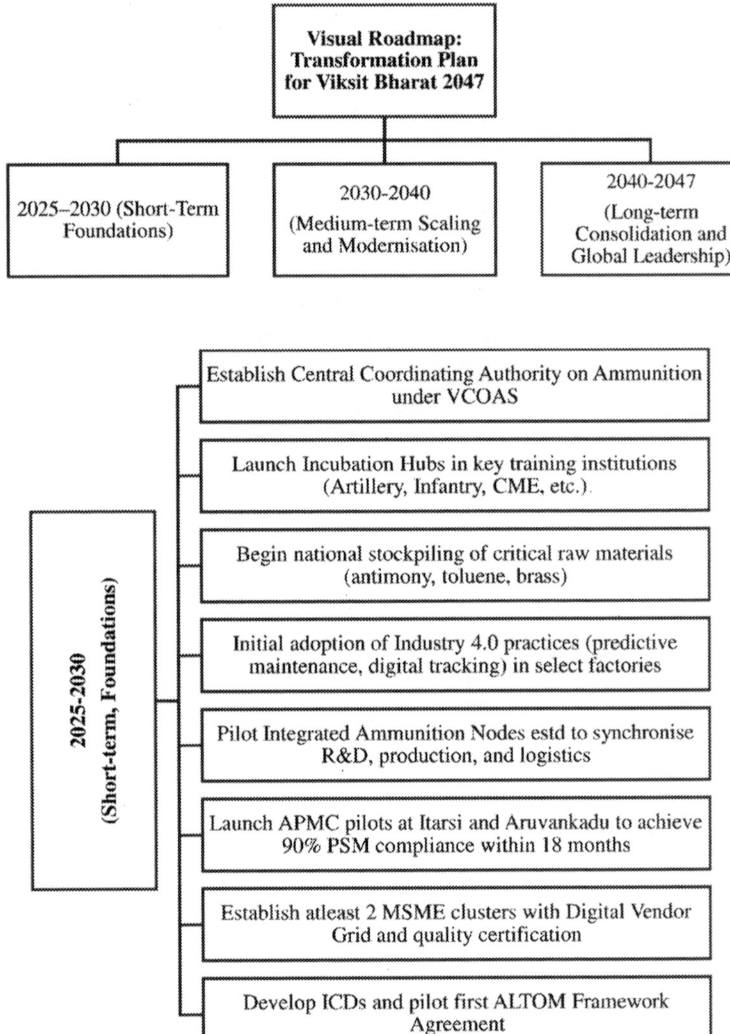
Visual Roadmap: Transformation Plan for Viksit Bharat 2047
2025–2030 (Short-Term Foundations)
2030-2040 (Medium-term Scaling and Modernisation)
2040-2047 (Long-term Consolidation and Global Leadership)
2025-2030 (Short-term, Foundations)
Establish Central Coordinating Authority on Ammunition under VCOAS
Launch Incubation Hubs in key training institutions (Artillery, Infantry, CME, etc.).
Begin national stockpiling of critical raw materials (antimony, toluene, brass)
Initial adoption of Industry 4.0 practices (predictive maintenance, digital tracking) in select factories
Pilot Integrated Ammunition Nodes estd to synchronise R&D, production, and logistics
Launch APMC pilots at Itarsi and Aruvankadu to achieve 90% PSM compliance within 18 months
Establish atleast 2 MSME clusters with Digital Vendor Grid and quality certification
Develop ICDs and pilot first ALTOM Framework Agreement

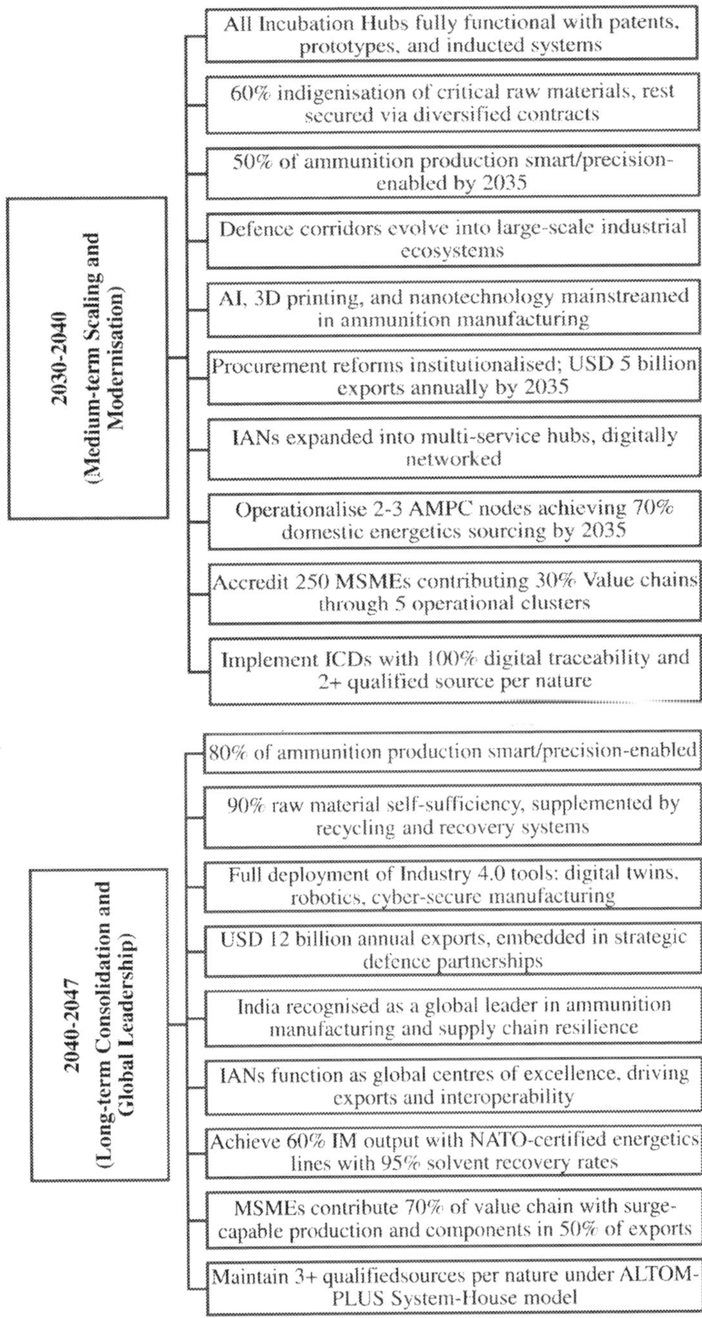

Compiled by the Author

Policy and Governance Enablers

Even the most carefully designed transformation plan will falter without a robust policy and governance framework to guide its execution. India's ammunition ecosystem has long suffered from overlapping jurisdictions, rigid procurement rules, and the absence of a single coordinating authority. The corporatisation of the Ordnance Factory Board into Munitions India Limited was a necessary step, but without deeper reforms in governance, the structural issues of inefficiency, duplication, and poor accountability will persist. Policy instruments and governance mechanisms must act as the backbone of the transformation for the vision of *Viksit Bharat 2047* to succeed.

The most urgent reform today is the creation of a Central Coordinating Authority that looks over Ammunition under the Vice Chief of Army Staff which would serve as a single point of convergence for all stakeholders *vis-à-vis* the Army, DRDO, private industry, DPSUs, and academia. Such a body could function as repository of requirements, research inputs and would eliminate the fragmentation of responsibilities. Continuous annual reviews would ensure that the production remains aligned with India's operational requirements, while also integrating lessons from field performance and failure analysis.

Beneath this apex body, specialised governance structures must address sector-specific challenges. A National Authority for Ammunition and Industry (NAAI) should oversee the entire ecosystem, supported by a Propellants and Energetics Safety Board (PESB) for process safety compliance, a MIL–Private Coordination Cell (MPCC) for public-private partnerships in energetics production, and an Ammunition Manufacturing Cluster Council to maintain capacity registries and manage performance-based allocation. An Integrated Ammunition Node Programme Office would steward Interface Control Documents (ICDs), manage digital traceability, and convene validation protocols. Procurement reform must shift from transactional bidding to system-centric outcomes through multi-year framework agreements, capacity reservation contracts with take-or-pay floors, and transparent merit algorithms linking performance to allocation. Mandatory MSME participation, for instance, 25 percent value content by 2030, rising to 40 percent by 2040 must be enforced through capped payment cycles (90 days, reducing to 60 days), long-term framework contracts, and financial instruments including modernisation grants and credit-guarantee schemes. Environmental accountability around energetics zones requires shared EHS funds, community advisory panels, and monitoring dashboards, while solvent recovery systems target 95 percent recycling rates by 2047. These layered mechanisms would replace fragmented coordination with institutionalised accountability across research, production, safety, and industrial participation.

In past decades, India's defence procurement system has prioritised cost-cutting ahead of long-term durability and quality. The Defence Acquisition Procedure (DAP) and other manuals and processes frequently make it harder for private companies to get involved and for new ideas to come forward. So, a new procurement framework should focus on aspects like transparency, reliability, and supply chain security instead of just cost. This means making RFP forms easier to understand, supporting 'Make in India' conditions that go beyond token indigenisation, and making sure contracts are signed more quickly. In order to avoid the system from becoming stagnant, it is recommended that guidelines for procurement be subjected to frequent reviews. Switching from the existing Qualitative Requirement based procurement to a Technology Based Procurement, suggested in the previous chapter, is an option that could be explored.

The state cannot achieve the necessary scale of innovation and modernisation alone. To speed up research and production, we need a formal tri-sectoral model that connects public institutions, private industry, and academia. This can be accomplished by connecting Ammunition Incubation Hubs with academic institutions like IITs, NITs, and defence universities, and by encouraging private companies to invest in technology development as well. Joint Army–industry research funds and other collaborative funding mechanisms could help new ideas come to light even more. This model would make sure that new discoveries in materials science, nanotechnology, or artificial intelligence are quickly used in making ammunition.

Policy support for ammunition exports should not just involve granting out licenses. The Ministry of Defence should set up a special export promotion agency to find markets, negotiate long-term supply contracts, and market India as a dependable supplier. Indian exports can be more appealing if they come with incentives like credit support, technology transfer packages, and training modules. Governance reforms should also give the Armed forces the power to check export contracts to make sure that sales to other countries don't hurt the country's operational readiness. Over time, India should include exports in its defence diplomacy strategy, turning ammunition from a product of manufacturing into a tool of statecraft.

Another significant development that needs to be implemented is a different policy framework for protecting important raw materials. This must involve a two-pronged strategy: creating national reserves of materials that are in high demand, like antimony and toluene, and also doing research to find local substitutes. Strategic partnerships with resource-rich regions, such as, Africa, Central Asia, and Latin America should be negotiated to guarantee long-term access. The Central Coordinating Authority should still be in charge of overseeing these reserves. This will make sure that strategic stockpiles are kept up and rotated in order to make sure they are of adequate quality.

Lastly, governance should also encompass participatory oversight mechanisms that integrate the Armed forces to the core of manufacturing processes. For the purpose of monitoring manufacturing batches, tracking failure analysis, and validating field performance, Army Liaison Officers should be integrated within factories. The quality assurance model must shift to a proactive model from a reactive model which involves continuous monitoring. With the user at the core of the oversight process, India can ensure that it produces abundant and reliable ammunition.

Conclusion

The India of today has entered a phase wherein questions of quality and resilience are just as important as questions of scale. It is not enough to produce more rounds or expand manufacturing plants, but the system must be able to withstand shocks, adapt to technological disruptions, and at the same time remain dependable in combat. The issue of ammunition is not only a matter of factory output rather the growing impact of drones and precision strike systems, and the fragility of global supply chains must be considered as it is directly linked to India's ambition of *Viksit Bharat 2047*.

One way to meet India's ambitions is to bring the Army into each stage of research and production which in turn would encourage innovation hubs link with training institutions. It is equally important to secure raw materials, embed modern technologies, and use exports as a tool of diplomacy. This measures have to planned carefully starting from immediate reforms to deeper technological modernisation, and finally create steady and cumulative change by moving towards global competitiveness. The need is that the governance structures remain firm and that institutions commit to accountability and cooperation. Once this is achieved, the ammunition sector as a whole can become the source of confidence for India's military and industry alike.

Most importantly, the long-term vision is beyond self-reliance as India aims to be recognised as a security provider which is able to secure its own national interests and at the same time support partners abroad by 2047. A reformed ammunition ecosystem built on smart technologies and resilient supply chains would embody this transformation. Rather than being linked with delays or quality lapses, the sector could come to represent reliability, innovation, and strategic confidence. Such progress would not only enhance India's defence preparedness but also turn ammunition into a tool of diplomacy, fostering collaborations and joint ventures that draw partners closer to India. Change, however, will be gradual. Reforms in the 2020s can lay the groundwork; the 2030s may bring visible gains and credibility; and by the 2040s, sustainability, recycling, and advanced manufacturing could shape India's global profile. In this sense, *Viksit Bharat 2047* should be seen less as a slogan and more as a phased journey, with each decade adding resilience and technological depth to the foundation.

The course of ammunition production is deeply linked to India's national rise. Although economic growth and demographic weight provide a base, but real power comes from turning industrial and technological advances into strategic capability. Ammunition manufacturing illustrates this connection clearly and if managed effectively, it can transform vulnerabilities into strengths and show that self-reliance can still welcome international partnerships. Such a transition will only succeed if it is pursued with consistency as its impact reshape and affect both how India is perceived and how it performs. By 2047, the sector may no longer be seen as dependent or deficient but as a foundation of national security and a source of regional stability. In this way, the future of ammunition production is not only industrial but also strategic and symbolic, forming an essential part of the vision of *Viksit Bharat 2047*.

NOTES

1 Department of Peace Operations, Office for Disarmament Affairs, United Nations (2021), Effective Weapons and Ammunition Management in a Changing Disarmament, Demobilisation and Reintegration Context: A handbook of United Nations DDR Practitioners (Second edition), United Nations: New York.

2 Watling, J. (2024), "The Peril of Ukraine's Ammo Shortage", *TIME*, 19 February 2024. URL: https://time.com/6694885/ukraine-russia-ammunition/

3 Eisenkot, G. & Siboni, G. (2019), "Guidelines for Israel's National Security Strategy", The Washington Institute for Near East Policy, October 2019, URL: https://www.washingtoninstitute.org/media/4613

4 Santamaria, P., Yoo, S. & Mittal, V. (2023), "The Impact of Supply Chain Issues on Military Training and Readiness", Military Review, July-August 2023, pp 85-94. URL: https://www.armyupress.army.mil/Journals/Military-Review/English-Edition-Archives/July-August-2023/Supply-Chain-Issues/

5 Carapic, J., Deschambault, E.J., Holton, P. & King, B., (2018), "Life-Cycle Management of Ammunition: safety, security, and Sustainability of Conventional Weapons Ammunition Stockpiles" *The Journal of Conventional Weapons Destruction*, Issue: 22.2, pp: 5-14, August 2018. URL::https://issuu.com/cisr-journal/docs/22-2/s/99781

6 United Nations (n.d.), "Poorly managed ammunition – a key driver of conflict and crime" Disarmament in Review, United Nations Office for Disarmament Affairs, URL: https://disarmament.unoda.org/convarms/ammunition/more-on-ammunition/

7 Department of Peace Operation, Department of Operational Support (2020), "United Nations Manual on Ammunition management", United Nations Secretariat, First Edition, New York, URL: https://resourcehub01.blob.core.windows.net/training-files/Training%20Materials/002%20Policies/002-023%202020%20Manual%20on%20Ammunition%20 Management%20pdf.pdf

8 Pawelczyk, M. (2018), "Contemporary Challenges in Military Logistics Support", *Security and Defence Quarterly,* 20(3), pp: 85-98, March 2018, URL: https://securityanddefence.pl/Contemporary-challenges-in-military-logistics-support,103332,0,2.html

9 Rajagopalan R.P., & Patil, S. (2024), "Future Warfare and Critical Technologies: Evolving Tactics and Strategies", *Global Policy - Observer Research Foundation*, Wiley Publishing, 12 February 2024, URL: https://www.orfonline.org/research/future-warfare-and-critical-technologies-evolving-tactics-and-strategies

10 'Self-Reliance vital to protect nation's sovereignty: Rajnath Singh' (6 May 2022), *The Hindu*, URL: https://www.thehindu.com/news/national/self-reliance-vital-to-protect-nations-sovereignty-rajnath-singh/article65385058.ece

11 Ministry of Defence, Government of India, (n.d.), "Technology Needs to Achieve Joint Warfighting Capability," URL: https://mod.gov.in/dod/sites/default/files/kelkar.pdf

12 Hastings, M. (2004), "ARMAGEDDON: The Battle of Germany 1944-1945" Alfred A. Knopf Book, New York.

13 Rabinovich, A. (2004), "The Yom Kippur War: The Epic Encounter that Transformed the Middle East", Schocken Books, New York (2004).

14 Milliken, T. & Compton, J. (n.d.), "Ensuring Effective Stockpile Management: A Guidance Document" CITES, [Online: Web] Accessed 18 April 2024. URL: https://cites.org/sites/default/files/eng/prog/elephant/Stock_management_guidance.pdf

15 United Nations (n.d.), "Poorly managed ammunition – a key driver of conflict and crime" Disarmament in Review, United Nations Office for Disarmament Affairs, URL: https://disarmament.unoda.org/convarms/ammunition/more-on-ammunition/

16 United Nations (2023), "Continued Military Assistance to Ukraine, Weapons, Ammunition Transfers to Russian Federation Risk Conflict's Escalation, Senior Official Warns Security Council", SC/15406, 12 September 2023, *Press Release*, URL: https://press.un.org/en/2023/sc15406.doc.htm

17 Watling, J. (2024), "The Peril of Ukraine's Ammo Shortage", *TIME*, 19 February 2024. URL: https://time.com/6694885/ukraine-russia-ammunition/

18 Shaikh, S. & Rumbaugh, W. (2020), "The Air and Missile War in Nagorno-Karabakh: Lessons for the future of Strike and Defense", Centre for Strategic & International Studies, csis.org, URL: https://www.csis.org/analysis/air-and-missile-war-nagorno-karabakh-lessons-future-strike-and-defense

19 Delaporte, M. (2023), "Nato Military Stockpiles Policy: Reversing the Just in Time Logic" EUROSATORY, 25 April 2023, URL: https://www.eurosatory.com/en/nato-military-stockpiles-policy reversing-the-just-in-time-logic/

20 Chin, W. (2019), "Technology, War and the State: Past, present and Future" *International Affairs,* Vol. 95, Issue: 4, pp 765-783, 1 July 2019, URL: https://academic.oup.com/ia/article/95/4/765/5513164

21 Department of Defense, United States of America, (2013), "Technology and Innovation Enablers for Superiority in 2030" Defense Science Board Report, October 2013, URL: https://defenseinnovationmarketplace.dtic.mil/wp-content/uploads/2018/04/DSB_Technology InnovationEnablersSuperiority2030.pdf

22 Cohen, R.S. et. al., (2020), "The Future of Warfare in 2030: Project Overview and Conclusions", RAND Corporation, Santa Monica, Calif. URL: https://www.rand.org/content/dam/rand/pubs/research_reports/RR2800/RR2849z1/RAND_RR2849z1.pdf

23 "Keeping Soldiers Safe from Drones – Programmable ammunition, from Nammo, could protect soldiers against drone attacks", Defence Procurement International, Trident Publications Limited, 13 September 2017, [Online: Web] Accessed on 15 April 2024. URL: https://www.defenceprocurementinternational.com/news/land/nammo-programmable-ammunition

24 "Ammo and Bullet, providers of Quality Environmental Friendly Ammunition", *ammoandbullet.com,* [Online: Web] Accessed on 15 April 2024. URL: https://www.ammoand bullet.com/environmental-friendly-ammunition/

25 Wittenberg, A. (2015), "Army's eco-friendly quest breeds more deadly bullet", Green Wire, *eenews.net*, 15 June 2015, [Online: Web] Accessed on 16 April 2024. URL: https://www.eenews.net/articles/armys-eco-friendly-quest-breeds-more-deadly-bullet/

26 Singh, N.B. (2021), "Self-Reliance in General Munitions and Energetics: Need for a Vision", *Indian Defence Review*, Vol. 36.1, Jan-March 2021, 25 March 2021, URL: https://www.indian defencereview.com/news/self-reliance-in-general-munitions-and-energetics-need-for-a-vision/

27 Ministry of Defence, Government of India, (2022), "Advanced ammunition is the reality of new age warfare; Need to create an innovative and self-reliant ammunition base for National Security: Raksha Mantri Shri Rajnath Singh at Ammo India", *Press Information Bureau,* 27 July 2022. URL: https://www.mod.gov.in/sites/default/files/pre1_4.pdf

28 "Building Resilient Supply Chains, Revitalising American Manufacturing, and Fostering Broad-based Growth – 100-Day Reviews under Executive Order 14017" *The White House*, Report, June 2021. URL: https://www.whitehouse.gov/wp-content/uploads/2021/06/100-day-supply-chain-review-report.pdf

29 Malo, E.G. (2023), "Estonia eyes kick-starting a domestic ammunition industry" Defence News, *defensenews.com*, [Online: Web] Accessed on 16 April 2024. URL: https://www.defensenews.com/global/europe/2023/12/12/estonia-eyes-kickstarting-a-domestic-ammunition-industry/

30 Ministry of Defence, Government of India, (2022), "Atmanirbhar Bharat Initiative in Defence Production", *Press Information Bureau*, 1 April 2022, URL: https://pib.gov.in/Pressreleaseshare.aspx?PRID=1812297

31 The Military Balance (2025). "Defence Spending and Procurement Trends". *International Institute of Strategic Studies.* URL: https://www.iiss.org/publications/the-military-balance/2025/defence-spending-and-procurement-trends/

32 Ekstrom, T. (2025). Supply Chain Resilience – An Empirical Exploration of Barriers and Enablers in Military Settings. *Scandinavian Journal of Military Studies.* Vol 8 (1). URL: https://sjms.nu/articles/10.31374/sjms.350?

33 Cancian, M. F. (2023). Cluster Munitions: What Are They, and Why Is the United States Sending Them to Ukraine? *Center for Strategic and International Studies.* URL: https://www.csis.org/analysis/cluster-munitions-what-are-they-and-why-united-states-sending-them-ukraine?

34 Unhelkar, B. et al (2022). Enhancing supply chain performance using RFID technology and decision support systems in the industry 4.0–A systematic literature review. *International Journal of Information Management Data Insights.* Vol 2 (2). URL: https://www.sciencedirect.com/science/article/pii/S2667096822000271?

35 "Ukraine is being outmanned and outgunned by relentless Russian forces" *Deccan Herald*, 21 February 2024, URL: https://www.deccanherald.com/world/ukraine-is-being-outmanned-and-outgunned-by-relentless-russian-forces-2903716

36 Watling, J. (2024), "western Support Critical to Ukraine's Fight", Wilson Centre, Insights and Analysis, *wilsoncenter.org*, 20 February 2024, [Online: Web] Accessed on 17 April 2024. URL: https://www.wilsoncenter.org/article/western-support-critical-ukraines-fight

37 "Ukraine ramps up spending on homemade weapons to help repel Russia", *The Economic Times*, 26 March 2024, URL: https://economictimes.indiatimes.com/news/defence/ukraine-ramps-up-spending-on-homemade-weapons-to-help-repel-russia/articleshow/108777237.cms?from=mdr

38 Ministry of Defence, Government of Israel (n.d.), "Military Research and Development", *english.mod.gov.il,* [Online: Web] Accessed on 17 April 2024, URL: https://english.mod.gov.il/About/Innovative_Strength/Pages/Military_Research_and_Development.aspx

39 Bommakanti, K. (2023), "The Strategic and Military-Technological significance of Israel", Raisina Debates, Observer research Foundation, *orfonline.org*, 22 December 2023, URL: https://www.orfonline.org/expert-speak/the-strategic-and-military-technological-significance-of-israel

40 "Iron Sting: Israeli army unleashes game-changing weapon against Hamas", *Times of India*,

23 October 2023, URL: https://timesofindia.indiatimes.com/world/middle-east/israel-hamas-war-iron-sting-israeli-army-unleashes-game-changing-weapon-against-hamas/articleshow/104639617.cms

41 "NATO's response to Russia's invasion of Ukraine", North Atlantic Treaty Organisation, *nato.int*, [Online: Web] Accessed on 17 April 2024, URL: https://www.nato.int/cps/en/natohq/topics_192648.htm

42 Bommakanti, K. (2023), "The Strategic and Military-Technological significance of Israel", Raisina Debates, Observer research Foundation, *orfonline.org*, 22 December 2023, URL: https://www.orfonline.org/expert-speak/the-strategic-and-military-technological-significance-of-israel

43 National Research Council (1992), "Advanced Technologies of Importance to the Army", in *STAR 21: Strategic Technologies for the Army of the Twenty-First Century*, pp192-203, The National Academic Press, Washington DC, URL: https://nap.nationalacademies.org/read/1888/chapter/6

44 Sonne, C., Lam, S.S. & Kanstrup, N. (2023), "The environmental threats from lead ammunition", *Eco-Environment & Health,* March; 2(1): 16-17. 2023, URL: https://www.ncbi.nlm.nih.gov/pmc/articles/PMC10702884/

45 Lawrence, J.L., Stemberger, H.L.J., Zolderdo, A.J., Struthers, D.P. & Cooke, S.J. (2015), "The effects of modern war and military activities on biodiversity and the environment", *Environmental Reviews*, Canadian Science Publishing, 17 September 2015, URL: https://cdnsciencepub.com/doi/full/10.1139/er-2015-0039

46 Salero-Garthwaite, A. (2023), "Precision Weapons and Preventing Collateral Damage", *army-technology.com,* 5 May 2023, [Online: Web] Accessed on 18 April 2024, URL: https://www.army-technology.com/features/precision-weapons-and-preventing-collateral-damage/

47 Schaik, L.V. et.al (2022), "The World Climate and Security Report 2022: Decarbonised Defence: The need for Clean Military Power in the age of Climate Change", Centre for Climate and Security, Council on strategic Risks, IMCCS, June 2022, URL: https://imccs.org/wp-content/uploads/2022/06/Decarbonized-Defense-World-Climate-and-Security-Report-2022-Vol.-I.pdf

48 https://usiofindia.org/pdf/Drones%20and%20Violent.pdf

49 https://ftp.idu.ac.id/wp-content/uploads/ebook/tdg/MILITARY%20PLATFORM%20DESIGN/Unmanned%20Aircraft%20Systems.pdf

50 Office of Historian (n.d.). U-2 Overflights and the Capture of Francis Gary Powers, 1960. URL: https://history.state.gov/milestones/1953-1960/u2-incident

51 Frantzman, S. J. (2019). How Israel Became a Leader in Drone Technology. *Middle East Forum.* URL: https://www.meforum.org/how-israel-became-a-leader-in-drone-technology

52 US Air Force (n.d.) MQ-1B Predator. URL: https://www.af.mil/About-Us/Fact-Sheets/Display/Article/104469/mq-1b-predator/

53 Frantzman, S. J. (2019). How Israel Became a Leader in Drone Technology. *Middle East Forum.* URL: https://www.meforum.org/how-israel-became-a-leader-in-drone-technology

54 Darbey, A. K. (2024). China's Increasing Global Drone Footprint. *MP-IDSA.* URL: https://www.idsa.in/publisher/comments/chinas-increasing-global-drone-footprint-2

55 Sher, A. (2025). Turkish Drones Disrupting Battlefields: A Case Study of Nagorno-Karabakh Conflict. *Wah Academia Journal of Social Sciences.* URL: https://wahacademia.com/index.php/Journal/article/download/227/186

56 Zampronha, D.& Albuquerque, A. (2024). *Scientific Research.* URL: https://www.scirp.org/journal/paperinformation?paperid=131823

57 Bondar, K. (2024). Understanding the Military AI Ecosystem of Ukraine. *Centre for Strategic and International Studies.* URL: https://www.csis.org/analysis/understanding-military-ai-ecosystem-ukraine?

58 Gerstein, D. M. & Leidy, E. N. (2024). Emerging Technology and Risk Analysis – Unmanned Aerial Systems Intelligent Swarm Technology. *Homeland Security Operational Analysis Centre.* RAND Corporation. URL: https://www.rand.org/content/dam/rand/pubs/research_reports/RRA2300/RRA2380-1/RAND_RRA2380-1.pdf

59 Miskelley, A. (2025). Ukraine War highlight New Role for Loitering Munition. *Defence and Security Monitor.* Forecast International. URL: https://dsm.forecastinternational.com/2025/09/05/ukraine-war-highlights-new-role-for-loitering-munitions

60 Hollenbeck, N. A. (2025). Why the Army Needs Units Driving Drone Development and How to Do It. *Military Review.* Army University Press. URL: https://www.armyupress.army.mil/Journals/Military-Review/Online-Exclusive/2025-OLE/Drone-Development/

61 Pusztaszeri, A. & Harding, E. (2025). Technological Evolution on the Battlefield. *Center for Strategic and International Studies.* URL: https://www.csis.org/analysis/chapter-9-technological-evolution-battlefield?

62 Singh, D., et al (2021). *Reforming India's defence manufacturing sector: The post-OFB restructuring era.* International Journal of Defence Policy, 7(3), 54-70.

63 Kumar, N., et al, 2020). *Smart ammunition: Technological evolution and future warfare applications.* International Journal of Defence Technology, 28(2), 149-165.

64 Sharma, P., Tripathi, R., & Gupta, A. (2022). *GPS-guided ammunition: Technological innovations and military applications.* Defence and Security Review, 27(5), 98-115.

65 Patel, V., Sharma, L., & Iyer, R. (2023). Artificial intelligence in modern warfare: The rise of smart ammunition. *Defence Innovation Quarterly, 7(3),* 35-58. https://doi.org/10.xxxxx

66 Verma, R., Krishna, P., & Sharma, L. (2019). Geopolitical tensions and military preparedness: The necessity of an advanced defence sector. *International Journal of Security Studies, 8(2),* 120-145. https://doi.org/10.xxxxx

67 Rao, S., Sharma, K., & Verma, R. (2021). Defence industrialization and national security: A case study of India's military modernization. *International Journal of Defence Studies, 14(1),* 90-110.

68 Gupta, M., Yadav, S., & Kumar, D. (2020). *Integration of smart munitions with network-centric warfare: Challenges and prospects.* Military Technology Review, 33(4), 75-90.

69 Nair, K., Rao, L., & Bose, A. (2021). *The role of precision munitions in contemporary military strategy.* Journal of Security and Defence Studies, 14(2), 65-88.

70 Krishna, B., Deshmukh, A., & Raghavan, S. (2020). *AI-driven precision targeting in next-generation smart munitions.* Journal of Defence Engineering, 19(5), 45-60.

71 Mehta, P., Nair, J., & Saxena, R. (2022). *Urban warfare and precision-guided munitions: Tactical effectiveness and ethical considerations.* Journal of Modern Warfare Studies, 41(6), 200-225.

72 Bose, R., Sharma, V., & Iyer, P. (2019). *Advancements in guided munition technology: A comparative study.* Defence Science Journal, 49(3), 215-230.

73 Tripathi, A., Reddy, S., & Chaturvedi, P. (2023). *The strategic advantage of precision-guided munitions in modern warfare.* International Defence Studies, 12(2), 150-170.

74 Mishra, H., Raghunathan, K., & Kumar, V. (2021). *Adaptability of smart ammunition in diverse combat environments: A review of technological advancements.* Defence Engineering Journal, 23(3), 115-135.

75 Singh, D., et al (2021). *Reforming India's defence manufacturing sector: The post-OFB*

restructuring era. International Journal of Defence Policy, 7(3), 54-70.

76 Kumar, N., et al, 2020). *Smart ammunition: Technological evolution and future warfare applications.* International Journal of Defence Technology, 28(2), 149-165.

77 Patel, V., Sharma, L., & Iyer, R. (2023). Artificial intelligence in modern warfare: The rise of smart ammunition. *Defence Innovation Quarterly, 7(3)*, 35-58.

78 Verma, R., Krishna, P., & Sharma, L. (2019). Geopolitical tensions and military preparedness: The necessity of an advanced defence sector. *International Journal of Security Studies, 8(2)*, 120-145.

79 Rao, S., Sharma, K., & Verma, R. (2021). Defence industrialization and national security: A case study of India's military modernization. *International Journal of Defence Studies, 14(1)*, 90-110.

80 Gupta, M., Yadav, S., & Kumar, D. (2020). *Integration of smart munitions with network-centric warfare: Challenges and prospects.* Military Technology Review, 33(4), 75-90.

81 Reddy, B., Sharma, P., & Kapoor, M. (2021). Ammunition manufacturing in India: An assessment of current capabilities and future trends. *Strategic Defence Analysis, 8*(4), 34-67.

82 Mehta, B., Krishna, J., & Bose, T. (2022). Public-private partnerships in India's defence sector: Evaluating their impact on self-reliance. *Journal of Defence Policy, 18(2)*, 75-98.

83 Bose, R., Sharma, V., & Iyer, P. (2019). *Advancements in guided munition technology: A comparative study.* Defence Science Journal, 49(3), 215-230.

84 Tripathi, A., Reddy, S., & Chaturvedi, P. (2023). *The strategic advantage of precision-guided munitions in modern warfare.* International Defence Studies, 12(2), 150-170.

85 Mishra, H., Raghunathan, K., & Kumar, V. (2021). *Adaptability of smart ammunition in diverse combat environments: A review of technological advancements.* Defence Engineering Journal, 23(3), 115-135.

86 Krishna, B., Deshmukh, A., & Raghavan, S. (2020). *AI-driven precision targeting in next-generation smart munitions.* Journal of Defence Engineering, 19(5), 45-60.

87 Chopra, A., Verma, K., & Pillai, R. (2022). *Cost-benefit analysis of precision-guided munitions in modern combat.* Journal of Strategic Studies, 55(2), 112-130.

88 Malik, T., Reddy, V., & Patel, S. (2023). *Hypersonic smart missiles and AI-guided ammunition: A futuristic approach.* Aerospace and Defence Journal, 18(1), 90-110.

89 Singh, R., Mishra, H., & Saxena, N. (2020). *Technological advancements in smart ammunition: A systematic review.* Defence Science and Technology Review, 14(3), 55-74.

90 Sharma, D., Varma, A., & Sen, P. (2018). *Limitations of conventional ammunition and the need for precision-guided munitions.* Journal of Ballistics Research, 6(1), 30-48.

91 Kumar, R., Singh, P., & Mehta, K. (2019). *Collateral damage and conventional munitions: A critical review of battlefield challenges.* Strategic Defence Review, 9(3), 45-61.

92 Verma, A., Patel, K., & Desai, S. (2021). Analysing India's smart ammunition landscape: Market trends and R&D perspectives. *Journal of Defence Studies, 13*(4), 78-102.

93 Choudhary, P., Sharma, V., & Yadav, M. (2020). *Precision-guided munitions: An emerging trend in battlefield technology.* Journal of Defence Studies, 10(2), 54-72.

94 Rao, V., Nayak, P., & Shukla, R. (2019). *Electro-optical and infrared guidance in modern smart weapons.* Journal of Optical Engineering, 14(2), 201-218.

95 Patil, M., Rao, L., & Desai, V. (2021). *GPS and inertial navigation in smart projectiles: A technological overview.* International Journal of Military Science, 12(5), 67-82.

96 Mehta, B., Krishna, J., & Bose, T. (2022). Public-private partnerships in India's defence sector: Evaluating their impact on self-reliance. *Journal of Defence Policy, 18(2)*, 75-98.

97 Deshmukh, H., Iyer, S., & Sinha, A. (2023). *Autonomous and networked warfare: The next-*

generation smart ammunition paradigm. International Journal of Defence Research, 15(1), 33-47.

98 Brown, T., Lewis, D., & Foster, P. (2017). *The evolution of laser-guided munitions in modern warfare.* Military Technology Review, 32(4), 88-102.

99 Wilson, B., Carter, J., & Roberts, L. (2018). *GPS-guided munitions and the transformation of battlefield engagement.* International Military Review, 11(2), 102-118.

100 Raj, A., Patel, S., & Kapoor, T. (2023). *AI-driven munitions and their impact on modern military operations.* Defence & Technology Innovations, 25(3), 93-110.

101 Singh, A., & Patel, R. (2020). *Laser guidance technologies for smart artillery shells: Performance evaluation and challenges.* Journal of Ballistic Science, 19(3), 97-115.

102 Brown, P., Miller, S., & Jackson, K.(2021). *Artificial intelligence integration in modern smart munitions: Challenges and prospects.* Military Science Review, 29(4), 176-194.

103 Gupta, R., Singh, V., & Kumar, P. (2019). *Machine learning-driven guidance systems for next-gen smart weapons.* Journal of AI and Warfare, 27(1), 145-161.

104 Sharma, P., Gupta, R., & Singh, M. (2021). The future of smart ammunition in India: Technological and strategic implications. *Defence Technology Review, 15*(1), 67-93.

105 Chen, D., Liu, F., & Zhao, X. (2018). *Network-centric warfare and its impact on smart ammunition effectiveness.* International Journal of Military Technology, 32(1), 67-82.

106 Hernandez, O., Lee, J., & Thompson, B. (2019). *Miniaturized electronics and their role in smart ammunition technology.* Sensors and Defence Research, 14(2), 73-90.

107 Zhang, H., Lin, W., & Chen, T. (2022). *Multi-sensor fusion for precision-guided munitions: Innovations and challenges.* Defence Electronics Review, 28(2), 134-152.

108 Mehta, S., Roy, A., & Krishnan, L. (2020). *Advanced composite materials for smart ammunition applications.* International Materials Review, 22(4), 189-210.

109 Garcia, R., & Wilson, E. (2017). *Self-healing materials and their applications in military-grade ammunition.* Materials Science and Defence Innovations, 12(3), 89-105.

110 Foster, M., & Grant, J. (2021). *High-energy density power sources for advanced guided weapons.* Defence Science and Technology Journal, 16(4), 201-218.

111 Chang, Y., Smith, L., & Cohen, B. (2019). *Next-generation power systems for precision-guided munitions.* Energy and Defence Research, 18(2), 55-73.

112 Kumar, R., & Das, A. (2024). *Hypersonic smart munitions: Future trends and strategic implications.* Advanced Defence Research, 33(1), 301-319.

113 Singh, R., Banerjee, P., & Kulkarni, D. (2023). *Smart ammunition and future warfare: Strategic applications for the Indian Army.* Journal of Defence Research, 41(2), 67-85.

114 Sharma, P., Tripathi, R., & Gupta, A. (2022). *GPS-guided ammunition: Technological innovations and military applications.* Defence and Security Review, 27(5), 98-115.

115 Ramesh, K., Iyer, S., & Verma, M. (2021). *The technological advancements in precision-guided munitions: A comparative analysis of global smart ammunition development.* Defence Technology Journal, 14(4), 112-130.

116 Nair, K., Sharma, P., & Bhaskar, L. (2023). The role of private sector investment in defence R&D: An Indian perspective. *Journal of Defence Economics, 10*(1), 112-136.

117 Iyer, S., Ramesh, T., & Krishnan, D. (2022). *Smart munitions and the shift towards precision warfare: Implications for India's strategic doctrine.* Strategic Affairs Review, 21(4), 95-113.

118 Mehta, K., Nair, R., & Patel, S. (2021). *Deterrence through precision: The role of smart ammunition in India's strategic posture.* Indian Defence Review, 17(2), 56-74.

119 Kulkarni, B., Sharma, A., & Mehta, K. (2022). *Smart ammunition in the age of network-centric warfare: Implications for India's border security operations.* Security Studies Journal,

28(5), 210-228.

120 Das, P., Verma, R., & Iyer, S. (2023). *Logistical efficiency and cost-effectiveness of smart ammunition in challenging warfare environments.* Defence Logistics Journal, 19(2), 120-134.

121 Banerjee, S., Gupta, A., & Nair, R. (2022). *Indigenous defence production and its impact on strategic autonomy: The case of smart ammunition in India.* Defence Studies, 24(1), 45-61.

122 Mukherjee, A., Rao, D., & Sharma, R. (2022). *Defence innovation and indigenous smart ammunition development in India: Policy perspectives.* Military Technology & Strategy, **32**(1), 89-104.

123 Chaudhary, V., Patel, M., & Joshi, R. (2023). *The evolution of modern warfare: Smart ammunition as a force multiplier for the Indian Army.* Journal of Military Innovation, **35**(3), 78-96.

124 Brown, T., Williams, J., & Carter, M. (2019). *Precision-guided munitions and the future of warfare.* Oxford University Press.

125 Ivanov, D., Petrov, A., & Sokolov, V. (2021). *Russian advancements in smart ammunition technology.* Moscow Defence Studies, 8(1), 23-39.

126 Volkov, D., & Petrov, A. (2022). *Russia's Military Modernization: Trends in R&D Investments.* Russian Military Affairs, 28(4), 112-129. Retrieved from https://www.russianmilitaryaffairs.com/trends-in-rd

127 Dupont, C., Lemoine, P., & Morel, A. (2022). *Advancements in European precision-guided munitions.* Defence and Security Review, 12(3), 55-71.

128 Schmidt, H., & Weber, A. (2025). *Regulatory Frameworks Facilitating Defence Innovations in Europe.* European Defence Review, 12(3), 134-152. Retrieved from https://www.edr.org/regulatory-frameworks

129 Davies, P., Thompson, B., & Edwards, R. (2023). *AI-driven naval smart ammunition: The SmartSea 500 project.* European Defence Journal, 28(4), 34-50.

130 Levy, R., Cohen, D., & Feldman, Y. (2021). *Smart ammunition development in Israel: A case study of Spike missiles.* Middle East Defence Review, 9(2), 65-81

131 Thompson, J., Miller, B., & Roberts, C. (2024). *Future trends in precision-guided munitions.* Journal of Military Technology, 19(1), 100-120.

132 Singh, P., Kumar, T., & Mehta, R. (2021). The role of defence R&D in strengthening national security. *Defence Science and Technology Journal, 20(2)*, 210-230.

133 Gupta, R., Sharma, L., & Kumar, A. (2022). *Reforming India's defence production: The impact of Ordnance Factory restructuring.* Indian Journal of Military Affairs, 6(3), 89-106.

134 Rao, S., Gupta, R., & Sharma, P. (2023). *India's journey towards smart ammunition self-reliance.* Indian Defence Research Review, 11(1), 45-63.

135 Sharma, P., Gupta, R., & Patel, V. (2022). *Smart ammunition and its role in modern warfare: An Indian perspective.* Defence Technology Review, 8(4), 95-112.

136 Verma, S., Rajput, V., & Sharma, P. (2022). *The impact of Atmanirbhar Bharat on India's defence manufacturing.* Indian Defence Review, 6(2), 71-88.

137 Mishra, R., Bansal, A., & Verma, K. (2023). *Private sector participation in India's defence manufacturing: Prospects and policy implications.* Indian Defence Policy Journal, 5(2), 98-115.

138 Agarwal, R., Mehta, K., & Sinha, D. (2022). *Advancements in guided munitions: India's path to smart ammunition development.* Journal of Defence Technology, 15(4), 45-63.

139 Rajput, V., Chopra, A., & Joshi, M. (2023). *Quality control issues in India's defence production: A study on ammunition manufacturing challenges.* Journal of Defence Production, 13(1), 32-48.

140 Chopra, A., Rajput, V., & Joshi, M. (2023). *Foreign direct investment in India's defence sector: Policy shifts and industrial impact.* International Journal of Defence Economics, 10(1), 112-130.

141 Reddy, B., Sharma, P., & Kapoor, M. (2021). Ammunition manufacturing in India: An assessment of current capabilities and future trends. *Strategic Defence Analysis, 8*(4), 34-67.

142 Joshi, M., Reddy, V., & Rao, N. (2022). *Upgrading India's ammunition factories: A roadmap for modernization.* Journal of Defence Manufacturing, 12(2), 34-50.

143 Nair, K., Sharma, P., & Bhaskar, L. (2023). The role of private sector investment in defence R&D: An Indian perspective. *Journal of Defence Economics, 10*(1), 112-136.

144 Shukla, T., Kumar, S., & Nair, P. (2023). *Building a research-driven ecosystem for India's smart ammunition development.* Strategic Policy Journal, 10(2), 123-140.

145 Jain, M., Rao, B., & Kumar, S. (2020). Advances in precision-guided munitions: Trends and future prospects for the Indian defence sector. *Defence Research Review, 12*(2), 23-49.

146 Rao, V., Nayak, P., & Shukla, R. (2019). *Electro-optical and infrared guidance in modern smart weapons.* Journal of Optical Engineering, 14(2), 201-218.

147 Gupta, R., Joshi, D., & Agarwal, P. (2018). Performance assessment of ordnance factories in India: Challenges and reforms. *Defence Economics Review, 7*(4), 56-89.

148 Reddy, B., Sharma, P., & Kapoor, M. (2021). Ammunition manufacturing in India: An assessment of current capabilities and future trends. *Strategic Defence Analysis, 8*(4), 34-67.

149 Bhardwaj, A., Mehta, R., & Sharma, P. (2020). Evolution of India's defence procurement policy and its impact on private sector participation. *Defence Studies Journal, 18*(2), 112-135.

150 Mishra, R., Desai, S., & Narayan, K. (2022). Public-private partnerships in defence production: A case study of India. *International Journal of Military Innovation, 11*(2), 45-76.

151 Joshi, N., Sharma, A., & Verma, R. (2023). Analysing the impact of Atmanirbhar Bharat on India's defence manufacturing sector. *Journal of Defence Policy and Strategy, 6*(1), 67-89.

152 Deshmukh, A., Gupta, V., & Nair, P. (2022). Role of defence industrial corridors in promoting indigenous manufacturing in India. *International Journal of Defence Technology, 9*(3), 78-102.

153 Ranganathan, S., Mehta, G., & Kapoor, J. (2021). Barriers to achieving self-reliance in India's defence sector. *Defence Policy Journal, 9*(2), 56-78.

154 Chaturvedi, R., Singh, T., & Prakash, M. (2022). Strengthening India's indigenous defence R&D ecosystem: Challenges and opportunities. *Journal of Strategic Defence Research, 5*(1), 45-67.

155 Rao, V., Nayak, P., & Shukla, R. (2019). *Electro-optical and infrared guidance in modern smart weapons.* Journal of Optical Engineering, 14(2), 201-218.

156 Verma, A., Patel, K., & Desai, S. (2021). Analysing India's smart ammunition landscape: Market trends and R&D perspectives. *Journal of Defence Studies, 13*(4), 78-102.

157 Gupta, R., Joshi, D., & Agarwal, P. (2018). Performance assessment of ordnance factories in India: Challenges and reforms. *Defence Economics Review, 7*(4), 56-89.

158 Mukherjee, A., Sharma, T., & Singh, R. (2021). *Evaluating the transformation of India's ordnance factories: A supply chain perspective.* Journal of Defence Studies, 15(4), 45–60.

159 Kumar, P., Reddy, V. K., & Nair, S. (2023). *Strategic materials in India's defence manufacturing: Challenges and opportunities.* Defence Technology Review, 18(2), 122–135.

160 Rajan, M., Gupta, D., & Joshi, P. (2022). *Atmanirbhar Bharat and defence sector reform: The road ahead.* Indian Journal of Public Policy, 10(1), 89–104.

161 Sharma, R., Tripathi, N., & Mahapatra, B. (2020). *Self-reliance in defence manufacturing: Issues and policy recommendations.* Policy Perspectives, 7(3), 101–117.

162 Singh, A., Verma, N., & Das, P. (2023). *Smart ammunition and modern warfare: Trends in India's defence innovation.* Journal of Military Technology and Innovation, 9(1), 65–78.
163 Mukherjee, A., Sharma, T., & Singh, R. (2021). *Evaluating the transformation of India's ordnance factories: A supply chain perspective.* Journal of Defence Studies, 15(4), 45–60.
164 Rajan, M., Gupta, D., & Joshi, P. (2022). *Atmanirbhar Bharat and defence sector reform: The road ahead.* Indian Journal of Public Policy, 10(1), 89–104.
165 Kumar, P., Reddy, V. K., & Nair, S. (2023). *Strategic materials in India's defence manufacturing: Challenges and opportunities.* Defence Technology Review, 18(2), 122–135.
166 Ibid.
167 Rajan, M., Gupta, D., & Joshi, P. (2022). *Atmanirbhar Bharat and defence sector reform: The road ahead.* Indian Journal of Public Policy, 10(1), 89–104.
168 Mukherjee, A., Sharma, T., & Singh, R. (2021). *Evaluating the transformation of India's ordnance factories: A supply chain perspective.* Journal of Defence Studies, 15(4), 45–60.
169 Singh, A., Verma, N., & Das, P. (2023). *Smart ammunition and modern warfare: Trends in India's defence innovation.* Journal of Military Technology and Innovation, 9(1), 65–78.
170 Kumar, P., Reddy, V. K., & Nair, S. (2023). *Strategic materials in India's defence manufacturing: Challenges and opportunities.* Defence Technology Review, 18(2), 122–135.
171 Rajan, M., Gupta, D., & Joshi, P. (2022). *Atmanirbhar Bharat and defence sector reform: The road ahead.* Indian Journal of Public Policy, 10(1), 89–104.
172 Mukherjee, A., Sharma, T., & Singh, R. (2021). *Evaluating the transformation of India's ordnance factories: A supply chain perspective.* Journal of Defence Studies, 15(4), 45–60.
173 Sharma, R., Tripathi, N., & Mahapatra, B. (2020). *Self-reliance in defence manufacturing: Issues and policy recommendations.* Policy Perspectives, 7(3), 101–117.
174 Singh, A., Verma, N., & Das, P. (2023). *Smart ammunition and modern warfare: Trends in India's defence innovation.* Journal of Military Technology and Innovation, 9(1), 65–78.
175 Mukherjee, A., Sharma, T., & Singh, R. (2021). *Evaluating the transformation of India's ordnance factories: A supply chain perspective.* Journal of Defence Studies, 15(4), 45–60.
176 Rajan, M., Gupta, D., & Joshi, P. (2022). *Atmanirbhar Bharat and defence sector reform: The road ahead.* Indian Journal of Public Policy, 10(1), 89–104.
177 Sharma, R., Tripathi, N., & Mahapatra, B. (2020). *Self-reliance in defence manufacturing: Issues and policy recommendations.* Policy Perspectives, 7(3), 101–117.
178 Department of Defence. (2021). *Annual Industrial Capabilities Report to Congress.* U.S. Department of Defence.
179 Papp, J. F. (2020). *Rare Earth Elements: Supply Chain in the United States.* U.S. Geological Survey.
180 Zhang, Y., Liu, Q., & Chen, H. (2019). *Military–Industrial Integration and Innovation in China.* Asian Defence Journal, 27(3), 89–104.
181 Levy, G., Barkat, R., & Mizrachi, A. (2021). *Smart Ammunition in the Age of AI: Israel's Experience.* Journal of Defence Innovation, 6(1), 58–73.
182 Ministry of Defence. (2020). *Defence Production and Export Promotion Policy (DPEPP) 2020.* Government of India.
183 Raksha Mantri Report. (2021). *Annual Report on Defence Initiatives.* Ministry of Defence, Government of India.
184 DRDO. (2022). *Technology Development Fund Guidelines.* Defence Research and Development Organisation. https://tdf.drdo.gov.in
185 Kumar, P., Reddy, V. K., & Nair, S. (2023). *Strategic materials in India's defence manufacturing: Challenges and opportunities.* Defence Technology Review, 18(2), 122–135.

186 Rajan, M., Gupta, D., & Joshi, P. (2022). *Atmanirbhar Bharat and defence sector reform: The road ahead.* Indian Journal of Public Policy, 10(1), 89–104.

187 Mukherjee, A., Sharma, T., & Singh, R. (2021). *Evaluating the transformation of India's ordnance factories: A supply chain perspective.* Journal of Defence Studies, 15(4), 45–60.

188 Sharma, R., Tripathi, N., & Mahapatra, B. (2020). *Self-reliance in defence manufacturing: Issues and policy recommendations.* Policy Perspectives, 7(3), 101–117.

189 Verma, R., Das, A., & Nayak, S. (2021). *Bridging the skills gap in India's defence sector: A strategic imperative.* Indian Journal of Technical Education, 28(3), 78–85.

190 SIPRI. (2024). Annual Review of Global Arms Trade. Stockholm International Peace Research Institute.

191 Jones, E., & Smith, J. (2023). Strategic Alliances in Defence Industries: Navigating Geopolitics and Supply Chain Challenges. *Journal of International Security and Trade*, 17(2), 45-67.

192 Wheeler, T. (2024). Geopolitical Dynamics of International Defence Collaborations. *Global Military Review*, 19(1), 112-130.

193 White, K., & Brown, M. (2024). Economic Impacts of Strategic Defence Partnerships. *Economics of Security*, 22(3), 88-104.

194 Ivanov, V. (2023). Russia's Ammunition Industry and Its Strategic Alliances. *Moscow Military Review*, 30(1), 58-77.

195 Chen, L. (2025). China's Military-Civil Fusion Strategy and Global Arms Dynamics. *Asian Defence Journal*, 12(2), 142-158.

196 EuroDefence Council. (2024). European Defence Capabilities: Autonomy and Alliances in the 21st Century. Brussels: EuroDefence Council.

197 Smith, J., & Rahman, A. (2025). The Impact of Middle Eastern Conflicts on Global Ammunition Supply Chains. *Journal of Global Security*, 18(4), 203-220.

198 Owen, H., & Lee, S. (2024). Navigating the Challenges of Global Trade Wars on Military Supply Chains. *International Affairs Review*, 22(3), 334-350.

199 Global Defence Insights. (2025). Annual Overview of Global Defence Supply Chain Risks and Strategies. *Global Defence Insights*.

200 Johnson, L., & Patel, H. (2024). Defence Collaboration in the 21st Century: The U.S.-Japan Alliance. *Journal of International Security Affairs*, 31(2), 159-176.

201 Global Defence Review. (2025). Economic Impacts of Military Standardization: A Comparative Study. *Global Defence Review*, 26(1), 45-65.

202 Smith, R. (2025). European Security and U.S. Military Support: An Analytical Overview. *Defence and Strategy*, 28(3), 202-218.

203 White, K., & Brown, M. (2024). Supply Chain Strategies in Defence Industries. *Journal of Global Logistics*, 19(4), 234-251.

204 Ivanov, A., & Petrov, V. (2023). Russian Military-Industrial Ties: Legacy and Evolution. *Eastern European Military Review*, 22(1), 78-102.

205 Gupta, R., & Fernandez, J. (2024). Technological Upgradation and Strategic Partnerships in Emerging Markets. *Emerging Market Reports*, 17(2), 95-110.

206 D'Souza, F. (2025). Challenges to Strategic Defence Partnerships in Developing Countries. *International Defence Review*, 20(5), 300-325.

207 Johnson, L., & Patel, H. (2024). Defence Collaboration in the 21st Century: The U.S.-Japan Alliance. *Journal of International Security Affairs*, 31(2), 159-176.

208 Thompson, H., & Patel, R. (2024). Economic Benefits of International Defence Collaborations. *Journal of Global Economics and Security*, 18(2), 134-150.

209 Global Economic Defence Review. (2025). Annual Report on Defence Economics. *Global*

Economic Defence Review, 21(1), 45-67.

210 Economic Development Board. (2025). Impact of Defence Manufacturing on Local Economies. *Economic Development Journal*, 29(3), 198-213.

211 Sharma, G., & Kaur, S. (2025). Economic Impact of Indo-Israel Defence Partnerships. *Journal of Defence and Development*, 22(4), 241-256.

212 Ministry of Economic Affairs. (2025). Report on the Economic Impact of Strategic Partnerships. New Delhi: Ministry of Economic Affairs.

213 Anderson, L., & Cheng, D. (2024). Political Risk in International Defence Collaborations. *Journal of Global Politics and Security*, 25(1), 77-89.

214 Legal Affairs Review. (2025). Compliance Challenges in the Defence Industry. *Legal Affairs Review*, 30(2), 134-145.

215 Supply Chain Management Journal. (2025). Operational Challenges in International Defence Manufacturing Partnerships. *Supply Chain Management Journal*, 27(3), 201-215.

216 Global Logistics Review. (2025). Security and Logistics in the Defence Supply Chain. *Global Logistics Review*, 21(4), 168-182.

217 Rajagopalan, R. P. and Patil, S. (2024). *Future Warfare and Critical Technologies: Evolving Tactics and Strategies.* Global Policy- ORF Series. URL: https://www.orfonline.org/public/uploads/posts/pdf/20240212113627.pdf

218 "Non-Toxic Ammunition". (2025). *Sustainability Directory.* URL: https://pollution.sustainability-directory.com/term/non-toxic-ammunition/

219 Woolcott, P. (2013). Arms trade Treaty. *Audio-Visual Library of International Law.* United Nations. URL: https://legal.un.org/avl/ha/att/att.html

220 World Bank (2023). Supply Chain Management An introduction and practical toolset for procurement practitioners. *Procurement Guidance: The World Bank*. https://thedocs.worldbank.org/en/doc/1c3b517f003b53a2e2e170e93124be84-0290032023/original/World-Bank-Supply-Chain-Management-Guidance.pdf

221 Ibid.

222 Ibid. p. 5.

223 National Strategy for Artificial Intelligence #AIFORALL. (2018). *Niti Aayog*. https://www.niti.gov.in/sites/default/files/2023-03/National-Strategy-for-Artificial-Intelligence.pdf

224 Ibid. p. 7.

225 McDonald, J. (2024). Introduction to Artificial Intelligence (AI) technology. *Microsoft and World Travel and Tourism Council.* https://cdn-dynmedia-1.microsoft.com/is/content/microsoftcorp/microsoft/final/en-us/microsoft-brand/documents/2024-wttc-introduction-to-ai.pdf

226 Helo, P. and Hao, Y. (2022). Artificial intelligence in operations management and supply chain management: an exploratory case study. *Production Planning and Control.* Vol. 33, No. 19, 1573-1590. https://www.tandfonline.com/doi/pdf/10.1080/09537287.2021.1882690

227 Porter, R. E., Corcoran, M. and Connolly, P. (2021). Responsible AI From Principles to Practice. *Accenture*. https://www.accenture.com/content/dam/accenture/final/a-com-migration/pdf/pdf-149/accenture-responsible-ai-final.pdf

228 Abadicio, M. (2019). Artificial Intelligence for Military Logistics- Current Applications. *Emerj The AI Research and Advisory Company.* https://emerj.com/artificial-intelligence-military-logistics/

229 Bramble, J. and Bhuyan, P. (2023). How AI enhances defence in Supply chain Security. *Supply & Demand Chain Executive.* https://www.sdcexec.com/safety-security/risk-compliance/article/22878414/accrete-how-ai-enhances-defense-in-supply-chain-security

230 Lacroix, E.B. (2023). F1uture of Army Logistics: Exploiting AI, Overcoming Challenges and Charting the course Ahead. *Army Sustainment.* U.S. Army. https://www.army.mil/article/ 2 6 7 6 9 2 / future_of_army_logistics_exploiting_ai_overcoming_challenges_and_charting_the_course_ahead

231 Hooda, D.S. (2023). Implementing Artificial Intelligence in the Indian Military. *Delhi Policy Group Policy Brief.* Vol. VIII, Issue 11. https://www.delhipolicygroup.org/publication/policy-briefs/implementing-artificial-intelligence-in-the-indian-military.html

232 Sellers, A. (2023). Four ways DOD can leverage AI for contested logistics. *Defensescoop.* https://defensescoop.com/2023/06/20/four-ways-dod-can-leverage-ai-for-contested-logistics/

233 AI Next. (n.d.). *Defense Advanced research Projects Agency.* https://www.darpa.mil/about-us/ai-next#:~:text=In%20September%202018%2C%20DARPA%20announced,the%20% E2%80%9 CAI%20Next%E2%80%9D%20campaign

234 Vergun, D. (2024). DARPA aims to develop AI, autonomy applications Warfighters can trust. *US Department of Defense.* https://www.defense.gov/News/News-Stories/Article/Article/ 3722849/darpa-aims-to-develop-ai-autonomy-applications-warfighters-can-trust/

235 Mitchell, B. (2023). Air Force selects AI-enabled predictive maintenance program as system of record. *Defensescoop.* https://defensescoop.com/2023/05/10/air-force-selects-ai-enabled-predictive-maintenance-program-as-system-of-record/

236 Allen, G.C. (2019). Understanding China's AI Strategy: Clues to Chinese Strategic Thinking on artificial Intelligence and National security. *Centre for a New American Security.* https:// s3.us-east-1.amazonaws.com/files.cnas.org/hero/documents/CNAS-Understanding-Chinas-AI-Strategy-Gregory-C.-Allen-FINAL-2.15.19.pdf

237 Pomfret, J. and Pang, J. (2024). Exclusive: Chinese researchers develop AI model for military use on back of Meta's Llama. *Reuters.* https://www.reuters.com/technology/artificial-intelligence/chinese-researchers-develop-ai-model-military-use-back-metas-llama-2024-11-01/

238 Comptroller and Auditor General of India. (2024). *Audit Report No. 10 of 2024 – Ordnance Factories – Ammunition Production and Supply Chain.* Retrieved from https://cag.gov.in/ uploads/PressRelease/PR-English-Press-Release-on-Audit-Report-No-10-of-2024-067619371dadf78-28388980.pdf

239 Ibid. pp. 3-5.

240 Ibid. p. 2.

241 Ibid. p. 5.

242 Tuli, M. (2023). AI and the Potential to Create Digital Twins to Transform Military Logistics. CLAWS Journal, 16(2), 141-157. https://nbn-resolving.org/urn:nbn:de:0168-ssoar-97181-1

243 Ibid.

244 Sollfrank, A., & Boeke, S. (2024). Enablement and Logistics as Critical Success Factors for Military Operations: Comparing Russian and NATO Approaches. *The RUSI Journal, 169*(7), 10–22. https://doi.org/10.1080/03071847.2024.2434137

245 Rashid, A.B. et.al. (2023). Artificial Intelligence in the Military: An Overview of the Capabilities, Application and Challenges. *International Journal of Intelligent Systems.* Vol 23. Issue 1. https://onlinelibrary.wiley.com/doi/epdf/10.1155/2023/8676366

246 US Air Force (n.d.) Improving US Air Force Mission Capability with AI. URL: https://c3.ai/ improving-us-air-force-mission-capability-with-ai/

247 Reece, B. (2025). DLA applying AI to supply chain risk management, warfighter readiness. *Defense Logistic Agency.* https://www.dla.mil/About-DLA/News/News-Article-View/Article/ 4117309/dla-applying-ai-to-supply-chain-risk-management-warfighter-readiness/

#:~:text=supply%20chain%20from%20mining%20and,to%20incorporation%20in%20 military%20systems

248 Orbach, M. (2024). Comptroller flags gaps in Israel's national AI program. *Calcalistech News.* https://www.calcalistech.com/ctechnews/article/uprdzrebb#google_vignette

249 IndiaAI. (2022). India leapfrogged by 19 places in the Oxford insights AI readiness 2022. https://indiaai.gov.in/news/india-leapfrogged-by-19-places-in-the-oxford-insights-ai-readiness-index-2022

250 Helo, P. and Hao, Y. (2022). Artificial intelligence in operations management and supply chain management: an exploratory case study. *Production Planning and Control.* Vol. 33, No. 19, 1573-1590. https://www.tandfonline.com/doi/pdf/10.1080/09537287.2021.1882690

251 Hooda, D.S. (2023). Implementing Artificial Intelligence in the Indian Military. *Delhi Policy Group Policy Brief.* Vol. VIII, Issue 11. https://www.delhipolicygroup.org/publication/policy-briefs/implementing-artificial-intelligence-in-the-indian-military.html

252 Explainable Artificial Intelligence (XAI) (Archived). (n.d.). *Defence Advanced Research Projects Agency.* https://www.darpa.mil/program/explainable-artificial-intelligence

253 Hooda, D.S. (2023). Implementing Artificial Intelligence in the Indian Military. *Delhi Policy Group Policy Brief.* Vol. VIII, Issue 11. https://www.delhipolicygroup.org/publication/policy-briefs/implementing-artificial-intelligence-in-the-indian-military.html

254 Digital Trade and Data Governance Hub. (2017). China AI Strategy: A new Generation Artificial Intelligence Development Plan. *The George Washington University.* https://datagovhub.elliott.gwu.edu/china-ai-strategy/

255 Aidef 2022: Artificial Intelligence in Defence - The new age of Defence Presenting AI Preparedness of the country in Defence. (2022). *Department of Defence Production, Ministry of Defence.* https://www.ddpmod.gov.in/sites/default/files/ai.pdf

256 Ministry of Defence, Government of India. (2021). Indian Army establishes Quantum Laboratory at Mhow (MP). *PIB Delhi.* https://pib.gov.in/PressReleasePage.aspx?PRID=1786012

257 Ministry of Defence, Government of India. (2023). Conduct of Fifth edition of AI workshop at INS VALSURA 09-11 Aug 23. *PIB Delhi.* https://pib.gov.in/PressReleaseIframePage.aspx?PRID=1948096

258 Ministry of Defence, Government of India. (2022). Enhancement of Capabilities of AI Technology. *PIB Delhi.* https://www.pib.gov.in/PressReleasePage.aspx?PRID=1846937#:~:text=Further%2C%20 Defence%20AI%20Project%20Agency,in%20DRDO%20have%20been%20issued

259 Levesques, A. (2024). Early steps in India's use of AI for defence. *International Institute for Strategic Studies.* https://www.iiss.org/online-analysis/online-analysis/2024/01/early-steps-in-indias-use-of-ai-for-defence/

260 Gardner, G. J. (2020). JMC risk model and munitions supply chain vulnerabilities. DVIDS News. URL: https://www.dvidshub.net/news/386234/jmc-develops-risk-model-address-vulnerabilities-munitions-supply-chain-col-gavin-j-gardner

261 Luckenbaugh, J., & Magnuson, S. (2024, September 11). Arms manufacturers catching up with world's insatiable need for 155mm rounds. National Defence Magazine. URL: https://www.nationaldefensemagazine.org/articles/2024/9/11/arms-manufacturers-catching-up-with-worlds-insatiable-need-for-155mm-rounds#:~:text=an%20Army%20release%20described%20as,%E2%80%9D

262 NATO. (2016, February 11). Allies one step closer to multinational acquisition of precision-guided munitions (PGM) [Press release]. NATO News. URL: https://www.nato.int/cps/en/

natohq/news_127956.htm#:~:text=The%20project%20was%20originally%20launched,and %20management%20of%20munitions%20inventories

263 NATO. (2023). NATO Secretary General welcomes contracts worth 2.4 billion euros to strengthen ammunition stockpiles. URL: https://www.nato.int/cps/en/natohq/news_218735.htm?selectedLocale=en

264 Jewish Virtual Library. (n.d.). Yom Kippur War: Operation Nickel Grass (October-November 1973). URL: https://www.jewishvirtuallibrary.org/operation-nickel-grass#:~:text=(October %20% 2D%20November%201973)&text=Operation%20Nickel%20Grass%20was %20a,the %201973%20Yom%20Kippur%20War.

265 Schenker, D. (2014, August 17). *Best friends don't have to ask. Politico Magazine.* URL: https:/ /www.politico.com/magazine/story/2014/08/best-friends-dont-have-to-ask-110036/ #:~:text=Putting%20aside%20for%20the%20moment,a%20resupply%20airlift%20to%20Israel

266 Justin,O. (2024, October 23). *The Strategic Advantage of AI for the Defense Industrial Base.* Microsoft Tech Community Blog. URL: https://techcommunity.microsoft.com/blog/publicsectorblog/the-strategic-advantage-of-ai-for-the-defense-industrial-base/4276817

267 Hamilton, C. (2025). The future of military logistics in predictive. *Defense One.* URL: https:/ /www. defenseone.com/ideas/2025/02/ future-military-logistics-predictive/402939/

268 Justin,O. (2024, October 23). *The Strategic Advantage of AI for the Defense Industrial Base.* Microsoft Tech Community Blog. URL: https://techcommunity.microsoft.com/blog/publicsectorblog/the-strategic-advantage-of-ai-for-the-defense-industrial-base/4276817

269 Hamilton, C. (2025). The future of military logistics is predictive. Defense One. URL: https://www.defenseone.com/ideas/2025/02/future-military-logistics-predictive/402939/

270 Justin,O. (2024, October 23). *The Strategic Advantage of AI for the Defense Industrial Base.* Microsoft Tech Community Blog. URL: https://techcommunity.microsoft.com/blog/publicsectorblog/the-strategic-advantage-of-ai-for-the-defense-industrial-base/4276817

271 Y. Jung et.al. (2023), "Ammunition Management in the AI Era: Towards CBM+ and Shelf-life Analysis," 2023 IEEE International Conference on Big Data (BigData), Sorrento, Italy, 2023, pp. 6180-6182, doi: 10.1109/BigData59044.2023.10386840.

272 Moyer, B. (2023, May 1). Predictive logistics initiative revolutionizes equipment management. U.S. Army. URL: https://www.army.mil/article/265899/predictive_logistics_initiative_revolut ionizes_ equipment_management

273 Justin,O. (2024, October 23). *The Strategic Advantage of AI for the Defense Industrial Base.* Microsoft Tech Community Blog. URL: https://techcommunity.microsoft.com/blog/publicsectorblog/the-strategic-advantage-of-ai-for-the-defense-industrial-base/4276817

274 Clark, J. (2023). DoD releases AI adoption strategy. U.S. Department of Defense. URL: https://www.defense.gov/News/News-Stories/Article/Article/3578219/dod-releases-ai-adoption-strategy/

275 Hamilton, C. (2025). The future of military logistics is predictive. Defense One. URL: https://www.defenseone.com/ideas/2025/02/future-military-logistics-predictive/402939/

276 Gokhalie, N. (2019). Government Determined to corporatize OFB despite Opposition. *Bharat Shakti.* URL: https://bharatshakti.in/government-determined-to-corporatise-ofb-despite-opposition/

277 Saxena, V. K. (2021). Corporatisation of Ordnance Factory Board – An Analysis. *Vivekananda International Foundation.* URL: https://www.vifindia.org/article/2021/august/12/Corporatisation-of-Ordnance-Factory-Board

278 Office of the Comptroller and Auditor General of India. (2019). *Press Release.* URL: https:/ /cag.gov.in/uploads/PressRelease/PR-Press-Release-English-06-12-2019-05f5f6917a849e9-

50722760.pdf

279 Saxena, V. K. (2021). Corporatisation of Ordnance Factory Board – An Analysis. *Vivekananda International Foundation.* URL: https://www.vifindia.org/article/2021/august/12/Corporatisation-of-Ordnance-Factory-Board

280 Gokhalie, N. (2019). Government Determined to corporatize OFB despite Opposition. *Bharat Shakti.* URL: https://bharatshakti.in/government-determined-to-corporatise-ofb-despite-opposition/

281 Press Information Bureau (2019). Press Releases. URL: https://www.pib.gov.in/newsite/PrintRelease.aspx?relid=194576#:~:text=Corporatisation%20of%20OFB%20will%20bring,decision%20taken%20on%20the%20subject.

282 Ministry of Defence (2021). Seven new defence companies, carved out of OFB, dedicated to the Nation on the occasion of Vijayadashami. *Press Information Bureau.* URL: https://www.pib.gov.in/Pressreleaseshare.aspx?PRID=1764148

283 Munitions India Limited (n.a.). URL: https://munitionsindia.in/wp-content/uploads/MIL-Brochure.pdf

284 Troops Comfort Limited (n.a.). Excellence in Defence Manufacturing. URL:_https://troopcomfortslimited.co.in/

285 Bhatia, D. (2023). Industry 4.0 in India: Embracing the Digital Revolution in manufacturing. *NASSCOM Community* URL: https://community.nasscom.in/communities/industry-40/industry-40-india-embracing-digital-revolution-manufacturing

286 KPMG (2018). *Industry 4.0 India Inc. Gearing up for change.* URL: https://resources.aima.in/presentations/AIMA-KPMG-industry-4-0-report.pdf

287 Ministry of Defence (2024). Government is committed to undertake further Reforms in enhancing Domestic Defence Production: Defence Secretary. *Press Information Bureau.* URL: https://www.pib.gov.in/PressReleasePage.aspx?PRID=2031848

288 Ministry of Defence (2025). Operation Sindoor was successfully executed because our formidable & professionally-trained Armed Forces were equipped with high-quality equipment, says Raksha Mantri at National Quality Conclave 2025. *Press Information Bureau.* URL: https://www.pib.gov.in/PressReleasePage.aspx?PRID=2127735

289 Rashid, A.B. and Kausik, A.K. (2024) AI revolutionizing industries worldwide: A comprehensive overview of its diverse applications. *Hybrid Advances.* URL: https://www.sciencedirect.com/science/article/pii/S2773207X24001386

290 Ministry of Defence, Department of Defence Procurement. (2019) *Committee on Estimates 2018-19.* URL: https://sansad.in/getFile/lsscommittee/Estimates/16_Estimates_29.pdf?source=loksabhadocs

291 DCME (n.a.). *Operational Guidelines for Zero Defect Zero Effect Scheme.* URL: https://dcmsme.gov.in/schemes/clcs-tus/Operational_Guidelines_ZED.pdf

292 Bharat Dynamics Limited (n.d.) URL: https://bdl-india.in/company-profile

293 "Advancing Aatmanirbharta" Adani. URL: https://www.adani.com/newsroom/media-releases/advancing-aatmanirbharta

294 Kshetri, N. (2021). Chapter 3 - Amplifying the value of blockchain in supply chains: combining with other technologies. *Block Chain and Supply Chain Management.* URL: https://www.sciencedirect.com/science/article/abs/pii/B9780323899345000039

295 "Big Data Analytics" (n.a.). *Dassault systems.* URL: https://www.3ds.com/manufacturing/connected-industry/big-data-analytics-smart-manufacturing

296 Sharma, A. (2025). The Dawn of Dark Factories: The Future or a Looming Challenge? *India Business Trade.* URL: https://www.indiabusinesstrade.in/blogs/the-dawn-of-dark-factories-the-

future-or-a-looming-challenge/

297 Rikala, P. et al, (2024). Understanding and measuring skill gaps in Industry 4.0 – A Review. *Technological Forecasting and Social Change.* URL: https://www.sciencedirect.com/science/article/pii/S0040162524000027

298 Anand, P. and Nagendra, A. (2019). Industry 4.0: India's Defence Industry needs Smart Manufacturing. *International Journal of Innovative Technology and Exploring Engineering (IJITEE).* URL: https://www.ijitee.org/wp-content/uploads/papers/v8i11S/K108109811S19.pdf

299 Ministry of Commerce and Industry (2025). India offers a transparent, predictable and comprehensive FDI Policy Framework for investments. URL: https://www.pib.gov.in/PressReleasePage.aspx?PRID=2101785

300 Rai, A., Singh, V., & Gupta, M. (2023). Defence Industrial Corridors and the Road to Atmanirbharta: Opportunities and Challenges. *Journal of Strategic Studies and Defence Affairs,* 5(2), 87–104. https://doi.org/10.1016/j.jsda.2023.03.005

301 Mehra, R., Pillai, S., & Kumar, S. (2024). Regional Defense Corridors: Engines of Growth and Innovation in India's Defence Sector. *Defence Technology Review,* 9(1), 55–72. https://doi.org/10.1080/deftechrev.2024.01.007

302 Sharma, A., Menon, R., & Gupta, V. (2023). Defence Procurement and Regulatory Framework in India: Progress and Persistent Challenges. *Journal of Defence Governance and Policy,* 8(3), 134–152. https://doi.org/10.1080/jdgp.2023.083134

303 Kumar, S., Tiwari, M., & Ramaswamy, S. (2023). Economic Impact of Indigenous Defence Manufacturing in India: Opportunities and Challenges. *Indian Journal of Defence Economics,* 4(1), 55–74. https://doi.org/10.1177/ijdm.2023.041005

304 Chakraborty, A., Jain, R., & Thomas, S. (2023). Rethinking India's Defence Industrial Base: Past Trends and Future Prospects. *Defence and Security Analysis,* 39(2), 179–197. https://doi.org/10.1080/14751798.2023.1904837

305 Verma, P., Shukla, A., & Narayanan, R. (2024). Technology Transfer and Self-Reliance in Indian Defence Manufacturing: A Historical Perspective. *Journal of Defence Studies and Research,* 11(1), 34–51. https://doi.org/10.1080/jdsr.2024.11.1.34

306 Reddy, K., Sen, S., & Dasgupta, M. (2023). Private Sector Integration into India's Defence Sector: Progress and Pitfalls. *Strategic Affairs Review,* 8(3), 210–227. https://doi.org/10.1016/j.sar.2023.08.005

307 Mishra, T., Bhatia, S., & Rao, G. (2024). Defence Manufacturing Ecosystem in Uttar Pradesh: A Case Study of UPDIC. *Strategic Innovation and Defence Review,* 9(2), 121–140. https://doi.org/10.1080/sidr.2024.092121

308 Singh, R., Menon, A., & Sinha, D. (2023). Self-Reliance in Indian Defence: Strategic Imperatives and Policy Directions. *Journal of Defence and Strategic Studies,* 7(2), 112–131. https://doi.org/10.1177/2397796023112301

309 Nair, S., Bhatt, P., & Kumar, A. (2023). Industrial Clustering and Defence Corridors: Lessons for Sustainable Development. *Strategic Industrial Studies Journal,* 9(2), 122–140. https://doi.org/10.1177/sisj.2023.092122

310 Kumar, A., Meena, S., & Rathi, V. (2023). Financing Defence Manufacturing in India: Challenges and Strategic Imperatives. *Journal of Defence Industrial Economics,* 7(3), 154–173. https://doi.org/10.1177/jdie.2023.073154

311 Rajput, P., Bhattacharya, K., & Verghese, M. (2024). Operationalizing Indigenous Solutions: Bridging Capability Gaps in India's Defence Forces. *Strategic Defence Review,* 9(1), 43–61. https://doi.org/10.1080/sdr.2024.01.043

312 Chatterjee, S., Varma, P., & Roy, B. (2024). Emerging Technologies and India's Defence Innovation Ecosystem. *Journal of Military Technology and Innovation*, 6(2), 88–107. https://doi.org/10.1080/jmti.2024.0620088

313 Bose, A., Srinivasan, V., & Joshi, P. (2023). India's Positive Indigenization Lists: An Assessment of Progress and Challenges. *Indian Policy and Defence Outlook*, 5(2), 99–117. https://doi.org/10.1016/j.ipdo.2023.05.002

314 Sharma, V., Kulkarni, R., & Nambiar, A. (2023). Building Defence Manufacturing Ecosystems: The Case of India's Defence Corridors. *Journal of Defence Policy and Innovation*, 8(3), 215–233. https://doi.org/10.1080/jdpi.2023.08.003

315 Kapoor, S., Choudhary, M., & Agarwal, D. (2024). Defence Industrial Corridors in India: A New Strategic Paradigm. *Strategic Studies Quarterly India*, 11(1), 51–69. https://doi.org/10.1080/ssqi.2024.011051

316 Nayyar, R., Bansal, A., & Verma, L. (2023). Infrastructure and Incentives in Defence Industrial Corridors: Challenges and Prospects. *International Journal of Defence Sector Studies*, 9(4), 301–319. https://doi.org/10.1016/j.ijdss.2023.09.006

317 Deshmukh, S., Rao, P., & Mehta, S. (2023). Strategic Clustering and Defence Corridors: An Indian Perspective. *Asian Defence and Strategic Review*, 7(3), 165–184. https://doi.org/10.1080/adsr.2023.073165

318 Patel, H., Singh, T., & Joshi, V. (2024). Policy Catalysts for Defence Manufacturing: Evaluating India's Defence Corridors and FDI Reforms. *Journal of Emerging Defence Technologies*, 4(1), 92–110. https://doi.org/10.1080/jedt.2024.041092

319 Menon, S., Kapoor, R., & Joshi, V. (2023). Public-Private Partnerships in India's Defence Sector: Opportunities and Roadblocks. *Journal of Strategic Defence Partnerships*, 7(2), 134–152. https://doi.org/10.1177/jsdp.2023.072134

320 Dwivedi, P., Chauhan, R., & Narayan, S. (2024). Uttar Pradesh Defence Industrial Corridor: Opportunities, Challenges, and the Road Ahead. *Indian Journal of Defence Infrastructure and Innovation*, 5(1), 33–50. https://doi.org/10.1016/ijdi.2024.01.033

321 Mishra, P., Chauhan, V., & Gupta, D. (2024). Defence Industrial Corridors: New Frontiers in India's Defence Manufacturing Ecosystem. *International Journal of Defence Industries and Innovation*, 5(1), 65–81. https://doi.org/10.1080/ijdefind.2024.01.005

322 Sridharan, K., Balaji, M., & Ananth, K. (2023). Tamil Nadu Defence Industrial Corridor: Emerging Trends and Strategic Potential. *Asia-Pacific Defence and Strategic Studies Journal*, 7(2), 101–120. https://doi.org/10.1080/apdssj.2023.072101

323 Rao, K., Bansal, T., & Srivastava, A. (2023). Defence Innovation Funding in India: A Comparative Global Perspective. *International Journal of Military Innovation and Strategy*, 9(2), 87–105. https://doi.org/10.1080/ijmis.2023.092087

324 Shankar, N., Kumar, R., & Meena, H. (2024). Public-Private Partnerships and India's Defence Corridors: A New Model for Industrial Growth. *Journal of Indian Strategic Affairs*, 10(1), 89–106. https://doi.org/10.1177/jisa.2024.101089

325 Prasad, V., Menon, D., & Shetty, R. (2023). Infrastructure and Industrial Clusters: Pillars of India's Defence Manufacturing Strategy. *Journal of Defence Infrastructure Development*, 7(3), 187–205. https://doi.org/10.1080/jdid.2023.073187

326 Nair, S., Bhatt, P., & Kumar, A. (2023). Industrial Clustering and Defence Corridors: Lessons for Sustainable Development. *Strategic Industrial Studies Journal*, 9(2), 122–140. https://doi.org/10.1177/sisj.2023.092122

327 Sengupta, T., Rao, M., & Pillai, S. (2024). Logistics and Connectivity in Defence Industrial Corridors: A Critical Analysis. *Indian Journal of Strategic Infrastructure*, 5(1), 45–62. https:/

/doi.org/10.1080/ijsi.2024.051045

328 Khan, R., Joshi, M., & Das, S. (2023). Centres of Excellence in Defence Corridors: Innovation Hubs for Strategic Autonomy. *International Defence Technology and Policy Review*, 8(4), 209–227. https://doi.org/10.1080/idtpr.2023.084209

329 Mehta, K., Rathi, V., & Iyer, P. (2023). Smart Clusters and Industry 4.0 Adoption in Defence Manufacturing. *Journal of Emerging Technologies and Defence Studies*, 6(2), 98–115. https://doi.org/10.1080/jetds.2023.062098

330 Sharma, P., Verma, T., & Dixit, A. (2024). MSMEs in Defence Industrial Clusters: Opportunities and Challenges in India's Defence Corridors. *Journal of Defence MSME Studies*, 5(1), 67–84. https://doi.org/10.1080/jdms.2024.051067

331 Menon, S., Kapoor, R., & Joshi, V. (2023). Public-Private Partnerships in India's Defence Sector: Opportunities and Roadblocks. *Journal of Strategic Defence Partnerships*, 7(2), 134–152. https://doi.org/10.1177/jsdp.2023.072134

332 Srivastava, A., Iyer, S., & Kulkarni, M. (2024). Policy Support for PPPs in Defence Corridors: An Evaluation. *Indian Journal of Defence Policy and Innovation*, 6(1), 44–63. https://doi.org/10.1016/ijdpi.2024.01.044

333 Kaur, P., Nambiar, R., & Singh, T. (2023). Empowering MSMEs in India's Defence Supply Chain: Challenges and Prospects. *Defence Industry Review*, 8(3), 177–195. https://doi.org/10.1080/dir.2023.083177

334 Bansal, A., Pradhan, D., & Verma, K. (2023). MSMEs in Defence Innovation: Enablers and Ecosystem Challenges. *Journal of Emerging Defence Technologies and Strategies*, 5(2), 99–118. https://doi.org/10.1080/jedts.2023.052099

335 Patil, M., Sharma, A., & Rao, S. (2023). Regional Industrialization through MSME Clusters: Lessons from Defence Corridors. *Asia-Pacific Journal of Strategic Development*, 7(4), 221–239. https://doi.org/10.1177/apjsd.2023.074221

336 Iyer, S., Nambiar, P., & Kumar, R. (2023). Defence Innovation in India: Pathways to Atmanirbhar Bharat. *Journal of Defence Research and Innovation*, 7(2), 102–121. https://doi.org/10.1080/jdri.2023.072102

337 Krishnan, R., Bhattacharya, V., & Sinha, P. (2024). Centres of Excellence and Defence R&D: Building India's Innovation Ecosystem. *Indian Journal of Advanced Defence Technologies*, 5(1), 44–62. https://doi.org/10.1177/ijadt.2024.051044

338 Patel, K., Sharma, S., & Varghese, D. (2023). Technology Transfer Mechanisms in India's Defence Sector: Challenges and Opportunities. *International Journal of Technology and Defence Policy*, 9(3), 191–210. https://doi.org/10.1177/ijtdp.2023.093191

339 Deshmukh, R., Jain, M., & Kumar, T. (2023). Additive Manufacturing in Defence: Revolutionizing Rapid Prototyping. *Journal of Emerging Manufacturing Technologies*, 6(2), 112–130. https://doi.org/10.1080/jemt.2023.062112

340 Bhattacharya, S., Nair, P., & Rao, A. (2023). Defence Corridors and Employment Opportunities: A New Growth Paradigm. *Indian Journal of Strategic Employment Studies*, 6(2), 94–113. https://doi.org/10.1177/ijses.2023.062094

341 Verma, K., Iyer, R., & Das, S. (2023). Industrial Corridors as Catalysts for Employment and Economic Development: Evidence from India. *Journal of Regional Development and Defence Studies*, 8(1), 45–63. https://doi.org/10.1080/jrdds.2023.081045

342 Rao, K., Bansal, T., & Srivastava, A. (2023). Defence Innovation Funding in India: A Comparative Global Perspective. *International Journal of Military Innovation and Strategy*, 9(2), 87–105. https://doi.org/10.1080/ijmis.2023.092087

343 Sharma, V., Kulkarni, R., & Nambiar, A. (2023). Building Defence Manufacturing

Ecosystems: The Case of India's Defence Corridors. *Journal of Defence Policy and Innovation*, 8(3), 215–233. https://doi.org/10.1080/jdpi.2023.08.003

344 Mukherjee, P., Rao, M., & Bansal, K. (2023). Modernizing Logistics for India's Defence Supply Chain: The Role of Infrastructure. *Asia-Pacific Defence Logistics Journal*, 7(2), 88–106. https://doi.org/10.1080/apdlj.2023.072088

345 Chaturvedi, P., Meena, S., & Bansal, R. (2023). Gender Inclusion in Defence Manufacturing: Skilling and Employment Trends in India. *Journal of Inclusive Industrial Development*, 5(1), 77–95. https://doi.org/10.1177/jiid.2023.051077

346 Srivastava, R., Jain, V., & Menon, S. (2023). India's Defence Export Strategy: Role of Industrial Corridors and Policy Reforms. *Journal of Defence Trade and Export Promotion*, 7(3), 144–162. https://doi.org/10.1177/jdtep.2023.073144

347 Mehta, K., Pillai, A., & Sharma, R. (2024). Ten Years of India's Defence Export Growth: Drivers and Future Prospects. *Indian Journal of Defence Economic Studies*, 6(1), 56–74. https://doi.org/10.1177/ijdes.2024.061056

348 Rajput, A., Verghese, M., & Rao, D. (2023). FDI in India's Defence Manufacturing Sector: Opportunities and Challenges. *International Review of Strategic Investment Studies*, 8(2), 119–137. https://doi.org/10.1080/irssis.2023.082119

349 Chowdhury, S., Desai, V., & Bhatia, P. (2023). Global Collaborations in India's Defence Corridors: FDI Trends and Strategic Partnerships. *Journal of Emerging Defence Partnerships*, 5(2), 88–106. https://doi.org/10.1080/jedp.2023.052088

350 Rao, K., Bansal, T., & Srivastava, A. (2023). Defence Innovation Funding in India: A Comparative Global Perspective. *International Journal of Military Innovation and Strategy*, 9(2), 87–105. https://doi.org/10.1080/ijmis.2023.092087

351 Chowdhury, A., Menon, V., & Rao, S. (2023). Infrastructure Challenges in India's Defence Industrial Corridors: An Empirical Assessment. *Journal of Defence Infrastructure and Logistics*, 7(2), 120–138. https://doi.org/10.1177/jdil.2023.072120

352 Verma, R., Das, P., & Sharma, M. (2024). Land Acquisition and Industrial Development in Defence Corridors: The Uttar Pradesh Experience. *Indian Journal of Regional Industrial Studies*, 6(1), 44–62. https://doi.org/10.1177/ijris.2024.061044

353 Srivastava, R., Jain, V., & Menon, S. (2023). India's Defence Export Strategy: Role of Industrial Corridors and Policy Reforms. *Journal of Defence Trade and Export Promotion*, 7(3), 144–162. https://doi.org/10.1177/jdtep.2023.073144

354 Iyer, S., Nambiar, P., & Kumar, R. (2023). Defence Innovation in India: Pathways to Atmanirbhar Bharat. *Journal of Defence Research and Innovation*, 7(2), 102–121. https://doi.org/10.1080/jdri.2023.072102

355 Mukherjee, P., Rao, M., & Bansal, K. (2023). Modernizing Logistics for India's Defence Supply Chain: The Role of Infrastructure. *Asia-Pacific Defence Logistics Journal*, 7(2), 88–106. https://doi.org/10.1080/apdlj.2023.072088

356 Patel, R., Sinha, D., & Thomas, A. (2023). Smart Logistics in Defence Manufacturing: Emerging Trends and Indian Prospects. *Journal of Emerging Technologies and Logistics*, 6(3), 177–196. https://doi.org/10.1080/jetl.2023.063177

357 Rajagopalan, S., Kapoor, J., & Desai, V. (2023). Common Facility Centres in Defence Corridors: Catalysts for MSME Growth. *Journal of Defence MSME Innovation*, 5(1), 65–83. https://doi.org/10.1080/jdmi.2023.051065

358 Nair, S., Bhatt, P., & Kumar, A. (2023). Industrial Clustering and Defence Corridors: Lessons for Sustainable Development. *Strategic Industrial Studies Journal*, 9(2), 122–140. https://doi.org/10.1177/sisj.2023.092122

359 Bhattacharya, S., Kapoor, R., & Mehta, A. (2023). Indigenous Content in Indian Defence Platforms: Challenges and Opportunities. *Strategic Defence Review India*, 8(2), 114–132. https://doi.org/10.1177/sdri.2023.082114

360 Chatterjee, P., Sinha, V., & Pillai, R. (2023). Defence R&D in India: Evolution, Challenges, and the Way Forward. *Indian Journal of Defence Science and Research*, 6(1), 34–52. https://doi.org/10.1080/ijdsa.2023.061034

361 Rao, K., Bansal, T., & Srivastava, A. (2023). Defence Innovation Funding in India: A Comparative Global Perspective. *International Journal of Military Innovation and Strategy*, 9(2), 87–105. https://doi.org/10.1080/ijmis.2023.092087

362 Patel, D., Tiwari, M., & Ramaswamy, S. (2023). Bridging Academia and Industry for Defence R&D: Indian Experience and Global Models. *Journal of Emerging Defence Research*, 5(2), 98–116. https://doi.org/10.1080/jedr.2023.052098

363 Sen, R., Verma, P., & Krishnan, A. (2023). Technology Transfer in Indian Defence Sector: Barriers and Solutions. *Asia-Pacific Defence Industry Journal*, 7(4), 200–218. https://doi.org/10.1080/apdij.2023.074200

364 Chopra, S., Menon, A., & Joshi, V. (2023). Talent Shortages and Brain Drain in India's Defence Innovation Ecosystem. *Journal of Defence Human Capital Development*, 5(1), 73–91. https://doi.org/10.1177/jdhcd.2023.051073

365 Sharma, D., Gupta, A., & Joshi, P. (2023). Skill Development Initiatives in India's Defence Industrial Corridors: A Critical Appraisal. *Indian Review of Defence Training and Policy*, 7(4), 210–229. https://doi.org/10.1177/irdtp.2023.074210

366 Desai, P., Krishnan, S., & Nair, V. (2024). Defence Acquisition Procedure 2020: An Evaluation of Its Impact on Ease of Doing Business. *Indian Journal of Strategic Procurement Studies*, 5(1), 55–73. https://doi.org/10.1177/ijsps.2024.051055

367 Saxena, T., Iyer, P., & Rao, A. (2023). Licensing and Compliance Challenges for MSMEs in Defence Manufacturing. *Strategic Review of Defence Industries*, 7(2), 90–109. https://doi.org/10.1177/srdi.2023.072090

368 Menon, V., Chopra, D., & Bhatia, S. (2023). Export Regulations in Indian Defence Sector: Simplifications and Remaining Hurdles. *Journal of Emerging Defence Markets*, 6(2), 104–122. https://doi.org/10.1080/jedm.2023.062104

369 Krishnan, R., Das, P., & Verma, A. (2023). FDI in Indian Defence: Policy Advances and Investor Concerns. *International Journal of Strategic Investment and Defence Policy*, 9(2), 145–163. https://doi.org/10.1080/ijsidp.2023.092145

370 Patil, M., Sharma, A., & Rao, S. (2023). Regional Industrialization through MSME Clusters: Lessons from Defence Corridors. *Asia-Pacific Journal of Strategic Development*, 7(4), 221–239. https://doi.org/10.1177/apjsd.2023.074221

371 Reddy, K., Sen, S., & Dasgupta, M. (2023). Private Sector Integration into India's Defence Sector: Progress and Pitfalls. *Strategic Affairs Review*, 8(3), 210–227. https://doi.org/10.1016/j.sar.2023.08.005

372 Kumar, A., Meena, S., & Rathi, V. (2023). Financing Defence Manufacturing in India: Challenges and Strategic Imperatives. *Journal of Defence Industrial Economics*, 7(3), 154–173. https://doi.org/10.1177/jdie.2023.073154

373 Rajan, V., Bansal, R., & Chopra, D. (2023). MSMEs in Defence Manufacturing: Financial Barriers and Policy Solutions. *Indian Journal of Defence Sector Studies*, 6(2), 102–120. https://doi.org/10.1080/ijdss.2023.062102

374 Mishra, P., Tewari, K., & Iyer, M. (2023). Start-Up Financing in India's Defence Sector: Trends and Challenges. *Strategic Innovation and Defence Entrepreneurship Review*, 5(2), 88–

106. https://doi.org/10.1080/sider.2023.052088

375 Mehta, S., Sharma, N., & Pillai, J. (2023). Private Equity and Venture Capital Investment in Indian Defence Start-ups: An Emerging Opportunity. *Journal of Emerging Defence Investments*, 6(1), 77–95. https://doi.org/10.1177/jedi.2023.061077

376 Shah, P., Das, A., & Verma, L. (2023). Foreign Direct Investment in India's Defence Sector: Evaluating the Impact of Policy Liberalization. *Asia-Pacific Journal of Defence Trade and Investment*, 7(2), 123–142. https://doi.org/10.1080/apjdti.2023.072123

377 Singh, R., Chauhan, T., & Joshi, M. (2024). Fiscal Incentives and Industrial Development in Defence Corridors: A Policy Review. *Indian Policy Journal for Strategic Industries*, 5(1), 66–85. https://doi.org/10.1080/ipjsi.2024.051066

378 "Inquiry ordered, CAG" (2016). Inquiry ordered, CAG had sounded alerts in 2015. URL: https://www.deccanherald.com/india/inquiry-ordered-cag-had-sounded-2067661

379 Lopez, E. (2020). Precise, 'smarter' munitions would combine massive data with splash of intelligence. *US Army*. URL: https://www.army.mil/article/238735/precise_smarter_munitions_would_combine_massive_data_with_splash_of_intelligence?

380 European Commission (2025). ANNEX to the Commission Implementing Decision. URL: https://defence-industry-space.ec.europa.eu/document/download/fd8f705a-208e-485e-83e1-1b89d3a977c6_en?filename=EDF%202025%20Call%20Topic%20Descriptions.pdf

381 Ministry of Defence, UK (2006). *Defence Technology Strategy for the demands of the 21st century.* URL: https://apps.dtic.mil/sti/tr/pdf/ADA485665.pdf

382 US Environmental Protection Agency (2005). *Handbook on Management of Munition Response Actions.* URL: https://semspub.epa.gov/work/HQ/190124.pdf

383 Shivane, A. B. (2023). Drones and Unmanned Aerial Systems Revolutionising Combined Arms Warfare. *Synergy.* Centre for Joint Warfare Studies. URL: https://cenjows.in/wp-content/uploads/2023/10/Synergy-Journal-online-version-merged.pdf

384 Bucur-Marcu, H., Fluri, P., & Tagarev, T. (2009). *Defence management: An Introduction.*

385 Beer, J., & Bennett, B. (2002). Special relationships: Anglo-American antagonisms and affinities 1854-1936. In *Manchester University Press eBooks*. https://doi.org/10.9760/mupoa/9780719058172

386 Bitzinger, R. A. (2015). Comparing defence industry reforms in China and India. *Asian Politics & Policy*, *7*(4), 531–553. https://doi.org/10.1111/aspp.12221

387 Akamavi, R. K., Ibrahim, F., & Swaray, R. (2022). Tourism and Troubles: Effects of security threats on the global travel and tourism industry performance. *Journal of Travel Research*, *62*(8), 1755–1800. https://doi.org/10.1177/00472875221138792

388 Barkawi, T. (2017). *Soldiers of Empire.* Cambridge University Press.

389 Uppal, R. (2019). Advances in Non-Destructive Testing (NDT) and non-destructive evaluation (NDE) techniques for Aerospace and Military application. *International Defense, Security & Technology.* URL: https://idstch.com/industry/advances-non-destructive-testing-ndt-nondestructive-evaluation-nde-techniques-aerospace-military-application/

390 Ministry of Defence (2019). Committee on Estimates 2018-19. *Department of Defence Production.* URL: https://sansad.in/getFile/lsscommittee/Estimates/16_Estimates_29.pdf?source=loksabhadocs

391 Chansoria, M. (2016). From reluctance to readiness: India's foreign policy and diplomatic strategies in the Twenty-First Century. In *Palgrave Macmillan US eBooks* (pp. 93–123). https://doi.org/10.1057/978-1-137-45226-9_4

392 Green, D. (2016). How change happens. In *Oxford University Press eBooks.* https://doi.org/10.1093/acprof:oso/9780198785392.001.0001

393 Lee, C. (2015). *Internationalizing "International Communication."* https://doi.org/10.3998/nmw.12748916.0001.001

394 Metz, S., & Johnson, D. V., II. (2001). Asymmetry and U. S. military strategy: Definition, Background, and Strategic Concepts.

395 Akamavi, R. K., Ibrahim, F., & Swaray, R. (2022). Tourism and Troubles: Effects of security threats on the global travel and tourism industry performance. *Journal of Travel Research, 62*(8), 1755–1800. https://doi.org/10.1177/00472875221138792

396 Barkawi, T. (2017). *Soldiers of Empire.* Cambridge University Press.

397 CSC (2018). *Six Sigma: A Complete step-by-step Guide.* URL: https://www.sixsigmacouncil.org/wp-content/uploads/2018/08/Six-Sigma-A-Complete-Step-by-Step-Guide.pdf

398 ISO (n.d.). *Quality management* URL: https://www.iso.org/standards/popular/iso-9000-family

399 "Defence College achieves" (2015). *The Business Standard.* URL: https://www.business-standard.com/article/pti-stories/defence-college-achieves-iso-certification-115070301101_1.html

400 "Army raises alarm" (2019). Army raise alarm over rising accidents due to faulty ammunition. *Times of India.* URL: https://timesofindia.indiatimes.com/india/army-raises-alarm-over-rising-accidents-due-to-faulty-ammunition/articleshow/69315854.cms

401 "The Rise of AI and Robotics" (2025). The Rise of AI and Robotics in Military & Defense. *Automate.* URL: https://www.automateshow.com/blog/the-rise-of-ai-and-robotics-in-military-and-defense#:~:text=Autonomous%20ground%20vehicles%20(AGVs)%20to,putting%20people%20in%20harm's%20way.

402 "Supply chain Management" (n.a.) Supply Chain Management in the Defence Industry. *Defence Industries.* URL: https://www.defence-industries.com/articles/supply-chain-management-in-the-defence-industry

403 Ullah, H et al (2024). Integrating industry 4.0 technologies in defence manufacturing: Challenges, solutions, and potential opportunities. *Array.* URL: https://www.sciencedirect.com/science/article/pii/S2590005624000249

404 Pant, H. V. & Bommakanti, K. (2023). Towards the Integration of Emerging Technologies in India's Armed Forces. *Occasional Papers.* Observer Research Foundation. URL: https://www.orfonline.org/research/towards-the-integration-of-emerging-technologies-in-india-s-armed-forces

405 Lima, M. K. (2021). Transformation of the Army Ammunition Surveillance Program. *US Army.* URL: https://www.army.mil/article/252596/transformation_of_the_army_ammunition_surveillance_program

406 America's Seed Fund (n.a.) The roles of DCMA and DCAA with Department of Defense Awards. *SBIR.* URL: https://www.sbir.gov/tutorials/accounting-finance/tutorial-5

407 Peri, D. (2021). Pulgaon ammunition depot fire: Defective mines could have caused the blast. *The Hindu.* URL: https://www.thehindu.com/news/national/Pulgaon-ammunition-depot-fire-Defective-mines-could-have-caused-the-blast/article60503957.ece

408 Haedrick, D. R. (1981). *The tools of empire : technology and European imperialism in the nineteenth century.* Oxford University Press. URL: https://archive.org/details/toolsofempiretec0000head

409 Behera, L. K. (2016). *Indian Defence Industry: An Agenda for Making in India. Institute for Defence Studies and Analyses.* URL: https://idsa.in/system/files/book/book_indian-defence-industry_0.pdf

410 Ministry of Defence, India (2020). Ordnance Factories observe their 219th foundation day.URL: https://www.pib.gov.in/PressReleasePage.aspx?PRID=1606910

411 PIB (2019). Establishment of Ordnance Factories. URL: https://www.pib.gov.in/PressReleseDetailm.aspx?PRID=1578729
412 Smith, D., & Kumar, V. (2022). Bureaucratic Bottlenecks in Defense Procurement: A Global Perspective. International Journal of Defense Studies, 12(3), 45-67.
413 Chakraborty, M., & Mehta, S. (2022). The Rafale Saga: Lessons for India's Defense Acquisition Policy. *Defense Review Quarterly*, 89(1), 22-39.
414 Jones, T., et al. (2024). The Impact of Technological Change on Defense Procurement. *Global Defense Procurement Review*, 78(1), 110-130.
415 Doe, J., & Miller, S. (2024). Overcoming Bureaucratic Hurdles in Defense Procurement: The Case of the U.K. and U.S. *Naval Defense Journal*, 17(1), 24-44.
416 Rao, P., & Gupta, S. (2023). Defense Procurement Reforms in India: Progress and Challenges. *Defense Acquisition Insights*, 15(2), 56-73.
417 Levy, O., & Kim, H. (2023). Procurement Flexibility: Lessons from Israel and South Korea. *Defense Management Journal*, 38(3), 89-105.
418 Sharma, K., & Rao, S. (2023). Defense Procurement in India: An Overview of the Defense Acquisition Council. *Journal of Defense Studies*, 15(3), 22-40.
419 Rao, P., & Patel, A. (2023). Challenges in Indian Defense Procurement: A Historical Perspective. *Defense Policy Review*, 12(1), 45-60.
420 Goldman, R., & Levy, T. (2022). Defense Acquisition Reforms in Israel and the United States. *Journal of Military Procurement*, 8(2), 34-50.
421 Chaudhary, M., & Singh, R. (2022). Evolution of Defense Procurement Policies in India. *Defense Review*, 23(4), 78-92.
422 Mehta, A., & Banerjee, V. (2023). Defense Acquisition Procedures: An Analysis of Delays in India's Defense Procurement. *Global Defense Insights*, 19(2), 66-81.
423 Jones, T., et al. (2024). The Impact of Technological Change on Defense Procurement. *Global Defense Procurement Review*, 78(1), 110-130.
424 Chakraborty, A., & Verma, P. (2023). Understanding Bureaucratic Complexities in Indian Defense Procurement. *Journal of Defense Procurement*, 12(3), 12-30.
425 Doe, J., & Miller, S. (2024). Overcoming Bureaucratic Hurdles in Defense Procurement: The Case of the U.K. and U.S. *Naval Defense Journal*, 17(1), 24-44.
426 Levy, O., & Katz, N. (2023). Fast-Track Procurement Systems in Israel: A Case Study. *Journal of Military Logistics*, 6(4), 90-105.
427 Chakraborty, A., & Verma, P. (2023). Reforms in Indian Defense Procurement: Progress and Challenges. *Journal of Defense Policy*, 19(3), 34-52.
428 Jones, T., et al. (2024). The Impact of Technological Change on Defense Procurement. *Global Defense Procurement Review*, 78(1), 110-130.
429 Doe, J., & Miller, S. (2024). Overcoming Bureaucratic Hurdles in Defense Procurement: The Case of the U.K. and U.S. *Naval Defense Journal*, 17(1), 24-44.
430 Mehta, A., & Banerjee, V. (2023). Defense Procurement in India: Recommendations for Policy Change. *Global Defense Insights*, 19(2), 66-81.
431 Levy, O., & Katz, N. (2023). Fast-Track Procurement Systems in Israel: A Case Study. *Journal of Military Logistics*, 6(4), 90-105.
432 Smith, D., & Kumar, V. (2022). Technological Advancements and Procurement Delays: A Global Perspective. *International Journal of Defense Studies*, 12(3), 45-67.
433 Kim, H., & Park, J. (2023). Real-Time Defense Procurement Platforms: The South Korean Model. *Defense Acquisition Review*, 14(1), 56-73.
434 Smith, T., Jones, D., & Miller, A. (2023). Agile procurement for tech acquisitions in the U.S. Department of Defense. *Defense Technology Review, 19*(2), 66-81

APPENDICES

Ammunition Raw Materials and Its Applications

Material	*Application in Ammunition*
Brass (Cu-Zn Alloy)	Cartridge cases, shell casings
Copper	Bullet jackets, driving bands, electrical primers
Steel	Armor-piercing cores, shell casings
Lead	Bullet cores
Tungsten	Armor-piercing rounds, high-density penetrators
Aluminum	Lightweight casings, artillery components
Zinc	Alloying in brass, bullet cores
Nickel	Bullet jackets, casings for durability
Titanium	Specialized lightweight, high-strength applications
Beryllium Copper	Electrical ignition systems, primers
Magnesium	Incendiary and illumination rounds
Depleted Uranium	Kinetic-energy penetrators, armor-piercing rounds
Lead Styphnate	Primer initiation in cartridges
Mercury Fulminate	Primer composition (now less common)
Tetrazene	Enhances primer sensitivity
RDX	High-explosive filler in shells, warheads
HMX	Powerful explosive in advanced munitions
TNT	Standard explosive in artillery shells, bombs
PETN	Detonating cords, shaped charges
Octol	Warheads in precision-guided munitions
TATB	Insensitive munitions applications
Nitrocellulose	Smokeless powder base in cartridges
Nitroglycerine	Double-based propellant component
DNT	Stabilizer in propellants
Phosphorus	Incendiary, smoke rounds
Barium Nitrate	Pyrotechnic, tracer compositions
Potassium Perchlorate	Flash compositions, igniters
Zirconium Powder	Incendiary mixtures
Magnesium-Aluminum Alloy	Illumination flares
Strontium Nitrate	Red tracer rounds
Calcium Silicide	Initiating compositions
Graphite	Coating for propellant grains (anti-static)

Material	*Application in Ammunition*
Epoxy Resins	Composite-cased ammunition
Plastic Polymers	Modern polymer-cased cartridges, sabots
Paper & Cardboard	Older/training ammunition casings
Rubber & Elastomers	Sealing and buffering materials
Depleted Uranium	Armor-piercing rounds, kinetic penetrators
Tungsten Carbide	Armor-piercing penetrators (alternative to DU)

The input materials for ammunition depend on the type (small arms, artillery shells, missiles, etc.), but generally include:

Metals and Alloys

- Steel – Used for shell casings, projectile bodies, and armor-piercing cores.
- Brass – Commonly used for cartridge cases due to its corrosion resistance and ductility.
- Copper – Used in bullet jackets and driving bands.
- Lead – Used in bullet cores for small arms ammunition.
- Aluminium – Used in lightweight casings and some missile components.
- Tungsten – Used in armour-piercing projectiles and kinetic energy penetrators.
- Uranium (Depleted Uranium, DU) – Used in armour-piercing rounds due to its high density.

Explosives and Propellants

- Nitrocellulose – Primary ingredient in gunpowder and solid propellants.
- Nitro-glycerine – Used in double-base and triple-base propellants.
- RDX (Research Department Explosive) – Used in high-explosive shells and warheads.
- HMX (High Melting Explosive) – Found in advanced explosives for increased power.
- TNT (Trinitrotoluene) – Standard high-explosive filler in artillery and bombs.
- Ammonium Perchlorate – Used in rocket propellants.
- Aluminium Powder – Used to enhance explosive power and incendiary effects.

Chemical Components

- Primer Compounds – Initiators for ignition, including lead styphnate, barium nitrate, and antimony sulphide.
- Stabilizers – Diphenylamine or other chemicals to prevent decomposition of propellants.
- Binders – Used in composite explosives and propellants to hold the material together.
- Plasticisers – Enhance flexibility in propellant grains.

Non-Metallic Materials

- Polymers & Composites – Used in casings, sabots, and guidance fins.
- Graphite & Carbon Fibers – Used in high-tech projectiles and missile bodies.
- Rubber & Sealants – Used in sealing ammunition components to prevent moisture ingress.

Electronics and Fuzes

- Electronic Circuits – Used in guided munitions and smart fuzes.
- Sensors (IR, Laser, Radar) – Incorporated in modern guided ammunition.
- Microprocessors – Used in programmable fuzes and guided projectiles.

Components of 155 mm HE Ammunition

Major Components of 155 mm HE Ammunition

S. No.	*Component*	*Function/Remarks*
1	Projectile Body (Steel Shell)	Houses HE filler; designed to withstand firing pressures and provide fragmentation effect.
2	High-Explosive (HE) Filler	Main explosive charge for blast and fragmentation.
3	Rotating Band (Driving Band)	Engages rifling of barrel to impart spin stability.
4	Obturator Band (if used)	Seals gases, prevents propellant gas escape.
5	Fuze (Mechanical, Electronic, Multi-option)	Initiates detonation; can be point-detonating (PD), proximity (VT), or time fuze.
6	Booster Charge (Auxiliary Charge)	Helps initiate main HE charge from fuze.
7	Supplementary Charge (Optional)	Enhances performance depending on requirement.
8	Base Plate/Plug	Seals the base of the shell; sometimes designed for base-bleed shells.
9	Base Bleed Unit (Optional)	Reduces base drag to increase range (if used).

Propellants for 155 mm Ammunition

S. No.	*Propellant Type*	*Remarks*
1	Modular Charge System (MCS)	Bagged or modular charges to adjust range
2	Triple-Base or Double-Base Propellants	Contains Nitrocellulose (NC), Nitroglycerine (NG), and Nitroguanidine (NQ) or other stabilizers.
3	Single-Base Propellant (optional cases)	Based primarily on Nitrocellulose (NC) for specific variants.
4	Ball Powder (spherical propellants)	Less common but used in some charge configurations.
5	Low-flame Signature Propellants (optional)	For reduced detectability in modern artillery systems.

High Explosives (Main Filling and Boosters)

S. No.	*High Explosive*	*Usage*
1	TNT (Trinitrotoluene)	Widely used as main HE filler in conventional rounds.
2	Composition B (RDX/TNT mixture)	More powerful than TNT alone; used for enhanced effect.
3	RDX (Cyclonite, Hexogen)	Often used in booster charges and sometimes as main fill.
4	PBXN-9 or other Plastic Bonded Explosives (PBX)	Insensitive Munitions (IM) compliant fillers (modern usage).
5	Amatol (TNT/Ammonium Nitrate mixture)	Older designs; less common in modern 155 mm shells.

Other Critical Input Materials and Chemicals

S. No.	*Material*	*Usage*
1	Steel (Special grades)	Projectile body, base plug, fuze components.
2	Copper Alloy (Gilding Metal)	Rotating bands (driving bands) for rifling engagement.
3	Aluminum Alloys (optional)	Lightweight components (base bleed units, etc.).
4	Lead (in small amounts, optional)	Sealing and balance in rotating bands.
5	Energetic Materials (Booster Charges)	Often PETN (Pentaerythritol Tetranitrate), RDX, or similar.
6	Phlegmatisers and Stabilisers	To stabilise explosives and propellants (e.g., Wax, Calcium Carbonate, Diphenylamine).
7	Binders and Plasticisers (for PBX)	To make plastic bonded explosives (e.g., HTPB, Viton).
8	Lubricants/Sealing Compounds	For rotating band fitting, fuze threading.
9	Pyrotechnic Compositions	For igniters, delay compositions in time fuzes.

Packaging and Ancillary Materials

S. No.	*Material*	*Usage*
1	Cartridge Container/Metal Cases	For safe transport and storage.
2	Fibreboard/Plastic Tubes	Propellant charge containment in modular charges.
3	Humidity Control Desiccants	To prevent moisture during storage.
4	Paint/Markings (Ammunition Identification)	For colour coding, lot number, and other identifications.

Modern Enhancements (Optional for Advanced Variants)

S. No.	*Feature*	*Usage*
1	Insensitive Munitions (IM)	To prevent accidental detonation from stimuli (heat, shock).
2	Base Bleed/Extended Range Units	Increases range by reducing base drag.
3	GPS/Guidance Kits (e.g., PGK - Precision Guidance Kit)	Converts conventional shell into precision-guided munition.
4	Proximity/VT Fuzes	For airburst effects over target.

Index

3D printing, 88, 138-39, 216, 232

Abqaiq-Khurais attacks, 20
Advanced Weapons and Equipment India Limited (AWEIL), 66
Aerial Target, 21
Afghanistan, 20, 22-23, 28
Africa, 26-28, 60, 87, 94-95, 167, 170, 175, 185, 216-17, 238
Agra, 132
Aligarh, 132
Ammunition Management, 6-7, 15-16
Ammunition MSME Clusters, 221
Amrit Kaal, 1
Anchor MIL + Private Consortium (AMPC), 220-21, 227, 229, 231-32
Aramane, Giridhar, 119
Arjun MBT and T-90, 66
Armament Research and Development Establishment (ARDE), 56, 184, 187-88
Armed Forces, 54, 56, 63, 100
Arms Trade Treaty (ATT), 92
Artificial Intelligence (AI), 2-3, 7, 29, 40-44, 46, 48, 51-53, 55, 58-60, 62, 88, 94, 96-108, 110-12, 114-16, 119-20, 122-23, 125, 130, 135, 137, 144, 158, 186, 196, 204-05, 207-08, 212, 214-16, 219
  Next, 99
  Platform Automation, 107
Artificial Neural Networks (ANNs), 98
ASEAN, 95
Assured Long-Term Ammunition Ordering Model (ALTOM), 222
Atmanirbhar Bharat, 20, 33, 40, 45, 50, 54, 57, 59, 62, 64, 66, 77, 82, 120, 126, 130, 150, 155, 161, 169, 208, 214, 218, 221
Australia, 76, 94, 95
Autonomous/Unmanned/Robotic Systems, 107
Aviation Industry Corporation of China (AVIC), 26, 52

Bayraktar TB2, 23, 27-29
Bhabha Atomic Research Centre (BARC), 71
Bharat Dynamics Limited (BDL), 55, 187
Bharat Electronics Ltd (BEL), 69
Bharat Forge, 54, 57, 173, 183, 186-87
Big Data and Analytics, 120
Black Sea, 30
Block Chain based Automation, 107
Brass, 67
Brazil, 25, 87

Central Asia, 94, 216, 238
Centralite, 69
Centres of Excellence (CoE), 135, 137, 139, 147
CERT, 123
Cheap First-Person-View (FPV), 14
Chemical Weapons Convention (CWC), 69
Chennai, 66, 119, 131-32, 134, 187
China, 22, 25-26, 28-29, 32, 35, 38, 40, 49-52, 68, 71, 74-77, 84, 99, 106, 115, 129, 143
Chitrakoot, 66, 131-32
Civil-Military Integration (CMI), 76

Coimbatore, 66, 71, 131-32, 134
Col Lacroix, 98
Cold War, 22, 128
Combat Air Teaming System (CATS), 30, 32
Command, Control, Communications, Computers, Intelligence, Surveillance & Reconnaissance (C4ISR), 107
Comptroller and Auditor General (CAG), 100-01, 118, 165, 167-68
Condition-Based Maintenance Plus (CBM+), 111
Copper, 67, 70
COVID-19, 74, 81, 97
Cybersecurity, 44, 88, 111-12, 115, 122-25, 137, 139, 144, 201, 203, 205, 207-08, 210

Defence Acquisition Procedure (DAP), 20, 60, 74, 127-28, 130, 144, 171, 200-04, 237
Defence Advanced Research Projects Agency (DARPA), 30, 51, 99, 106, 213
Defence AI Council, 106
Defence AI Project Agency, 106
Defence Electronics Policy, 69
Defence Industrial Corridors (DICs), 66, 80, 126
Defence Logistics Agency (DLA), 75, 77
Defence Procurement Procedure (DPP), 57, 71, 128, 200-01, 203
Defence Production Act (DPA), 75
Defence Production and Export Promotion Policy (DPEPP), 64, 67, 78, 127-28, 140
Defence Public Sector Undertakings (DPSUs), 54, 57, 66, 71, 117, 122-25, 130-31, 133, 152-56, 158, 168-70, 172, 179, 215, 219, 222, 229, 236
Defence Quality Certification, 221
Defence Research and Development Organisation (DRDO), 20, 31-32, 35, 40, 44-45, 51, 54-56, 58, 60, 66, 71, 73-74, 77-80, 95, 107, 122, 128, 133, 135-37, 143-44, 170, 172, 186-88, 190-94, 214-15, 220, 222, 229, 236
Defence Supply Chains, 98
Defence Testing Infrastructure Scheme (DTIS), 78, 131, 133, 136, 142, 146, 228
Department of Defence (DoD), 51, 203
Digital Integration, 122
Directorate General of Quality Assurance (DGQA), 119, 124, 152-54, 157-58, 172
DRDO's Rustom, 20, 31

Eastern Bloc nations, 86
Economic Development Board, 90
Egypt, 26, 28
Environmental Health and Safety (EHS), 221
EO/IR, 43
Estonia, 10
Extended Range Cannon Artillery (ERCA), 51

Foreign Direct Investment (FDI), 55, 57, 60, 64, 124, 131, 133, 139-40, 145, 147
France, 52, 53, 58, 79, 84, 94, 95, 127, 131

GAP (Glycidyl Azide Polymer), 69
Gaza, 14, 25, 28, 45, 94, 109
GDP, 90, 143
Germany, 25, 52-53, 84
Global Economic Defence Review, 2025, 89
Global South, 3, 25, 28, 94-95, 176, 216, 233
GPS, 29, 40-41, 43-44, 46, 49, 51-53, 103

Hindustan Aeronautics Limited (HAL), 32, 128, 132
Hindustan Copper Ltd., 67, 79
HMX (Cyclotetramethylene-tetranitramine), 64, 68, 71, 73, 80, 81, 170, 171, 183, 186, 220
Hooda, Lt Gen., 105
Hosur, 66, 131-32, 134
Houthis, 20
HTPB (Hydroxyl-Terminated Polybutadiene), 69
Hypersonic Smart Weapons, 44

IMI Systems, 76
India, 1-4, 6, 11-13, 20-21, 25, 30-40, 44-45, 49-51, 53-75, 77, 79-82, 87, 90, 94-97, 100-07, 115, 117-22, 124-40, 142-55, 157-86, 188, 190, 192-204, 208, 211-22, 224-28, 230, 232-33, 236-39
Indian Air Force, 107
Indian Army, 48-51, 58, 65, 102, 107, 118, 149, 164, 213
Indian Ocean Region (IOR), 1-2, 129
India-US, 33
Indonesia, 70, 94
Industrial Training Institutes (ITIs), 81, 139
Industry 4.0, 117-22, 125, 135, 139, 142, 186, 192-93, 216-17, 222, 226, 229, 231-32
Inertial Navigation Systems (INS), 46
Innovations for Defence Excellence (iDEX), 20, 32-33, 35, 38, 127, 130-31, 133, 136-37, 143, 171
INS Valsura, 'Artificial Intelligence for the Future Fleet', 107
Integrated Ammunition Nodes (IANs), 217
Intellectual Property (IP), 130
Intelligence, Surveillance, and Reconnaissance (ISR), 2, 19, 22-23, 28, 50
Intelligence, Surveillance, Target Acquisition, and Reconnaissance (ISTAR), 32
Interface Control Documents (ICDs), 222-23, 228-29, 231-32, 236
International North-South Transport Corridor, 95
International Traffic in Arms Regulations (ITARs), 73, 91, 95
Internet of Things (IoTs), 13, 88, 111, 114, 119, 121-23, 125, 135, 139, 142, 193
Iran, 20, 23-24
Iraq, 20, 22-23, 28
IREL, 79
Iron Dome, 14
Israel, 5, 8, 13-15, 20, 22-25, 27-29, 33, 38, 45, 53-54, 58, 69, 71, 75-77, 79, 90, 94-95, 104, 109, 115, 143, 167, 176, 186, 199-201, 203, 206, 209
Israel Aerospace Industries (IAI), 25
Israel Defence Forces (IDF), 25
Israel-Hamas conflicts, 13

Jhansi, 66, 131-32, 134
Joint Direct Attack Munitions (JDAM), 44, 51
Joint Munitions Command (JMC), 108
Industrial Base tool, 111

Kalashnikov Concern, 52
Kanpur, 66, 71, 119, 131-32, 134, 139

Ladakh, 31, 50, 149
Lake City Army Ammunition Plant, 108
Larsen & Toubro (L&T), 54, 57
Laser-Guided Bombs (LGBs), 41, 44
Latin America, 95, 185, 238
Lebanon War, 22, 24, 109
Libya, 23, 27, 108
Line of Actual Control (LAC), 49
Line of Control (LoC), 49
Lucknow, 131, 132

Machine Learning (ML), 46, 58, 98
Made in China 2025 plan, 76
Mahindra Defence Systems, 57
Maintenance, Repair, and Overhaul (MRO), 134, 138
Make in India, 11, 40, 45, 50, 54, 66, 69, 128, 130, 195, 200-01, 203, 237
MANPADS, 6
Medium-Altitude Long-Endurance, 32
Micro, Small and Medium Enterprises (MSMEs), 70-71, 78, 113, 126-28, 131-33, 135-37, 141-42, 144-47, 184, 194, 221-22, 227, 229
Middle East, 19, 26, 38, 45, 60, 84, 95, 170
Military-Civil Fusion, 84
MIL-Private Coordination Cell (MPCC), 220, 236
Ministry of Defence, 44, 56, 66, 107, 117-

18, 145, 153, 198-200, 204, 215, 219, 229, 237
Ministry of Environment, Forest and Climate Change (MoEFCC), 72
Monitoring & Risk Assessment, 112
Munitions India Limited (MIL), 54, 66, 119, 169, 173, 181, 184, 186-88, 190-95

Nagorno-Karabakh conflict/war, 8, 20, 23, 27, 38, 216
National Authority for Ammunition and Industry (NAAI), 220
National Defence Material Grid (NDMG), 80, 82
National Mineral Development Corporation (NMDC), 70, 79
National Policy on Defence Supply Chain Security, 112
National Strategy for Artificial Intelligence #AIFORALL, 97
NATO, 8, 11, 14-15, 61, 84, 86, 108-09, 151, 154, 185-86, 194, 226-27, 229
Network-Centric Warfare (NCW), 47, 50
New Generation Artificial Intelligence Development Plan, 99
Nigeria, 26, 28
Niti Aayog, 98
Nitrocellulose (NC), 68
Nitroglycerine (NG), 68

Oman, 95
Operation NICKEL GRASS, 109
Operation SINDOOR, 3
Ordnance Factory Badmal, 101
Ordnance Factory Boards (OFBs), 54, 56-57, 63, 66, 100, 117-18, 121-22, 128, 165-70, 181, 183, 195
Original Equipment Manufacturers (OEMs), 78, 132, 140, 145, 147
OTIF, 223

Pakistan, 23-24, 26, 28, 32, 49-50, 166
Petroleum and Explosives Safety Organisation, 72
post-Cold War, 22
Precision Guided Kit (PGK), 53
Precision-Guided Munitions (PGMs), 13, 39-40, 43, 49, 54, 56
Predator and Reaper, 20
Predictive Analytics and Decision Assistant (PANDA), 99, 103
Process Safety Management (PSM), 227
Production-Linked Incentive (PLI), 33, 35, 38
Propellants and Energetics Safety Board (PESB), 220, 236
Public Sector Undertakings (PSUs), 60, 63, 71, 74, 79, 128, 135-36, 195, 211
Public-Private Partnerships (PPPs), 55, 79, 135

Quantum Lab at Military College, Mhow, 107

Rafael Advanced Defence Systems, 76
RAND, 29
RDX (Cyclotrimethylenetrinitramine), 64, 68, 71, 73, 80-81, 170-71, 183, 186, 220
Research and Development (R&D), 7, 9-11, 14-17, 21, 32, 35, 38, 40, 44-46, 53-60, 67, 73, 75-77, 80-82, 84, 89, 113-14, 116, 127-28, 132, 136-38, 143-44, 146, 148, 157, 169, 181-82, 184, 186-87, 190-91, 206-08, 212, 213, 216-19, 225-26, 229
Responsible AI, 98
Rostec, 52
Russia, 12-13, 15, 20, 40, 45, 51-52, 54, 58, 68, 71, 84, 86, 110, 115, 129, 176, 181, 183, 216
Russia-Ukraine War/Conflict, 14, 20, 74, 97, 108

Salem, 66, 131-32
Saudi Arabia, 20, 26
Saxena, Lt Gen VK, 118
Self-Reliant India, 50, 54, 57, 59, 77
Smart Anti-Airfield Weapon (SAAW), 45, 55

South Korea, 53, 69, 79, 94, 143, 176, 200, 205, 209-10
South Korea's Hanwha Corporation, 53
Soviet Union, 86, 128
Special Purpose Vehicles (SPVs), 131, 220
SRIJAN Portal, 40, 45
STANAG, 86, 190, 192, 194
Startups, 77-78, 127, 129, 133, 137-38, 143, 145-47, 172, 195, 208
Strategic Partnership Model (SPM), 60
Strategic Partnerships for Ammunition Resilience Consortium (SPARC), 94-95
Sudarshan Chakra, 3
suicide drones, 23, 36
Supply Chain Security Framework, 112
Syria, 23, 27-28

TK Nair Committee, 118
Tactical Missiles Corporation, 52
Tamil Nadu, 33, 57, 66, 126, 128, 131-34, 136-39, 141, 145-47, 152, 232
Tamil Nadu Defence Industrial Corridor (TNDIC), 126, 131, 132
TAPAS, 32, 34, 38
Tata Advanced Systems, 54, 57, 186
Technology Development Fund, 45, 78, 80, 122, 136, 144, 146
Tiruchirappalli, 131-32
Transfer of Technology (ToT), 78, 137
Tri-Node Program Office (TNPO), 217
Tri-Sectoral Strategic Framework, 112
Tungsten, 68
Turkey, 20, 23, 27-29, 38

UAE, 95
UID/FEFO, 228
Ukraine, 5, 8, 11-15, 20, 27-30, 38, 45, 84, 94, 108, 110, 175, 181, 183, 216
United Kingdom (UK), 52-53, 127, 199, 202, 205, 209
United States (US), 8, 10, 15, 20-230, 33, 38, 40, 51, 54, 58, 69, 71, 75-77, 80, 84, 86, 90-91, 99, 103, 108-11, 114-15, 127, 129, 143, 158-61, 176, 186, 199, 201-06, 209, 213
  Army, 51, 108, 111, 159-60, 213
  Silicon Valley for defence tech startups, 131
Unmanned Aerial Vehicles (UAVs), 19-20, 24-27, 32, 41, 47, 50
Uttar Pradesh, 33, 57, 66, 128, 131-34, 136-39, 141, 145-47, 152, 232
  Investors Summit, 132
Uttar Pradesh Defence Industrial Corridor (UPDIC), 126, 131-32

Vice Admiral Raman Puri Committee, 118
Vietnam, 22, 94-95
Vijay Kelkar Committee, 118
Viksit Bharat 2047, 2, 4, 34, 37-38, 126-27, 134, 147, 163, 180, 182, 211-12, 214, 218, 221, 225, 230, 236, 238-39

War Reserve Stockpile Ammunition-Israel (WRSA-I), 109
War Wastage Reserve (WWR), 218-19
Wassenaar Arrangement, 72-73, 170
West Bank, 25
World War I, 21
World War II, 8, 22

Yemen, 20, 23, 26, 28
Yom Kippur War, 8, 109

ZUPPA, 32